THE MARTHA MANUAL

HOW TO DO (ALMOST) EVERYTHING

MARTHA STEWART

This book, an edited compilation of many of the many thousand "Good Things" and helpful articles I and my extremely talented staff of *Martha Stewart Living* have worked on for three decades, is dedicated with love and thanks to those very colleagues who always find the time to do everything in the best possible fashion! Thank you all very, very much.

THE MARTHA MANUAL

HOW TO DO (ALMOST) EVERYTHING

MARTHA STEWART

Houghton Mifflin Harcourt
Boston New York 2019

Produced by Melcher Media

INTRODUCTION

Not to be boastful, but I believe I can write a book like this, a manual on how to do (almost) everything, without feeling as if I am overstepping my expertise, or taking on a subject too large for any one person.

In fact, "how-to" could be my middle name: I have always been on the lookout for the most practical, appealing, efficient, and sensible way to accomplish everyday and meaningful tasks, and I have devoted my life to discovering and sharing those solutions. Once I find the smartest way to vacuum a room, the most sensible way to plant a tree, the finest way to organize a drawer, or the most beautiful way to decorate a cake, I am committed to teaching that method until I learn another, better way to do such a task. And I am always aware there might be a better way!

I do not know when I became so task oriented, but I do remember how quickly my lovely mother, "Big Martha," could pick string beans; how easily she could iron a shirt, as if it came from a professional dry cleaner; or how organized she could be in preparing our huge, delicious Thanksgiving dinner each year. She was a remarkable teacher, and so was my father, who (like the fictional father in his favorite movie, *Cheaper by the Dozen*) was an efficiency expert. There was no time for wasted actions—personal flair could exist, as well as creativity, but only if no time was squandered.

We are now constantly told that we are too busy to learn anything new—that we cannot possibly fit a gardening lecture or a sewing lesson or a painting tutorial into our schedules. I vehemently disagree! Put down the cell phone and pick up some knitting needles, a trowel, or even a screw-driver—and make, plant, fix. You'll be glad you did.

—MARTHA STEWART

A well-organized home—whether yours is a country house, a city apartment, a cabin in the woods, or a cottage by the sea—makes living well that much easier.

If the kitchen is smartly arranged, cooking and baking will be more enjoyable. If your bathroom is appropriately stocked and well-appointed, then even guests can use it and feel as if the space is their own. When your closet is well designed—with designated places for shoes, bags, suits, dresses, and pants—then getting dressed will be a pleasure. And when kids' rooms are neat, with toys and games and learning materials within easy reach, children will stay happily busy (and may even be more likely to pick up after themselves).

Good organization applies to all the spaces in one's home, starting with the entryway, but also including those areas that some of us tend to neglect, such as the garage, attic, and basement. I have spent a lot of time organizing and reorganizing my homes for photo shoots, for television shows, and for my family and myself. This has afforded me the opportunity to test innumerable ideas for making each space livable, workable, and comfortable. In the following chapter, we share some of the very best of those ideas, room by room—even and especially the all-important, hardworking laundry room. We have also distilled decades of organizing advice into what we call the golden rules, which I myself find to be highly effective. My number one organizing principle? Give everything its own place; start there, and you will find the rest comes all the easier.

THE GOLDEN RULES OF ORGANIZING

It's easy to be seduced by the promise of order. So the thinking goes, as long as our keepsakes are tucked away, our desks neat and tidy, and our closets jumble-free, our lives will be similarly serene.

Yet most organizing manifestos bear the familiar battle cry—Combat clutter! Conquer chaos!—as if life were a no-win war against all our belongings. Instead, here's a radical proposition: Toss out the old mantras and view organizing as less a problem to be solved and more an opportunity to embrace.

In that spirit, keep these guiding principles in mind as you put (and keep) your own home in tip-top shape.

1. BE TARGETED
Rather than tackle the whole house, target one room at a time. Focus first on high-use areas—such as the bathroom or home office. Next address the places you usually ignore. If there's an overflowing drawer that makes you wince every time you open it, remind yourself that it's probably less taxing to sort through it than to feel frustrated every day.

2. PARE DOWN
It's impossible to have a well-organized space when there's too much stuff to fit into it. Take a hard look at your rooms and then edit out what you don't use (see Four-Box Formula below).

3. UNIFY STORAGE
No matter their contents, matching containers make any space more organized. Use woven baskets, metal bins, canvas cubbies, or wooden crates. If you want a matching set, paint them a uniform color.

4. RETHINK FURNISHINGS
Furniture need not be used for its original purpose. If you no longer require an armoire to store clothes, turn it into a home office; a bookcase can be an entryway bench.

5. CONSIDER PROXIMITY
Keeping items near where they are used will make each room more efficient. Tuck infrequently used items away to clear visual (and mental) clutter.

6. GROUP STRATEGICALLY
In other words, stash things that are used together in the same spot. Think spare candles with matches, wrapping paper with ribbon and scissors, and so on.

7. MAXIMIZE SPACE
Look high and low for space-making inspiration. Mount a ledge over a door; carve out a nook beneath a kitchen cabinet; put under-furniture spaces to work.

8. STAY FOCUSED
Avoid having to start from scratch with your organizing goals each year. Instead, implement a system for staying on top of your spaces, scheduling time on your calendar, and then sticking to that plan (see opposite page).

FOUR-BOX FORMULA
It's hard letting go of our possessions, so systematize the process. Set up four boxes and label them "Keep," "Toss," "Donate," and "Sell." Then get to work.

 KEEP
Keep important items and put them in their proper places—or assign them permanent homes.

 TOSS
Toss out products that are no longer useful and paperwork that's no longer required (see How Long Should You Keep Records?, page 35).

SCHEDULE IT IN

Establishing a regular maintenance regime is essential to keeping your home in order. The following timeline is a good place to start.

DAILY

Sort incoming mail to keep counters clear and paper piles minimal; recycle all junk mail and newspapers immediately.

Clear your desk or other workspaces.

Hang up and put away clothing, shoes, handbags, and backpacks.

Put away toys to keep kids' rooms tidy.

Straighten up the kitchen before going to bed; clear away dirty dishes from the sink and empty the dishwasher, if possible; wipe down counters and sink.

WEEKLY

Discard any food in the refrigerator that's past its prime.

Empty your wallet of receipts and either file or shred them.

Sort through or discard invitations and other notices, jotting down important dates in your calendar and tossing outdated items.

File away schoolwork, such as art projects and returned homework.

MONTHLY

Recycle magazines and catalogs you no longer want; store all others.

File paid bills.

File important documents for long-term storage (see page 35).

Delete unnecessary digital files and back up the rest.

TWICE ANNUALLY

Toss out old cosmetics and grooming products.

Dispose of expired medications.

Discard pantry items that are past their use-by date.

Replenish first-aid kit.

ANNUALLY

Sort through clothing, shoes, and toys; give unwanted items to charity.

After filing your tax return, do a thorough inventory of stored financial documents; shred anything you no longer need.

Sort through spices and discard expired ones; replenish as needed.

Go through utility spaces; restock equipment, tools, and batteries as needed.

TIME-MANAGEMENT TIPS

The key to staying organized is taking advantage of the occasional spare moments in your regular routine. If you have …

10 minutes

Clean out your handbag, purse, or backpack.

Organize credit-card receipts.

Sort through catalogs and magazines.

Clear your email inbox.

Bag up recyclables.

Take an inventory of cleaning supplies.

30 minutes

Refold sweaters.

Straighten a linen-closet shelf.

Organize one drawer.

Update a bulletin board.

Sort through toys and redistribute them.

Update labels for containers.

60 minutes

Take an inventory of your pantry.

Clean out the refrigerator and/or freezer.

Sort through clothes closets, looking for items to repair, clean, or donate.

Rearrange books.

Sort through financial records.

Back up photos or computer files.

Straighten out boxes or bins in the garage, attic, or basement.

3 DONATE

For everything that remains, ask yourself, When was the last time I used it? Do I need it? If you can't remember or aren't sure, the item can go (see Donation Guidelines, page 43).

4 SELL

Sell anything of value, either on-line or via a tag sale (see How to Organize Tag Sales, page 43).

HOW TO ORGANIZE
ENTRYWAYS

Clutter in the entrance can stifle the flow of your home well beyond the front door. What to do with all the sundries that need stashing? Create a space that's practical as well as pleasing to the eye. An all-in-one unit such as the one shown opposite is just one very convenient option. Read on for other ways to make your own entry (and exit) point as pulled together as can be.

THE FIVE "ESSENTIALS"

Whether you have a grand foyer or no real entry at all, you can maintain order and a consistent routine with a few simple elements. Just how you go about implementing these entryway items will depend mostly on the physical footprint of your space. For example, if you have a dedicated hall closet, you may be able to forgo the hooks; if you don't have room for a console or other table, you can mount a shelf or a floating ledge.

1. HOOKS

Even if you do have a coat closet, wall-mounted hooks are an efficient way to hold everyday items such as scarves and dog leashes; plus they allow raincoats to dry off. Be sure to arrange some hooks within reach of any little ones, too.

2. BASKETS

Corral items big (such as umbrellas and soccer balls) and small (like loose change and sunglasses) in coordinated containers. You can even designate a cubby for each member of the family, or for each category of gear—sports, pets, beach, and such.

3. TABLE OR SHELF

You'll need a horizontal surface to house small items, as well as a place to set down bags and totes as you come and go. Console tables have slender profiles; credenzas offer hidden storage. Shelves allow for customization. Or let a bench do double duty (see page 14).

4. BENCH OR OTHER SEATING

Besides being an inviting addition to any entry, a seat has the practical purpose of providing a place to sit when putting on and taking off shoes. Many benches offer storage underneath, either with built-in cubbies for shoes and other everyday items or space for tucking in your own baskets or containers.

5. DOORMAT OR SMALL RUG

A mat or rug protects your floors from the elements and provides a soft spot for weary feet. Plus, it affords another way to personalize the space. Choose durable, easy-to-clean wool or indoor-outdoor rugs, or you can stick with coconut-husk or other traditional doormat fibers. Shoes and boots can go in a boot tray to catch any drips.

MARTHA MUST

I keep a basket of nonskid socks by the entrance as part of a no-shoes policy, a custom I picked up when visiting Japanese homes many years ago. Besides keeping your floors clean, it is a cozy option for colder months.

MORE IDEAS
AND INSPIRATION

If you don't have a dedicated entryway in your home, improvise by making use of space-saving storage: A bench can double as a hallway organizer and a bookcase can divide a room.

BOOKCASE TO BENCH

Turn a minimal bookcase on its side, fit it with casters for easy transport, and top with a custom cushion that plays nicely with the surroundings—above, a patterned floor and graphic wallpaper in the same shade of green. Tuck baskets, shoes, and other items in the open compartments, and hang hooks on the wall above for holding coats, bags, and umbrellas. Add a pillow and it becomes a decorative, utilitarian, and mobile piece with a bevy of uses.

PARTITION PLUS

A prefab storage unit divides the room visually, creating the illusion of a hallway (a runner also helps). Store shoes in the lower cubbies for easy access, collectibles and other decorative objects up top and out of reach of kids, and anything you'd rather hide in matching bins and drawers, making them your own with leather-tab pulls (simply drill a hole in each drawer and attach a piece of folded leather with a nut and screw). Mount hooks on the side for your most-used garments and accessories.

PROJECT

CREATE A COMMAND CENTER

Shopping and to-do lists, kids' school reminders, and other flotsam and jetsam of everyday life tend to pile up fast. That's why every organized home needs a command center—whether in an entryway, the kitchen, a home office, or some other well-chosen spot. A command center provides a place for everything that needs one (see box below). For a message board that's equal parts form and function, consider upgrading to Homasote—an affordable fiberboard that's sold at hardware shops, office-supply stores, and home-improvement centers—or corkboard with inexpensive overlays from radiator covers, also available at home-improvement stores.

SUPPLIES

Radiator cover

Homasote board
(see page 41 for the how-to)

Grommet set with screws

Extra-long thumbtacks

Holders, clips, and other optional supplies

1. Mount radiator cover over Homasote board, securing it with grommets and screws in far corners.

2. Use extra long thumbtacks to reach through the cover.

3. Attach attractive holders and binder clips for loose odds and ends.

COMMAND CENTER ESSENTIALS

- Incorporate a month-at-a-glance calendar to keep track of schedules.
- Corral business cards, invitations, and homework in easy reach.
- Add decorative touches such as photos and postcards to keep it from being too utilitarian.
- Edit the board regularly to keep it up-to-date and prevent it from becoming overburdened.

HOW TO ORGANIZE
CLOSETS

What do prewar apartments, vintage farmhouses, mid-century ranches, and cute cottages have in common? A dearth of designated closet space—if any at all. Even modern-day dwellings can test the limits of our organizing abilities when it comes to finding space for clothes, linens, and accessories. Take inspiration from these ideas, then tweak them to create smart solutions for your space.

EDITING YOUR CLOSET

It's a good idea to do a wardrobe walk-through at least twice a year—such as in the spring and fall, when switching out the seasonal items. Sort everything according to the Four-Box Formula (see page 10).

Start with unused or broken costume jewelry, matchless socks and gloves, and shoes that haven't seen the light of day in a year. Gather up these things and put them in a pile.

Then sort through every article of clothing and all your accessories, weeding out pieces that might be taking up valuable space. As you go, be on the lookout for anything you might be keeping using the following common (erroneous) justifications:

IT MIGHT FIT AGAIN: Try on items that you think might be too small or large, and then pass those along to others who can use them.

IT WAS EXPENSIVE: Buyer's remorse is never a good reason to keep something that has no value to you. Assuage the guilt by giving it to someone who will appreciate it (or sell it at a consignment shop).

IT MIGHT COME BACK INTO FASHION: That might very well be the case, but you might not like it as much—and it might not flatter you as well—the next time around. Hold on only to classic pieces that still fit, as these never go out of style.

IT WAS A SPECIAL GIFT: There is no expectation that you keep every gift you have ever received. Instead, honor the giver by finding a good home for the wearables; there is always someone who can use the item, even if you can't.

CLOSET-ORGANIZING PRINCIPLES

For such a small space, closets have to accommodate a big mix of belongings. How you arrange them makes all the difference.

WHAT TO HANG: Anything that is likely to wrinkle (linen, rayon, cotton dresses) or slide around in a drawer (silks and satins should get a hanger), as well as garments that are pressed or have pleats.

MARTHA MUST

I installed valet bars to organize the outfits I will be wearing on trips or to special events, using my own laminated tags to sort the items by laundering method. Tags include Launder by Hand, Do Not Put in Dryer, and Dry Clean.

HOW TO HANG: Use the right type of hanger to extend the life of your clothes.

- Coats need broad wooden hangers to keep shoulders aligned and garments in shape.

- Silk blouses, cotton shirts, and vests need smaller (but still sturdy) wooden hangers.

- Pants made of wool and other sturdy fabrics are best suspended from the waist on hangers fitted with clips (as shown on page 18); more delicate items can be folded over a wider hanger's bar, preferably one that's lined with cushioning velvet.

WHAT TO FOLD: All knitwear, cotton T-shirts, and sportswear (preferably in a separate drawer) should be neatly folded, plus jeans and casual slacks if there's not enough room to hang them.

WHAT TO PUT AWAY: Lingerie, scarves, ties—anything you aren't planning on hanging or stacking on open shelves can be tucked into compartments.

For storing these items, drawers are just one option; lining up bins on a closet shelf is another alternative. Either way, sort these items by type or color (such as the socks on page 18).

TIP

When editing your wardrobe, it can be hard to be objective, especially when parting with sentimental items. Invite a trusted friend over to help make the tough decisions.

CUSTOM-CLOSET CONFIGURATIONS

If you are considering having a closet built to suit, start by taking stock of your wardrobe. The guidelines in this chart should help you get a sense of how much space you'll need, but be sure to leave extra room for future purchases—and space-hogging winter clothes.

VERTICAL SPACE PER CLOTHING CATEGORY

Dresses	48–66 inches
Skirts	34–44 inches
Women's blouses	30–36 inches
Women's suit jackets	32–42 inches
Pants	46–52 inches (by cuff)
	28–32 inches (folded)
Coats	46–66 inches
Jackets	40–44 inches
Men's shirts	38–39 inches
Men's suit jackets	39–42 inches

ROD SPACE (HORIZONTAL) PER ITEM

Shirts and blouses	1 inch
Pants and skirts	1½ inches
Dresses, suits, and jackets	2–2½ inches

MARTHA MUST

Clothing needs room to breathe, as overcrowding causes wrinkles. That's why wooden hangers are the only option for me, not those skinny hangers that are reputed to fit two or three times as many garments in a closet.

FORM AND FUNCTION

Design your closet with equal parts efficiency and enjoyment in mind. Grouping items lets you achieve that goal.

■ Arranging like items together creates visual harmony in your closet. It also eliminates the need to hunt anything down—and lets you put together an ensemble with ease.

■ You could group by kind—tops, pants, skirts, and dresses, for example—or by color, from light to dark. The optimal method? Do both, using the pants shown opposite as inspiration.

■ Apply the same organization to accessories, keeping frequently worn items on open shelves and the rest stored. At right, the shoes are further grouped by kind (ankle boots vs. high-heeled sandals). Change the selection according to the season.

■ Don't overlook any tucked-away items, which are also amenable to being similarly arranged. First do so by type—dress socks and athletic socks in separate compartments, tights and hosiery in yet another—and then by color. Ties, belts, and scarves work the same way.

TIP

Round up all your clothes-keeping necessities—sewing kit, sweater combs, shoe polishes—in one place, either a box or a basket, and place it in or near your closet. The more accessible they are, the more likely you are to sew, shine, and spiff up your clothes.

MORE IDEAS
AND INSPIRATION

If you're tired of untangling your trinkets or hunting down your favorite hat, or you've run out of shoe storage, here are ways to put all your accessories in their place.

DIY JEWELRY DISH

Small, decorative plates provide ample opportunity to store your trinkets—and show off your creativity. Try splattering, outlining, or stenciling the patterns shown above, or improvise to make your own designs. You can also vary the sizes and shapes of the dishes (try miniature bowls) to accommodate your collection.

DOOR-MOUNTED DOWEL

Mount a thin wooden dowel, available at craft-supply stores, inside an armoire or cabinet door and use S hooks to hang necklaces, bracelets, and even rings in a manageable, accessible display. Coat the dowel with semi-gloss paint to keep the hooks from sliding and to blend in with the furniture.

CAFÉ-ROD DOOR RACKS

Keep your favorite winter woolens within easy reach by mounting two café rods on the back of a door. Hang hats and gloves from the top bar using curtain clips; drape scarves over the lower one. Come spring, swap them out with seasonal hats, visors, and wraps.

PICTURE-RAIL SHOE RACK

For artful storage for your fanciest heels, line a wall with molding (sold at home-improvement centers). Have preprimed pieces cut to length; paint as desired. Attach (a foot apart) to wall with construction adhesive. Hammer finishing nails every 18 inches (no studs needed), countersink nails, spackle, and touch up with paint.

HOW TO ORGANIZE
BATHROOMS

Mornings are hectic enough without having to search for your favorite lipstick. Touch up this busy space with some paring down and a few simple updates. Then you and your powder room can get off to a fresh start.

STREAMLINE STORAGE

The biggest challenge in keeping even the smallest of bathrooms in order? Taming all the stuff.

■ At least twice each year, weed out expired makeup and beauty products and eliminate any duplicates, forgotten items, or impulse purchases that you've never used.

■ Take this opportunity to also rotate out any seasonal items—sunburn-soothing aloe in summer, moisturizing creams for itchy, dry winter skin.

■ After decluttering, arrange only the most-used products on shelves or easy-to-access spots. Put all the rest in a cabinet or coordinated bins (or even in a nearby linen closet).

■ Decant bulk toiletries into manageable, uniform containers, like the ones shown opposite, which are stored smartly within an adjustable bathtub rack.

■ If storage is scarce, make use of free vertical space. Mount shelves in a narrow nook, as shown opposite, or on the wall above a toilet. Don't overlook the back of the door, too (look for over-the-door units at housewares stores).

■ Plan for just two bath towels per person— one in use while the other is being laundered. This not only cuts down on the need for storage, it also reduces your laundering load (and water usage).

■ Tuck a small stool in the bathroom to reach items kept up high.

KEEP IT TIDY

Where to put the spare towels and toothbrushes? The following are some ways to keep these and everything else in order.

■ Apply the grouping principle to store like with like, corralling combs and brushes, shaving products, nail polishes, and other often-used and odd-shaped items in separate containers.

■ In the same vein, assign a separate shelf or bin to each category of toiletries, as an easy way to keep track of them (and for others to know where to find and replace them).

■ A single large bin is harder to keep orderly than two (or three) smaller ones; those that stack have the same footprint. Label them or choose bins with clear lids so there's no guesswork required.

■ Between lotions, potions, and other spill-prone liquids, bathroom shelves can get dirty. Line each shelf with easy-to-clean, cut-to-size sheets of Plexiglas, or use clear or patterned shelf liner so it blends in with the decor.

■ Strategically placed hooks happen to be great space-savers, keeping towels within easy reach of the bath or shower. Mount towel bars inside the door for out-of-the-way drying after each use.

MARTHA MUST

Keep a small squeegee in your shower and use it to wipe down the walls, and doors if you have them, after each use; even my grandchildren know to do this. It helps prevent moisture buildup and makes weekly cleaning easier to do.

MORE IDEAS
AND INSPIRATION

When outfitting a bathroom to gain extra storage, don't be afraid to borrow some fixtures from elsewhere in the home.

STORAGE CART

A bar cart makes a superlative stand-in for heftier fixtures. Plus, it's easy to roll to and fro when cleaning—and the handlebar doubles as a place for hanging a hand towel. You can even (finally) solve the blow-dryer dilemma by looping the cord around an S hook. To make the cart more stain resistant, coat it with glossy paint.

WOODEN TUB SHELF

To keep your bathing essentials close at hand, simply cut a board—either reclaimed or from the lumber yard, like this knotted Douglas fir—a few inches wider than your tub. Sand it smooth, then seal with a waterproof finish. Or search out antique versions made of metal, which often expand and have built-in soap dishes.

MULTI-USE BASKETS

These old-fashioned three-tiered baskets may have been designed for separating produce in the kitchen, but they are just as brilliant at storing toiletries in the bathroom. Group like items (paper goods, exfoliators, and salves are shown above) in each tier to keep it neat.

SPACE-SAVING HOOKS

Indispensable in the kitchen (for hanging pots) and the garage (for hanging tools), oversize S hooks are also handy in the bathroom: They let you hang more towels than a single rod allows and can be shifted to meet your needs. Plus, brass hooks pop against a bronze bar and a dark wall.

HOW TO ORGANIZE
KITCHENS

There's no need to undertake an all-out renovation to breathe new life into your kitchen. Employing time-tested strategies will ensure the hardest-working area of the house is also the most productive—and the most inviting. Start with these tenets: Make the most of every inch, clear out what you don't need, and design a space that works for you. Then keep in mind the following lessons.

KEEP THINGS WHERE YOU USE THEM

Consider this the platinum rule of kitchen organization. Storing things near where they'll be most used saves on time—important when trying to feed the family during the morning rush hour, getting dinner on the table on a busy weeknight, and even having friends over for a home-cooked meal. Take the open shelves, opposite: Their placement is conveniently located within arm's reach of the dishwasher for easy unloading.

Also, creating "stations" will help streamline your daily to-dos. The following are meant as examples; pinpoint your most-common prep and cooking activities to devise your own.

COFFEE AND TEA TIME: Ease your morning routine by congregating mugs, stirrers, coffee beans, the electric grinder, and sugar and other sweeteners next to your coffeemaker of choice (French press, espresso machine, or otherwise). Keep assorted teas, tea balls and sachets, and teapots in the same vicinity.

BREAKFAST NOOK: Stow the bread box by the toaster; have the juicer out on the counter.

STOVE SUPPLIES: Stash cooking oils, salt and pepper, preferred spices, and key utensils near the stove. Rest assorted items on a tray for a tidy appearance (and to catch drips). Separate metal and wood tools in crocks.

BAKING GOODS: Keep canisters of flour, sugar, oats, spices, and other staples near the stand mixer, along with baking tools and dry-measuring cups.

DON'T HIDE EVERYTHING

Besides providing easy access, open shelving helps make the space feel light and airy. It's less expensive and easier to customize than closed cabinetry. Shelving can also put underused space to work, fitting in where a cabinet wouldn't. If you don't want everything on view, opt for a mix: open shelving for items you use often or enjoy having on display, behind-closed-doors for the rest.

MARTHA MUST

I use a rolling cart (above) for portable storage, so I can wheel it to the stove during cooking and park it out of the way other times. I store dog treats and medicine on the bottom shelf, oversize pots and pans in the middle, and crocks of utensils on the top, within easy reach.

MAXIMIZE DRAWER SPACE

Deal with a hodgepodge of implements in a multitude of shapes, sizes, and storability by providing each tool its own place. Make use of housewares-store compartments, dividers, and liners, and take a step back to think about how best they can be used.

POTS AND PANS: Deep drawers can be a convenient alternative to a cabinet for some items, allowing you to reach them more easily. Add a divider on one side for the lids.

SPICES: Because spices should not be exposed to heat or light, drawers make smart storage options. Arrange the spices in low racks, as shown above, decanting them into clear same-size jars and adding labels with dates.

UTENSILS AND KNIVES: Fit out a drawer with bamboo inserts, picking the dimensions to match your needs. You can even find inserts with knife slots (called knife docks) for protecting sharp blades.

LINENS: Fold and stack napkins, tea towels, and runners to keep them orderly, using dividers to hold napkin rings or place cards. Tuck pot holders and trivets in a drawer near the stove, where they are needed most (above, they share a drawer with spices, separated by a divider).

PLATES AND BOWLS: If you don't have enough cabinet space for all your dishware, consider storing it in a sizable drawer; the one above has a cut-to-fit pegboard liner (sold at home-improvement stores) with tall pegs holding each stack in place. Some drawers even come with pegs already installed.

BAKING PANS AND CUTTING BOARDS: Stacking these items is often the default choice, but not the most conducive to frequent use. Instead, stand them up in a deep drawer (or over-the-oven cabinet), using sturdy metal dividers from an office-supply store or those intended for pot lids.

"JUNK" DRAWER: What to do with all the stuff that doesn't belong anywhere else? Store it in a special drawer—and then tidy it every few months. Keep it from looking messy by giving each type of "junk" (batteries, rubber bands, and the like) its own container.

PUT YOUR PANTRY TO WORK

The organizing principles that apply to your cooking supplies also work for your foodstuffs—store like with like and get creative with containers. If you don't have a walk-in pantry, you can rely on cabinets, open shelving, and other clever contrivances, such as the nook shown at right. No matter your space, the principles are the same.

- Decant dry goods into matching canisters, and label and date each one.

- Group foods according to their use or by type. At right, condiments live on one shelf, beans and legumes on another, baking goods and extra cooking oils on a third.

- Use valuable floor space for holding long-lived vegetables such as onions and potatoes, keeping them in separate baskets or open bins (never closed containers).

- Reserve a shelf for small appliances, tea towels, and other odds and ends.

- Use a nail to hang twine or other kitchen staples.

MORE IDEAS
AND INSPIRATION

Just because your kitchen is tight on space doesn't mean it's short on potential. Rather, maximize your kitchen's efficiency with these counter-clearing solutions.

MAKESHIFT ISLAND

A kitchen island offers a handy workstation. If your space can't accommodate a permanent fixture, refashion one from a slender table. Screw casters onto legs for added height and movability; top with concrete, Silestone, or other countertop material (cut to size at the store). Finally, install rods (cut with a tube cutter) between the legs for hanging baskets, and towel bars on the sides for hanging essentials with S hooks.

VERTICAL SPACE

Pot racks keep often-used cookware within reach but away from foot traffic. The above rack is actually a repurposed vintage ladder, which has been hung over a kitchen island, and makes use of S hooks to keep pots and pans close at hand. It adds a rustic touch to a bright and cheery space.

PROJECT

PEGBOARD STORAGE

Made famous by Julia Child, pegboard is a practical and presentable way to house multiple wares in the kitchen. This stylish update swaps out particleboard for plywood; larger holes yield a graphic result, and long pegs can support shelves or accommodate larger items.

SUPPLIES

¾-inch-by-4-foot-by-8-foot birch plywood sheet

1-inch-thick wood dowel

Circular saw (optional)

Hacksaw

Measuring tape

Pencil

Handheld electric drill

1-inch paddle or Forstner drill bit

Fine grade sandpaper (220-grit)

2 French cleat brackets

Wall-mounting screws

Shelves

1. Cut the plywood sheet with a circular saw to fit your space (or have the lumber-yard do it). Cut the dowel into 12-inch pegs using a hacksaw.

2. Measure and mark a grid of 1-inch holes on plywood (as shown at right).

3. Drill the holes with a 1-inch paddle or Forstner drill bit. Lightly sand pegs and board.

4. Mount board on wall using two French cleat brackets.

5. Add pegs and shelves (the pegs' tight fit will hold them steady).

TIP

Mount the adjustable shelves according to their contents, placing frequently used items (such as a smart device, for recipes) on a lower one, pantry staples in the middle, and more decorative objects on top. Include single pegs for hanging tea towels, measuring spoons, cutting boards, and other essentials.

HOW TO ORGANIZE
LAUNDRY ROOMS

Augment this no-nonsense area with some sensible solutions—versatile wall shelves being the most space-expanding enhancements. Read on for more smart ways to upgrade your wash, dry, and repeat routine.

ORGANIZING ELEMENTS

Any size laundry "room" can be every bit as functional as a much larger space if you employ a few basic principles.

SHELVES

Deep shelving units expand storage space upward; aim for at least 12 inches to fit all your laundry essentials.

■ If you like the look of custom-built shelves but don't like their price point or permanence, consider this next-best-thing solution: Install open wooden shelves on stylish and substantial brackets, and add a rounded edge for a more finished look. The ones shown opposite are painted the same shade as the wall in easy-to-clean semi-gloss paint, for a harmonious effect.

■ You could also opt for an affordable and convenient shelving system whereby shelves hang from a wall-mounted bracket; this allows you to easily reposition the shelves over time.

■ No wall space? Use a bookcase or cabinet, applying the same storing suggestions below to keep it orderly.

SUPPLIES

Prevent provisions from looking chaotic by decanting and other simple steps.

■ Keep regular supplies within easy reach; place extras and incidentals on a high shelf or in another out-of-the-way spot.

■ Store unsightly items in baskets and bins. Lightweight baskets are also great for transporting clothes to closets or other areas of the home.

■ Corral everything you need to treat stains in one bin or tray (see page 132 for a handy chart); place mending items in another.

■ A fold-up drying rack can be tucked between the washer and dryer or hung on the wall when not in use.

SURFACES

Consider other aspects of getting the laundry done, like folding and hanging.

■ Include a flat surface for folding clothes right out of the dryer (or off the clothesline). Place a plank atop side-by-side units, either painted to match, as shown opposite, or left plain. If that's not an option—say, for stackable units—you could mount a drop-down ledge. Or use your ironing board.

■ A system for hanging freshly laundered garments is key, as is a place to keep a steady supply of hangers. The under-shelf rod, opposite, is simply a metal drapery rod; to mount it, drill a hole slightly larger than the rod's diameter on the inside of each bracket. Rolling carts are also easy to find, come in affordable options, and offer where-you-need-it convenience.

TIP

Once towels and linens are neatly folded, you'll want to keep them that way. Use upturned brackets as shelf dividers to keep them from toppling over, as shown opposite. This idea works for linen closets, too.

HOW TO ORGANIZE
HOME OFFICES

Today's home office needs to fulfill a number of roles—household command center, creative work space, and personal refuge. Design an area that works for you, whether it's a dedicated room, a corner of the kitchen, or even a customized bookshelf (see page 37).

START WITH THE SURFACES

A clutter-free desk is much more conducive to getting down to business.

- Clear your desk of all but the must-haves, such as your computer and task lamp.

- Cull each shelf and drawer in your office and remove outdated and unnecessary items.

- Keep supplies within easy reach, whether in drawers or on a surface near your desk.

- Design an inspiration board that provides even more storage opportunities; the graphic grid (pictured opposite) lends style and substance to the room.

- For a polished look, gather loose items in matching metal canisters (which can also be hung on the grid, as shown opposite) or trinket bowls.

TIP

To make the sleek hanging folders shown opposite, cut a 14-by-18-inch piece of faux leather and fold it in half, leaving 1 inch extending on one side. Mark spots ⅝ inch from the top and side of front flap, then punch holes through both flaps. Insert grommets into holes, then hang with J hooks.

KEEP ON TOP OF PAPERWORK

Follow the "touch once" rule for paperwork: Either act on it, file it away, or discard it (by shredding or recycling).

- Place paperwork in designated bins or files labled as "to-do" or "in progress."

- Stash papers and file folders in magazine holders. Personalize them with numbered or lettered stencils, as shown opposite, or give them custom labels of your own design.

- Assign colors (as in red for "do today") or categories ("personal") to folders or paperwork using Post-it notes, stickers, or washi tape. If you share a work space or a filing cabinet, assign a color to each family member.

STRIVE FOR COMFORT

Create a warm and pleasant space by adhering to the following tips and guidelines.

- Set up your computer ergonomically: When you sit down and straighten your arm, your pointer finger should be at the center of the screen. Elevate a laptop to the proper height and use an external keyboard and mouse to avoid hunching your back.

- Add human touches to keep the space from feeling too sterile. Beloved family photos, framed artwork, pretty pottery, travel keepsakes, or other personal mementos can add some style and substance without cluttering the space.

- Plants are proven stress-reducers, plus foliage brightens any room. If you lack sufficient light for potted plants, consider "bouquets" of freshly cut mint or other herbs.

HOW LONG SHOULD YOU KEEP RECORDS?

1 YEAR
Paid bills

Copies of checks for non-tax-deductible items

Annual investment statements

7 YEARS
IRS tax records

Bank and credit card statements

Records of deductible expenses

FOR AS LONG AS THEY ARE ACTIVE
Contracts

Mortgage records

Real-estate deeds

Home-improvement receipts

Paid bills for insurable purchases

Stock or bond certificates

Vehicle titles

INDEFINITELY
Birth certificates

Marriage and divorce papers

Social Security cards

Passports

Education records

MORE IDEAS
AND INSPIRATION

These clever innovations prove that you can carve a fully functional workstation out of a former closet, a blank wall, or even one section of a bookcase.

STUDIO IN A CLOSET

This former closet is now an orderly artist's studio with all the elements of the creative process (as well as a place to keep track of bills). The double doors are lined on the inside with cork linoleum for tacking up pieces of inspiration—and can hide it all away when the workday is done. This same idea can also be applied to fashion a sewing or crafting space.

WALL UNIT

This all-in-one piece turns a desk nook into a more practical place. The three vertical steel standards allow you to raise or lower bracketed shelves according to your needs. DIY touches help to up the efficiency: Large holes drilled into one shelf fit containers for small supplies (plus essentials like flowers); leather strips attached with brass tacks soften the edges; a "drawer" under the desktop is ideal for personal devices.

DIY FOLD-AWAY DESK

This desk system maximizes square footage by fitting into a modular bookshelf. It also neatly hides away so your work is out of sight, out of mind (see also page 83 for how to turn shelves into matching felt-covered cubbies).

SUPPLIES

Modular shelf system

Measuring tape

Birch plywood, ¾-inch wide

Circular saw

Eggshell paint

Wool felt

Multipurpose spray adhesive

2 desk hinges with screws

2 lid-stay hinges with screws

1. Measure width and height of opening you want to use for pull-down desk. Using a saw, cut a piece of plywood to those dimensions. Paint to match shelf; let dry completely.

2. Cut felt to dimensions of plywood. Spray one side of plywood with adhesive, press felt onto surface, and let dry.

3. Remove shelf and cut down back edge by ¾ inch (or have it cut at your local lumberyard).

4. Align plywood desk with shelf. Screw two desk hinges into desk and then to shelf.

5. Place shelf and plywood desk in bookcase. Screw lid-stay hinges into shelf and desk.

HOW TO ORGANIZE
KIDS' ROOMS

When little ones enter the picture, they bring big changes—and not just to your routine. Even the most stalwart tidy-uppers will find new challenges. Read on for how to embrace kid-friendly organizing habits.

FIVE STRATEGIES FOR SUCCESS

Involve your kids in the process, letting them help define certain spaces in their rooms. This way, you'll also be able to better see the room from their—shorter—perspective.

1. Sort belongings and store like with like. Categories include clothing, toys, books, and other gear, such as sports or crafts supplies.

2. Once sorted, corral smaller items into containers before storing; this is especially helpful for arts-and-crafts supplies.

3. Label boxes, bins, and everything else so the kids know where everything goes—they'll be more likely to return things to their designated spots.

4. Opt for open storage solutions whenever possible, as these are easier for little hands to maneuver. Consider bookshelves and bins rather than dressers and chests for clothes and toys. You might also want to remove a closet door and use the upper part for infrequently used items, leaving lower shelves for everyday objects.

5. Purge periodically—at least twice a year (and use the Four-Box Formula on page 10). Some parents swear by the "one in, one out" rule of new toy–buying; let your child choose which toy is out.

CURATING ARTWORK

Kids' creative endeavors can quickly accumulate, but there are ways to keep it under control—and the budding artist feeling inspired.

- Go through the collection with your child every so often to pare it down.

- Choose the ones you want to display (see page 41 for one idea).

- Try to keep only one piece per week, then at the end of the month, pick your favorites to stow away.

- Decide what to do with the rest: send to grandparents, recycle for craft projects and gift wrapping, and/or donate to a children's hospital or other place in need of charm and cheer.

MARTHA MUST

Stowing at least some toys within reach encourages curiosity and keeps children engaged. I prefer to buy colorful wooden toys, both old- and new-fashioned, that can also serve as a focal point in my grandchildren's playroom.

MORE IDEAS
AND INSPIRATION

Put cherished keepsakes on display to keep them off the floor
(or wherever your child tosses them).

PICTURE-BOOK LIBRARY

A ready-made plate rack can be easily trans-
formed into a child's bookshelf, displaying toys
and books. The forward-facing covers make
it easy for kids to find the current favorite and
create an ever-changing wall of artwork.

TOY EXPO

Some picture rails are just deep enough to hold
miniature models. If your kids are not the build-
it-to-knock-it-down sort, mount the floating
shelves in his or her room. You can always add
more shelves as the collection grows.

PROJECT

PIN-UP PANEL

What to do if your child is a prolific artist? Show off all that handiwork in a gallery-worthy display. Originally made for Martha's grandchildren, this double-height bulletin board was made from Homasote, then covered with fabric for an ever-changing exhibit.

SUPPLIES

Utility knife

Straightedge (such as a ruler)

Homasote

Scissors

Fabric (such as burlap, linen, or canvas)

Staple gun

Craft knife

Power drill with ¼-inch and ⅜-inch drill bits

Grommet set (⅜-inch)

Plastic anchors and flathead screws (#12)

1. STRETCH FABRIC

Using utility knife and straight-edge, cut Homasote to fit your space. With scissors, cut fabric 3 inches larger than Homasote board on all sides; lay fabric right-side down. Center board on fabric. Wrap fabric around one side of board and staple once in center back. Pull taut, then staple opposite side. Repeat with other 2 sides. Continue stapling, adding pairs of staples along opposite sides, working toward corners. Stop a few inches before corners.

2. AFFIX CORNERS

At corners, fold fabric as flat as possible. Staple one side all the way to corner, then fold perpendicular side on top. Pull taut and staple. Flip board over.

3. SCORE FABRIC

With a craft knife, score four ½-inch Xs in fabric, 1 inch in and 1 inch down from each corner.

4. DRILL HOLES

At Xs, create pilot holes by drilling through board with a ¼-inch bit. (Fold fabric away first, so bit doesn't come into contact with fabric.) Using holes as guides, drill through board again with a ⅜-inch bit.

5. SET GROMMETS

Set a ⅜-inch grommet shank in each drill hole. (If it's a tight fit, tap in with a hammer.)

6. MOUNT TO WALL

Set anchors in wall, then use screws to mount the board.

TIP

To keep the board from getting overwhelmed by paper, periodically remove all the art and file it. But first, snap a photograph of the fully covered board to document the kids' progress, phases, and favorites.

HOW TO ORGANIZE
GARAGES

We ask a lot of this space beyond parking the car. Just think: gardening gear, lawnmowers and weeders, sporting goods and lawn games, recycling bins, and more. Here's a plan to get this hardworking space in order.

MAKE THE MOST OF WALL SPACE

Achieving garage nirvana is all about keeping as many things off the floor as possible (lawnmowers being an exception). To help you do this, you'll want to stock up on hooks of all shapes, sizes, and strengths (e.g., loads).

- There's a screw-hook for every type of item; rubber-coated utility hooks like the ones shown at right protect surfaces from scratches. A sideways hook can accommodate certain items, such as a dustpan.

- Use two-pronged hooks for heavier items like outdoor furniture, large shovels and rakes, ladders, lawn feeders, and motorized edgers, as well as for smaller items (such as bike pumps) that can't be hung on a single hook.

- Garden hoses can be mounted on special hose (or ladder) hooks, which come in a variety of finishes and styles; be sure to buy one that is deep enough to fit your particular hose length. The one shown at right also holds a broom.

- Bungee cords help restrain heavy, awkward items that can't stand up straight on their own (such as a wheelbarrow). Strap each end of the cord to a hook in the wall.

- Pegboard is tailor-made for utilitarian spaces like this, too; mount hook brackets to hold adjustable shelving, and use S hooks to hang small tools, bins, and baskets.

STORE LIKE WITH LIKE

Separating the space into zones—gardening, recycling, sports gear, etc.—will help keep it orderly.

- Organize containers by type, whether for hardware, paint supplies, or gardening tools.

- Keep recycling and garbage bins in an easy-to-access spot.

- Mount a drop-down shelf on a hinged bracket for a garden and compost station.

- If you are storing boxes, invest in a sturdy shelving unit to protect them from moisture and temperature fluctuations.

- A tall freestanding cabinet can hold extra pantry items and cleaning supplies, or seasonal gear such as ski boots or beach towels.

- Include a wall-mounted clipboard with a notepad for reminders about lawn care (watering, fertilizing, and planting) as well as car maintenance.

HOW TO ORGANIZE
TAG SALES

Whether you're planning a major move or just simplifying your home, a tag sale helps you earn points on the recycle-and-reuse scorecard and may also put some money back in your pocket. Plan well in advance and be strategic to make the most of your time, effort, and stuff.

PREP FOR SUCCESS

You'll want to get as many people to your sale as possible, so plan ahead—and spread the word.

PURGE: Go through every room and set aside all the things you don't love, don't use, or don't even remember owning—all indications that an item has passed its expiration date. For more tips, see page 10.

PLAN: Decide on a weekend for your sale. June through October tends to be the busiest time for yard sales—meaning there will be stiff competition. It's a good idea to invite neighbors and friends to participate, since multifamily sales attract more customers. Check with your town to see if a permit is required, and also if you need special permission for on-street parking.

BE RAIN-READY: Plan an alternate rain date or be prepared to sell out of your garage. Die-hard yard-sale shoppers will show up rain, snow, or shine.

PROMOTE: Post "save the date" notices a few weeks ahead, and then announce the sale the week before. Use Craigslist and local websites, social media, and any local circulars or neighborhood groups. Give the date and time, a rain date if there is one, and the exact address. Specify "no early birds" if that's your policy.

POST SIGNS: Make easy-to-read posters to place around the neighborhood and a large eye-catching sign for your yard, too, so people will know they've found the right place.

PRICE IT RIGHT: Set your prices high enough to allow for bargaining but not so high that you'll scare off buyers. And let people know that you're willing to negotiate. Put a price tag on everything, no matter how small, and if an item is noteworthy, label it as such—"mid-century modern Eames chair," for example. Having tables or bins with "Two for $5" and other bargains will help ratchet up the sales.

STRATEGIZE FOR SALES

Creating an inviting scene will go far in getting people to browse—and buy.

THINK THROUGH DISPLAY OPTIONS: Gather as many picnic and card tables as you can (your neighbors are bound to have some). First assemble everything you want to sell on the ground, then plan table displays. Group like items by color for visual interest. Use existing clotheslines to display clothes and linens, or rent (or borrow) rolling racks.

OFFER REFRESHMENTS: Have the kids set up an old-school lemonade stand. Or consider offering coffee and tea to early risers and first-comers, who are most likely going to be your biggest buyers.

BY AFTERNOON, CONSOLIDATE: By midmorning of your sale, much will be gone, so regroup and reprice your tables. Move items closer to the street for impulse buyers passing by, and reduce prices during the last two hours of the sale.

PACK UP THE REST: Pack up boxes for donating and consider putting "free" signs on the rest.

DONATION GUIDELINES

Many places will not accept the following:

- Cribs
- Car seats, walkers, or other products that do not meet the current safety standards of the U.S. Consumer Product Safety Commission
- Mattresses or box springs
- Carpet or carpet padding
- Household chemical products: pesticides, paint, paint thinner, drain cleaner, oven cleaner, aerosols, and other hazardous-waste products
- Automotive hazardous waste: tires, lead acid batteries, additives, gasoline, oils, antifreeze, etc.
- Large appliances: refrigerators, ovens, washer-dryers, air conditioners, furnaces, water heaters, etc.
- Personal care and fragrance items
- Plumbing fixtures or building materials
- Recyclables
- Weapons of any kind

FIX
AND
MAINTAIN

Every home needs repair at some point—drains get clogged, faucets drip, and windows crack. And so, every homeowner should have at least some of the basic skills necessary to do common fixes.

You might be surprised that many problems can be remedied with a simple toolkit and a bit of rudimentary know-how—and without relying on a professional, saving you much money over the years. Of course, even if you never plan to fix anything yourself, you'll benefit from knowing what each repair entails so you can determine if the work is being done correctly, efficiently, and cost effectively.

As the owner of several homes with complex operating systems, I can offer you this advice: When you notice something is wrong, or beginning to falter, you should address the problem immediately. Ignoring things invariably results in more extensive (and expensive) repairs. Equally important: Rather than waiting for problems to arise, take simple steps to prevent them from cropping up in the first place. And if you haven't done so already, familize yourself with your home's mechanicals, including water shut-off valves and circuit breakers.

Follow the step-by-step instructions in this chapter to become self-sufficient, self-confident, and knowledgeable about what needs to be done, when it needs to be done.

THE ALL-PURPOSE TOOLBOX

Before you can tighten a doorknob, hang a picture, or fix a leaky faucet (or attempt the myriad DIY projects throughout this book), you'll need to equip yourself with the right tools. This first-aid kit for the home will cover the typical pounding and prying jobs that crop up. There's no problem, in other words, that you won't be prepared to handle. For how to create a plumbing repair kit, see page 53.

POWER DRILL

A lightweight (9.6-volt), cordless model is versatile and easy to use, and offers go-anywhere drilling. Plug-in models are often more powerful and may be a better option for certain jobs. Most drills come with basic drill bits; supplement as needed.

HAMMER

A 16-ounce curve-claw hammer is the go-to size for most people; test out other sizes and weights to find one that's comfortable. A hammer with a smaller head is better for driving nails into a wall.

SCREWDRIVER

You'll need both small and large versions of the flat and Phillips-head models. Multi-head drivers conveniently feature interchangeable tips. A "ratchet action" model doesn't require resetting after each turn.

STAPLE GUN

A light-duty staple gun lets you repair window screens, replace upholstery, and hang holiday lights (among other decorating tasks). For heavy-duty tacking like installing insulation or weather stripping, look for an electric staple gun with a safety switch.

WRENCH

For everyday assemble-it-yourself needs (furniture, bicycles, etc.), an adjustable (or crescent) wrench is about all you need. Pros prefer socket wrenches for speed and maneuvering in tight spaces, and most come with different-size sockets.

DO YOUR HOMEWORK

Don't wait for a power failure or flooded basement to figure out your home's inner workings, such as valves and power sources.

LOCATE WATER VALVES

The main shutoff valve will usually be next to the meter. Every fixture has its own local valve, too.

LABEL YOUR WATER PIPES

Print the name of the water source on a peel-off label; affix the labels to copper plant tags, and wrap them around the appropriate pipes.

PLIERS

Having a variety will cover most jobs. Slip-joint pliers (above, top) are a general go-to; needle-nose pliers (above, bottom) twist and bend wire and reach into tight spaces; groove-joint pliers (not shown) are great for nuts, bolts, and irregular shapes.

SCISSORS

A sturdy pair of scissors is essential for so many everyday tasks such as cutting kraft paper, tape, and twine. Stainless steel fights rust; those with a non-stick coating will be resistant to adhesives.

HEX KEYS

These usually come in sets of five or more, with the most convenient being held together in a sleeve with a slot for each size. The smallest keys are helpful for electronics and toys, the others for assembling prefab furniture and working on bicycles.

TAPE

Stock an assortment of tapes in 1- to 2-inch widths: blue painters', for low-tack adhering to painted walls and delicate surfaces; all-purpose masking, for small jobs; duct, for holding items together temporarily; plumbers' (thread-seal), to help seal pipe threads; and electrical, for wrapping wires and cables.

MEASURING TOOLS

A 1-inch-wide, 25-foot-long measuring tape with a locking mechanism lets you measure most anything. A 9-inch torpedo level (named for its shape) is also a must for hanging anything. A ruler is still a great straightedge, though a yardstick offers more coverage.

UTILITY KNIFE

Basic models will do, as long as they have a retractable blade to prevent accidents. Buy plenty of extra blades and replace often—dull blades are more likely to cause injury by slipping during use. Some models offer tool-free blade replacement.

PUTTY KNIFE

Opt for a few different sizes. Besides its primary role—to smooth putty when filling holes and dents in walls—it can be used as a scraper; just be sure to reserve separate ones for either smoothing or scraping.

ASSORTED HARDWARE

Keep assorted sizes of screws (both flat- and Phillips-head), nails, picture hangers, and anchors and bolts (see pages 74–75 for more information on those) neatly organized in a compartmented tray or container that fits inside your toolbox.

---

3 **LABEL YOUR CIRCUIT SWITCHES**

If your electrician hasn't already done so, label each circuit switch in your fuse box or circuit breaker with the room or area of the house it controls. Attach a flashlight to the box (using magnets or Velcro).

4 **MAKE A FLOOR PLAN**

It should include the location of shutoff valves, fuses, circuit breakers, or power sources for everything that uses water, gas, or electricity. Apply color-coded stickers for each utility. Keep this somewhere safe and visible.

HOW TO FIX
FAUCETS

That steady drip may not seem like much, but over time you could potentially be wasting thousands of gallons of precious water. Most likely it's caused by one of three culprits—worn-out washers, faulty O-rings, or built-up sediment—though other problems can also be to blame. How you go about fixing the faucet depends on its type.

FIRST THINGS FIRST

Start by identifying which faucet you have from the four basic types below.

COMPRESSION FAUCETS are the most affordable and the most likely to leak; they are also common in older homes. To stop the water flow, you need to screw down, or compress, the separate hot and cold handles. The compression faucet is the only type that relies on a rubber washer to close off the valve seat.

BALL FAUCETS have a ball-shaped cap above the base of the spout, and a single handle on top that you rotate for hot and cold water. Beneath the rounded cap, a slotted plastic or metal ball controls the water flow and temperature. The ball faucet tends to need more repairs than other washerless types, usually on account of worn springs, or dried-out O-rings or rubber seals around the rotating ball.

CARTRIDGE FAUCETS are a bit tricky to spot, since they can be either single- or double-handled. On a single-handled model, the cartridge moves up and down to control water flow and left or right to adjust temperature. Two-handled models look like compression faucets, except in the closed position a cartridge faucet will turn off smoothly, without having to tighten the handles. Worn-out O-rings and cartridges are the most common cause of leaks.

DISK FAUCETS are easily identified by having a single handle on top of a wide cylindrical cartridge. Two ceramic disks (one stationary, the other not) control the flow of water. In the unlikely event these faucets need repairs, a worn-out cartridge or seal is probably to blame.

BEFORE YOU BEGIN

- For any sink repair, turn off the water locally by closing the shutoff valve.

- Line the sink or tub basin with a towel to protect the surface, cover the drain, and provide a safe spot to place the disassembled parts, in order of removal.

MARTHA MUST

I always wrap the teeth of pliers and wrenches with painters' or masking tape to keep those tools from scarring fine metal surfaces. I also wrap the faucet or other hardware, for extra protection.

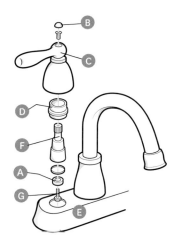
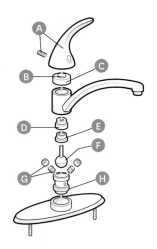
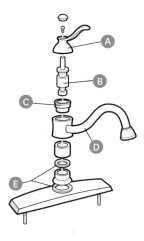
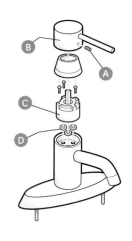

SUPPLIES

Screwdriver

Groove-joint pliers, or a wrench

Replacement parts (likely washer)

SUPPLIES

Wrench or screwdriver

Groove-joint pliers

Needle-nose pliers

Utility knife

Replacement parts

SUPPLIES

Screwdriver

Needle-nose pliers (optional)

Utility knife

Replacement parts (likely O-rings)

SUPPLIES

Screwdriver

Replacement parts (likely seals or cartridge)

White vinegar (optional)

COMPRESSION FAUCETS:

1. To replace the washer (A), pry off the decorative cap (B) on the handle (C), then use a screwdriver to remove the handle. With pliers or a wrench, loosen the faucet's large bonnet nut (D) in a counterclockwise motion. Hold the faucet seat (E) securely to avoid wrenching it loose from the sink.

2. With the nut loosened, unscrew the faucet stem (F) from the seat. Remove the screw (G) and the washer at the end of the stem. Refit with a new washer.

3. Screw the stem back into the seat, and retighten the bonnet nut.

BALL FAUCETS:

1. With a wrench, unscrew faucet handle (A), or unscrew handle-set screw with a screwdriver, and lift off handle.

2. For a leaking handle, tighten adjusting ring (B) with groove-joint pliers.

3. For a leaking spout, use groove-joint pliers to take off adjusting ring and cap (C). Remove cam (D), cam washer (E), and rotating ball (F). With needle-nose pliers, remove inlet seals and springs (G). Cut off O-rings (H) with a utility knife. Replace parts as needed.

4. Reassemble the faucet.

CARTRIDGE FAUCETS:

1. Unscrew the handle (A) and remove the cartridge (B). Remove the retaining clip (found inside C), if it has one, using needle-nose pliers.

2. Remove the spout (D). Cut off the O-rings (E) using a utility knife. Replace the O-rings with new ones.

3. If O-rings are not worn, you may need to replace the cartridge. Some faucet brands, such as Moen, require a special cartridge remover (at faucet dealers) to take out the cartridge.

4. Reassemble the faucet.

DISK FAUCETS:

1. Remove the set screw (A) from the side of the handle (B). Unscrew the cartridge (C). With a screwdriver, lift out the seals (D) from the cartridge.

2. If the seals are damaged, replace them. If the cartridge itself is badly worn, replace it. Otherwise, clean it with equal parts white vinegar and water, rinse, and let dry.

3. Reassemble the faucet.

HOW TO FIX
DRAINS

Stopped-up sinks or showers are bound to happen—it's no surprise they rank near the top of home plumbing predicaments. But rather than calling in a professional (at least just yet), it's worth trying to diagnose—and quickly resolve—the problem yourself.

SUPPLIES

Cup plunger

Drain auger

Bucket

Pipe wrench

Bottle brush

Plumbers' tape

PREVENT CLOGS FROM HAPPENING IN THE FIRST PLACE

Taking these small, simple steps will help keep drains working properly.

- Place a mesh screen on every sink drain in your home.

- In the kitchen, never pour fat down the drain, and wipe oil and grease from pans before rinsing them in the sink.

- In the bathroom, brush hair before getting into the shower. And go easy on products (especially hair conditioners) that contain oils, which can lead to drain-clogging residue.

BEFORE YOU BEGIN

Before you pour any commercial liquid product down your drain—and into the waterways—read the label. Avoid anything made with toxic chemicals and opt for one of these earth-friendly methods instead:

- Pour ½ cup baking soda, followed by ½ cup white vinegar, down the drain, and cover with a drain plug or wet rag. Also cover any overflow hole or the other drain in a double sink. Let this mixture do its work for about 5 minutes, then flush with a kettle of boiling water (or tap water at its hottest setting, to avoid damaging more delicate pipes), followed by cold tap water for about 30 seconds.

- Try using enzymatic drain openers, such as Super Digest-It or Rid-X, another safe way to help dissolve clogs. They contain mighty microorganisms that eat away at the interfering material, turning it into carbon dioxide and water.

NEXT STEPS

PLUNGE AWAY: Fill about one-third of the sink or tub with water, then cover the overflow hole or double-sink drain and begin plunging the drain vigorously with a cup plunger, working the plunger cap up and down four to five times before quickly pulling up. Make sure to use the right kind of plunger: Anything will work for a sink or tub drain, but toilets require a flange type in order to seal properly (see page 53). Keep at it; you may need to plunge off and on for 10 minutes. If that doesn't work …

ACTIVATE THE AUGER: Feed the long, thin steel coil, or "snake," down the drain in a twisting motion and through the blockage; then work the auger back and forth to loosen the clog. You'll need to plunge again, then run water for a few minutes. If you still face slow draining, hear a gurgling sound, and/or see water bubbling up into the sink …

CHECK THE TRAP: The U-shaped bend at the lowest point of the drainpipe under the sink stays filled with water to keep sewer gases out; it also traps solids that accidentally slip down the drain. To clear it, turn off the sink's water supply and place a bucket under the trap. With a pipe wrench, loosen the nuts at either end, and remove and empty the trap. Run a bottle brush through it to clean the walls. Replace the trap and the nuts after wrapping the threads with plumbers' tape. If you are unable to resolve the matter yourself …

CALL A PLUMBER: And remember: Plunging too forcefully, or tinkering with the wrong pipes, can cause more damage than good, especially to older plumbing systems.

HOW TO FIX
TOILETS

Because they are subjected to frequent use, toilets are bound to malfunction once in a while. Before they do, make sure you have a reliable plunger, familiarize yourself with the inner workings, and read through the steps for the two most-common toilet conundrums.

SUPPLIES

Rubber gloves

Replacement parts (flapper and/or chain)

Fine steel wool

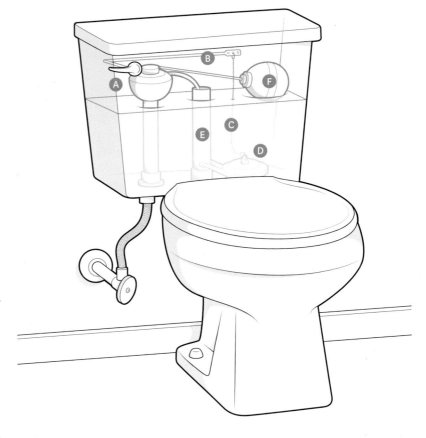

ANATOMY OF A TOILET

It helps to understand what's hiding under the lid of the tank: The flush handle (A) is connected to a lever (B) attached to a chain (C) descending to the flapper (or stop) valve (D) that's hooked to the bottom of the overflow tube (E). When the handle is depressed, the flapper valve opens, releasing water from the tank and causing the toilet to flush. As the tank refills, the float (F) rises to a certain level until the float-arm position triggers the refill to stop.

HOW TO STOP A RUNNING TOILET

When a little jiggling doesn't do the trick, it's time to don some gloves and tackle the tank.

1. First try bending the float arm to adjust the height of the float; if it is too high, the water will keep filling the tank. Also check that the chain is not hooked on something.

2. If that fails, turn off the water and flush toilet to drain tank. If it empties without flushing, the flapper or stopper is broken.

3. Disconnect chain, remove damaged stop valve, and replace (use model name and number of toilet to purchase the right one).

4. While the flapper is off, clean the valve's seat with fine steel wool to secure the seal. Make sure the new flapper is seated flush in the water tank's drainage hole.

5. Then turn the water back on, make sure the tank is holding it, and flush to confirm the flapper seats properly.

6. If not, adjust the length of the chain, which should fix the issue.

SUPPLIES

Flange plunger

Toilet auger (optional)

HOW TO UNCLOG A TOILET

Don't panic; do grab your plunger (be sure to use a flange style) and follow these steps. And take note: It's not how hard you plunge but how efficiently you get the proper seal.

1. With the flange extended, lower the plunger into the bowl at an angle so the flange fills with water and not air, then press down until it's fully compressed.

2. Pull up quickly; then work the plunger in a quick push-and-pull manner four or five times. If you notice air coming out the side of your plunger cup, shift it until you get a proper seal. Repeat plunging until the water drains on its own.

3. Remove the lid from the tank and locate the flapper (D in the diagram on opposite page). Flush the toilet using the usual lever. If everything appears normal, you're all set. If not, shut off the water by pushing the flapper over the drainage hole in the bottom of the tank.

4. Continué to plunge or use a toilet auger (a drain auger can scratch the porcelain): Place the auger end into the bowl, then hold the shaft steady as you crank the handle to feed the cable (or snake) up through the trap. Continue cranking—being careful not to be too forceful—until the cable is fully extended before reversing the motion to reel the cable back in. Flush the toilet. Still sluggish? Time to call in a pro.

TIP

To keep a just-used plunger off your clean bathroom floor, first fill a bucket with a solution of your usual disinfecting cleaner and hot water. After using the plunger, swish it around thoroughly in the hot-water mixture, rinse, then set on a rag to air-dry.

PLUMBING REPAIR KIT

Because plumbing problems crop up fairly frequently, it helps to devise a special repair kit for tackling any leaks and clogs right away. At the very least you'll need both types of plungers and a pair of rubber gloves; the rest is optional, though highly recommended—and helpful in an emergency. In a large bucket, stock the following:

- Cup (or sink) plunger with at least a 6-inch-diameter cup
- Flange (or toilet) plunger
- Pipe wrench
- Standard adjustable wrench
- Groove-joint pliers
- Flexible drain auger, or "snake"

- Toilet auger (optional)
- Assorted washers and O-rings
- Small piece of thin rubber sheeting
- Hose clamps
- Plumbers' tape
- Masking tape
- Small, powerful flashlight
- Rubber gloves

HOW TO FIX
TILE GROUT

Those tiles in your kitchen and bathroom are built to last, but not so the grout anchoring them. Grout is typically made from a porous mixture of cement, sand, polymers, and water, meaning it's a magnet for dirt and prone to discoloration.

SUPPLIES

Safety goggles

Miniature rotary tool with a grout-removal attachment, or grout saw

Small chisel

Hammer

Putty knife

Vacuum with crevice-tool attachment

Sponge

Grout (unsanded for joints less than $1/8$ inch; sanded for all else)

Rubber grout float (or old toothbrush)

Grout-haze remover

Grout sealer

HOW-TO

1. USE A STEADY HAND: Remove the old grout with a rotary tool or a chisel and hammer, then remove any remaining bits with a putty knife. Always take care to avoid letting the tool come in contact with the tile. If you can't get to all grout without endangering the tiles, leave some in place—the new material will disguise it.

2. CLEAN AND PREP: Once the old grout has been removed, vacuum up any dust with the crevice-tool attachment, and wipe the edges of the tiles with a damp sponge. Mix your new grout with water, following the package instructions.

3. APPLY, THEN LET DRY: Use a rubber grout float (or an old toothbrush if just replacing around a few tiles) to spread the mixture evenly over the tiles, pushing it into the spaces in between. Immediately clean off excess with a damp sponge, and allow to dry for at least 24 hours. Apply haze remover, then grout sealer, as directed on label.

HOW TO FIX
SHOWERHEADS

If your morning shower has lost some of its usual power, blame it (most likely) on hard-water mineral deposits that tend to clog those tiny openings in the nozzle. The following fix is easy to do.

SUPPLIES

Wrench or groove-joint pliers

Painters' or masking tape

Distilled white vinegar

Plumbers' tape

Old toothbrush

HOW-TO

1. Use wrench or pliers (wrapped in masking or painters' tape to prevent scarring; see Martha Must on page 48) to remove showerhead. Some experts recommend running water at full force while the showerhead is removed to clear out any debris that might be clogging the pipe.

2. Submerge the showerhead in a bowl of distilled white vinegar overnight.

NOTE: *If the showerhead is a Tuscan brass or an unlacquered finish, refer to the manufacturer's instructions for cleaning, as vinegar can damage the surface.*

3. Wrap plumbers' tape clockwise around the pipe thread to ensure a tight seal.

4. Remove showerhead from vinegar and use a toothbrush to scrub its face. Screw it on by hand, and then adjust with pliers to make snug.

5. If the above doesn't solve the problem, replace the showerhead with a new one, removing the existing one as described in step 1 and then following manufacturer's instructions to mount the new showerhead.

HOW TO FIX
DRAFTS

Windows are great for letting the sunshine in—and for letting much-wanted warm or cool air right back out. Doors, floors, attics, and basements? Guilty as charged. That energy loss translates to unnecessary utility costs during the winter and summer months. Here are some tricks for trapping the desired temperature inside.

GAPS BETWEEN MOLDINGS AND BASEBOARDS

Check for leaks by moving a lit candle around perimeter of a closed window or door frame and around baseboards. A flickering flame indicates a trouble spot. Fill with caulk.

SPACES UNDER OUTSIDE OR BASEMENT DOORS

The rubber strip along the bottom of a door should be snug when the door is closed. If not, replace with a new strip, available at home-improvement stores. A door sweep is needed for gaps larger than ¼ inch.

DUCTS IN UNFINISHED BASEMENTS, ATTICS, CRAWL SPACES, AND ATTACHED GARAGES

Ducts and chases in these areas can allow hot or cold air to enter and escape the home. Patch any cracks or holes with a water-based adhesive (such as duct mastic, available at hardware stores) or hire a contractor.

THE ATTIC HATCH

Use a weather-stripping kit (sold at home-improvement stores) to seal the perimeter of the hatch; this will keep hot air in during the winter and out during the summer. If you have pull-down stairs, use an insulated attic-stair cover.

WINDOWS

Winter, spring, summer, fall: Windows should be your number one priority for keeping your home at the most comfortable temperature.

- If you have single-pane windows, adding storm windows will reduce your heating and cooling costs significantly (as much as 33 percent during the winter).

- Tack clear low-emissivity (or "low-e") films onto indoor window panes; they're inexpensive, long-lasting, and energy-saving. If you're considering replacing your windows, you can have this coating applied during the manufacturing stage, too.

- Install draperies made from tightly woven fabrics, such as broadcloth, wool and wool blends, velvet, tapestry, and tweed, preferably with an insulated lining. Mount them close to the window pane and hang them from ceiling to floor. Keep them closed at night and on especially chilly or sunny days.

MARTHA MUST

I place a "snake" (also called a draft dodger) at the base of each of my drafty windows and exterior doors during the colder months. The simple snakelike shapes are easy to sew yourself, using batting or cat litter as the filler, or look for them at housewares stores.

HOW TO FIX
WINDOW SCREENS

Punctures, tears, and gashes can result over time, especially to a screen door in a well-trafficked home. The good news is that a screen is easy to replace with the right tools, following some basic steps.

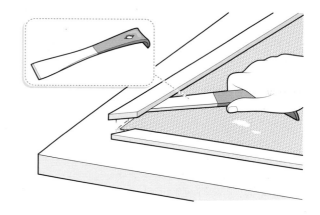

SUPPLIES

Utility knife

Metal spatula or hive tool

Flat-head screwdriver

Needle-nose pliers

Paintbrush

Fine-grade sandpaper

Replacement screening

Push pins

Staple gun

Hammer

Small brads (slender wire nails with minimal heads)

Nail set

Wood filler

HOW-TO

If you have the time, do all other needed repairs (patching paint, tightening hinges and other hardware) after removing the old screen and before replacing with the new one.

1. If there are moldings around the screen, use a utility knife to cut away any paint that might keep you from lifting up the molding; score along the seam all the way around the opening. To pry up the molding, insert spatula or hive tool under molding and gently lift it up as you again work around the opening, taking care as there will be nails (see diagram above). Set the molding strips aside (you will use them again).

2. First loosen all the staples with tip of screwdriver, then use pliers to pull out staples, being careful not to break them.

3. Clean the opening with a paintbrush, then gently sand the rough wood and brush again to remove dust.

4. Cut replacement screen to fit with utility knife (or have screening cut to fit at the home-improvement store); leave a ½-inch border around the perimeter when measuring. Place it over the opening, pulling taut and tacking in place in the corners with push pins.

5. Starting in the center of one side, use staple gun to staple screen at even intervals, anywhere from 1 to 2 inches apart. Once you finish one side, repeat on remaining sides, pulling taut and pinning to frame with push pins as needed.

6. Trim any excess screening with utility knife along outside edge.

7. With a hammer, tap out nails from removed molding strips, then replace the strips in the opening; hammer in place with brads, doing this at a slight angle; use nail set to countersink each brad. Fill in holes with wood filler.

MARTHA MUST

My favorite tool for prying up the molding is a hive tool (made for beekeeping) that has a thin flat end that slips easily under the frame, to loosen, and a large hooked end for lifting it off.

HOW TO FIX
WALLS

When a slip of the hammer leads to an unsightly hole in your wall, or when cracks appear over the course of time, skip the toothpaste and glue and use joint compound and drywall joint tape instead. Look for premixed, all-purpose compound at hardware stores.

SUPPLIES (HOLES AND DENTS)

Paintbrush

Putty knife

Joint compound

Fine-grade sandpaper (120- to 150-grit)

Primer and paint

Drywall joint tape (for small holes)

Self-adhesive mesh patch (for larger holes)

SUPPLIES (HAIRLINE CRACKS)

Scraper or 5-in-1 tool

Fine-grade sandpaper (120- to 150-grit)

Primer sealer

Paintbrush

Taping knife

Joint compound

Drywall joint tape

Primer and paint

FIRST THINGS FIRST

The following instructions for holes, dents, and cracks are for repairs to drywall. If your walls are made of plaster, you can simply fill small holes with fast-drying patching plaster or plaster of Paris: First mix the plaster powder with water according to the package instructions, then wet the surface area of the hole before filling in. Let dry before priming and painting.

PATCH HOLES AND DENTS

FOR TINY HOLES (LESS THAN ½ INCH):

1. Begin by brushing away any loose material in and around the hole with a dry paintbrush.

2. Using a putty knife, fill the hole with joint compound, erring on the side of overfilling (you will sand the surface later). Scrape off any excess compound with the knife, and let dry. Repeat as needed to fill.

3. Sand the area until it's smooth and level with the surrounding surface. The area is ready to prime and paint.

FOR SMALL HOLES (UP TO 2 INCHES):

1. Clean area around hole, then cut a piece of drywall joint tape to just cover the hole. Apply a thin layer of joint compound to the wall, and lay joint tape in place.

2. Using a putty knife, cover tape with compound, feathering it out to a 6-inch-diameter circle. Let dry.

3. Sand as above.

FOR LARGER HOLES (UP TO 6 INCHES):

1. Clean area around hole, sand lightly, then brush away dust.

2. Cover hole with a self-adhesive square mesh patch, which comes in a range of sizes.

3. Using a putty knife, fill with two or three coats of spackling, (allowing each to dry in between), feathering to a circle that's about 3 inches larger in diameter than the patch.

4. Sand as above.

REPAIR A HAIRLINE CRACK

1. Remove any loose material around the crack with a scraper or 5-in-1 tool.

2. Sand any raised spots and apply a primer sealer with a paintbrush; let dry.

3. Using a taping knife, cover entire crack with a thick coat of joint compound.

4. Place a piece of drywall joint tape over the compound, covering the entire length of the crack. With your taping knife, go over the tape to press out excess compound. Let dry.

5. Apply a thin coat of joint compound with the knife, spreading it to about 5 inches wider than the tape on either side. Let dry.

6. Sand lightly, and the wall will then be ready to prime and paint.

HOW TO REPLACE
DOORKNOBS

It's easy to take doorknobs for granted—that is, until, they start misbehaving. These functional fixtures are prone to failing to latch, getting stuck, or slipping out of place. And doorknobs are attached to doors, which if made of wood will warp over time, especially in high-humidity bathrooms. Keep these tips in mind.

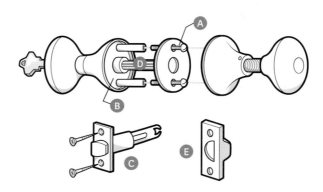

SUPPLIES

Screwdriver (most likely Phillips-head)

Replacement set

HOW-TO

For some doorknobs, you will need to first remove the "rose" (or cover), or even the actual knob; look for a small hole or slot in the cover, then insert a nailset or thin screwdriver to release.

1. REMOVE THE LOCKSET: Use a screwdriver to remove backing screws (A) on one (or both) sides of door, then pull out both knobs from either side along with backing plates (B), latch (C), and spindle (D). If latch doesn't automatically slide out of the mortise (try nudging it a little), there may be screws on edge of door that need removing.

2. REPLACE THE STRIKE PLATE: Remove screws holding old strike plate (E) in place with screwdriver, then install new plate in same position.

3. INSTALL THE NEW SET: Slide new latch into mortise (using provided screws, if included). Position locking side of knob onto door, matching square peg up with latch assembly. Then mount knob to other side of door. Tighten screws with screwdriver.

WHEN THE LATCH DOESN'T CATCH

If your door isn't staying closed—a more common occurrence than you might think—replacing the knob is not necessarily the answer. To diagnose the cause, watch how the latch bolt meets the strike plate while slowly closing the door. Is the bolt hitting above, below, or to one side of the strike plate? If so, the two are misaligned.

First, tighten the door hinges, as too-loose screws can be the culprit for doors that don't latch. You should also check to make sure the latch screws are holding it securely in place.

FOR A MINOR (LESS THAN ⅛-INCH) MISALIGNMENT: Try filling behind the inside edge of strike plate with wood filler until it is better aligned with the latch. Or use a rounded metal file to enlarge the opening enough to catch the latch.

FOR ANYTHING LARGER: Remove strike plate and extend the mortise higher or lower as necessary. Replace the plate, then fill the remaining gap in the mortise with wood filler, refinishing that area as necessary.

IF THE LATCH AND PLATE LINE UP JUST FINE, but the latch can't fully penetrate the plate, the door may have shrunk over time. Try building out the plate by attaching a shim (a thin piece of metal or wood) in the plate's position before replacing the plate. You may also need to do this for the door's hinges.

TIP

Use this gentle soaking solution to restore doorknobs and hinges to their former beauty: In an old saucepan—one you'll never use for food—mix 4 tablespoons baking soda with 1 quart water. Place hardware in the pan, then simmer for 20 minutes. Once water has cooled, remove pieces. Gently scrub stuck-on paint with a brass brush or steel wool. Repeat process if necessary. Let dry thoroughly before resetting the knobs.

HOW TO MAINTAIN
WOOD FLOORS

Despite all your conscientious sweeping, mopping, vacuuming, and buffing, you can't expect hardwood floors to gleam quite like when they were first installed. You can, however, extend their life—and appreciate their beauty—for years to come. Rule number one: Promptly clean up spills and anything else undesirable afoot.

SUPPLIES

Fine-grade sandpaper (220-grit) or floor scrub pads

Polyurethane-flooring cleaner

Soft cloth

Polyurethane-flooring finish (same as what's on floor)

Foam paint pad

Paintbrush

BEFORE YOU BEGIN

The proper treatment for common problems (see opposite) depends on the flooring's finish, if any. Polyurethane, a hard film coating, is more durable—and harder to repair—than the age-old wax application. If you aren't sure, do a spot test in a clean, inconspicuous area, preferably near a window: Rub some mineral spirits (or paint thinner) with a white cloth over the area; if the cloth picks up a glaze, or stains amber or brown, odds are the floor is waxed. If not, the coating is likely polyurethane, which can be water- or oil-based. To test, apply a small amount of the solvent Xylene, let sit for about 10 seconds, and wipe away; if floor is sticky, the finish is water-based; if nothing happens, it is oil.

SPOT-REPAIR WOOD FLOORS

When the treatments (see opposite) fail to work on polyurethane finishes, you can tackle blemishes with the following three steps.

1. Lightly sand the damaged area with sandpaper or floor scrub pads, being careful to avoid cutting into the wood itself (and making color-matching difficult).

2. Wipe away dust with a commercial cleaner formulated for polyurethane, rubbing it over the surface with a soft cloth.

3. Apply the same polyurethane finish as what's already on the floor, using a foam paint pad to evenly cover the area and then a dry paintbrush to feather the edges.

NOTE: *If the floor was treated with a wood stain, you will need to restain the sanded area before applying the finish.*

PROTECT & PREVENT

Your best course of action is to keep those nicks and scratches from happening in the first place.

- Always place self-adhesive furniture pads (such as by EZ Glide) on the feet of chairs, tables, sofas, and other portable pieces to keep them from scraping and scuffing the floor.

- To avoid scuffed floors when moving heavy pieces of furniture, fold two clean towels, place one under each end, and slide the piece across the floor.

- Before you spend an afternoon rearranging the furniture, do a trial run with a set of paper templates. Measure dimensions of each piece, then transfer them onto kraft paper. Cut out the templates, label them, then lay them on the floor in the intended spots.

PROBLEM	SOLUTION
LIGHT SCRATCHES	**POLYURETHANE FINISH:** Camouflage scratches with wax sticks or wood-stain markers; both are available at hardware stores and come in many common floor shades. Or mop with floor polish (such as Old English Scratch Cover) in the appropriate shade. **WAX FINISH:** Eliminate (not just mask) scratches by rubbing them with extra-fine steel wool (#000). Then reapply paste wax with a soft cloth, let dry, and buff with a clean cloth. To fix divots left behind from heavy furniture, lay a damp flannel cloth over the area and use an iron to heat it briefly; the wood fibers should expand and bounce back into shape.
WHITE SPOTS	**POLYURETHANE FINISH:** Rub the spots (most likely dried spills) with a just-damp cloth, or use a commercial cleaner made especially for polyurethane. **WAX FINISH:** Use extra-fine steel wool (#000) to rub the area, reapply wax, and let dry. Buff with a clean cotton cloth.
DARK SPOTS (INK, PET STAINS, AND WATER)	**BOTH FINISHES:** For minor stains, rub with fine steel wool (#00). Then spot-refinish. Deeper stains on polyurethane require oxalic acid (a common ingredient in deck brighteners), available at hardware stores. Stir together with water to make a paste, apply and let sit for 5 to 10 minutes, then wipe away with a damp cloth. Use the same paste on wax finishes, but wipe with a dry cloth, then rub on wax and buff with a cloth.
GUM	**BOTH FINISHES:** Cover the area for five minutes with a plastic bag filled with ice, and then scrape with a credit card or spoon. For polyurethane finishes, follow with a polyurethane-specific cleaner; buff waxed floors with a dry cloth.
WAX STAINS (CANDLE OR CRAYON)	**BOTH FINISHES:** Try the ice trick (above). If it doesn't work on a wax finish, soften with a blow-dryer set to warm, scrape with a credit card or spoon, and buff with a dry cloth.
OIL AND GREASE	**POLYURETHANE FINISH:** Dampen a soft cloth with a cleaner formulated for polyurethane. Wipe the damaged spot. **WAX FINISH:** Dampen a soft cloth with mineral spirits. (Look for odor-free mineral spirits, which are less toxic than the standard version because benzene and other aromatic hydrocarbons have been removed). Wipe the area dry, rewax, and buff with a dry cloth.

HOW TO FIX
FLOORBOARDS

If there's a stubborn squeakiness in certain areas of your home, odds are your floorboards are rubbing against one another, or it could be your subflooring sidling up against its nails—or a little of both. Either scenario is much more common in older houses, because wood flooring and subflooring settle and react to changes in temperature and humidity throughout the years. Subflooring also loosens with time, while swelling can loosen the nails that secure it, causing a veritable cacophony of creaks.

HOW-TO

In most cases, the noises do not indicate a structural problem, and they can be cured in one of the following ways:

IF YOU DON'T HAVE ACCESS TO FLOOR FROM BELOW: Before any other remedy, try this simple trick: Sprinkle talcum powder or other lubricant (such as powdered soapstone or graphite) on the area of the floor that squeaks. Sweep the powder into the cracks between the boards, then place a cloth on the floor and step on the boards repeatedly to work in the powder. If the problem is two boards rubbing against each other, this method can help reduce the friction—and the noise.

IF YOU DO HAVE ACCESS TO FLOOR FROM BELOW: First have someone walk on the floor above so you can pinpoint the problem.

- If the noise coincides with a gap between the subfloor and a joist, use a shim (or shims if necessary), or slender wedge of wood, to bridge that gap (and keep the floor from bouncing). Affix it with wood glue, being careful not to drive it in too hard and widen the gap.

- Use construction adhesive specially designed for subflooring on longer gaps that run along a common joist.

- If the noise occurs between the joists, most likely what you are hearing is the friction between floorboards and subflooring. Drill short screws—they should be ½-inch shorter than the floor's total thickness—up through the subflooring where there's squeaking and see if that helps. Screws that are too long can cause a whole other problem.

MARTHA MUST

When my antique wooden furniture develops squeaks, I apply a coat of wood-swelling solvent to the joints. Waxing the furniture once a year with color-matched paste also helps by keeping the wood from drying out.

HOW TO FIX
WOOD FURNITURE

Scuffs, scratches, and spills: Think of them as adding character rather than as flaws, and learn how to help mask and even remove certain unsightly spots.

PROBLEM	SOLUTION
LIGHT SCRATCHES	Shoe polish offers easy coverage and is reversible (just wipe it off with mineral spirits). To use, squirt some polish in a color that matches the surface onto a soft cloth, then rub it over the scratch. For more permanent color, there are lacquer sticks, though these are not for antiques.
CANDLE WAX	Scrape off hardened wax with a credit card or a rubber spatula, then buff the remainder away with a soft cloth and paste wax. To harden freshly dripped wax, rest a plastic bag of ice cubes against the wax for about five minutes before scraping.
WATER MARKS	If you catch the spill soon enough, you can try one of these solutions: • Place a smooth white cloth on the surface and run a medium-hot iron (or bottom of a hot pan) back and forth over the area, lifting it as you go to monitor progress—you want to stop as soon as the mark is gone. Be sure to use a cloth without weave, which will otherwise leave an impression. Once the furniture is clear, polish the area. • Apply an equal-parts mixture of baking soda and plain (non-gel) toothpaste to the area, rubbing with a soft cloth until you no longer see a mark. Wipe and buff.
RINGS FROM GLASSES OR MUGS	A white ring means moisture or heat has reached only the wax and the spot just needs a thorough cleaning. First try rubbing the area with a thick paste of olive oil and table salt, let sit 30 minutes, then wipe off paste with a soft cloth. If that doesn't work, rub the ring with mineral spirits or odorless paint thinner (both found at hardware stores) until it disappears; you may want to go over the rest of the table while you're at it. Then apply paste wax, using a soft cloth in a circular motion (i.e., buffing) to spread in an even layer. If the ring is darker than the wood, moisture or heat has actually permeated the finish and it requires professional refinishing.

HOW TO MAINTAIN
FIREPLACES

In addition to having annual professional chimney sweeps, you should give your fireplace a thorough cleaning at the end of the season to keep it spotless until the next year.

SUPPLIES

Newspaper or drop cloth

Protective mask

Rubber gloves

Cleaning agent of choice

Nylon brush

Fireplace shovel and tin (or fireplace vacuum)

Dirt-removal sponge

Stiff-bristled brush (if using green cleaner)

TIP

Hire a professional chimney sweep once a year (ideally at the end of your fire-burning season) to manage creosote, a thick brownish-black residue that can build up on the inner surface of the chimney and is a major cause of chimney fires.

FIRST THINGS FIRST

Cover surrounding surfaces with newspaper or a drop cloth, and wear a protective mask to avoid breathing in the particles.

CHOOSE YOUR CLEANING AGENT

TRISODIUM PHOSPHATE (TSP):
Long the cleaner of choice for tackling soot, TSP comes with many drawbacks—it can be harmful to both you and the environment (by entering waterways). When using TSP, take these extra precautions: Work only in a well-ventilated area; wear gloves, long sleeves, and pants to protect skin; and dispose of used sponges or cloths.

FOR A GREENER CLEANER:
Mix together a paste of cream of tartar and water and apply as you would TSP, or combine equal parts white vinegar and water in a spray bottle. You'll have to do a lot more—and harder—scrubbing to remove all the soot, but you might find that the better option.

HOW-TO

1. Wearing rubber gloves, remove andirons and grate; place on drop cloth. Add water to TSP powder to create a paste, or use one of the greener options. Apply to andirons and grate and scrub with a nylon brush. Rinse completely with water; wipe dry.

2. Scoop out any leftover piles of ash and debris with a fireplace shovel, or use a special vacuum for fireplaces, and discard. Make sure there are no burning embers; it can take up to 72 hours for those to die out.

3. With nylon brush or hand broom, sweep down walls, then sweep out ashes. Scrub fireplace walls from top down with cleaner and a dirt-removal sponge. If using a green cleaner, you may find it necessary to first scrub with a stiff-bristled brush before applying the cleaning solution.

4. If the fireplace or insert has a glass door, use your regular glass cleaner or diluted white vinegar.

HOW TO REPLACE
WINDOWPANES

If your window cracks or shatters, you'll need to order the replacement glass from a local glass repair shop or home improvement store; measure the dimensions of the opening precisely and have a new pane cut ⅛ inch smaller in height and width.

SUPPLIES

Work gloves

Chisel

Hair dryer (optional)

Stiff-bristled brush

Primer

Waterproofing solution (optional)

Replacement pane and glazier's points

Glazing compound

Putty knife

FIRST THINGS FIRST

Wear thick gloves anytime you are working with broken glass. You may want to tape newspaper to the inside of the pane to keep the glass from falling in, and have ready a piece of cardboard or a drop cloth to collect debris on the outside.

HOW-TO

1. Working from outside of window, use a chisel to pry existing compound from recessed edges surrounding panes (called rabbets). Soften stubborn compound with a hair dryer.

2. First locate the glazier's points, the minuscule metal triangles holding the pane in place, working the chisel (or the tip of a small flat screwdriver) around the frame; then pry them out. Now you can gently slip out the pane.

3. Use a stiff-bristled brush to thoroughly strip any compound and paint from around the frames. Apply a paint primer to seal the wood; you can also apply a waterproofing solution, available at paint-supply stores.

4. Carefully place the new pane in the frame. Then, with chisel, push new glazier's points as far as they can go into rabbets where the old ones were. Knead a lump of glazing compound to form a long rope, then press it along one side of the frame with your fingers; smooth compound with a single corner-to-corner pass of the putty knife to create a beveled edge. Let compound set for about a week before repainting sash.

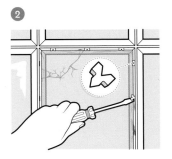

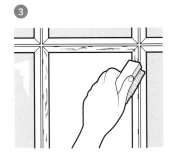

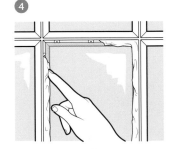

HOW TO MAINTAIN
GUTTERS

With clogged gutters, your home could suffer floods, rotting wood and roof shingles (and, consequently, termites and carpenter ants), and soil erosion—all easy enough to prevent.

SUPPLIES

Work gloves

Ladder

Gutter scoop (or old rubber spatula)

Biodegradable bags

Garden hose with a spray nozzle

Stiff-bristled brush

HOW-TO

1. Wearing gloves and working your way around entire house, remove leaves and other items with a gutter scoop and deposit them in a bag, moving the ladder as you work. Also, be sure to remove any debris from the top of the downspout opening.

2. While clearing downspout openings, look to see if there is anything lodged inside the spout itself. If so, unscrew or jiggle free the elbow at the base. If the downspout is attached to an underground drain, you'll need to take apart the connection.

3. Spray water up through the base of the downspout until it is clear. Replace elbow (or underground connection).

4. Loosen any remaining dirt and particles with a brush.

5. With the hose, spray the gutter to remove dirt. Also gently spray a little water on the roof, directing the flow down from above; do not aim the stream underneath shingles, because this can cause them to break off.

6. Make any necessary repairs as discussed at right.

NOTE: *Always heed safety tips when using a ladder, avoiding uneven ground, and preferably with someone there to hold it steady.*

REPAIRS FOR LEAKS

The next time it rains, check your roof for seepage signs, including leaks along the lines and water dripping from the back of the gutter—both problems that should be addressed right away. Consider replacing the gutter if there are a lot of leaks; otherwise, here's your game plan:

■ For small holes in metal gutters, use a wire brush followed by steel wool to scrub the area, then patch holes with roofing cement or a special cement made for gutter repairs, applied with a putty knife.

■ For larger holes, use a piece of flashing—made of the same metal as your gutters—cut to size with shears. Press it firmly over the cement. Caulk can seal leaky joints.

■ If water dribbles (or worse, cascades) from back of gutter, the roof and gutter may not be aligned properly. Ask a roofer to install drip-edge flashing—a piece of metal, shaped like an upside-down L, that fits beneath the edge of the roofing and prevents water from running down back of gutter.

■ When the water has stopped flowing, check to see if any puddles remain inside the gutter. This indicates that the trough is not angled properly toward the downspout. Correct the alignment by adjusting the gutter brackets or have a roofer or gutter-repair service install new ones.

REFRESH
AND
EMBELLISH

Ever since I painted the walls (and ceilings) of my first apartment as a newlywed in New York City, I have gone about painting each of my homes as a way to make it my own—and to keep the rooms from looking tired over time.

For anyone who shares this sensibility, you know how a fresh coat of paint can instantly transform a space or an entire home. Really, painting is enjoyable and offers great satisfaction—and it is a cost-effective way to revive less-than-perfect wood floors and even flea-market furniture. Start with a small area or simple project if need be, but do give painting a try.

Painting is merely one way to refresh and embellish your home. As someone who takes many photographs and collects a variety of artwork, antique mirrors, and other objects worthy of display, I've learned the importance of plotting out the position with templates, and using the appropriate hardware for the weight of the object as well as the wall's surface. I am also an ardent fan of using wall-mounted shelves to increase storage in a smaller space, such as my laundry room, and of using wallpaper to highlight sections of a room.

Of course, window treatments, floor coverings, and lighting all contribute to the look and feel of a living space, but only if they are hung, sized, or placed correctly; look to those sections for tips on achieving a cohesive, coordinated result.

While this chapter does not cover more extensive renovations, you will find all the pointers, tips, and techniques needed to embellish and adorn your home so that it reflects your own style—whether it be your first home or one of a number.

SIZE UP
YOUR SPACES

When it comes to embellishing your home, an overarching goal is to aim for the right placement and proportion, from the ground up. That means before you can give your home a professional-quality paint job, create a gallery wall, or choose the right rug—all covered on the following pages—you first need to arm yourself with the right measuring tools for each job. Then consider the following expert tips for creating stylish rooms with the necessary know-how.

FIRST THINGS FIRST: MEASURE UP

Stock your toolkit with the following supplies:

- A level guarantees proper alignment when you're mounting things to the wall.

- A folding ruler is great for vertical heights where there's no wall (e.g., for a pendant light over a table).

- A soft measuring tape works for round items, like lampshades, and a stiff metal tape for long expanses or tall heights.

- Thick twine or ribbon is effective for an object that is just too shapely for even a soft measuring tape. First "measure" it with thick twine or ribbon, using adhesive to secure it as you work your way around the area to be measured. Then remove the twine and straighten it on a measuring tape to determine the length.

REASSESS YOUR ROOMS

All the pretty paint colors and throw pillows in the world won't be able to mask an ill-fitted-out space. Even if you do nothing else to spruce up your home, take a good (objective) look around each room, starting in the common areas—specifically the living room, where the most people tend to congregate and where you have the most freedom to switch up the arrangement. Do this once a year, or more often if your household changes (a new baby arrives or a graduate goes off to college, for example). Often it's not that you "need" a new sofa, but that the sofa needs a new position.

FURNITURE GOES FIRST: When setting up a cohesive space, you'll want to begin with the key components. For a living room, this means the sofa, coffee table, accent chairs, side table, and media console. A bed (or beds), side tables, and bureaus are the main pieces in a bedroom; the dining table and sideboard are the workhorses of a dining room. Once these pieces are in place, you can embellish the space with rugs, lighting, and decorative accents.

SIZE UP YOUR SPACE: If your living room is small, have the sofa close to (but not touching) a wall. If you have a larger space, create separate zones with sofas floating and rugs helping to define those spaces. Then arrange side chairs with conversation in mind.

PRINCIPAL POINT OF VIEW: Every room should have a focal point. In the living room, it could be the fireplace, the view out the window, or a stunning piece of artwork. An eye-catching pendant works over a dining table; or an arrangement of art does the trick above a bed. Don't overlook the power of a pretty shower curtain (or a clawfoot tub) in a bathroom.

COLOR TELLS A STORY: Many people feel they have to decide on paint colors from the outset, before they've picked out the upholstery or other textiles. But each element is part of the narrative, and a favorite fabric or an heirloom rug can (and often should) inspire a room's palette, from the walls to the trim and the accent colors. If you are wary of using bold colors in big ways, reserve them for small spaces (a hallway or powder room), or to punctuate a room (by painting only the door or window frame).

MIND THE NUMBERS

The following are suggestions for creating a comfortable and visually appealing living room (see diagram at right).

1. Leave 14 to 18 inches between the coffee table and the sofa (the larger the sofa, the farther away the table).

2. The height of the coffee table should be within 4 inches (either way) of the sofa's seat height, depending on how you use it most; the length should fall between one-half and less than three-quarters the length of the sofa.

3. Sofa tables placed behind floating sofas should never be taller than the

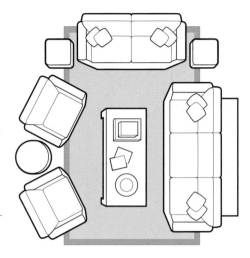

back of the sofa, and should be at least 12 inches shorter than its length (to prevent bumping into the corners).

4. Place a table within easy reach of all chairs; pairs can of course share one in between. The table should be no higher than the arm of the chair, or 8 inches above the seat if armless, and never lower than the seat height.

5. Allow at least 30 inches for pathways, including around dining tables.

MARTHA MUST

When designing a room, I start by plotting the dimensions on graph paper, with each square unit equal to some measurement (depending on the room's size). Note the placement of doors, windows, fireplaces, and other structural features. Then, sketch the furniture pieces to scale in the desired arrangement.

WHEN TO CALL IN A PRO

Even if you're redesigning only one or two rooms, you may want to enlist some help. Here are some different ways you can call in an expert:

BY PROJECT

A designer can come up with a concept for just one room (especially a new kitchen or bathroom) or the whole space, editing down all the many options on your behalf.

BY THE HOUR

Reach out to an expert for help with choosing paint colors, tiles, flooring, and other options (upholstery and such), to achieve a cohesive result.

ONLINE

Online services pair clients with designers for video or phone chats and offer a range of packages, depending on your needs.

BY STORE

Many national home-improvement stores offer (usually free) in-home consultations for kitchen and bathroom remodels, custom window treatments, and more (including exterior upgrades).

HOW TO
HANG ANYTHING

Paintings, mirrors, and shelves understandably get all the attention, but what about the hardware that holds those weighty details in place? Those are just as essential. Save yourself some time and trouble by using the chart on pages 74 to 75 to choose the right anchor for the job; make sure to match the weight of the object to be hung with the shear-load rating of the anchor (noted on the package). The how-tos for the most common hardware follow.

HARDWARE HOW-TOS

It's important to pair the screw with the anchor according to its thread, whether machine (tight) or coarse. Often, screws and anchors come in the same package, but other times you'll have to make the match yourself. Ask someone at the hardware store for assistance.

ANCHOR HOW-TO

The same method applies to both plastic and lead expansion anchors.

1. Make a small pilot hole using an awl to prevent the drill bit from wobbling.

2. Drill a hole sized according to anchor packaging. (Use a carbide-tipped bit on tile, and a masonry bit for brick or stone.)

3. Insert the anchor by tapping carefully with hammer until it is flush with the wall.

4. Insert the mounting hardware into anchor and tighten.

TOGGLE BOLT HOW-TO

These vary in their application, but the following steps cover the most basic type (strap toggles being the exception); see specific instructions on pages 74 and 75.

1. Predrill holes if necessary, making sure to properly measure, mark, and level the anchor position.

2. Assemble mounting hardware onto the toggle according to packaging, then thread onto screw.

3. Fold back toggle wings completely, then slip bolt into the hole; push until the wings pop open.

4. Pull back on the assembled unit so wings are tight against the inside of the wall (to prevent them from turning). Tighten mounting hardware with a screwdriver, being careful not to overtighten.

MARTHA MUST

For my heavy mirrors, paintings, and cabinetry, I only trust metal French cleats. Each cleat comes with two interlocking beveled pieces, one that attaches to the wall, the other to the item being hung.

MIRRORS

When hanging a mirror (especially a heavy one), double its weight before choosing the hardware; this allows for the extra load when cleaning them.

PLACEMENT

If the mirror is not hung at the right height, you may see only the top of your head; too low, and you'll have to stoop to get a look at yourself. Have an average-size person stand in front of the mirror, and hold it up at an appropriate level, leaning it on a table or stool if necessary. Then decide where it should go. Mirrors can be hung horizontally over a sofa or mantel, too.

MOUNTING

Anchors should always be used, even if the mirror comes with its own hanging hardware. Two hangers, one on each side of the mirror, are better than one, especially when placed lengthwise. If the mirror is backed with wood, look for Z clips; screw one strip into the wall and the other into the back of the mirror.

TYPES OF HANGING HARDWARE

FOR SOLID SURFACES

For surfaces such as brick and tile, the hole must be the same width as (or slightly smaller than) the anchor; always use the proper bit for your surface. On masonry, try a hammer drill.

FOR HOLLOW SURFACES

Determine the thickness of hollow surfaces, such as drywall and plaster walls and ceilings, by drilling a small hole into them and probing with a wire or nail.

SOLID SURFACES		HOLLOW SURFACES	
PLASTIC EXPANSION ANCHORS	**LEAD EXPANSION ANCHORS**	**TOGGLE BOLTS**	**STRAP TOGGLES**
WHEN TO USE THEM: This hardware works for lightweight items, such as towel bars and shelves that aren't weight-bearing. Some of the anchors have ribs or teeth for additional grip. They come in assorted sizes.	**WHEN TO USE THEM:** This heavy-duty anchor is appropriate for weighty items—such as mirrors, shelves, and light fixtures—that will be mounted to masonry walls and ceilings. Avoid them on delicate tile.	**WHEN TO USE THEM:** Use these for very heavy objects (cabinets and bookshelves) that will be permanently installed; the toggle will drop off after the mounting hardware is removed. Also good for ceilings.	**WHEN TO USE THEM:** Unlike standard toggle bolts, this one stays in place after mounting hardware is removed, so it's good for objects that will be replaced, or if you tend to take down items frequently for repainting and the like.
HOW THEY WORK: Outward pressure forces the anchor to conform to the sides of the hole for a tight fit as the mounting screw is tightened (see page 73 for the step-by-step how-to).	**HOW THEY WORK:** The same principle applies as with their plastic counterparts (see page 73). Use care with these, as they are more prone to snapping.	**HOW THEY WORK:** After inserting the toggle bolt into the predrilled hole, the spring-activated wings open inside the wall, keeping items tight (see page 73 for the step-by-step how-to).	**HOW THEY WORK:** Push the metal flange through the predrilled hole, then pull it against the inside of the wall while sliding the ring on plastic straps toward the wall. Snap off the straps once the ring is flush with the wall; insert and tighten mounting hardware.

TIP

To choose the right anchor for the job, make sure to match the weight of the object to be hung with the shear-load rating of the anchor (noted on the package).

HOLLOW SURFACES (CONTINUED)			
MOLLY BOLTS	**SELF-DRILLING TOGGLES**	**COLLAPSIBLE TOGGLES**	**THREADED ANCHORS**
WHEN TO USE THEM: A molly bolt is often used to affix coat or towel hooks to walls or hollow-core doors. It isn't as strong as a toggle bolt or strap toggle because its wings don't open as wide against the inside of the wall.	**WHEN TO USE THEM:** Metal versions can withstand the weight and regular use of shelves and coat racks. Plastic ones are not as sturdy; use them only in predrilled drywall (and never on harder plaster).	**WHEN TO USE THEM:** This plastic, cost-efficient choice is substantial enough for medium-weight objects, including curtain rods. Since plastic can break, avoid this type with valuable items.	**WHEN TO USE THEM:** This anchor comes in plastic and metal and is a cinch to install. Use for lightweight items such as small picture frames that won't be handled a lot (jiggling can loosen its grip). Do not use on ceilings.
HOW THEY WORK: Insert them into the hole or drive them into the wall; tighten mounting hardware. The sleeve on the bolt will fold in on itself, drawing tight against the wall. Some molly bolts require predrilling, but drive types (with pointed ends) may be hammered into drywall.	**HOW THEY WORK:** Drive the toggle into the wall and insert and tighten the mounting screw. Once the threads engage with the wall, the toggle will open on its own and draw tight against the inside of the wall.	**HOW THEY WORK:** First insert the anchor into a predrilled hole. Then tighten the screw, which will force its wings to fold up and draw tight against the inside of the wall. Don't use too much force, as the plastic threads are easy to strip.	**HOW THEY WORK:** The coarse threads keep a steady grip on drywall, keeping the anchor in place. Make a small pilot hole with a drill or an awl according to packaging; screw in anchor. Insert mounting hardware into anchor, and tighten. Avoid overtightening.

HOW TO
ARRANGE ART

Hanging artwork is as much about the "eye of the beholder" as it is an exact science. As shown here, there are many ways to display your pictures with panache; but, keep in mind that a little advance planning will go a long way toward achieving your desired result.

THE BASICS

Before you nail or drill anything into your wall, you need to know what the wall is made of. Homes built before 1945 typically have plaster walls; otherwise drywall is the default.

- Picture hooks are more secure than nails. You can nail these to the wall for light- to medium-weight pictures. For heavier items, you'll want to use anchors (see page 74). Toggle bolts work best in drywall, molly bolts with more fragile plaster.

- Buy the right type of hardware for the picture it will hold. Picture hooks are usually one of three types: a one-nail hook will hold up to 30 pounds; two-nail hooks hold up to 50 pounds; and three-nail hooks up to 75 pounds (or more). Go by what's on the package and err on the side of caution.

- Use two hooks per picture to avoid tilting. This will also provide extra security against too-heavy objects.

- For the same reason as above, consider mounting two D rings on the back of the pictures, as these are more stable than picture wire. They are also less forgiving, so weigh your options.

- If you prefer picture wire, you'll need to have wire that's 8 inches longer than the width of the frame. Thread it through the D rings, and pull 4 inches of wire through either side; fold the short end back, and twist it tightly around the main wire several times.

TIP

Leave 8 to 10 inches between bottom of artwork and a sofa back or headboard. If hanging just one piece, it should be about two-thirds the furniture's width.

HOLE-FREE HANGING

If you'd rather not drive nails into your walls, you've got options. You can lean the artwork against the wall (resting it on a shelf or furniture). Or try one of the following items, sold at home-improvement centers.

PICTURE MOLDING (common in traditional homes) allows you to hang pictures using S hooks.

FRENCH RODS (common in art galleries) are installed near the ceiling; metal hooks rest over the bar and slide along, for changeable placement.

PICTURE RAILS (convenient for small spaces) are just that: slender ledges just deep enough to rest pictures on.

PLACEMENT TIPS AND TECHNIQUES

Keeping artwork at eye level will allow you to best appreciate its beauty. That said, there's nothing wrong with mounting items lower or higher, such as to create intimacy in a reading nook, or to add an element of surprise above a doorway or window frame. In other words, the following are guidelines to consider as a starting point as you create a display that's personal to you and your space.

- Hang art so its midpoint is 57 to 60 inches from the floor, a little higher in rooms with ceilings that are over 8 feet. Once you pick the midpoint, stick with it for consistency. For art that's taller than 72 inches, forget the midpoint rule; just make sure the bottom edge is about a foot from the floor—or simply rest it on the floor.

- To select a midpoint for a gridded grouping, think of the collection as one piece of art (see page 79 for more).

- If the display will feature multiple sizes and shapes (and won't be arranged in a grid), choose your center spot and then work out from there.

- If hanging two or three pictures in a column, treat them as one piece and position the center point at 57 to 60 inches.

- Space medium to large artwork (anything larger than 15 inches) about 2 inches apart on all sides; smaller pieces can be closer, or even joined, together.

- If you're hanging a smaller work over a large furniture unit, try adding sconces or other art to fill out the composition.

HOW TO
CREATE A
GALLERY WALL

There's no best way to display photos—in a grid or loosely arranged, with uniform frames or a mixed-and-unmatched selection—but there are considerations to keep in mind for a cohesive and impressive display. The following are ideas intended to inspire, along with some tips to help you along the way.

COMPOSE

The first step is to decide on the tone you are hoping to achieve, arranging—and rearranging—the pieces until you find the desired composition. Consider these options:

■ A common thread will help unify the different pieces, if that's your goal. That could be the type of artwork (botanicals, for example), the frames (see at right, with one unexpected addition), the color of the mats, or some other element.

■ Sometimes not having a linking element is itself the unifying theme, and it creates a less formal display; these often require even more careful planning to keep the display from looking haphazard.

■ Arranging the items in a precise grid creates a graphic look, while those in a square or rectangle are still tidy but less formal.

■ Rows of pictures can be aligned at their center for a traditional look, or at the top or bottom for a more modern effect.

■ As a general rule, keep smaller pieces lower to allow for more intimate viewing.

TEMPLATE

Take the time to plot out your arrangement on the wall before you grab the hammer and nail holes:

1. Trace around frames on kraft paper to make a template for each piece of art, then cut out.

2. Measure distance from D rings or top of hanging wire's arc to top of frame. Make a corresponding mark on template. Lay picture hook on template so bottom of hook is on mark; make another mark where nail hole will go.

3. Use painters' tape to hang templates. When you're satisfied with placement, hammer nails through picture hooks and into wall over marks on kraft paper. Remove the paper, leaving nails and hooks in place, and hang your frames.

TIP

For lightweight artwork, use adhesive picture-hanging strips, such as Command Strips by 3M. Because they do not damage the wall, they are also perfect for hanging wreaths and other decorations during the holidays, or for testing the placement of a more permanent piece.

MORE IDEAS AND INSPIRATION

Let the space itself and your own sense of style be your guides in grouping artwork. Below, the shape of a hallway and stairwell dictate the arrangements.

STAIRWAY ARRANGEMENT

What keeps this composition neat and orderly is the way the photos are grouped in distinct "columns" that climb the walls, with the wooden stair railing "framing" the arrangement. Look at the large butterfly at the top left above, for instance, and the pairs of pictures arranged closely underneath. Having the columns consist of different sizes of photos keeps the overall effect feeling organic, not overly staged.

GRAPHIC GRID

Precise measuring is essential when creating an intricate arrangement like this one. To achieve this surround-scene effect, mark walls with painters' tape in the desired grid based on size of art, using the midpoint rule and spacing the pieces no more than 2 inches apart on all sides. What keeps this display from looking too composed are the variances among the photographs' sizes and orientations.

HOW TO
INSTALL SHELVES

Shelves turn walls into workhorses, and even novices can construct and install them. But besides being sturdy, these ledges can also be stylish, uniting form and function.

FIRST THINGS FIRST

You'll need to mount the shelves securely, while also considering their appearance. Let the surroundings dictate the materials.

SEARCH FOR STUDS: If you prefer to mount your shelves by screwing directly into the wall, you'll need to pinpoint the wall studs.

FIND A FASTENER: Alternatively, use anchors or bolts that spread out once they're in the wall to create a strong hold. The type of fastener you should use depends on the type of wall you have (see page 73).

CHOOSE THE BRACKETS: You can find a seemingly endless supply of support systems, some utilitarian, others more decorative. The brass brackets shown opposite and others like them can be found at housewares shops and online retailers.

PICK THE PLANKS: Wood, glass, stone—they are all viable options for the ledges. The shelf ledges opposite are precut marble windowsills, an affordable alternative to custom stone—and they happen to be the same depth as many brackets.

SUPPLIES

Measuring tape

Painters' tape

Level

Shelving

Shelf brackets

Screws and anchors

Drill

HOW-TO

Follow these simple steps to install bracketed shelves, using mounting hardware (if any) that comes with the brackets.

1. First figure out how many shelves you want. Space them as desired, from top to bottom. Start with 12-inch intervals, which is what is shown opposite (and which will accommodate a variety of decorative objects and also standing books); opt for less or more space between to suit your needs and space.

2. Use painters' tape to mark the wall where the shelves will go, making sure it is level.

3. Measure the space and purchase shelving to match (or have the shelving cut to fit at your local home-improvement center).

4. Install the brackets first (two brackets per shelf), using studs or anchors; mark the position of the holes on the wall at even measurements from either end of shelf.

5. Rest the shelf on top of brackets and check that they are level.

MORE IDEAS
AND INSPIRATION

Use shelves anyplace where sufficient surfaces can be lacking, such as in bathrooms and bedrooms. They can also redefine an empty space—even a window.

ELEVATED WINDOW LEDGE

Give a prime window new purpose by hanging a ledge across its span (mount the support brackets to the frame or adjacent wall). Pull up a pair of chairs for a breakfast nook; opt for counter or bar height, around 34 or 40 inches, respectively. Or use the spot to grow sun-loving potted plants that are too wide for the windowsill.

SPACE-SAVING SOLUTION

Milk-glass shelves are a step up from regular glass shelves in a bathroom—and they coordinate well with white tub and tile. These shelves are 9 inches deep—just deep enough to hold towels and toiletries. (Standard shelving sizes are between 8 and 12 inches.) The powder-coated metal brackets complete the streamlined design.

PROJECT
TURNING SHELVES INTO CUBBIES

Create pull-down "shades" for modular shelving or storage units using felt, Velcro, and basic hardware-store supplies (see also page 37 for creating a built-in pop-up desk).

SUPPLIES

Measuring tape

Wool felt

Fabric scissors

1-inch square balsa-wood strip

Velcro tape

Handsaw

1¼-inch nails

Hammer

Craft scissors

Leather ribbon (½-inch wide)

Fabric glue

FELT COVERS HOW-TO

1. Measure width and height of shelf opening; cut felt to same dimensions. Cut balsa wood and Velcro to width of opening.

2. Line up wood beneath top of shelf opening; gently nail in from below. Stick one piece of Velcro to top edge of felt and other to mounted wood. Velcro felt into place.

LEATHER PULL HOW-TO

1. For each felt shade, cut a 2-inch strip of leather ribbon. Fold in half lengthwise, and glue ends together.

2. Glue leather tab to back of felt in the center of shelf, leaving the folded side extending.

3. Let glue dry before using (clamp with a clothespin to help secure while drying).

TIP

What's behind those felt shades is up to you, but make sure to keep the cubbies without the covering neat and tidy. Here, books are stacked vertically and horizontally in some, artwork and other decorative objects are arranged in others—and, for more hidden storage, coordinated bins (see bottom middle and right cubbies) house periodicals and more.

HOW TO
DISPLAY A
COLLECTION

If you're like most collectors, you've amassed belongings you love to look at and live with, not hide away for fear of damaging the goods. After all, collections are meant to be admired. But should there come a time when your stockpile exceeds your space, you'll want to store your trinkets and treasures the right way. The following methods allow you to approach both sides of collecting.

DISPLAYING

Your particular collectibles will largely dictate the display options, but there are some general tips to keep in mind when showcasing any wares.

■ Group smaller objects together on a designated shelf or table, or in a wall-mounted shadow box.

■ Frame flatter items, either individually (patterned tea towels or fabric swatches) or as a whole collection (think shells, buttons, or vintage spoons).

■ Larger items, including trays and quilts, can also double as wall art when hung over a sofa or bed, or along the wall of a staircase. Rotate your collection over time while putting the rest to their intended use.

■ Consider arranging items within a single collection—or even across multiple collections—by color, for a display that's harmonious and not at all cluttered.

TIP
The collectible itself can suggest its display method, such as hanging copper cookware on a large pot rack over a kitchen island, with others tucked into shelves underneath. This way, the items are able to be appreciated for their beauty while also being within easy reach for everyday usage.

STORING

Here's what to do with all the items that are too valuable to let go of—even if you can't find the room to show them off.

- Be sure to use archival-quality storage boxes and other supplies, available at most home-supply stores, to protect paper, photographs, and other delicate items from breaking down.

- It's important to sweep, scrub, and otherwise clean the storage area before using it.

- You also should clean the objects you are storing before putting them away.

- Make an inventory of your objects before you devise a system, and measure roughly how much space is required. That way, you can tailor your storage space to fit your boxes, bags, and bins, not the other way around.

- Even with the best storage system, some things require occasional monitoring. Refold a linen tablecoth along different creases periodically; air out upholstered items on a sunny day.

WHERE TO STORE

- China, glassware, and other objects made of durable materials are impervious to the damaging conditions found in unfinished basements and attics. Be sure to check frequently for leaks, especially after a heavy rainfall or extended periods of snow on the ground or roof.

- Never store photographs and other precious family documents in the attic or basement, as they cannot withstand temperature extremes. Fine silks and tapestries are vulnerable, too. Put these items in a spare closet or the backs of cabinets—even if you have to move other things to do so.

- Finished basements and garages also have more temperate conditions for storing collectibles, even more delicate ones.

METAL MATTERS

Not all metals are created equal. Here are special considerations for the more common collectibles.

BRASS

Because this alloy of copper and zinc tarnishes easily, many pieces are coated in clear lacquer. Problem is, the lacquer can chip and the metal underneath can begin tarnishing—and then the coating must be removed. That's why most collectors choose the unlacquered variety. As a general rule, liquids and polish-soaked cloths work well for light to medium tarnish; pastes and creams do a better job on heavier tarnish. Or you can make your own polish by mixing equal parts salt and flour with enough white vinegar to make a paste; apply it to the piece, let dry, rub off with a soft cloth, then wash and dry.

COPPER

Outdoor decorations made of copper are often left to develop a green patina. Cookware is usually polished: Sprinkle the cut side of a lemon half with salt, then rub it over the copper, which will soon gleam.

SILVER

To remove light tarnish, handwash your silverware (do not place in the dishwasher) and buff dry with a soft cloth. Use commercial polish for deeper stains. When silver isn't in use, you can hinder the tarnish process by storing it in anti-tarnish or acid-free tissue paper, or protective cloth bags.

MARTHA MUST

I fell in love with copper cookware decades ago while in Paris. The pink-gold color is just gorgeous, and the metal is also superior to other materials for many cooking chores. My vast collection of pots, pans, bowls, and more is not just for show. I put the items through the regular round of use, polishing them each time until they are gleaming again.

MORE IDEAS
AND INSPIRATION

Don't feel constrained by tradition when curating an arrangement. The examples below reflect the personality of the collector as much as the collectibles.

KITCHEN CREAMWARE

A sizable collection of mix-and-match creamware storage crocks and serving pieces looks right at home on a vintage sideboard in a kitchen or dining area, where at least some of the items can be called to duty at a moment's notice. An all-white arrangement like this also looks wonderful in contrast to the rich, dark wood of the furniture piece, for welcome warmth.

TOP-SHELF BARWARE

This assortment of barware is sublime in its simplicity, and fittingly arranged for open access at cocktail hour. What makes the DIY display dramatic and functional are the white three-sided shelves (letting the colorful glasses pop) and brass rods (attached by drilling holes into the shelf's sides), which keep the valuables safe. The shelves free up valuable floor space, too.

PLATE-WALL UPDATE

No more strictly matching china. What makes this potpourri so appealing is the ivory, blue, and brown color scheme, as well as the unstructured symmetry.

There are many types of plate hangers to choose from. Look for ones that are sturdy but discreet, such as brass models. For delicate antiques, use a V-shaped hanger instead of a spring-operated one, which can put too much pressure on the rim.

Mapping out your display with templates (see page 78) will help keep the holes in the wall to a minimum.

SUPPLIES

Plates

Kraft paper

Wax pencil

Craft scissors

Painters' tape

Plate hangers

Hammer

1. Turn each plate over onto kraft paper, and trace its edges with a wax pencil; cut out. Use templates to try different formations.

2. Tape templates to wall.

3. Carefully attach an appropriately sized plate hanger to the back of each dish. (If necessary, bend back hanger clips slightly to prevent them from scratching the plate.)

4. Place plate over template, and mark where the hook will go on the template. Hammer the hook directly through template; remove paper and hang plate.

HOW TO
PAINT WALLS
AND CEILINGS

Paint has the capacity to transform in many ways: It can make a room feel larger or smaller, shorter or taller, or take it from bright and cheery to warm and cozy (for a bedroom or reading nook), or just the reverse (the goal of most kitchen or playroom updates). If you don't want to paint your entire living room a bold shade, consider a pop of color on an accent wall, or only on the trim (a terrific way to frame a room).

FIRST THINGS FIRST

Always test several paint shades (even so-called white hues) on your wall before committing to one. Do this in different spots of the wall or areas of the room to account for variances in light; for the same reason, be sure to consider how the paint looks at different times of day and on sunny versus cloudy days.

When painting your swatches on the wall, "feather out" the edges to avoid creating a ridge that will have to be sanded later. Or, better yet, paint the swatches on poster board and then rest that against the target wall; this makes it easy to test the color in numerous locations.

You'll need to choose the finish—e.g., shine factor—of the paint before getting an accurate read, too. Latex paint is the default paint for covering entire rooms, though oil-based paints (see opposite page) are also available and used in certain projects that follow. These finishes are for latex.

■ Flat, aka matte, has the least shine—hence, it is the most adept at hiding imperfections and the hardest to clean, making it a good choice for ceilings. Flat is recommended for bedroom and living area walls but not for high-trafficked areas (hallways, stairwells, mudrooms, bathrooms, and so on).

■ Eggshell, aka satin, is an all-purpose choice for walls (and also ceilings), falling between flat and glossy. It's especially popular in bathrooms and kitchens.

■ Semi-gloss is just that: It has a higher sheen than eggshell without coming on too strong. Because it resists stains better than the other finishes, semi-gloss is often reserved for busy common spaces as well as kids' rooms and playrooms.

■ Glossy tops the charts for shine and cleanability, making it the best choice for trim. It also dries to a hard, shiny coat on furniture, if the lacquered look is what you're aiming for.

To determine how much paint you will need, first calculate the square footage of the area. For each wall, multiply height times width, then add up the walls for the total coverage. Double this number for two coats. Allow at least 10 percent extra for future touch-ups. Divide square footage by 450 (1 gallon of paint typically covers 450 square feet).

PREP SUPPLIES

Drop cloth

Screwdriver

Masking paper

Spackling paste, wood filler, and putty knife

Joint tape, joint compound, and taping knife

Sandpaper, sanding sponge, and dust mask

Caulk and caulking gun

Vacuum and sponges

Painters' tape

Primer

Brushes

Paint rollers and sleeves

PREP HOW-TO

Plan to devote a full day to the four Ps that lead up to painting a room: protecting floors and furnishings; patching holes, fissures, and gaps; prepping walls (cleaning, taping them off); and, finally, priming.

PROTECT: Gather large objects in the center of the room, removing any small objects, and cover with a drop cloth (plastic or canvas). Unscrew switch and outlet face plates. Lay masking paper over floors and tape to secure. Cover carpeting with drop cloths.

PATCH: Repair any holes or cracks in the wall as described on page 58. Cracks between the baseboard—or any trim—and the wall should be treated with latex caulk (which can be painted). Apply with a caulking gun, following the manufacturer's instructions. Use a damp sponge to even caulk out and wipe off excess immediately after applying. (It is impossible to do this after caulk dries.)

PREP: Vacuum the room and wash the walls with a sponge and warm water.

PRIME: Tape off the ceiling if not painting it the same color as walls. If you'll be covering a light-colored wall with dark paint, use a gray primer, or have one custom-mixed to match your paint shade. Follow the method on page 102 when coating surfaces with primer, and let dry thoroughly.

OIL-BASED VS. LATEX PAINT

Because oil-based paints are durable and long-lived, they were long the go-to choice for floors and trim among many experts. These traits can now be found in good-quality latex paints, which dry in half the time of oil-based paints and resist chipping and cracking better. Oil-based paints are also less forgiving when applying and cleaning up after, requiring the use of mineral spirits rather than soapy water for cleaning brushes and other tools. What's more, many states have laws restricting the sale of oil-based varieties because of environmental concerns. That said, oil-based paints provide a smooth coat that is still preferred for certain projects, including in this book.

If you're in doubt about which kind of paint to use, consult the paint store or home center where you plan to buy your paint. Whichever type of paint you decide to use, buy the best quality within your budget.

TIP

Additives such as Floetrol emulate the smooth look of oil paint by rendering brush and roller marks less prominent. Mix a pint of conditioner with a gallon of latex paint. Test a swatch on the wall. For an even cleaner finish, add up to 1 pint more conditioner.

Wooden stir sticks

Cardboard box (optional)

Small plastic containers
(optional)

Brushes

Paint rollers and sleeves

Roller tray and liner

Extension pole

Painters' tape

PAINT HOW-TO

In most cases, you'll paint walls before trim,
so you have to tape off only once. Apply at
least two coats, allowing four hours of drying
time in between; let the final coat of wall
paint dry overnight before taping off and
painting trim. When buying brushes, look
for those with flexible (not stiff) bristles and
flagged, or split, ends. Use a 3- or 4-inch
brush on walls (anything larger is unwieldy);
angled 1- to 2-inch ones are ideal for windows, trim, and cutting in.

DECANT: Place a flattened cardboard box
under paint containers to give floors an extra
layer of protection. After mixing paint with a
wooden stir stick, pour some into a smaller
plastic vessel, filling about halfway. (Spouts
on newer containers make this easier.)

DIP: To minimize the risk of drips, insert the
bristles about 2 inches into the paint, then
tap them against the sides of the container to
remove excess.

CUT IN: Paint part of a corner or around the
trim (edges you won't be able to reach with
a roller) with a 2-inch angled brush. This is
called cutting in. Do only 4-foot sections at
a time to avoid the marks that appear when
paint starts to dry.

ROLL: Pour paint into your roller tray. Dip in the
roller, then move it back and forth on the tray
bed until it's saturated but not dripping. To
ensure even coverage, paint a 2-foot-wide V
on the wall, and, without lifting the roller, fill it
in with tight vertical strokes. Repeat, working
top to bottom, until the wall is completed.

FINISH: Let wall paint dry overnight; then use
painters' tape to tape off around the trim,
burnishing tape with your fingertips as you
go for proper adhesion. Apply paint to trim
with an angled 2-inch brush. Although some
people prefer to wait until paint is dry before
removing tape, most experts say to remove
it as soon as you are finished painting, when
there's less risk of causing the paint to peel
off along with the tape. Either way, pull off the
tape slowly at an angle.

TO PAINT A DOOR: First, sand and prime the
door's surface (after removing all hardware).
With a 3-inch roller, paint one section of the
door, such as an inset panel, then immediately
brush over it with a 3-inch brush. Continue
working in sections until you've finished the
main body of the door, then do the vertical
and horizontal framing.

TIP

To keep paint from drying
out between coats (two
or three days tops), cover
can with plastic wrap
before replacing the lid;
wrap wet brushes and
roller sleeves with plastic
wrap and then place in
resealable plastic bags (or
a plastic bag that's twisted
to seal). Also, be sure to
snap a photo of the label
affixed to the can's lid in
case you need to buy more
paint in a pinch.

CLEANUP HOW-TO

Paint can dry out quickly, so be sure to store it properly and tackle brushes (and reusable trays) right away. Roller sleeves should be discarded after finishing up a project.

STORE: Transfer leftover paint to smaller airtight plastic containers; paint kept in opened cans is prone to drying out.

LABEL: Mark each container with the paint color and room it was used in. Keep the paint on hand for touch-ups.

WASH: Rinse each brush with lukewarm water. Then add a few drops of liquid dish soap and continue rinsing. Dislodge any dried bits of paint with a metal brush comb. Wrap the bristles in paper towels to maintain their shape, and lay flat to dry. You can also wash out paint trays with warm, soapy water and allow to dry completely before storing.

TIP

Paint can be used to draw your eye through a vantage point like the one at left, where each room visible is given a different shade. Note how the bookcase in the foreground is painted in yet another harmonious hue. When going this route, it's wise to consult a color wheel to find complementary colors.

MORE IDEAS AND INSPIRATION

Rather than covering an entire wall, use paint (and the same techniques on the previous pages) to define a small space, frame a room, or provide a small but striking pop of color.

BOLD CONTRAST

Painting the trim a darker color than the walls frames the room in a wonderful way, as demonstrated by this living room-slash-library. The edges of the shelves and the adjacent doorframe and molding are painted peacock blue, the walls a light gray, the palette inspired by the colors in the area rug.

LACQUERED LINEN CLOSET

Liven things up by painting a nondescript space a gleaming sunny yellow, or other vibrant hue of your choosing. You'll need to apply several coats of high-gloss paint—preferably with a brush and not a roller to keep it from looking too candy-coated (any visible brush strokes are all the better).

PROJECT
GLAZED WALL "TILES"

These painted-on "tiles" give dimension to a wall; alternating the directions of the lines creates a sense of movement. The magic lies in a special combing tool and the translucent glaze, tinted with a contrasting shade of paint (darker than the base for warmth, lighter for coolness).

SUPPLIES

Latex paint

Latex or acrylic glazing liquid

Pencil

Level

China bristle brush

Combing tool (a triangular rubber tool with narrow teeth, sold at most paint stores)

1. Begin by applying a base coat in the desired color, as instructed on page 90. Let dry thoroughly.

2. To make the glaze, mix 1 part latex paint (in contrasting color) with 1 part latex or acrylic glazing liquid and 2 parts water.

3. Using a pencil and a level, mark 18-inch-square sections on dried base coat. Apply a thin layer of glaze with a China bristle brush to one square at a time. Pull the combing tool through the glaze. Alternate the direction of stripes with each square, and repeat in remaining sections. Let dry. Repeat with remaining squares.

MARTHA MUST

As an inexpensive alternative to wallpaper, I like to cover painted walls with special effects, using a tinted glaze. I covered a painted gray wall with my favorite faux-bois pattern, using a wood-grain combing tool sold at home-improvement and craft-supply stores.

HOW TO
PAINT FLOORS

Painting has long been a way to extend the life of less-than-perfect wood floors—costing much less money and involving much less effort than refinishing them would. But it is more than just practical; painted floors can also transform an entire space. An all-white floor both softens and enlarges a bedroom or living area, while a bright shade lends sparkle and shine to a bathroom. What's more, this decorating update can be applied to modern and traditional homes in equal measure.

FIRST THINGS FIRST

Good prep yields great results. Start by removing all furniture and objects from the room and opening up all windows.

1. Lightly sand entire surface with 100- to 200-grit sandpaper, just to remove existing finish and help paint adhere well. Fill any holes with wood putty. (Or, to cut down on sanding time, first apply a deglosser and follow that up with a light sanding.)

2. Clean floors thoroughly, first by vacuuming, then by damp-mopping with soapy water or going over floor with a tack cloth.

3. Seal floors with a primer coat and let dry completely before painting with two or three coats of paint, depending on the color and the space; let each coat dry thoroughly.

NOTE: *Oil-based paint is better able to withstand wear and tear than latex; many experts use porch paint for this reason. If you are concerned about fumes, you can go with latex paint, but be prepared for scuffs and scratches. It's a trade-off that many people are willing to make. The same goes for brush versus rollers: The former provides the most desirable surface, while the latter gets the job done more quickly.*

TIP

To achieve the glossy color shown above, apply two to three coats of any kind of paint (in any finish), then top with two applications of high-gloss polyurethane, which adds luster and also helps protect against water spots.

FLOOR PAINTING HOW-TO

The goal is not perfection but preparation. As in, be prepared to make mistakes, most of which you won't notice in the final result, the rest lending the project more character. If you make a mistake that feels essential to fix, simply wipe the area with a clean cloth and start over. And if this is your first foray, it's a good idea to gain confidence by painting an out-of-the-way bedroom or an upstairs hall before tackling a more prominent area.

1. Tape off the baseboard and door sashes with painters' tape.

2. Apply the first coat: Start by cutting in the edges with a brush, then use a brush or roller to work your way toward the door, applying paint in a thin layer. Allow the paint to dry for 24 to 48 hours, until it's dry enough to walk on.

3. Apply the second coat in the same manner as the first. Once dry, determine if you need a third coat of paint. Let dry completely.

4. Add decorative details, using painters' tape if needed for stripes or a pattern, like the gingham shown at right. Let dry.

5. Seal floor with a clear polyurethane, if desired. This is helpful in high-traffic areas, but you may want to skip this step in a bedroom.

6. Let the paint cure completely. This may take as little as three days or as long as two weeks depending on the humidity. You should be able to walk gently on the paint after a few days; use care when moving furniture back into rooms.

MAINTENANCE

Dirt and grit act like sandpaper on painted floors, so the key is to vacuum the surface regularly (and enact a no-shoes policy). Clean up any spills as soon as possible. Clean dirty spots with a damp cloth or mop wrung out in a mild household cleaner. If the floors are scuffed, use your go-to spray cleaner or, if necessary, a gentle abrasive, making sure to dry the floors immediately.

TIP

To create a gingham floor like the one pictured above, start by measuring the dimensions of the floor and making a scale drawing of the pattern. Measure the room carefully, and disregard the width of the floorboards, so the pattern is even.

HOW TO
APPLY WALLPAPER

Wallpaper delivers instant texture, color, and pattern that cannot be achieved by paint alone. There's a wallpaper to suit every space, style, and budget, too. Rest assured: Learning the ins and outs—from purchasing the proper amount to applying it to walls—is entirely doable, and doesn't even require many special tools (though a partner helps).

FIRST THINGS FIRST

HOW TO CHOOSE: Beginners may well want to stick with "random pattern" papers such as textured solids like grasscloth, stripes, or close-packed overall patterns. These make matching easier, as do "straight-across match" patterns, which are matched along the sides. Hold off on "drop repeat" patterns, which need to be matched both horizontally and vertically, until you've mastered the basic techniques.

HOW MANY ROLLS: The numbers in the chart at right are based on a "double" roll, which typically covers about 66 square feet. To calculate how many rolls you need per room, divide the total square footage of the walls (including windows and doors) by the square footage of one roll. Buy extra paper to accommodate for errors and adjustments (at least 10 percent more paper). For difficult-to-match patterns, buy substantially more paper. Save leftovers for future repairs.

HOW TO PREP: Group furniture in the middle of the room and cover belongings and floor with plastic drop cloths. Spackle and sand the wall to smooth any imperfections, following the instructions for painting prep on page 89.

HOW TO APPLY: Use a straightedge, a level, and a pencil to mark top to bottom where each cut strip will fit on the walls. When the last strip meets the first, be aware that you probably won't achieve a perfect pattern match. To soften this mismatch, hang the first strip in a discreet corner, and then work around the room, back to where you started. Or begin by centering the pattern at a focal point, and proceed in opposite directions, making sure the last two strips meet in an inconspicuous corner location.

WALLPAPER ROLL CALCULATOR

WALL HEIGHT (FEET)	8	9	10	11	12
24	3	4	4	4	5
32	4	5	5	6	6
40	5	6	7	7	8
48	6	7	8	8	9
56	7	8	9	10	11
64	8	9	10	11	12
72	9	10	11	12	14
80	10	11	13	14	15
88	11	12	14	15	16
96	12	14	15	16	18
104	13	15	16	18	19
112	14	16	17	19	21
120	15	17	19	20	22
128	16	18	20	22	24
136	17	19	21	23	25
144	18	20	22	24	27

ROOM PERIMETER (FEET) — labels the left column of perimeter values above.

GLUING AND BOOKING

Booking, or folding, wallpaper strips makes them much easier to handle once they've been glued (and before they are hung), so don't be tempted to skip this easy step.

NOTE: *If any glue gets on the table, it will mar the next sheet. Slide the paper all the way to the edge of the table to apply glue to the ends and edges. Cover the floor underneath with a drop cloth, and clean the table as you go.*

1. Using a large paint roller, coat wall with wallpaper primer and let dry thoroughly.

2. With scissors and straightedge, cut vertical strips 4 inches longer than the wall height. Arrange wallpaper strips side by side on the floor to ensure that the pattern lines up correctly.

NOTE: *If you're making a shape (as with a headboard), cut it out on a cutting mat with a utility knife.*

3. Use a tape measure, level, and pencil to mark where on the wall the paper will be placed. For example, mark the top edge of a chair rail or sides of a rectangle.

4. Pour premixed clear wallpaper glue into a paint-roller tray. Lay the first strip on a clean work table, pattern side down, with excess hanging over one end. Make a pencil mark at midpoint.

5. With a small paint roller, roll glue thinly over half of strip, then book (or fold) the strip by lifting the bottom edge of the glued half to the midpoint of the strip. Press this edge down so the paper sticks to itself, but don't crease the fold. The pattern will be facing up. Glue and book the other half of the strip.

6. Set aside to let cure according to package instructions (typically about 15 minutes before the glue begins to dry, enough time to hang the strip).

HANGING AND TRIMMING

You may need to use a ladder to reach the top corner; if so, you may want to enlist a helper to hand you what you need rather than schlepping up and down.

1. Carry the first glued and booked strip to the wall, and unfold the upper half of the strip. Align one of the edges of the strip with the appropriate pencil line, and place the top edge so that it slightly overlaps the ceiling (or the base of the crown molding).

2. Smooth the paper against the wall with your hands, moving sideways and downward until you reach the midpoint.

3. Affix the bottom half.

4. Using a wide scraper as a straightedge, trim the edges with a utility knife.

5. Flatten any wrinkles with a plastic smoother; wipe away excess glue with a sponge.

MAKING SEAMS

There are two methods: A butting seam is the neatest, while overlapping seams are used in a pinch—in a corner, for instance.

BUTTING SEAM: Place the new strip as close as possible to an affixed strip. With your hands flat on the new strip, push it gently up or down to align the pattern, keeping fingertips away from the edge to avoid tearing. Push the new strip toward the old one until the edges of both strips touch and just begin to buckle. Then go over the seam with a smoother. After 10 to 15 minutes' drying time, run a seam roller along the seam in short up-and-down strokes.

OVERLAPPING SEAM: Position the new strip to overlap an affixed strip by $1/16$ inch and press as for butting seam. For thicker, fabric-covered papers, run a single-edge blade through both layers of the overlap, and peel away the underlying layers.

REMOVING WALLPAPER

If your goal is to remove the paper and then paint the wall instead, follow these steps.

1. Cover the floor with a drop cloth. Add hot water to wallpaper remover (which you can find at home-renovation stores) as directed.

2. Pierce wallpaper with a perforation tool to create holes that will allow the solution to get behind the paper and soften the adhesive.

3. Apply the solution to the wall with a paint roller or sponge. Let it soak in (timing will depend on the manufacturer's instructions).

4. Once the paper has loosened, peel it using a wide plastic taping knife.

5. After the paper is removed, rinse the wall with clean water (dampen, don't saturate) and let it dry thoroughly.

TEMPORARY WALLPAPER

If you fear you'll tire of wallpaper before long, or if you aren't in a position to put up permanent paper, there are many removable—and repositionable—options that will achieve the same result. They usually come in tiles that are designed to match up side to side. Though easy to use, there are a few tips to make them more manageable: Rather than pulling off the entire backing from each tile or strip, start by peeling back about 4 inches from the top section only; press this section against the wall, then pull off the rest of the backing as you work down the strip, pressing the paper smoothly. If possible, have one person do the pulling and the other do the smoothing. Work from the center of the strip out, to push any bubbles to the edge; should there be any remaining bubbles, simply lift up that section and press smooth. You'll need to cut the paper with a utility knife to accommodate any windows or doors, so consider that as you do your initial planning.

MORE IDEAS
AND INSPIRATION

Wallpaper can be a big commitment, as it's not as easy to replace as a tired paint color. With that in mind, use wallpaper in small doses—or give existing paper new life with a little paint.

METALLIC UPDATE

Shimmery dots give this botanical pattern a more modern aesthetic. Use a mix of metallic paint and matte medium in desired shade and proportions (the more medium used, the more transparent the result). Apply it to wallpaper with a craft stencil (secure with drafting tape, if desired) and a natural sea sponge; start in a corner or along molding and let dry for two minutes before removing stencil.

FURNITURE CONNECTION

In this makeshift home bar, wallpaper combines two disparate pieces—a cabinet and a desk—into one. Adhere wallpaper to the wall above the desk and mount the cabinet (above, with brackets as decorative details). Remove the cabinet shelves and line the back with wallpaper. Be sure to align the center of cabinet panel with center of wall panel below. The same would work for hutches, bookcases, china cabinets, and more.

COVERED BULLETIN BOARD

Consider covering a bulletin board (or piece of Homasote) with wallpaper, which can be swapped out easily over time. The board shown above is cut to fit a narrow nook over a built-in desk, then covered in a whimsical design—perfect for a kid's room. Even better, using magnetic paper makes the board pretty and practical. Adapt the motif and idea for a home command center (see page 15).

PAPERED-CLIPBOARD ORGANIZER

Here's a great way to use wallpaper samples and scraps: Trace a clipboard's shape onto card stock, making a notch for the clamp (hold clamp open with a zip tie while working). Place template on back of paper; cut out with a craft knife. Spread a thin layer of découpage glue onto clipboard with a craft brush. Adhere paper and smooth air bubbles with a craft scraper. Brush with more glue. Hang several in place of a bulletin board.

HOW TO PAINT FURNITURE

Paint can turn flea-market finds, unfinished new pieces, or even well-worn favorites into display-worthy delights. As always, doing the requisite prep work will ensure the most professional results.

SUPPLIES

Drop cloth

Screwdriver or other tools, for removing hardware

Painters' tape

Sandpaper (120- and 220-grit)

Vacuum

Tack cloth

Wood filler or spackling compound

Putty knife

Paintbrush

Primer

Paint

TIP

When painting chairs, sofas, tables, and other furniture with legs, you'll want to raise those off the floor; a nail hammered into the bottom of the leg does the trick, but for valuable antiques, rest the legs on wooden blocks instead.

PREPARING AND PRIMING

Always work in a well-ventilated area and place the furniture being painted on a drop cloth.

1. Remove all hardware. If that's not possible, mask it with painters' tape before priming.

2. Lightly sand the entire surface with 120-grit sandpaper, following the grain. This will remove worked-in dirt and loose bits of original finish; most important, it will degloss the old, shiny finish so the primer has something to grip. Vacuum the piece, then wipe with tack cloth.

3. Fill any dents or deep scratches by pushing wood filler or spackling compound into the hole and scraping away excess with the putty knife. Once the patches have dried, fill again, if necessary, and then sand with 220-grit sandpaper. Vacuum and wipe clean with a tack cloth.

4. Prime one surface at a time. Brush on primer, following the grain, in long, steady strokes. Never work so far from your wet paint edge that you drag the brush through paint that is already drying.

PAINTING

You can use basic latex paint in the finish of your choice; milk paint, oil paint, chalk paint, or craft paint are other options.

1. After the primer has dried for the time recommended by the manufacturer, check for drips and any grit that may have gotten caught in the wet surface. Correct imperfections with 220-grit sandpaper; vacuum and wipe clean using a tack cloth.

2. Apply your finish coat as you did with the primer.

3. When painting a chest or anything with drawers, paint the rails between drawer openings and coat only the faces, not the sides. Paint all exposed portions of the drawer front, but not the rest of the drawer (this can cause sticking).

4. After the paint has dried, reattach (or replace) the hardware.

PROJECT

HERRINGBONE CHAIR BACK

A combing tool (see page 93) features the narrow teeth necessary to produce a herringbone pattern. Here it's been used on a simple chair with clean lines, though you could use it on dressers, bookcases, or even walls. Smooth irregularities as you work (they can catch the glaze and obscure its effect).

SUPPLIES

Paint roller (9-inch)

Latex paint

Glazing liquid (latex or acrylic)

Canister and paint stick (for mixing)

Painters' tape

Tinted glaze

China bristle brush

Triangular combing tool

1. Using a 9-inch paint roller with a ¼-inch nap, paint the surface in desired color using latex paint. Let dry thoroughly.

2. Mix 1 part latex paint (pearl finish or satin finish) with 1 part latex or acrylic glazing liquid and 2 parts water. (If using oil paint, mix 1 part oil paint with 1 part oil glazing liquid and 1 part mineral spirits.)

3. Use tape to mark 1-inch-wide sections, which eliminates the need for measuring. Affix a length of 1-inch-wide painters' tape down the center of item (base coat should already be applied and dried). Affix 2 more lengths of the tape to either side of the first strip. Remove middle strip.

4. Continue taping off, using middle strip as a spacer, until every other length is exposed.

5. Apply tinted glaze with a China bristle brush. Drag a triangular comb across surface at a 45-degree angle. Repeat until surface is covered. Let dry completely.

6. Remove tape strips. Apply fresh tape over combed strips to cover them completely.

7. Apply a second coat of tinted glaze. Drag comb through it at opposite 45-degree angle. Let dry. Lift the tape, and the herringbone pattern will be revealed.

HOW TO
RE-COVER A CHAIR

Before you toss out that tattered chair, consider giving it a fabric face-lift—especially if it's a family heirloom or sturdy antiquing score. Whether you hire out the job or tackle it yourself, there are a few important elements to keep in mind.

DETERMINING QUANTITY

Figuring out fabric amounts is tricky and depends on factors besides the furniture's dimensions—the shape of the piece, the pattern of the cloth, and any extras such as welting, to name the most common considerations. An average club chair, for example, requires about 6½ yards of fabric. See the chart, opposite, for more estimated guidelines.

CHOOSING A FABRIC

There are countless fabrics to choose from in a variety of sizes, patterns, and materials—all factors that will affect how much you need. Upholstery fabrics range in price greatly, with some costing upward of $350 per yard, so being able to estimate how much of it you'll have to buy will help you make an informed (and budget-minded) decision.

WIDTH

In the United States, the most common width for upholstery fabric is 54 inches; however, 48-inch-wide fabric is found both here and in Great Britain, and 40- and 42-inch widths are typical for many imported fabrics, like Indian silks. Other fabrics, such as garment textiles (less often used in upholstery), may be sold in 60- and 72-inch widths. Choose 54-inch-wide fabric when possible, as this will produce the least cutting waste, and upholsterers' yardage estimates assume this width.

PATTERN

Solid fabrics are the simplest to work with. Stripes, plaids, and other patterns must be matched at the seams. A smaller, evenly spaced stripe or plaid should not, however, require you to purchase more yardage. If you want welting—the cord that covers the seams—from the same fabric, you'll need to purchase significantly more. Consider choosing a solid fabric for welting that complements your patterned piece.

REPEAT

Depending on the repeat of the pattern, you may need to buy extra yardage. Some patterns have very small repeats, 3 inches or less; others are much larger. In general, an 18-inch repeat means you'll need about 20 percent more fabric; a 27-inch repeat means you'll need 40 percent more, and so on.

FABRIC ESTIMATOR

This chart should give you an idea of how much fabric you'll need for a particular chair. Keep in mind that these are estimated guidelines, not rules. The fabric's pattern, the upholsterer's work style, and variations in individual pieces of furniture can all influence the yardage. These estimates are based on 54-inch-wide fabric with a short repeat.

CHAIR FABRIC YARDAGE

SIDE CHAIR 2½ yards	**DINING CHAIR** 1½ yards	**ARM CHAIR** 1½ yards
BARREL CHAIR 4 yards	**SLIPPER CHAIR** 6 yards	**OTTOMAN** 2½ yards
BOUDOIR CHAIR 7 yards	**WING CHAIR** 8 yards	**CLUB CHAIR** 6½ yards

BUY PLENTY, BUT JUST IN CASE...

It's never a good idea to skimp on your initial fabric order because it's unlikely you'll get an exact fabric match the second time around. Better to give yourself at least a 5 to 10 percent overage. That said, if you do end up a bit short, here are ways to "cheat" the fabric:

- Cover the false platform (the fabric that covers the seat of the chair beneath the cushion) with a cheaper, solid fabric.

- Use "pulling strips" or "stretchers" to cover the hidden inches of material where the pieces covering the arms and back are pulled taut and tacked onto the chair frame.

TYPES OF FABRIC

When choosing fabric for upholstery, give due consideration to its durability, cleanability, and resistance to soiling and fading.

LINEN: A favorite for its natural fibers, linen does soil and wrinkle easily—and it won't withstand heavy wear. It also requires professional cleaning to avoid shrinkage. The pros are that linen does an admirable job of resisting pilling and fading, making it a good choice for chairs and settees.

LEATHER: This tough material can be gently vacuumed, damp-wiped as needed, and cleaned with leather conditioner or saddle soap. The only downside is that it shows scratches and scrapes, though you can chalk those up to the desirable patina.

COTTON: An affordable alternative to linen, cotton offers good resistance to wear, fading, and pilling, less so to spots and wrinkling (similar to linen). Surface treatments and blending with other fibers can make up for these weaknesses. Canvas cotton (duck and sailcloth) offer more durability than damask.

WOOL: The sturdiest of the bunch, wool stands up well to pilling, fading, wrinkling, and soiling. Rarely will you find 100 percent wool; more commonly this natural fiber is blended with a synthetic fiber to make it easier to clean and to reduce the risk of felting. Pure wool will need to be cleaned by a professional; blends can be spot-cleaned.

SILK: No surprise that silk is the most delicate fabric of all, subject to pulls and tears. It also must be professionally cleaned. If you want the same look but without the pricey upkeep, opt for synthetic (rayon or nylon).

TIP

Outdoor fabrics have made their way indoors for their ability to handle everyday spills and wear and tear. These weather-resistant fabrics come in an eye-catching array of colors and patterns—so they're tailor-made for the most highly trod areas of your home, inside and out.

PROJECT
RE-COVERING A CHAIR SEAT
If your wood-framed chair has good bones but a tattered seat cushion, refurbish it.

SUPPLIES

1-inch foam

Fabric pen

Scissors

Batting

Staple gun

Fabric

Interfacing or lining

Braid or ribbon (optional)

Hot-glue gun (optional)

NOTE: *If after removing the old cover, you discover a board with lots of staples or other signs of disrepair, you'll need to create a new one. Use the old board as a guide for cutting out the needed number of seat bottoms from quarter-inch plywood, using a jigsaw (or ask the lumberyard to do this for you).*

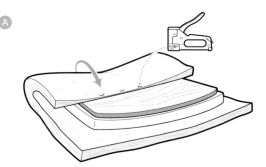

1. Create padding: Mark outline of seat bottom onto foam with a fabric pen, then use scissors to cut it ⅛ inch wider than outline.

2. Cut batting 3 to 4 inches larger all around than the seat bottom. Place seat bottom on top of foam, then center this on batting. Starting on one long end, fold batting up over the seat bottom and staple about 1½ inches from the edge, in the middle, then finish stapling the first side in 2-inch intervals (see figure A). Pull batting taut and staple the opposite side in the same way (this creates the smoothest results). Staple the short sides. Trim excess batting, leaving about ¼ inch (for a nicer finish to the underside).

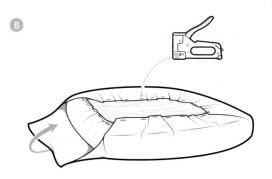

3. Cut fabric 3 to 4 inches larger than the covered seat bottom. With fabric wrong side up, center seat bottom on top, with front side away from you. Fold fabric over the front and staple in the center, about 1 inch from edge of fabric (this should also be about an inch beyond batting). Repeat on opposite side, pulling tight. Then go back to front and finish stapling all along that end; repeat to finish stapling opposite side. Pull the

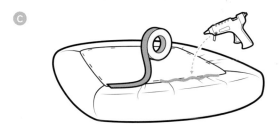

corners taut and staple the adjacent sides (see figure B).

4. To finish underside, cut interfacing about 2 inches smaller than covered seat, following the shape. Place it on the bottom of the seat and staple in place all around, in 3-inch intervals.

If desired, cover the raw edge of the interfacing with a ribbon and use a hot-glue gun to adhere (see figure C). Let dry completely before replacing seat bottom in chair frame and screwing into place.

HOW TO
CHOOSE THE RIGHT RUG

A too-tiny rug can shrink a room, while a too-large one can swallow it whole. A general rule of thumb is to measure the room and subtract 24 inches from the length and width to find the proper dimensions for the area rug. Because rules always have exceptions, you can also pick the size based on how you want the rug to frame the furniture.

MATERIAL MATTERS

Choose your rug's texture depending on where it will reside in the home. Note that a rug's "pile" refers to the height of its fibers; higher piles are softer than low piles, which are more durable and easier to clean.

- High-traffic areas (entryways, hallways, dining rooms) call for resilient fibers such as wool or flat-weave cotton, as well as synthetic options. Sisal and jute are long-lasting but stain easily and should not get wet.

- Reserve less durable fibers such as silk or hides for low-traffic spots (bedrooms, for example), as these also stain easily.

- For living rooms, you may choose comfort over other qualities, or layer a smaller, softer rug over a larger sisal for textural contrast.

LIVING ROOM (A)

The "right" size rug depends on the furniture layout.

- If your furniture is against the wall, you can either pick a size that lets your sofa and armchairs rest half on and half off the rug, or choose a smaller size so no part of the seating rests on the rug.

- For a large living room with floating furniture, choose a rug that's big enough for every piece to fully rest on it.

- Or use multiple smaller rugs to divide a large space into different zones, grouping furniture around (and completely off of) the rug or with just the front legs on it.

DINING ROOM (B)

The table and chairs should fully rest on the rug—even when the chairs are being used. An 8-by-10-foot or 9-by-12-foot rug should do.

BEDROOM (C)

Place a large rug (8 by 10 feet for a queen bed, 9 by 12 feet for a king) under the bed. Ideally it will peek out 2 to 3 feet on either side and at the foot. Nightstands needn't rest on the rug, which can start a few feet from the top of the bed. Another option is to place a runner on either side of the bed.

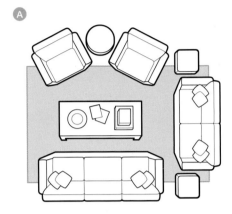

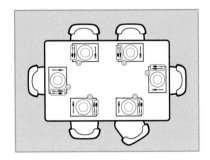

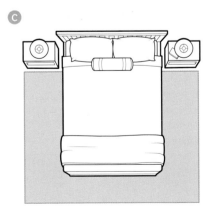

HOW TO
POSITION LIGHTING

There's more than just aesthetics at play when you consider where to install your sconces and pendants; their placement will ensure you bathe the room in a soft glow (or whatever your ideal lighting state may be). And remember that having a mix of lighting in a space—some overhead, some tabletop, for example—creates a more dynamic effect.

TABLE AND FLOOR LAMPS

In the living room, the bottom edges of the shades should typically be at or just above eye level when you're seated, so you and your guests have an unobstructed view of one another. On a bedside table, the bottom of the shade should be at chin level when you're sitting up in bed (the ideal reading level). When there are different lamps in the same room, keeping the tops of the lampshades at the same height will provide the most visual unity, though that's not a mandate—sometimes having varying heights provides more visual interest.

PENDANTS

When a pendant will be mounted over a kitchen island or bar, the bottom of the shade should hover 30 to 34 inches from the surface; same for any ceiling light that's over a dining table or banquette. Allow at least 7 feet of clearance for pendants that will be hung over areas where people walk underneath—or a few inches higher if your ceilings are higher than 8 feet.

SCONCES

The general rule is to mount this type of light at or above eye level, whether in a hallway (place them 8 to 10 inches apart) or on either side of a bathroom mirror (36 to 40 inches apart). These are space-saving alternatives to table lamps on either side of your bed, hung so they're at eye level when you're sitting up—or low enough to cast proper light when reading but high enough so that you don't see the light bulb from your usual sitting position.

TIP

Bulbs today are rated in terms of brightness, not wattage, and measured in lumens. The old 60-, 75-, and 100-watt bulbs are comparable to 800-, 1,100-, and 1,600-lumen bulbs, respectively.

HOW TO SWAG A PENDANT LIGHT

If you lack a ceiling junction for hanging a pendant lamp, you'll need to plug it in—and run the cord up the wall and over the ceiling, using a screw hook to suspend it. For the bedside setup shown above, the cord is also figure-eighted around a metal cleat (like the ones used to tether boats); or try looping it around brass or other knobs, for a polished look.

HOW TO
HANG CURTAINS

Done correctly, curtains can imbue bedrooms and living rooms with drama while also offering privacy with appeal throughout your home. They also insulate against the cold and heat from outside, and protect rugs and upholstery from being faded by extended exposure to the sun. The instructions that follow are for the type of bracket shown, but also apply generally to all types of brackets in terms of measuring and drilling.

MEASURE CORRECTLY

How you decide to hang the curtains depends on the size of the windows and the look you are after. If your windows are large, you may want to keep the rod closer to the top of the window frame. Otherwise, to create the illusion of a taller window, mount the rod as much as 6 inches above the frame, or even near the ceiling, and buy curtains that reach almost to the floor rather than near the bottom of the window. For café curtains, the idea is to have them fit inside the frame.

HOW TO MEASURE

The most important measurement is the rod's, and should be based on its width and its distance to the floor or bottom of the windowsill.

WIDTH: To allow for optimal light when the curtains are open, the rod should extend about 3 to 6 inches past the sides of the frame, wider if you want to make the windows appear larger. To get the right width for curtains, multiply the rod's measurement by 2 to 2.5. This will ensure that the curtains are drapey even when closed.

HEIGHT: The rod should be mounted at least 2 inches above the window frame. Standard curtain lengths are between 63 and 120 inches. Ideally, curtains will skim the floor or the sill. You can always have curtains hemmed, so it's better to err on the side of too long than too short.

HOW TO INSTALL

Use a level in the first step, when marking the holes.

1. Position the bracket on the wall next to the window and mark the top of the bracket with a pencil (use painters' tape to keep from marking directly on the wall).

2. Measure top of bracket to keyhole on back of bracket, then measure that same distance on the wall and mark the location.

3. Drill holes into the marked keyhole spot using a ⅛-inch bit.

4. Hammer in anchors and screw on the hardware.

5. Slide the bracket onto the screws.

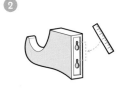

HOW TO
MOUNT SHADES AND BLINDS

Window shades and blinds can layer on color, texture, and even pattern. Choose between inside and outside mounting; the former looks neat and trim, while the latter enlarges windows and blocks out more light. For roller shades, you can choose either a forward or reverse roll, which is purely a matter of personal choice. This also applies to cord options; try cordless to avoid any entanglements.

HOW TO MEASURE

If you have an older home, be sure to measure each and every window, as there can be significant variances among them.

FOR INSIDE-MOUNTED SHADES AND BLINDS:

1. Measure the width at the top, middle, and bottom of the window and make a note of the smallest figure.

2. Unless specified by the manufacturer, do not measure for clearance; this will be accounted for when the blinds are cut to size.

3. Measure the height at the left and right sides and center; use the largest figure.

FOR OUTSIDE-MOUNTED SHADES:

1. Measure width to the outside edges of the molding.

2. Measure exact height of window from top edge of molding to bottom edge, or to top of sill if there is one.

HOW TO INSTALL

Use a level to make sure each set of holes is even with the others.

1. Hold the end brackets (and central bracket if included) in place and mark for pilot screw holes. (For some models, the same brackets are used for either inside or outside mounting.)

2. Drill the holes for the screws and install the brackets. If drilling into wood or wood framing, make the hole slightly smaller than the screw you'll use. If you aren't going into wood trim or wood framing, use wall anchors, toggle bolts, or other hardware.

3. Put the spring-loaded tip into the bracket, then insert the hook arms on the opposite side of the shade into the two hook-arm receiver holes. Or, if it's a simple head rail, simply lock that into place.

TIP

Taller shades are harder to raise and lower. For especially large windows, installing two or more shorter shades (with one mounted above the other) can do the trick—or, for windows in rooms where privacy is not a concern, just cover the lower parts of the windows and leave the top open to the view.

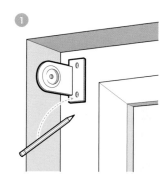

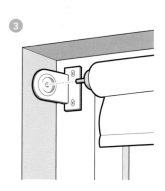

CLEAN

Housecleaning to me is not a chore. I find there's great satisfaction in putting things in order, and keeping spaces fresh and clean. And I've learned to implement some simple steps to make the whole process much more pleasant and efficient.

Having all the right supplies is important. Keep them in a central location so you can take what you need from room to room as you clean. Add labels to keep it all organized, and group like with like (all-purpose and glass cleaning solutions on one shelf, microfiber cloths and sponges on another, and so on).

To make sure no room or task is overlooked, I recommend posting a list of what should be done on a daily, weekly, monthly, or seasonal basis—and to be sure to do those tasks. Each and every day, for example, make the bed in the morning, put away clothes and dishes after each use, and sweep the floors before going to sleep.

I myself look forward to seasonal rituals such as window-washing in the spring, hosing down porches and patios in the summer, and polishing my silver in the fall, ahead of the holidays. You'll find advice on the following pages for tackling all those jobs, plus streamlining suggestions and time-tested cleaning techniques in sections dedicated to the kitchen and bathroom, and to your home's surfaces—walls, windows, floors, and even electronics.

If you establish good habits and follow a schedule, you may also learn to love housecleaning as much as I do.

ESTABLISH GOOD HABITS

Sweeping, scrubbing, dusting, doing the laundry: All these deeds pay such generous dividends. After all, a sparkling house (or studio apartment, for that matter) looks and feels more like a home. This chapter is filled with time-tested (and time-saving) tips and techniques so you can more efficiently go from "to do" to "done beautifully." Plus, you'll discover streamlining strategies and checklists that put the various tasks in perspective as you smoothly schedule them. Because whether it's the weekly refresher or the seasonal spiffer-upper, your efforts will leave your home (and your wardrobe) all the more enjoyable.

DAILY TO-DOS

Incorporate the following tasks into your everyday routine, and before long they'll become second nature—and your home all the easier to keep clean and fresh, week in and out.

MAKE THE BED: A crisply made bed at the start of the day garners the most welcome comfort at bedtime. Your tired self will thank you.

PUT AWAY CLOTHES: Don't let clean laundry pile up; stow it where it belongs. And pick up anything you may have discarded when getting dressed that morning.

TIDY AS YOU GO: Whenever you leave a room, put away anything that's not where it should be. It's hard to clean when there are too many things lying around.

SORT THE MAIL: Open, read, and sort mail as soon as you bring it inside. Keep a trash bin near your sorting area for junk mail. Drop other mail into one of four inboxes: personal correspondence, bills, magazines and catalogs, and filing.

DO THE DISHES: Wash and put away all pots and pans and other items as you use them, and load or unload the dishwasher.

SPOT-CLEAN SPILLS: Wipe up any tomato sauce on the cooktop or makeup on the bathroom counter (and other such spills) as soon as possible. Ditto for tackling small stains or smudges on clothes and upholstery.

WIPE DOWN SINKS: Because bathroom basins get a lot of use, it's a good idea to keep a spare cloth nearby for wiping them down once a day, either after your morning or nighttime routine.

CLEAN KITCHEN COUNTERS: It's worth the few minutes it takes to wipe down countertops after dinner. You'll be happy to wake up to a spotless kitchen.

CLEAN THE FLOORS: Crumbs can quickly accumulate in the kitchen and dining nooks, so use your method of choice to clean them up at the day's end.

FIVE KEYS TO A FRESH HOME

Make the most of your efforts by streamlining your routine, for top-to-bottom year-round satisfaction.

 Create a weekly, monthly, and seasonal schedule. Tackle certain tasks every day to keep ahead of the game (see above).

Regularly open windows to let air circulate and remove stale odors from the house.

SEASONAL STRATEGIES

In addition to your usual cleaning regimen, you'll want to schedule these every-so-often chores into your monthly calendars.

SPRING

This is the time for a thorough once-over, inside and out.

Start by taking inventory of cleaning supplies and replenishing as needed.

Deep-clean bathroom (see page 123) and kitchen and appliances (see page 117).

Clean area rugs; vacuum heavy curtains and upholstery.

Clean or replace outdoor mats.

Wash all windows; take down storm windows and replace with screens.

Store humidifiers, being sure to first drain and clean tank.

Steam sweaters and other winter garments before storing.

Air down comforters; clean and put away winter blankets.

SUMMER

Outdoor spaces and cooling systems require attention during these months.

Clean (or replace) air-conditioning filters; dust ceiling fans and standing fans. Have central air-conditioning units serviced by a professional.

To protect clothing from moisture, place packets of silica-gel crystals in drawers and storage boxes.

Spray porches, patios, and decks with a garden hose (or rent a power washer); rinse off outdoor furniture, as well as umbrellas, awnings, and other outdoor accessories; clean outdoor lighting.

Wash the exterior of your gas or charcoal grill with dishwashing liquid and water, and rinse; scrub burners or grates with a grill brush.

To prevent uneven fading, rotate lampshades, and move upholstery away from direct sunlight (or cover with slipcovers).

FALL

Spring is all about fresh-air cleaning, while fall is a good time for purging and organizing.

Organize kitchen cupboards and cookbook library.

Air down comforters; clean and put away summer linens.

Take down screens and install storm windows.

Clean and put away outdoor furniture.

Clean fireplace and schedule professional chimney sweep.

Touch up indoor paint while windows can be opened.

Pre-Thanksgiving, polish the silver, sharpen knives, and oil wooden cutting boards.

WINTER

Sleet and snow can play havoc on floors—and give you a good reason to hunker down with more time-consuming tasks.

Use two mats at each door—a rough one outside (to scrape off mud and snow) and an absorbent one inside (to soak up excess moisture).

Clean and wax floors; reseal stone surfaces.

Treat nicks in furniture with shoe polish.

Organize the attic, basement, and home office; curate your collection of books (including cookbooks) and periodicals.

Post holidays, clean and put away table linens; store decorations.

MARTHA MUST

There are certain chores I do at least once a season, including: cleaning out the refrigerator and freezer; organizing my clothes and linen closets; rotating all mattresses from head to toe; laundering pet bedding and soft toys; clearing the gutters; and washing the bird feeders.

 When cleaning your home, start at the top of the house and work your way down.

Clean each room from ceiling to floor, too, so dust will not fall on areas you've already cleaned.

 When vacuuming and mopping, start at the farthest point from a room's entryway so dirt isn't tracked over cleaned areas.

HOW TO CLEAN
KITCHENS

If you wash and put away the dishes, wipe down the counters, and sweep the floors each day, you'll stay steps ahead of the dirt, making your weekly routine that much easier to do. Every so often, however, you'll want to address the unseen (and unsightly) spots. Follow these essential tips, categorized for easy reference, to get your kitchen clean, down to the last detail.

MAJOR APPLIANCES

DISHWASHER

- For regular cleaning, wipe the door and control panel (including the rubber seal) with a damp soft cloth. Clean stainless steel surfaces with distilled white vinegar or appropriate cleaner.

- To battle stains and odors, sprinkle 1 cup baking soda on the bottom before running the machine on a short hot-water cycle.

- Once or twice a year, clean and descale inside of dishwasher by placing 1 cup vinegar on the top rack and running the (otherwise empty) machine at its hottest setting, often the "sanitize" or "heavy" cycle.

COOKTOP

- Wipe down the stove after each use, targeting any spills (especially greasy ones) right away. For glass cooktops, use a nonabrasive pad for routine cleaning; remove caked-on food with a baking-soda paste, and let sit before wiping with a soft damp cloth.

- Once a week, wash gas burner grates in hot, soapy water; use a soft sponge on coated grates, scouring pads on others.

- For electric burners, wipe off debris with a damp sponge. If residue remains, run the exhaust fan, turn the burners on high, and let the food burn off.

- Remove and wash the control knobs regularly in the sink with warm, soapy water; dry completely before replacing them.

- If gas burners aren't lighting, or if the flames are not blue at the tips, clear clogged ports with an opened paper clip.

OVEN

- For routine cleaning, wipe the door inside and out with warm, soapy water; clean the glass window with a mixture of warm water and white vinegar, then dry with a soft cloth.

- Every few months (or if the oven gives off smoke), remove the racks and run the self-cleaning cycle; once complete, wipe away residue with a damp cloth. For non-self-cleaning ovens, clog openings with foil, then spread a thick paste of ¾ cup baking soda, ¼ cup salt, and ¼ cup water over the interior (avoid bare metal); leave overnight. Scrape off with a plastic spatula and wipe clean.

- Twice a year (or as needed), soak racks in warm, soapy water for several hours; line your sink with an old towel to protect surface (or use a large plastic bin). Scrub with a scouring pad, then rinse and dry.

LOAD A DISHWASHER

Though machines differ, there are some general guidelines to follow:

TOP RACK

- Stack glasses, bowls, and dishwasher-safe plastics.

- Anchor lightweight items to prevent over-turning; load glasses on an angled row (not over the tines) to prevent spotting.

BOTTOM RACK

- Stack plates, pots, and pans closer to the water-spray unit.

- Orient items toward sprayer; don't let tall pieces block the unit.

FLATWARE BASKET

- Use the separator lids to prevent nesting, or alternate so pieces are handle-up and -down.

- Keep different metals separate to prevent discoloration.

VENT HOOD

- Wipe outside of hood with hot, soapy water and a soft cloth once a week; rinse with another hot, damp cloth, and wipe dry. Clean stainless steel hoods with vinegar or appropriate cleaner.

- Remove filters once a month, and soak them in hot, soapy water (do not put them in the dishwasher, even if so labeled). Brush gently with a plastic scrub brush to remove greasy particles; rinse and dry thoroughly before replacing.

REFRIGERATOR AND FREEZER

- Keep an open box of baking soda in refrigerator and freezer to help neutralize odors; replace every few months.

- Wipe up spills right away to prevent stains and odors.

- Discard expired food items regularly (perhaps before your weekly grocery shopping), especially from the refrigerator.

- Wipe exterior every week with a soft cloth and warm, soapy water; use vinegar or appropriate cleaner for stainless steel.

- Every few months, empty the refrigerator and wipe the interior with a solution of 2 tablespoons baking soda and 1 quart water; rinse with a damp cloth and dry. Remove shelves and drawers,

and wash them in the sink; let glass shelves come to room temperature before washing to avoid cracks. Dry thoroughly before replacing.

- Do the same for the freezer once each year.

- Twice a year (more frequently if you have pets), unplug the refrigerator and clean the condenser coils; these are typically found at the back or front bottom of unit. Use a long-handled brush or the crevice attach-

ment of your vacuum cleaner to remove dust and dirt.

ICE MAKER

- If ice cubes take on any unpleasant odors or flavors (which can happen over time), turn off the unit and wash the bin, as follows.

- Take the bin to the sink, melt the ice, and fill bin with a solution of 2 tablespoons baking soda for every quart of warm water. Wash and dry thoroughly before replacing the unit in the freezer.

COUNTERS AND BACKSPLASH

Clean surfaces every evening, using the appropriate method for the material.

ENGINEERED STONE (SUCH AS SILESTONE)

Use an all-purpose cleaner, wiping it dry with a microfiber cloth.

GRANITE

- Dampen a soft cloth in a mixture of warm water and pH-neutral stone cleaner and use this to wipe surface.

- Wipe up spills promptly; granite is very porous. Vinegar, citrus, tomato, and alcohol (and other acids) are particularly damaging.

- For tough stains, try a poultice treatment (available at hardware stores); reseal the stone afterward.

- When water no longer beads on the surface, it's time to reseal (check for the right sealant at hardware stores).

SOAPSTONE, MARBLE, OR LAMINATE

- Dampen a soft cloth in warm, soapy water for regular cleaning.

- Treat stains with a baking-soda paste.

STAINLESS STEEL

- Spray with a vinegar-water solution, or wipe with a baking-soda paste, using a soft cloth to avoid scratching.

- Dry thoroughly, buffing away streaks with a dry cloth.

UNFINISHED BUTCHER BLOCK

- Dampen a soft cloth in warm, soapy water for regular cleaning. Treat stains with lemon juice or vinegar. Let dry completely before lightly wiping with mineral oil.

- To revive butcher-block countertops, first wipe with a damp cloth, then let dry completely. Working in sections, squirt mineral oil generously and rub in with a soft cloth, using circular motions, to coat completely.

TILE

- Dampen a soft cloth in warm, soapy water for regular cleaning of tiles.

- Clean grout as needed with a baking-soda paste, using a soft-bristled brush; be careful not to scratch delicate tiles.

- Once or twice a year, protect grout lines, such as those between ceramic or natural-stone tiles, with a penetrating grout sealer (see page 55 for more tile and grout tips).

CABINETS

- Weekly cleaning will prevent grease and grime from building up. Wipe cabinets and hardware (hinges, pulls, and handles) with a sponge and warm, soapy water. Rinse with a damp sponge, and dry with a clean, absorbent cloth to prevent streaking.

- For wooden cabinets, use a product specifically designed for natural materials.

- To treat stubborn grime on hardware, unscrew if possible and soak in warm, soapy water for 30 minutes, then scrub lightly with a soft brush (or simply brush hardware that can't be unscrewed); wipe dry.

SINK AND FAUCET

- Wipe basin and fixtures at the end of each day with warm, soapy water and a soft cloth; dry with another cloth.

TIP

Keep the floor of your sink cabinet tidy by lining it with self-adhesive vinyl tiles (from a home-improvement store), which can be wiped clean in seconds.

- Once a week, sprinkle basin with a baking-soda paste and scrub with a soft cloth.

- Buff any water spots on faucet with a dry, soft cloth. For mineral deposits, mix equal parts white vinegar and water; apply with a soft cloth, rinse with a damp cloth, and then dry. Use a soft toothbrush to clean crevices around faucet.

- Flush drains with boiling water once a week, to prevent clogs. Deodorize drains at least twice a year by pouring in ½ cup baking soda, followed by ½ cup white vinegar; cover tightly with a plug or wet rag. Let sit for 5 minutes, then flush with boiling water.

- Sanitize the garbage disposal as needed by grinding frozen cubes of vinegar (made in an ice-cube tray), then rinsing with boiling water. Throw in a halved lemon or orange for a fresh scent.

FLOORS

- Sweep every night (or use a dry microfiber mop).

- Once a week, wet-mop the floors (see page 124).

FOR A FAST REFRESHER

1. Sweep floor, targeting corners and toe kicks of cabinets.

2. Clear off counters and wipe them down with a damp cloth. Let dry before replacing items.

3. Give faucet and sink hardware a quick polish with a damp cloth, then wipe down sink basin.

4. Clean any splatters or smudges from stovetop and refrigerator door.

SMALL APPLIANCES AND MORE

MICROWAVE

- Heat 1 cup water (with ½ cup lemon juice or vinegar in case of odors) on high for 3 minutes, then leave door closed for 5 minutes more; wipe clean with a soft cloth. (Avoid using harsh cleansers, as they can leave a strong scent that will permeate food during cooking.)

TOASTER

- Always start with an unplugged toaster.

- Every week, dispose of crumbs by turning the toaster upside down or emptying the crumb tray.

- Use a toothbrush to dislodge stuck-on pieces inside the toaster.

- Wipe exterior with a soft cloth and warm, soapy water (or use vinegar or appropriate cleaner on stainless steel). To remove rust spots from chrome, ball up dampened aluminum foil and gently scrub.

> **TIP**
>
> Adhere furniture pads to the base of your toaster to protect countertops and to make it easier to slide in and out (this trick works for all small countertop appliances).

COFFEEMAKER

- Wipe the exterior with warm, soapy water; rinse with a damp cloth and then dry. Wash carafes in the top rack of a dishwasher or by hand.

- Flush out interior once a month with a solution of equal parts vinegar and water (about 2 cups). With the carafe in place, run the machine for half a cycle, then switch it off. After an hour, turn the coffeemaker back on and finish the cycle. Rinse by running several cycles with fresh water.

COFFEE AND SPICE GRINDER

- Run soft bread or uncooked white rice through a grinder to pick up lingering spice particles and the oils they leave behind.

- To remove residue left behind by nuts, grind 1 tablespoon baking soda, then wipe thoroughly.

TEA KETTLE

- Dissolve mineral deposits in kettle every few months by boiling equal parts water and vinegar. Remove from heat; let sit a few hours before rinsing.

- Clean exterior with a damp sponge (wipe stainless steel with vinegar or appropriate cleaner).

KNIVES

- Wash and dry these by hand, using hot, soapy water (the dishwasher can warp and dull the blades). Dry well before storing.

- Avoid soaking knives with wooden handles, which can shrink.

CUTTING BOARDS

- Scrub wooden boards with hot, soapy water after every use; rinse with a damp cloth and wipe dry. (Never soak or wash in the dishwasher.)

- Once a week, sprinkle with coarse salt, rub with a halved lemon, and rinse with a damp cloth; dry.

- To sterilize, as needed, rub vinegar over surface, then rinse with a damp cloth and let dry.

- Place dishwasher-safe plastic cutting boards on the top rack and sterilize on the hot-rinse cycle. Wash other plastic boards by hand with warm, soapy water. For stubborn odors, use a baking-soda paste.

GARBAGE CAN

- Empty bin every day. Once a month (or as needed), take bin outside and rinse it with a hose.

- If it's especially grimy, use a long-handled brush to scrub inside bin with a mixture of vinegar and warm water; rinse and dry.

POTS AND PANS

CAST IRON (A)

- The trick is to remove residue without damaging the seasoned surface.

- Rinse after each use with a soft sponge and hot water; use mild dishwashing soap sparingly, if at all. Never put cast iron in the dishwasher. Dry well with a towel or over a low flame; oil it lightly before storing.

- For stuck-on bits, pour coarse salt on pan and scrub with a kitchen towel.

- To re-season a pan, scrub with steel wool and rinse with warm water, then rub with oil and bake upside down on the middle rack of a 350-degree oven for one hour. (Open the windows—it can get smoky.)

STAINLESS STEEL (B)

- Although stainless steel is dishwasher safe, it's also prone to stains from heat and hard water—so washing by hand is advised, rubbing the surface with vinegar and a soft cloth.

- For more stubborn stains, use a baking soda-paste and soft scouring pad. Always dry thoroughly after washing to prevent a film from forming.

Never soak stainless steel cookware; this will result in pitted surfaces.

ENAMEL-COATED (C)

- For routine cleaning, use a light-duty nylon sponge and warm, soapy water.

- For deeper cleaning, use a baking-soda paste and a bristle brush (enamel is scratchproof).

COPPER (D)

- Wash with warm, soapy water and a soft sponge.

- To get the outside gleaming, rub it with a halved lemon that's been sprinkled with coarse salt.

ALUMINUM (E)

- Handwash pan with warm, soapy water; rub tough spots with vinegar and a scouring pad.

- If that doesn't work, fill pan with water, adding 1 tablespoon cream of tartar for each quart; boil 10 minutes. Pour off water and scrub with a scouring pad.

NONSTICK

- Use the regular go-tos: mild dishwashing liquid and a nonabrasive sponge.

- If the coating is scratched or peeling, discard the piece to avoid exposure to toxic compounds.

HOW TO ELIMINATE STUBBORN SPOTS

Follow these tips for restoring pots and pans so they look brand-new (see left for how to care for cast iron).

TO REMOVE STUCK-ON BITS

Fill pot with water and ¼ cup baking soda. Bring to a boil, remove from heat, and let soak for an hour before scraping the pot clean with a wooden spoon or silicone spatula.

TO REMOVE BURN MARKS

With stainless steel, rub with a cloth dipped in vinegar (soaking can cause pitting). Fill other pots or pans with cold water and 2 to 3 tablespoons salt and let soak overnight; boil the water in the morning. If the marks remain, repeat the process.

HOW TO CLEAN
BATHROOMS

Banishing germs is the underlying goal; but having a fresh, sparkling-clean space is a satisfying reward.

BATHROOM BASICS

Moisture makes this room a welcome mat for unsightly (and unseen) developments.

- Color-code your sponges: One color for sink and bathtub, another for toilet. And reserve these sponges for bathroom use only.

- To discourage mildew growth, increase the amount of air circulation and light. Use fans during the shower and for about 30 minutes after, and open windows.

- Wipe shower walls with a squeegee after every use, and pull the shower curtain closed, so water can't sit in the folds.

- Spread towels over two hooks to dry, or hang them on rods.

ROUTINE CLEANING

TOILET

Skip the harsh chemicals and pour ½ cup vinegar (a natural disinfectant) into the bowl; let sit for several minutes. Brush interior with a toilet brush, then flush. If the toilet has a hard-water ring, let the vinegar sit for an hour, then brush clean. Spray outside of toilet (work from top to bottom) with equal parts vinegar and water, wiping with a soft cloth or sponge.

SINK & TUB

- Clean inside basins with a baking-soda paste and a soft sponge. (Never use a brush, which can damage the surface.)

- To tackle soap scum, use an acidic cleaner such as vinegar (or Lime-A-Way); rinse well, as acidic residue can etch surfaces if left on.

- Wipe faucets, handles, and other hardware with a soft cloth and vinegar or with non-ammoniated glass cleaner.

MIRRORS AND GLASS

Clean mirrors and other glass items, such as shower doors, cabinet fronts, or shelves, with a cloth dampened in glass cleaner or a mixture of vinegar and hot water. Wipe dry.

ACCESSORIES

Soap dishes can be washed in hot water in the sink—before cleaning the sink itself—or gently wiped down if mounted. Sanitize toothbrush cup holders in the dishwasher, or clean with vinegar and hot water.

FLOOR

Do this last (see page 124).

SPRING CLEANING

GROUT

Scrub with a soft-bristled brush and a baking-soda paste, being careful not to scratch delicate tiles. To treat mildew buildup, spray area with undiluted vinegar, let sit for a few minutes, then brush.

SHOWERHEAD

Submerge still-attached showerhead in a plastic bag filled with vinegar; secure with a rubber band. Let soak overnight. If clogs persist, see page 55.

FAN VENT

Remove vent cover and wash in warm, soapy water, scrubbing with a soft brush; vacuum the fan itself with the crevice tool. Let cover dry before replacing.

FOR A FAST REFRESHER

1. Straighen, fold, or hang all towels.

2. Wipe down mirror and sink along with the counter, if you have one.

3. Use an electrostatic duster to clean base-boards and toilet base.

TIP

A vinyl, nylon, cotton, or hemp shower liner can be machine-washed in hot water and mild detergent. Rehang the liner to dry. (And always pull the liner closed after showering.)

HOW TO CLEAN
FLOORS, RUGS, AND CARPETS

By far, the number one challenge for these surfaces is managing the dust and dirt and regular wear and tear. That's easy enough to do with basic supplies and a strategic approach (try a no-shoes policy). Read on for how to keep floors spotless, day in and day out.

CLEANING BARE FLOORS

There's no one-size-fits-all way to clean flooring; you'll need to match the solution to the surface. Before using any commercial cleaning product, read the label carefully and do a spot test.

HARDWOOD FLOORS

▪ Vacuum or use a microfiber mop regularly to prevent ground-in dust or dirt from wearing down a floor's finish. Push mop in one continuous motion, not back and forth.

▪ Water and wood generally don't mix, so only wet-mop sealed floors with a spray mop designed for wood floors, or with a regular (well-wrung-out) mop and a cleaner made for polyurethane; dry floor immediately afterward. Also, wipe up spills right away with a damp cloth, drying each time.

LINOLEUM AND VINYL

▪ Damp-mop surfaces with warm, soapy water weekly.

▪ Wax vinyl floors about every six months, applying wax sparingly onto floor, then spreading it into a thin coat using long, straight strokes with a sponge mop. Let dry to a shine, opening windows to speed the process. Remove wax buildup with stripper about once a year.

MARBLE, STONE, AND CERAMIC TILE

▪ Damp-mop with water and mild soap weekly; rinse with clean water and buff dry.

▪ Wax tiles once a year, following the same method as for vinyl (above).

CLEANING RUGS AND CARPETS

How you implement this action plan depends on what the floor covering is made of—and how dirty it is.

DAILY: Avoid treading on rugs and carpets with shoes by leaving them at the door. Also, tackle spills right away (see Removing Stains, below).

WEEKLY: Regular vacuuming will help to extend the life of floor coverings, using the appropriate setting for the pile's height. Avoid vacuuming any fringe around the edge.

SEASONALLY: Take area rugs outside and beat them with a rug beater or a broom handle; drape larger rugs over a clothesline and beat out dust in sections. Sweep or vacuum floor underneath rug before replacing it.

ANNUALLY: Treat the rug or carpet to a thorough deep-cleaning. Synthetic carpets can be steam-cleaned at home using a rented machine, but leave natural-fibers to a pro.

REMOVING STAINS FROM RUGS AND CARPETS

1. Blot liquid spills with white cotton towels or paper towels, so you can see when the stain stops pulling away. Rubbing will just make it all the harder to clean.

2. Apply a spot-cleaning solution, being careful not to saturate. You can buy natural sprays with live-enzyme cultures or mix your own: Dilute a few drops of clear dishwashing liquid in water (about ¼ teaspoon per quart). Blot gently (don't rub!), then rinse with clean water and blot again.

3. If the stain is persistent, dilute the spot with seltzer or club soda; let sit for a few minutes, then blot. Continue blotting with dry towels until the area is nearly dry.

4. Still no luck? Call in a professional. Never steam-clean anything with stains, as the heat could set them for good.

VACUUMING 101

Start at the farthest point of any room and work your way out.

1. Dust furniture and move it out of the way before you vacuum.

2. When vacuuming, use long, slow, overlapping strokes, and use the attachments to reach into corners and under furniture.

3. Change the vacuum bag when it's half to three-quarters full.

4. You can also use a vacuum on curtains and blinds, upholstered pieces, and other surfaces.

HOW TO CLEAN
WALLS

It's not only the visible splatters and smudges that dirty up our walls. Turns out dust (and dander) sticks to vertical as well as horizontal surfaces; grease can also build up in a kitchen. Remember to include walls in your regular cleaning regimen to keep them looking their best.

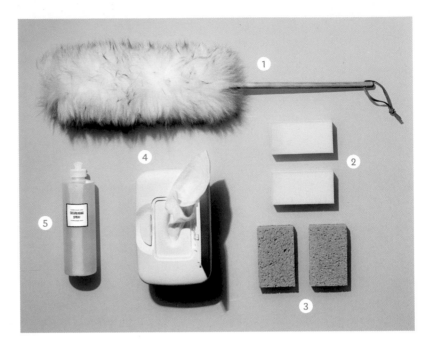

FIRST THINGS FIRST

When cleaning painted walls, you'll want to use only gentle products (mild dishwashing liquid works wonders) to avoid damaging the finish. It's especially important to avoid ammonia and other harsh chemicals, and even white vinegar (a major no-no with paint). Never use steel wool or other scouring pads, either; soft sponges and cloths only, please.

1. TO REMOVE DUST

Thoroughly go over walls once a month—more often if you have pets or people with allergies in the home. The bristle-brush extension of your vacuum cleaner does the job quickly, or use a lamb's-wool duster, which contains natural oils that help attract and hold the dust. Start with the ceiling (grab a ladder), then work your way down.

2. TO ERASE CRAYON MARKS

If you have little ones around, you may want to stock up on melamine-foam sponges (such as Mr. Clean Magic Eraser). These foam pads gently sand away scribbles and scrawls. Be sure to use light pressure to avoid erasing the paint, too.

3. TO TACKLE DIRT AND GRIME

Eradicate everyday dirt by wiping down walls at least twice a year with warm, sudsy water and a soft sponge. As always, start at the top and work in sections; rinse with a damp sponge and dry with a soft cloth as you work your way down. First test for streaks in an out-of-the-way spot, especially if the paint finish is flat or matte (see page 88).

4. TO WIPE AWAY SPLATTERS AND STAINS

The key is to act fast, cleaning up food splatters, fingerprint smudges, and other tough spots when they happen. Never scrub walls with an abrasive cleaner or scouring pad, lest you scrape right through the paint. Instead, use baby wipes, which are gentle on paint but more powerful than dishwashing detergent.

5. TO GO AFTER GREASE

If you have a washable paint finish (such as glossy or eggshell; see page 88), use a solvent-free degreasing spray. Wipe other surfaces with a dry cleaning sponge; just slice off the top layer with a sharp knife when it gets dirty, to expose the unused portion.

MARTHA MUST

Once a season, I clean my wallpaper with a vacuum's brush attachment on a low setting, working from the ceiling to the baseboards. This is especially important for flocked and fabric papers, which collect dust easily.

HOW TO CLEAN
WINDOWS

Rather than spend a substantial amount on a hired window-washer, do the job yourself. Caveat: If your windows are painted shut or otherwise impossible to budge open—or to reach safely on your trusty ladder or with a squeegee—it's probably better to call in a professional.

PANES

For streak-free results, wash windows on a day or at a time when the sun is not shining directly on the glass. Protect inside sills from drips with a rolled-up towel.

HOW-TO

1. First, use a soft-bristled brush to remove dust, dirt, and cobwebs from outside, being sure to hit hinges, sills, and mullions. Go over inside with a vacuum brush attachment.

2. For a homemade glass cleaner, mix equal parts white vinegar and hot water in a bucket. If your window frames are painted, use a mild dishwashing detergent or other gentle solution, as vinegar will strip the paint.

3. Using a large sponge, dampen (do not drench) the window panes, avoiding the frames. Change cleaning solution as needed.

4. Starting at the upper corner, run a dampened squeegee down the glass, then wipe the blade with a dry cloth. Repeat, slightly overlapping the strokes. Finally, pull the squeegee across the bottom of the pane.

5. To clean the frames, use a cloth dampened with non-ammoniated all-purpose cleaner. Rinse with a clean, damp cloth, then wipe dry with another clean cloth.

SCREENS

To get started, bag and label any loose hardware, noting the room and position ("bathroom, opposite sink"). Work in an area with lots of drainage, whether that's your backyard or near a drain in a garage.

HOW-TO

1. Lay the screens flat on the ground, prop them against a wall, or hold smaller ones at a slight angle.

2. Wet a scrub brush in a mixture of warm water and mild dishwashing liquid, and run it over the mesh and frame.

3. Rinse with a hose or under the faucet. Let dry completely (outside in the sun is best) before hanging.

MARTHA MUST

One of my favorite spring rituals is washing all the windows in my home. To make this chore easier to do, carry all the tools together in one bucket, and use a second bucket to mix the cleaning solution together.

TIP

Use a soft paintbrush to regularly remove debris from window screens between deep-cleanings.

HOW TO CLEAN
UPHOLSTERY

Regular vacuuming will help keep most pieces in top condition, as will treating spills as soon as they happen.

WEEKLY CLEANING

Put your vacuum's attachment to use in keeping up your upholstered furniture.

- First, check underneath cushions and remove any loose coins or other objects you don't want your vacuum to pick up.

- Next, use the crevice tool to reach into corners and other tight spots, such as between nonremovable cushions, around upholstered arms and seatbacks, and tufted areas.

- Then go over entire surface with the upholstery brush (or dust brush for leather furniture), using short, overlapping, side-to-side strokes, and working from top to bottom. Select the lowest suction setting for linen, silk, and other delicate fabrics.

DEEP-CLEANING

Just like rugs, upholstery can benefit from a thorough cleaning once or twice each year.

- For nonremovable upholstery, you may want to invest in a professional cleaning service (especially if it is a valuable antique); otherwise you can look into renting a steamer to do the job yourself.

- For removable cushion covers and slipcovers, check the care label and take to the dry cleaner or launder as suggested (typically washing with cold water on the permanent-press cycle and using only gentle heat when drying). Replace covers on the cushions or furniture while still damp (for less wrinkling) and let dry overnight before using.

SPOT TREATING

Prompt attention and the proper method are essential in tackling stains. Pretreat any removable covers while still on the furniture, then launder according to care label (see Stain Removal on page 132 for more tips).

WINE AND INK: Cover the area with coarse salt, patting gently, and let sit about 30 minutes (the salt should change color); vacuum and repeat. Blot any remaining stain with a cloth dampened in warm, soapy water.

OILY STAINS: Cover the area with baking soda and let sit until it absorbs oil; vacuum and repeat. Blot any residual stain with rubbing alcohol or dry-cleaning solvent.

TIP

To remove melted candle wax from upholstered chairs (and rugs and carpet), place ice on the spot; once it's hardened, scrape off what you can, then use an oil solvent or mineral spirits to remove residue. Rinse with iso-propyl alcohol, let dry, and dab (or wash) with an enzyme detergent.

HOW TO CLEAN
ELECTRONICS

Hands down, your keyboards and touch screens are among the grubbiest items in your home (or office). If you're not going to get off the grid, know how to keep them clean.

KEYBOARD

Never spray liquids (that includes water) directly onto the keyboard.

- Use a can of compressed air to dislodge particles, flipping the keyboard over and gently shaking out dirt. Angle the air so it blows dust out of a device (not into it). Fit the canister with an extension tube to get between the keys.

- As needed, moisten a microfiber cloth with a few drops of rubbing alcohol (use a medicine dropper), then rub this gently over the surface, until clean. Use a cotton swab dipped in alcohol (and dabbed to remove excess) to get into the nooks and crannies.

MONITOR

You can see smudges better on a black screen, so turn off the monitor before cleaning; heat can also set any streaks left behind.

- First dust the screen with a soft microfiber cloth (paper towels are too abrasive).

- Then dampen the cloth with a spray designed for LCD and plasma monitors (or use a special pre-wetted wipe) and erase any smudges and grime.

TIP

To remove tough grime on electronics, use a melamine-foam sponge, wiping gently to avoid scratching off the unit's surface.

TV SCREEN

For flat screens, experts advise using only special kits, which are sold at electronics stores. Spritz the screen when it is cool, as heat can cause permanent streaks, then very gently wipe away with a soft cloth.

PRINTER

Check the owner's manual for specific cleaning instructions for your make and model; some have self-cleaning options. The following are general tips:

- Wipe exterior surfaces and paper rollers with a soft cloth dampened with water. Use a damp cotton swab for hard-to-reach areas.

- Dust the corona wires (what attracts toner to paper) on laser printers using a dry cotton swab. Use toner cleanup cloths to remove any toner from your hands.

- Spray the fan and vent with compressed air to blow out dust.

DIY DISINFECTING

To rid handheld and hands-on gadgets and equipment such as phones, remote controls, keyboards, and computer mouses of germs, dip a soft cloth into rubbing alcohol, squeeze the cloth so that it's damp but not dripping, and thoroughly wipe down the surface. Or, even easier: Keep a container of sanitizing wipes on hand, and use them periodically.

LAUNDER

I actually (and perhaps not surprisingly) love to do the laundry—and I hope that after reading this chapter, you will, too.

Over the years, I have discovered the very best ways to wash and care for all types of things, from lingerie and fine linens to wool sweaters and scarves. Having a good washing machine and dryer in your home helps, as does a designated area in which to iron or steam.

I have learned (sometimes the hard way) to obey the rules covered in this chapter, being sure to always avoid mixing colors and putting too many items in the machine.

Also, because I like to have fresh white towels in most of the bathrooms and white dish towels in the kitchen, I have searched for the best detergents to keep them as bright and clean as possible—and insist on avoiding added scents and fabric softeners.

To dry my clothes, I use wooden drying racks in the laundry room, and have one large, flat surface covered in thick, padded muslin for blocking and flat-drying sweaters and scarves. Weather permitting, I dry sheets and tablecloths on my outdoor clothesline.

When you pay attention to how you do the laundry, your clothing and bedding will feel better, look better, and last longer. Read on for laundering guidelines, an effective stain removal chart, the proper way to iron, and mending techniques.

STAIN REMOVAL

When life leaves its inevitable marks, you'll want to act fast—and accurately. Use this as your basic guide to handle any stain.

STAIN-FIGHTING 101

The sooner you deal with the stain, the less time it has to set—and the more likely you will be to get it out.

1. First identify the spot:

- Blot liquids with a damp cloth, working from the outside in to avoid spreading the stain.

- Scoop up solids (jam, chocolate) with a spoon before blotting as above.

- Place ice on gum or candle wax to harden before scraping.

- Sprinkle cornstarch, salt, or talcum powder on oily stains, such as butter or cooking oil.

2. Next dampen entire area with tepid water, dabbing (never rubbing) it onto the stain. For oily stains and makeup, cover with undiluted dishwashing or laundry detergent (because oil and water don't mix).

3. Choose an appropriate solvent (see chart) and apply from the back of the garment to drive the stain to the surface.

4. Lay the garment right-side down on a clean white towel so it can soak up the stain for as long as an hour.

5. Always rinse the garment in lukewarm water to remove solvent before laundering.

6. Treat any residue with enzyme detergent or oxidizing (non-chlorine) bleaches.

7. Launder garment as soon as possible (preferably with enzyme detergent) in the hottest setting possible (see fabric-care label).

8. Check garment after washing and reapply solvent as needed; dry heat will set stains, so do not line-dry items in the sun or tumble-dry.

TYPE OF STAIN	ABSORBENTS • Cornstarch • Salt • Talcum powder	ACIDS • Distilled white vinegar • Lemon juice
ALL STAINS		
COFFEE/TEA		X
GRASS AND MUD		X
GUM AND GLUE		X
INK AND DYE		
MAKEUP		
OIL-BASED**	X	
PERSPIRATION	X	
RED WINE		X
TOMATO-BASED		X

* Leave undiluted for oily stains; use wool detergent for wool fibers.

** Be sure to use an absorbent first; then use a solvent.

TYPE OF SOLVENT						
DISHWASHING LIQUID*	**DRY SOLVENTS**	**GLYCERIN**	**ISOPROPYL ALCOHOL**	**OXIDIZING AGENTS**	**SHAMPOO**	**WOOL DETERGENTS**
Mix 1 tablespoon liquid soap with 2 cups water in a spray bottle	▪ Mineral spirits ▪ Acetone ▪ Use in a well-ventilated area	▪ Pure glycerin (sold at pharmacies) ▪ Stain sticks	Sold as 91% isopropyl or "rubbing alcohol"	▪ Hydrogen peroxide ▪ Commercial products (such as OxiClean)	Gentle formulas, such as baby shampoo	Special formulas for wool fibers, such as Woolite
X						X
	X			X		
				X		
		X	X	X		
	X		X	X	X	
X	X		X			
					X	
				X		

HOW TO WASH CLOTHES

Take a few minutes to brush up on some laundry basics to keep your whites whiter and darks darker.

1. SORT INTO LOADS

Begin by sorting whites from colors, and then by separating light colors from darks. Then sort further:

- Separate heavy fabrics (such as denim) from more delicate ones (such as workout gear).
- Wash very dirty clothes separately from the rest.
- Always wash brand-new brights on their own for the first few cycles, when they're most likely to bleed.
- Launder white towels and sheets on their own.

2. PREP INDIVIDUAL ITEMS

Empty pockets and turn them inside out, when possible. (Keep jars nearby for loose change.) Also do the following to protect your garments:

- Unroll socks and shirt and pant cuffs.
- Zip zippers, tie drawstrings, close snaps and hooks, and fasten Velcro.
- Leave shirt buttons unbuttoned.
- Treat any stains (see page 132). Soak any soiled whites in liquid oxygen bleach before washing.
- Check items for snags, holes, or other problem areas and mend before washing (see page 144).
- Turn items that are prone to pilling, such as cotton T-shirts and sweaters, inside out.
- Put any delicates in a mesh bag (or wash by hand).

3. CHOOSE THE WATER TEMPERATURE

To extend the life of your washables, use the coolest temperature and gentlest cycle for each load. Other considerations include:

- Hot water (120°F) is the best way to keep whites white and to clean very dirty, colorfast clothes (separately).
- Warm water (90°F to 110°F) is good for most average loads, and won't cause as much color fading as hot.
- Cold water (below 85°F) is the wise choice for delicates as well as bright colors that are likely to fade. Just keep in mind that detergents are not as effective in water that is below 65°F.

4. LOAD THE MACHINE

You may think you are saving on water and energy by packing items into the washing machine (for fewer loads), but overloading cuts down on efficiency. Make sure items fit loosely rather than being packed in tight. In addition:

- Avoid adding more than the suggested amount of detergent—it won't get your clothes any cleaner, and an excess might not be rinsed away.
- When washing whites, add a laundry booster, such as borax, oxygen bleach, or washing soda. Once a month (or when your whites become dull), wash them with a color remover (available at many supermarkets). Alternatively, soak non-shrinking items in boiling water and oxygen bleach in a sink or basin.
- For your darkest items, use liquid detergents—powders can leave behind residue. To prevent fading, wash with cold or warm water (never hot) and turn items (notably denim pieces) inside out before washing.

5. CONSIDER BEFORE DRYING

Never dry anything with a stain; the heat will set the stain.

- Always check for stains when items come out of the washer; treat any you find and wash again.
- If any color bleeding occurred, launder the clothes again separately.

FABRIC-CARE LABELS

Before you toss anything into the washer or dryer, check the item's care label for laundering instructions. Here's a guide to the most common symbols.

CARE LABEL SYMBOLS

WASH		BLEACH	DRY			IRON	DRY CLEAN
REGULAR/ NORMAL CYCLE	HOT	ANY BLEACH	NORMAL	ANY HEAT	LINE DRY	HIGH TEMPERATURE	DRY CLEAN
PERMANENT PRESS	WARM	NON-CHLORINE BLEACH	PERMANENT PRESS	HIGH HEAT	DRIP DRY	MEDIUM TEMPERATURE	DO NOT DRY CLEAN
GENTLE/ DELICATE	COLD	DO NOT BLEACH	GENTLE/ DELICATE	MEDIUM HEAT	DRY FLAT	LOW TEMPERATURE	
HANDWASH			DO NOT TUMBLE DRY	LOW HEAT	DO NOT WRING	NO STEAM	
DO NOT WASH				NO HEAT/AIR		DO NOT IRON	

6. WHEN DRYING

Air-drying—on a rack, towel, or clothesline—is easier on clothes and saves energy. See page 138 for drying on a clothesline. If you do tumble-dry your clothes, there are ways to minimize the wear and tear:

- Clean the lint filter before each load. Every so often, use a long-bristled brush that's designed just for the dryer to get past the machine's filter and remove excess lint.

- Don't overload the dryer, which promotes wrinkles and causes more wear and tear (especially on more delicate fabrics).

- Use the lowest temperature suitable for the material, as indicated by the care label; when in doubt, stick with low heat settings.

- Don't overdry; use your machine's moisture sensor, if it has one, to stop the dryer at the desired setting.

- Fold or hang items right away (or make beds with sheets) to prevent wrinkles.

TIP

Save energy when using the dryer by doing back-to-back loads, so the drum needn't heat up each time (a big part of a dryer's energy usage).

MARTHA MUST

I prefer not to tumble-dry clothing such as lingerie, cotton T-shirts, and workout wear. Instead, I hang them on wooden drying racks, which fold up for easy storage; they can be found at tag sales and flea markets.

137

HOW TO LINE-DRY LAUNDRY

There's something uplifting about seeing linens flapping in the summer breeze. This nostalgic scene is more than just idyllic; it's also practical (and cost saving, as the dryer uses more energy than all other household appliances). Whites will be all the brighter, sheets all the snappier, and your air-dried sundries all the sweeter-smelling.

LINE-DRYING TIPS AND TECHNIQUES

When it comes to pinning laundry on a line, stick to this guiding principle: Laundry will dry faster and with fewer wrinkles if a breeze can pass through it.

- Fold sheets and large tablecloths in half, then pin the corners of the hem to the line, allowing the fold to hang open at the bottom (this will prevent a crease in the middle). Then add pins along the hem between those corners to prevent sagging, creating gaps at the top to allow air movement.

- Hang shirts (including T-shirts) from their bottom hems; shorts and pants are also better pinned from the bottom of the legs rather than the waist.

- Soften towels by giving them a sharp snap just before pinning them to the line and once again before taking them down; you can also remove them from the line while still slightly damp and tumble them in the dryer for a few minutes on the lowest heat (or air-fluff cycle).

- Most sweaters need to be blocked and dried flat (see page 140), but cotton ones can be line-dried; hang them from the neck, with their arms horizontal and also pinned to the line (cover with a clean towel to prevent marks or snags from the clothespins).

- Turn colored items (especially darker ones) inside out or wrong side up to prevent fading.

MARTHA MUST

Wooden clothespins are the only option—they are sturdier than plastic, won't rust or leave stains on clothes, and look pretty on the line.

PROJECT
RIG A CLOTHESLINE

Now that you've decided the pros (sun-kissed clothes) outweigh the cons (all that pinning), here's how to construct your very own nature-drying nirvana.

This project calls for about half an hour of your time and 50 feet of line, but that measurement will depend on your environment.

SUPPLIES

Masking tape

2 large heavy-duty screw hooks

Cordless power drill with ¼-inch drill bit

Cotton clothesline rope (measure approximate distance before buying)

Line tightener

2 large pulleys

Line separator

Ladder or stepstool

Scissors or utility knife

1. First you'll need to determine the height of the line; it should be comfortably within reach but also high enough off the ground (keep in mind it will sag somewhat when fully loaded). Stretch your arm up fully and mark the spot on each tree or other strong support with tape accordingly.

2. Screw a hook into each marked spot; depending on the tree or post, you may need to start by drilling a pilot hole.

3. Slip one end of the rope through the loop on the line tightener. To secure, make a loop in the rope, bring the end of the rope up through the loop, around the standing part of the rope, then back down through the loop. Pull to secure. (This is called a bowline knot; see figure A.)

4. Run one end of the rope through the top of the first pulley. Pull the same end through the line separator, then pull the rope through the other pulley.

5. Slide the end of the rope through the center of the line tightener (cut first if end is frayed). Tie both ends of the rope into a simple knot.

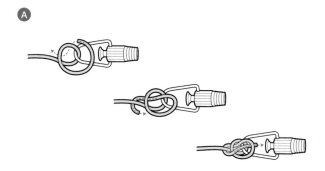

A

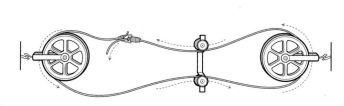

B

6. Attach a pulley to each post (a ladder may be required here). Use the line tightener to eliminate any sagging. Cut away excess rope, if necessary. (See figure B for assembled line and pulleys.)

7. Take the line down during the off-season (if you live in colder climates), to protect it from the elements.

TIP

Use a natural-fiber cotton line, which is strong and sturdy—unless, that is, you live in a very humid climate (then go with plastic). Cotton lines will last longer if first boiled, to tighten the fibers.

HOW TO
HANDWASH WOOLENS

Show your wool, cashmere, and other natural-fiber sweaters some TLC for fresh-scented, shrink-free, shape-preserving results. The best way to wash them? By hand, which is not only economical (no more dry-cleaning bills) but also eco-friendly.

PRE-WASH PREP

Do these simple steps before soaking, to help woolens keep their shape:

■ Button cardigans before washing; if there are snaps, hook closures, or zippers, fasten those properly, too.

■ Measure a sweater from shoulder to shoulder, across the bottom, and outside of each arm before washing so you can block the sweater (see step 4) back to those measurements before laying out to dry.

■ Remove pills with a fine-tooth comb or special pill remover (and never a razor).

> **TIP**
>
> When the sweater is dry, place it on a hanger and gently steam it to remove any wrinkles (or to freshen up a sweater between washings). Never store a sweater on a hanger, though; fold it neatly instead.

1. SOAK

Add a few drops of handwash detergent (preferably one specially designed for wool, such as Woolite) or a mild dishwashing liquid to running water to fill a sink or bucket. Use cool water to avoid shrinkage. Soak for 10 to 30 minutes, depending on how soiled the sweater is, gently swishing it to distribute suds and to avoid stretching.

2. RINSE

Gently ball up the sweater and squeeze out soapy water, then empty the basin and refill with fresh, cool water a few times, soaking the sweater until the water runs clear. Gently squeeze the sweater again to remove excess water, being careful not to wring or twist it.

3. ROLL

Lay the sweater on a clean white towel resting on a flat surface. Gently roll the towel and sweater together to remove moisture, pressing as you go. Unroll and repeat with a second white towel, if necessary.

4. DRY

Placing it on a dry towel, block the sweater by coaxing it back into shape: Square the shoulders, placing the sleeves parallel to the body, and square the hem. Dry flat.

HOW TO IRON

Ironing is a simple task that can transform a rumpled garment into one that's crisp and ready to wear. Following a few guidelines—like having a good-quality iron, knowing proper temperature settings for individual fabrics, and learning the basics below—will transform your wardrobe (and linens).

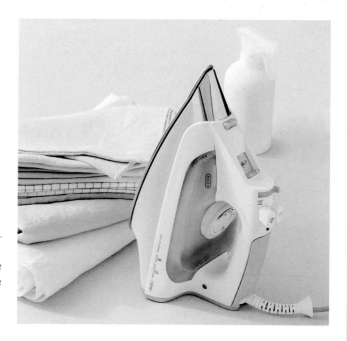

IRONING BASICS

- Go gentle on the heat, starting at the lower end of the range and increasing only as necessary to press out creases (reserve the highest temperatures for cotton and linen).

- On the other hand, be generous with the moisture and steam, using as much of both as the fabric can take according to the fabric-care label.

- Employ a pressing cloth (sold at sewing stores) or a plain white pillowcase on wool and other fabrics that are prone to shine; this can also help shield delicates from heat.

- Iron dark clothes inside out to prevent shine (or use a pressing cloth).

- Never iron in a circular motion, as this can stretch the fabric; instead, go with the grain.

- Keep the iron moving, but don't rush. After finishing one area, wait about 10 seconds before moving on, to set the press.

- Always hang a garment after ironing it (but fold sweaters). Let clothing rest for at least 5 minutes before wearing it or putting it away, so new wrinkles are less likely to form.

BEFORE YOU BEGIN

Take these steps before ironing anything, especially delicates.

1. PREP THE GARMENT: Steam irons generally provide plenty of moisture, but as a rule, cotton, linen, rayon, and silk should be damp when ironed. If you can't iron them right after laundering, use a spray bottle to dampen dry clothing before ironing. You'll also want to give the garment a careful once-over for stains, which can be set by the heat of the iron.

2. DIAL THE RIGHT SETTING: Most irons use a universal dot system to indicate temperature.

Low (·): synthetics
Medium (··): silk and wool
High (···): cotton and linen

3. LOOK FOR CLOSURES: Buttons and zippers don't necessarily need to be protected, but ironing over any fasteners can damage the garment and the iron. What's more, the heat from your iron can crack or melt buttons and plastic closures. Any rough or sharp edges on the garment are liable to scratch your iron's soleplate. Always close zippers before ironing, but make sure to leave buttons unbuttoned.

IRON A SHIRT

Begin with a damp shirt.

HOW-TO

1. Iron underside of collar first, gently pulling it away from iron to prevent puckering.

2. Next iron inside of cuffs, cushioning face-down buttons with a towel.

3. Then iron sleeves, using a sleeve board to avoid creases. Iron outside of the cuff after each sleeve.

4. Now iron the body, starting with inside of yoke (or shoulders) and back, then repeating on outside of both.

5. Iron inside and outside shirt front panels and placket. Do not iron over buttons.

6. Then iron on other side of collar.

7. Iron any details last: Iron ruffles on wrong side and pleats on right side, covering pleats with a pressing cloth.

8. Hang shirts and fasten top button.

IRON PANTS

Use a pressing cloth on wool trousers.

HOW-TO

1. Iron inside of waistband.

2. Turn back pockets inside out. Iron pockets flat. With pockets still inside out, iron outside of pants where pockets will lie. Tuck pockets back into place. Iron between, above, and around pockets. Repeat with front pockets.

3. Iron in pleats and touch up rest of front.

4. Match up all four seams in pant legs; lay along ironing board. Fold back top leg and iron inside bottom leg; do not press seam. Fold top leg back down; flip pants over. Fold back already-ironed leg and iron inside second leg.

5. Straighten out both legs, so they are together. Iron outside of top leg lightly, then flip and iron outside of other leg lightly.

6. Hang on clamp hanger.

IRON LINENS

As with shirts, it's best to start with just-laundered linens that are still damp from drying, or spray them lightly with water.

HOW-TO

1. Fold sheet or tablecloth in half lengthwise, squaring up the corners.

2. Then fold it in half or quarters, depending on the size.

3. Iron sheet or tablecloth until dry, being careful to avoid folds.

4. To iron pillowcases, simply press in sections as you go.

5. Fold item (see page 150 for how to fold a fitted sheet) or place on bed or table.

TIP

Once sheets are on the bed, you can quickly smooth out wrinkles with a garment steamer. (Photo stylists use this method often to make bedding picture-perfect.)

IRONING BOARD 101

Avoid wobbly ironing boards; a sturdy, well-made one will save you time and trouble. Look for an ironing board with rubber grips on the feet, for the most stability.

The size of the board also matters, both when using and storing. Standard (narrow) boards are ideal for ironing shirts and smaller-sized clothes; if space is tight, fold-down models can be mounted to a wall. Professional (wider) boards make it easier to iron pants as well as sheets and tablecloths.

You'll want to have a cover for the board, too. If you are using an older iron, or one without steam, consider a teflon- or silicone-coated cover, which allows the iron to move smoothly. Otherwise, a padded cotton cover is all you need, and you can find one in plain or patterned fabric at department and housewares stores.

EASY ALTERNATIVE: USE A STEAMER

Some fabrics (silk, velvet, knits, and synthetic blends) are prone to stretching, scorching, or flattening under the heat and weight of an iron. That's when a steamer can step in to do the job. It also works on drapes, valances, and duvet covers, without requiring the use of an ironing board (just steam them where they hang or rest).

■ Steamers are faster and will limit trips to the dry cleaner, which is particularly hard on clothes. (You'll still need to use an iron if your goal is a crisp crease.)

■ If you travel frequently or are short on storage space, buy a handheld steamer that's packable and tucks away easily.

■ First remove lint and pet hair with an adhesive roller and dab any dirty spots with a damp cloth. (Don't steam over stains, or they will become permanent.) Then run the steamer over the item in an up-and-down fashion.

MARTHA MUST

I use my steamer on all my garments after each wearing, to freshen them before storing. This also cuts down on the need for dry cleaning.

HOW TO MEND

Extend the life of your wardrobe with some basic sewing skills. Loose buttons and hems, snagged sweaters, and other common signs of wear and tear are best fixed before the garment is laundered, which can potentially make the matter all the harder to repair.

FIX A SNAG

Never cut a pulled thread, as this can leave behind a hole.

1. Turn garment inside out. If pulled thread has caused fabric to bunch, gently stretch it back into shape. (Some of the yarn will go back into place.)

2. Use a large blunt needle to gently work thread back into position (A).

3. Pull thread through to the next stitch and then the next, dispersing excess along the row (B).

4. Repeat on other side of snag.

5. Once thread is in position, smooth pulled area, and go over with a steam iron or steamer.

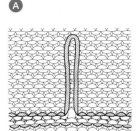

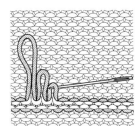

DARN A HOLE

A mushroom- or egg-shaped darner supports sweaters and socks as you darn them without stretching.

1. Place a darning mushroom or egg under hole for support. Create a vertical running stitch, starting ⅜ inch to the side of hole and extending ⅜ inch above and below it (A). Space rows as closely as possible, staggering stitches as you work. Once you reach the hole, pass yarn over it and stitch for another ⅜ inch. Change direction and continue; repeat until hole is covered vertically and stitches extend ⅜ inch past it.

2. Repeat horizontally (B); cover hole by weaving horizontal threads through vertical ones. Finish by weaving the end of thread into garment until hidden, then snip it.

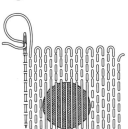

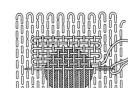

REPLACE A BUTTON

An all-purpose, cotton-wrapped polyester thread is durable enough for most fabrics.

1. Holding button in place, and with a 9-inch length of double-knotted thread, pass a needle from inside to outside and up through one hole in the button.

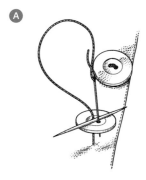

2. Hold button in place, and lay a toothpick across its center to create some space (A). Bring needle down, over toothpick and through second hole (if using a four-hole button, continue back up and down through third and fourth holes). Repeat four to six times, ending with the needle and thread between the button and the fabric. Remove toothpick.

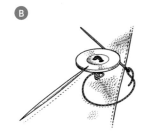

3. To create a shank that will allow room for fabric to close around button, lift button slightly, and wrap thread tightly around the shank several times (B). Slip the needle through one of the stitches and pull tight to secure. Trim thread.

REINFORCE A BUTTONHOLE

This how-to calls for a stitch that's similar to a blanket stitch (see page 189), only with the stitches right next to one another rather than spaced apart.

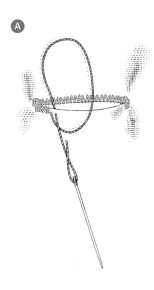

1. Thread a needle with a 9-inch length of double-knotted thread. With the outside of garment facing you and buttonhole positioned horizontally, pass needle from inside to outside, just below original stitching and about ⅛ inch below slit. Pass needle down through slit (A) and back up next to where you started, keeping the thread under tip of needle and holding it with your thumb as you pull thread gently until it lies flat. Continue stitching until you reach the end of the buttonhole.

2. To stitch the ends, shift the garment so the buttonhole is vertical. Create a horizontal stitch (perpendicular to slit) by passing the needle from right to left 3 times. Then stitch vertically until horizontal stitches are completely covered (B).

3. Shift garment so buttonhole is horizontal; repeat steps 1 and 2 to stitch the other side.

TIP

Keep an assortment of buttons in your sewing kit, so you're always prepared when a replacement is needed.

BUTTON UPDATES

You could simply replace a missing button, or take the opportunity to incorporate hits of color, using the same sewing skills. Try these three ideas:

1. CONTRASTING THREAD

Give an otherwise plain shirt more personality with bright thread. You'll need to remove all the buttons, but the extra effort is worth the end result. Sew the buttons back on with the desired shade of thread; or alternate hues if desired.

2. SLEEVE BUTTON-TAB

Some shirts come with convenient button enclosures to keep rolled-up sleeves in place and looking tidy. It's also easy to do this yourself: Cut a 12-inch piece of twill tape. Machine-sew a button hole at one end and hem that end. Sew twill tape to inside of sleeve, just above the elbow; sew on a button at the corresponding point on outside of sleeve.

3. MULTICOLORED BUTTONS

A classic blazer is instantly more stylish when same-colored buttons are replaced with a variety. Sew them on using thread that matches the shade of the jacket to keep it from looking jumbled.

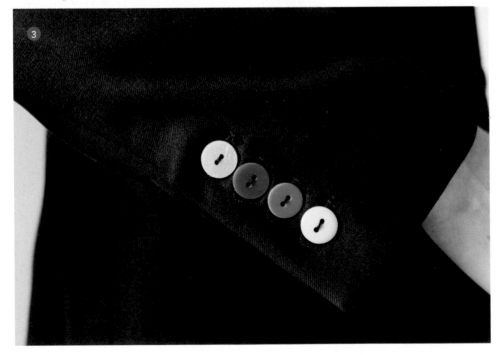

MEND A LOOSE PANT HEM

Choose a thread that matches the garment as some of the stitching will show.

1. Turn the pant leg or skirt inside out. Start and end your repair about 1/8 inch on either side of the loosened hem.

2. To secure the thread, make a short backstitch about 1/2 inch before the rip (no need to knot thread for mending): Piercing only the folded inner edge of the fabric, insert the needle in the hem, below the seam, and pull it out to make a 1/8-inch stitch. Reinsert the needle through the same stitch, and repeat once more to secure.

3. Just above the hem, insert the needle through fabric from right to left. Make the smallest possible stitch; it will show on the right side of the garment. Insert the needle through the inside of the hem, to the left of the first stitch. Bring the thread up and make a tiny stitch above the hem. Repeat, working from right to left. Continue stitching up and down the hemline until the rip is closed. As you sew, keep the tension of the thread slightly loose; pulling it too tight could break it or pucker the fabric.

4. When finished, secure the hem with a short backstitch, as at the start.

MEND A TORN SHIRT SEAM

This will work if there is a tear in the seam, but not in the garment itself.

1. Turn the shirt inside out. Tie off loose machine-stitched threads around the tear. To follow the original stitch line, draw a guideline with a marking pencil.

2. To secure the thread, make a short backstitch about 1/2 inch before the tear (no need to knot thread for mending): Taking stitch through both layers of fabric (and using straight pins to keep layers in place), insert the needle in the hem, below the seam, and pull it out to make a 1/8-inch stitch. Reinsert the needle through the same stitch, and repeat once more to secure.

3. To close the seam, continue to use the backstitch: Insert the needle about 1/8 inch (half a stitch length) behind the point where the thread emerges, then pull the needle and thread out about 1/4 inch (a full stitch length) forward. Continue stitching backward and forward until you've covered the area of the tear and stitched into the original seam for 1/2 inch. Finish again with a short backstitch.

4. Depending on the garment's original seam finish, you can open the seam and press it flat, or finish the seam with an overcast stitch: From underneath, pull needle and thread through both pieces of fabric; then come up and over the seam allowance, on a slight diagonal, and reinsert needle and thread (do not pull thread too taut). Repeat until repaired area is covered. Secure stitches with a short backstitch. Press seam.

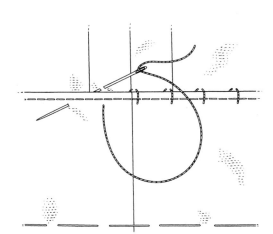

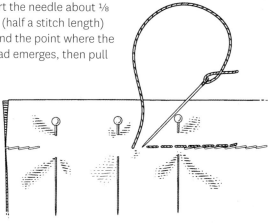

HOW TO
CARE FOR BEDDING

Your bedroom is your own private comfort zone: It's the first and last place you see each and every day— and you spend (on average) one-third of your life there. Make it count, and not just in terms of threads.

PILLOWS

The best way to extend the life of your pillows is to enclose them in pillow protectors, zippered covers that go under the cases. Even so, and this may surprise you, the pillows them-selves should also be cleaned at least once each year.

WASH: Wash pillow covers at least once a month following the fabric-care instructions. If the pillows are machine washable (check the care label), launder them in pairs to keep your machine balanced. Use liquid detergent rather than residue-leaving powder, and run them through the rinse cycle twice. Take other pillows to the dry cleaner.

DRY: Line-dry pillow covers when possible, or tumble-dry on low heat with towels or linens (never by themselves). Use the air-fluff cycle or low-heat setting for all pillows and always dry them completely; dampness left in down and feather pillows in particular can cause mold (you'll know it's dry when there are no longer any bunches of feathers).

COMFORTERS AND BEDSPREADS

Most down- or synthetic-filled comforters should have a cover. Bedspreads or coverlets are just fine on their own.

WASH: Launder comforter covers or bedspreads/coverlets monthly (weekly if you forgo a top sheet). When it's necessary, such as after a spill, launder comforters following the label's instructions (or take to a professional cleaner). Use gentle or delicate cycle and an extra rinse. If you opt to have them dry cleaned, take them to a place that avoids chemical solvents.

DRY: Moisture can lead to mold and mildew, so be sure to thoroughly dry comforters; most can be machine-dried, but always check the label. Bedspreads and coverlets can be line-dried or tumbled on the setting indicated on the care label; if unsure, use the lowest heat.

MATTRESS COVER

Mattresses should last at least eight to ten years, higher-quality ones over twice as long. Using a mattress cover will extend the life even more (and protect your investment).

WASH AND DRY: Wash the mattress cover at least once a month (along with your pillow covers), more frequently if you notice discoloration or dampness when changing the sheets. When possible, line-dry the cover outside; otherwise tumble-dry on the appropriate setting (check the care label).

MAINTAIN: Most mattresses (indicated by a designated top and bottom or head and foot) do not require flipping. You should, however, still rotate them once a month for the first six months and then once during each season after that. This is especially important if you sleep only on one side of the bed or if one partner is heavier than the other, to ensure that weight is distributed evenly.

> **TIP**
>
> Whenever you're leaving for a trip, air out your beds: Strip mattresses, remove duvet covers from comforters, and take pillows out of cases.

HOW TO MAKE A BED

For tight corners, follow these three easy steps when making your bed each morning:

1. Cover mattress with fitted sheet. Spread top sheet evenly over bed. Tuck in sheet along foot of bed, between mattress and box spring, leaving sides hanging at corners.

2. Make a hospital corner: Lift up an untucked corner to make a 45-degree angle to corner of mattress.

3. Holding sheet at that angle, tuck in the part that remains hanging.

4. Then fold down the angled part and tuck under mat-tress, forming the tight corner. Repeat on other side.

SHEETS

Whether you have a designated linen closet, a freestanding cabinet (see opposite), or just a few unused shelves, you'll need to solve a common dilemma: how to stow all your bedding so it looks its best come time for bed-making.

HOW TO FOLD

Fold sheets when they are freshly laundered to help them retain their shape—and save space when storing. Most people know how to crease the corners of flat sheets and pillowcases, but not so those oddball fitted sheets. Follow this foolproof method:

NOTE: *Instructions are for a right-handed person; reverse them if you're left-handed.*

1. Stand holding the sheet by the two adjacent corners of one of the shorter edges. With the sheet inside out, place one hand in each of these two corners.

2. Bring your right hand to your left, and fold the corner on your right hand over the one in your left, enveloping it. Next reach down and pick up the corner that is hanging in front and fold it over the other two corners in your left hand. This third corner will be inside out.

3. Bring the last corner up, and fold it over the others so it is right-side out.

4. Lay the sheet on a flat surface and shape as shown.

5. Fold two edges in, folding the edge with elastic first, so all the elastic is hidden.

6. Fold the strip of fabric into a rectangle. Continue folding until the rectangle is the desired size.

HOW TO STORE

The key to a well-ordered linen storage space is to sort and stack with a purpose, so you or anyone else—guests included—can match the sheets to the right bed.

1. Start by stacking each folded set—flat sheet on bottom, followed by fitted sheet and then pillowcases.

2. Slip each matched set into one of its pillowcases, a fabric bundle, or a basket; you can also stack sets by size or organize by room (helpful if you mix and match bedding).

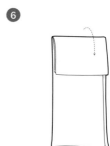

PROJECT
REPURPOSED LINEN CLOSET

If you don't have a closet to spare, consider repurposing an armoire as a designated linen storage. Customize it to meet your stacking needs by retrofitting it with DIY cubbies, sized to fit both pillowcases and larger quilts.

For a seamless look, paint the entire unit, including the separators, the same shade, inside and out. Or paint the cubbies in a contrasting hue, for pops of color.

SUPPLIES

Plywood, ½ inch thick

Table saw (or have wood cut for you when buying)

Fine-grade sandpaper

Paint and paintbrush (optional)

Red oak cove molding, ⅜ inch

Wood glue

Brads, ¾ inch

1. Determine number and placement of separators (A).

2. Cut plywood to height of space between shelves (B) and depth of shelves. Lightly sand and paint, if desired; let dry.

3. To create channels for separators to slide into, cut 4 lengths of molding for each separator.

4. Place separators where desired. Mount molding (C) on both sides of separator, as shown, and secure with wood glue and brads.

5. Slide separators into channels.

TIP

This same idea also works in a built-in closet for storing sweaters, scarves, and other foldable garments; winter hats and gloves can be stacked in smaller compartments.

CRAFT
AND
CREATE

I started sewing my own clothes and knitting my own mittens and scarves when I was very young. I learned these lifelong skills at home, from my mother and grandmother, who took great pride in making things with their hands.

Since then, I did not always have the time to sew or knit as often as I might have liked, but I always returned to these handcrafts before the holidays, when making gifts for family, friends, and colleagues. One year it was aprons with different pockets for gardening versus cooking; another year I made sweet little vests using the most beautiful black wool yarn spun from my own sheep.

Now that I am a grandmother myself, I have rediscovered the thrill of such creations. For instance, by taking simple fabrics—including my vast collection of vintage tea towels—and using uncomplicated patterns and basic stitches (and no zippers, snaps, or even buttons), I made sundresses with matching bloomers for my granddaughter.

I look forward to teaching my grandchildren how to sew, embroider, knit, and quilt, just as my grandmother taught me. Thanks to her—and my mother, who sewed a nightgown for me each year throughout her life—I'm inclined to make things that are unique, and that I could never find in a store. I hope you will learn to (re)discover the same satisfaction.

Remember to start with the best-quality materials for your budget, as they will determine the quality of what you make. And take the time to enjoy the process as much as the end result.

CREATE A CRAFT SPACE

When you carve out room (even a corner of a room, or a spare closet) for your crafting endeavors, you'll be more likely to spend time there—and that's always time well spent. A spare bedroom or closet will suffice, as will an underused attic or basement. If you lack any of the above, take heart—and get a cart for all your needs.

THE DETAILS

GENERAL WORKSTATION (A)

A desk or table works equally well, so long as it has enough room for measuring and cutting paper or fabric and other space-demanding tasks—and preferably provides even more storage opportunities.

- Here, the desk serves as a sewing station, complete with sewing machine (A) and frequently used items on top, drawers for keeping items out of sight below.

- The table at right provides a broader expanse, and has a lower shelf for housing scrapbooking materials and other bulky items.

ALL-PURPOSE COMPARTMENTS (B)

Wooden cubbyholes keep all the various supplies neatly organized.

- Some are left open, others have pull-out drawers, so you can take the items where you need them (or keep them hidden when not in use).

- For a seamless look, paint the cubbyholes to match the rest of the furniture. You can also find handsome store-bought units, many with adjustable shelves and other compartments.

DRAWER INSERTS

Keep sewing scissors, rotary cutters, hole punches, pom-pom makers, and other small tools in slide-to-fit acrylic drawer dividers, available at home-organizing stores.

- Spice-jar drawer inserts are great for containing jars of snaps, hooks, and other fittings (or glitter); they can also accommodate spools of thread.

SPOOL RACKS (C)

A wooden spool rack that rests on the desk holds machine thread; prewound disposable bobbins are stored in nearby jars. Still more spools in a full spectrum of colors are organized in wall-mounted racks.

FLAT-FILE DRAWERS (D)

These shallow, vertical organizers let you sort fabrics (and papers) by color and type, and also happen to be great for storing kids' artwork. They come in different sizes—and most often as freestanding units with an optional base or stand.

COMFORTABLE SEATING (E)

An office chair provides comfort in an ergonomic design. This vintage chair, retrofitted with charcoal-gray upholstery, also has wheels, for moving about the space.

UNIVERSAL CRAFT SUPPLIES

Most people (even non-crafters) will want to consider keeping the following basic items on hand, organized by purpose into stations.

WRAPPING

Keep supplies in one place: scissors, double-sided tape, ribbons, and wrapping paper, plus bows, tags, and toppers.

CUTTING

Keep a self-cutting mat, transparent ruler and/or straightedge, and craft knife on your work surface for cutting templates and other needs.

CORRESPONDENCE

3 When an email just won't do: It's easy to create your own stationery and thank-you cards from a cache of assorted papers (and blank envelopes), embossers, rubber stamps and ink pads, hole punches, bone folders, and colored pens and pencils.

MEMORY KEEPING

4 Scrapbooking is just the start; "scrapboxing" (using shadow boxes) and collages are other ways to display treasured keepsakes. Besides background paper, you'll need a hot-glue gun and a glue stick, plus markers and stamps.

SEW

It's a shame this life-affirming skill isn't taught in many schools anymore—with even the most rudimentary skills, you can rival any seamstress to make your own wearables and gifts.

SEWING BASICS

Begin building your sewing kit with the following, then add to it continually as you gain experience and work on different projects.

TAPE MEASURE (A): A flexible measure is a must for taking body measurements.

VARIOUS FASTENERS (B): Keep a steady supply of assorted buttons, snaps, Velcro fasteners, and hooks and eyes on hand.

SEWING SCISSORS (C): Choose scissors that are comfortable to hold, such as those with a cushioned, nonslip grip. Always designate a pair just for cutting fabric (tie a ribbon around the handle as a reminder); cutting paper and plastic will dull the blades.

EMBROIDERY SCISSORS (D): With their small blades and pointed tips, these can get at spots even thread clippers can't reach.

PINKING SHEARS (E): The jagged blade helps prevent fabric from fraying on finished seams and raw edges.

STRAIGHT PINS, GLASS PINS (F): Having pins with colorful tops makes them easy to spot when pinned to a project (or when you drop them). The flat-head types shown here can also be ironed over (plastic ones will melt).

PINCUSHION (G): You'll need a place to hold straight pins and make it easy to grab one when you need it. They come in all shapes and sizes, so pick what you like best.

SEAM RIPPER (H): Besides ripping seams, this tool removes all types of stitches. One with a fine tip will get at even small stitches.

ASSORTED SAFETY PINS (I): A must for sewing on elastic, sandwiching fabric layers, and other times a straight pin won't do.

THREAD CLIPPERS (J): Their odd shape lets you snip threads as you machine-sew.

BEESWAX (K): This sewing secret helps strengthen thread and keep it from snarling; run thread two or three times along length of beeswax, then "set" the wax by running thread through your thumb and forefinger.

THREAD (L): All-purpose thread works for most projects; buy in a range of colors. Heavy-duty (or "dual-duty") thread is good for sturdier fabrics and sewing on buttons.

NEEDLES (M): You'll need a range of sizes for sewing a variety of materials and with different types of thread.

THIMBLE (N): When sewing by hand, use a thimble (on your middle finger) to help push a needle through fabric.

NEEDLE THREADER (O): To help get thread through the tiny eye of a needle, slip the tool's loop through the eye, feed thread through this, then pull loop (and thread) out.

GRID RULER (P): A see-through (acrylic) ruler will help you cut straight lines and take accurate measurements for hems and buttons.

EXTRAS: Other tools that are helpful in the projects that follow: rotary cutter, for cutting around a template or pattern; craft knife, for making holes in sturdy fabric; assorted ribbon and cord, for decorative elements; bias tape, for finishing raw edges; grommet kit and mallet, for punching holes; plus a fabric pen and an iron and board.

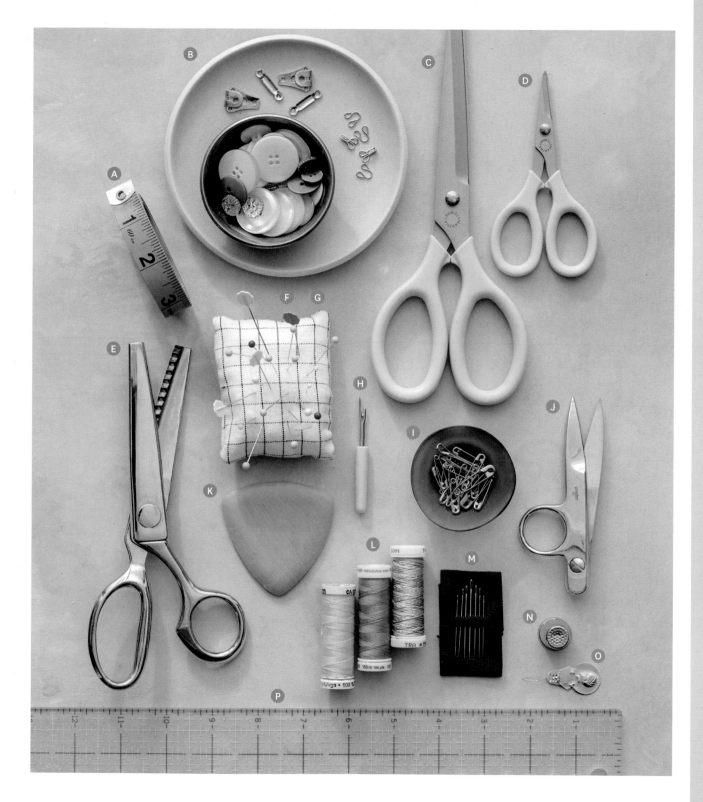

| SEW

BUYING A SEWING MACHINE

Whether you're looking to buy your first or fifteenth machine, you'll want to spend your money wisely. Here are some considerations to keep in mind:

■ Always give the machine a test-drive before purchasing. Comfort and simplicity count; look for one that's easy to operate, regardless of your skill set.

■ If you're an avid sewer, a computerized machine will make changing stitches easy— no fiddling with attachments required.

■ A more basic, less expensive model might suit a beginner's needs just fine, and avoid the distraction of functions that you aren't interested (or skilled) in using.

■ Depending on what you use the machine for, you may want one with additional features, such as automatic buttonholing, speed variables, and functions for sewing woven and knit fabrics.

■ Make sure the dealer offers technical support and training so you can utilize the machine's functions most efficiently. Many dealers allow you to trade in your model for an upgrade; it's worth buying from one of these.

■ To care for your machine, store it under a dustcover (either the one it comes with or one you sew yourself). Also, make a habit of dusting inside the bobbin case with a soft cosmetic brush (unplug the machine first). Check the owner's manual for advice on keeping the bobbin case lubricated, too.

BASIC SEWING STITCHES

These are the four sewing techniques (the fifth is the buttonhole stitch on page 145) that everyone should know—and that will allow you to create a variety of projects at home. Avoid tangles by cutting the thread the same length as your outstretched arm; the sharper the needle and the smaller the eye, the easier the needle will be to push through the fabric (and the harder it will be to thread, so use a needle threader). Always start by threading your needle and tying a knot at the end of the thread. You'll also typically begin from the wrong (back) side of the fabric, so the knot stays hidden.

1. RUNNING STITCH

The easiest of all stitches, the running stitch is also the fastest to do. Besides making seams, this versatile stitch is used for basting (temporary stitches to hold layers together) and mending.

Starting from the back side, insert the needle at evenly spaced intervals into the fabric, then pull the needle and thread through. Repeat. For shorter stitches and with thinner fabrics, try bunching up the fabric ahead of the needle and making as many stitches as will fit on the needle before pulling it through.

2. BACKSTITCH

Just as versatile as the running stitch, only stronger, the backstitch is great for repairing seams—and most closely resembles a machine stitch when made in tight intervals. As its name suggests, this stitch moves backward, not forward, creating a flexible but sturdy loop each time.

With front sides of the fabric together, bring the threaded needle through the two layers of fabric. Insert the needle back down through the fabric about ⅛ inch to the right; bring it back up the same distance to the left of where you started. Repeat.

3. SLIP STITCH

Because it is hidden (especially when using same-color thread), this stitch is ideal for hemming garments and curtains and also sewing pillow covers. When finished, the stitches resemble the rungs of a ladder, hence its alias: ladder stitch.

Make a small fold in the fabric, just enough to encase the raw fabric edge; press the fold. Then make another fold the size you want the hem to be. Put the needle inside the fold, push it through to the front, single layer of fabric, and pick up just a thread or two. Send the needle back into the fold, and repeat.

4. CATCH STITCH

When you are working on projects where the layers will require a little give, such as a full skirt or a round tablecloth, this crosshatch stitch offers flexibility and durability. Because these are not supporting the full weight of a garment or textile, but only the part of the fabric they are keeping intact, you can keep the stitches small and close together (which will help prevent snags).

Press the part of the fabric you will be stitching. Working from left to right, push the needle through to the front of the top fabric, then down about ⅛ inch back to the left on a diagonal through the bottom piece, then bring back up through the top fabric. Send the needle toward the bottom piece, crossing over original stitch, in a downward diagonal. Continue in this manner, sending each stitch in the opposite direction from the prior, to form a series of Xs. Do not pull taut, or fabric will pucker.

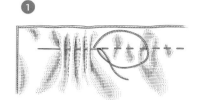

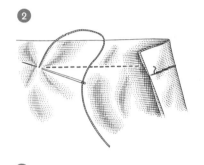

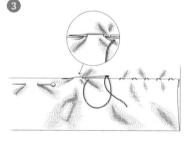

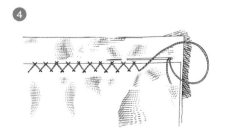

MARTHA MUST

I started sewing when I was very young, and still have my grandmother's machine in my craft room. I believe a sewing machine is as essential today as ever, which is why I often give basic models to kids for birthdays, graduations, and other occasions—along with patterns for simple projects such as tea towels or aprons.

HOW TO
SEW THREE GARMENTS FROM ONE PATTERN

Start with just one simple pattern, choose between two different crop marks, and use the three pieces—front, back, and sleeve—to make three fantastic designs. You can also play around with the length to make a midi or tunic—it's an easy enough project to undertake in a single afternoon.

SUPPLIES

Fabric

Iron

Sewing machine and supplies

2 yards ¼-inch-wide elastic or ribbon

Safety pins

Sewing scissors

MARTHA MUST

When cutting a piece of fabric from around a template or pattern, I find that a rotary cutter is easier to use, and does a more accurate job, than sewing scissors. With pattern pinned in place, just roll the cutter along the outline, no lifting required.

HOW-TO

Use a lightweight cotton or linen that drapes well. These instructions apply for a dress or a top.

1. See pattern and instructions for desired style and size at *marthastewart.com/968083/dress-blouse-how.* Buy appropriate amount of fabric, as indicated on pattern. Cut out fabric using pattern.

2. Prep neck hem: Fold over top edges of all pieces ⅜ inch and press with iron; fold over ⅜ inch again and press. Unfold. (You'll use pressed lines as guides later.)

3. Take one sleeve and, with right sides facing, sew to front, then back. Sew other sleeve to back, then front. Press seams open.

4. Sew along sleeve inseam, then down one side. Repeat on other side. Press seams open.

5. Fold over sleeve hem ⅜ inch and press; fold over ⅜ inch again and hem, leaving ½-inch opening at inseam.

6. Using guidelines from step 2, refold fabric to make neck tunnel. Sew, leaving ½-inch opening at center front (for ribbon) or center back (for elastic).

7. Using small safety pin, thread ribbon or elastic through neck and sleeve tunnels. Gather to desired tightness. If using elastic (as shown opposite for sleeves), overlap ends and sew; then sew opening closed. If using ribbon (shown in collars, above), tie to finish.

8. Fold bottom hem over ⅜ inch and press; fold over ⅜ inch again and hem.

HOW TO
SEW GIRLS' SUNDRESSES

The secret to these adorable kid-size garments? Crisp linen and cotton tea towels (these are vintage, but new ones work just as well) in sweet patterns. The tunic is easy enough for even novice sewers.

SUPPLIES

Tea towels

Sewing scissors

Sewing machine
and supplies

Bias tape

Iron

HOW-TO

A smock or tunic has a slight A-line shape. Its neck- and armholes are bound with bias tape. This pattern is sized for a 2-year-old. You may need to patch together towels before cutting the pieces, or supplement with linen yardage (vintage or store-bought).

1. Assemble pattern from *marthastewart.com/988814/tunic-dress*. Lay out on towels (you may need to play around with positioning) and cut out.

2. With right sides facing, sew back pieces together, leaving 3 inches unsewn at neck. Press seam open. Cut a 6-inch piece of bias tape; sew on at seam.

3. With right sides facing, sew seams at shoulders and sides. Press seams open.

4. Cut tape to fit around one armhole; sew on. Repeat on other side.

5. Cut tape to fit around neck, adding 12 inches on each end to create tie closure. Sew on. (Or cut tape to fit neck opening, sew on, and add a button and thread-loop buttonhole.)

6. Optional: Add ruffle. Baste along one long edge of the ruffle. Pull ends of thread to gather. With right sides facing, sew gathered edge to bottom of dress. Press seam open.

7. Press hem under by ¼ inch, then another ¼ inch. Sew.

HOW TO
SEW AN APRON WITH HIDDEN SEAMS

These aprons use a French seam, a clever way to conceal stitches that lets you color-block pieces of fabric together without any raw edges.

SUPPLIES

Craft knife

Ruler

Sewing scissors

Assorted mid-weight (6 to 8 ounces) denims, chambrays, and indigo linens

Sewing machine and supplies

Iron

Twill tape or ribbon, 1 inch wide (one 20-inch piece for neck strap, two 44-inch pieces for waist straps)

HOW-TO

1. Using the template on page 378, cut out two contrasting pieces of fabric for color-blocking the apron (or just cut out one piece for a solid apron); also cut out pocket piece(s).

2. For color-blocked apron: Align fabric pieces, wrong sides facing, and machine-stitch with a ¼-inch seam allowance. (Do not press open.) Flip fabric back other way, over seam, so right sides are facing (A). Stitch another seam with a ⅜-inch allowance to enclose the first (B). Flip fabric open and press seam to one side. On right side of fabric, topstitch along pressed seam (C).

3. To add pocket(s), fold top edge of fabric piece under ½ inch, press, then fold another ½ inch and press. Hem top edge. Fold all other sides under ¼ inch and press. Repeat for all desired pockets. Pin pocket to desired spot on apron (or to a larger pocket). Sew in place.

4. Press hem under by ⅜ inch, then another ⅜ inch; sew. Sew neck strap and waist straps (if desired) as indicated on page 378.

NOTE: *In the diagram, tan represents the right side of the fabric and white represents the wrong side.*

HOW TO
SEW TASSELS

Frilly or not, tassels can add a dash of homespun appeal to all sorts of objects (towels, blankets, shades, and hampers, for starters), both modern and traditional. While you can buy tassels from a fabric store, they are also worth making yourself—and in your favorite color combinations.

SUPPLIES

Craft knife

Heavy card stock

Thread in desired color

Craft scissors

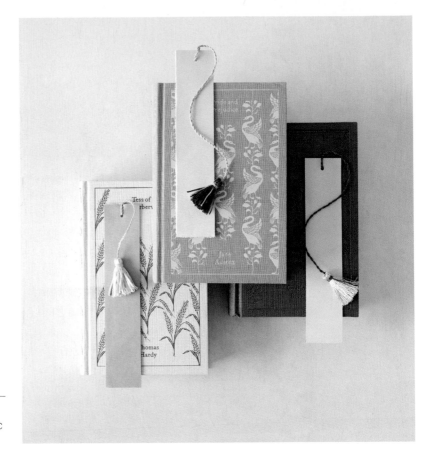

HOW-TO

Follow these four easy steps to create a basic tassel of any size.

1. Cut a winding board from heavy card stock, cardboard, or foam board; the board should be double the length of the finished tassel. Wind thread around board in taut loops until you reach desired fullness (tassel will be twice as full as the loop around board).

2. Lay a 5-inch piece of thread horizontally on work surface. Slide wound thread off board, and center it on 5-inch thread. Tie 5-inch thread into a tight knot around middle of looped thread.

3. Pull ends of 5-inch thread upward and wound threads downward. Cut through looped ends, and adjust into tassel shape.

4. Cut a 12-inch length of thread to wrap tassel neck: Fashion end of thread into a loop shape, then lay loop on tassel. Grasp the other end, and wrap it tightly around tassel and over the

top of the loop to secure it. Wrap slowly, working from the top of the neck down, so neck threads lie evenly next to one another. As you wrap, ensure all the threads in the head and skirt are neatly in place. After wrapping neck, pass end of thread through loop and gently close loop, tucking ends into the head of the tassel. Trim tassel ends, a few threads at a time, to even them if necessary. Use the tie-off threads on top of the tassel to attach it to your project.

HOW TO
SEW POM-POMS

Similar to tassels, opposite, pom-poms bring welcome bursts of color and soft texture to apparel and home décor, without too much extra effort. A clever little tool assists in putting all those yarn remnants to use in embellishing everything from hats (see page 166) and mittens to curtains, throws, and pillows.

SUPPLIES

Pom-pom maker (such as by Clover)

Yarn

Sewing scissors

Sewing supplies

Upholstery needle (optional)

HOW TO MAKE POM-POMS

1. Open up arms on both sides of center body of pom-pom maker. Holding one end of yarn against side of arm, begin wrapping yarn around the half-moon shape from outside end to the other. Close arm, running yarn through notch in center and then repeating to wind yarn around other arm in the same manner (A). Close up other arm and snip end of yarn with scissors.

2. Using scissors, cut through the loops, using the notch on the body of the pom-pom maker as your guide (B). Make sure arms are tightly closed when snipping.

3. Tie off the center with a length of the same yarn, sliding it in the opening between the two arms and then looping the ends to secure (C). Snip the ends as desired.

4. Open up arm pieces on either side, then pull apart center pieces to remove the pom-pom, trimming it as needed with scissors.

HOW TO ATTACH POM-POMS

1. To sew a pom-pom onto fabric, stitch straight through the pom-pom, being sure to pierce through the tied yarn at the center.

2. To attach to heavier textiles, such as a blanket or coverlet, leave a tail of about 8 inches when making the pom-poms; thread both ends of the tail through an upholstery needle, stitch through the blanket and then back through the center of the pom-pom, and tie.

3. Otherwise, use the loose strands to tie pom-poms to key chains, purses and totes (and other items with a zipper enclosure), and decorative objects that have a handle or other appurtenance (think baskets and bins, lamps and sconces, chairs and bedposts). Or just rest a bunch in a pretty bowl and keep on a bedside table or desk.

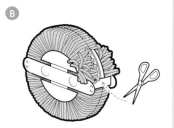

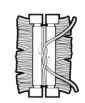

HOW TO
SEW HAT EMBELLISHMENTS

Four simple-to-stitch techniques can take your brand-new hat (or a thrift-shop find) from ordinary to extraordinary. Once you get going, you'll find a reason to make one for all your friends.

SUPPLIES

Sewing scissors

Felt

Large pom-pom

Sewing needle

SUPPLIES

3 (or more) small pom-poms

Thread

Sewing scissors

Yarn

SUPPLIES

Darning needle

Yarn

Sewing scissors

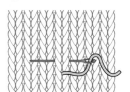

A

POM-POMS

1. Cut a 1-inch disk of felt. Place inside hat at desired spot for pom-pom.

2. Thread one tail of pom-pom onto a sewing needle, and stitch through hat and disk. Repeat with second tail. Tie tails tightly, using a square knot.

3. Optional: Repeat steps 1 and 2 for teddy-bear ear pom-poms.

BRAIDED POM-POMS

1. Tie off three pom-poms with strong thread, leaving 3- to 5-inch tails.

2. Cut three 30-inch pieces of yarn. Double-knot one set of pom-pom threads around middle. Clip off excess thread. Repeat for other two pom-poms.

3. Knot yarn strands together. Divide into three and braid; push end of braid through top of hat. Triple-knot to secure.

DUPLICATE STITCHES

1. This technique is best for stripes or monograms. Thread a darning needle with contrasting yarn. From inside of hat, push needle through base of stitch you're duplicating. Pass needle from right to left behind stitch directly above (A).

2. Insert needle through starting point, and back through base of next stitch up (B).

3. Fill in desired pattern (C). Stitches should be taut but not tight.

B

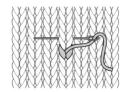
C

HOW TO
SEW TOTE BAGS

These multipurpose bags have buckles or grommets, with straps that run the gamut—ribbon, rope, and leather are shown opposite, but anything goes.

HOW TO MAKE A BASIC TOTE

Cut a piece of canvas twice the desired length of the bag plus 5 inches, and 1 inch wider all around. Fold it in half (right sides together) and sew both sides with a ½-inch seam allowance, then double-hem the top by folding the top edge ½ inch, then 2 inches, and edge-stitching all around. Turn the bag right side out.

> **TIP**
>
> When using leather handles, hand-stitch an X on each end using colorful waxed twine.

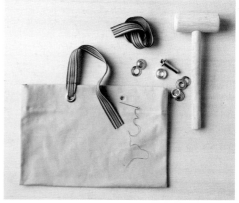

BUCKLE TOTE

SUPPLIES

Sewing supplies

4 buckles (⅝ inch)

Handleless tote

Rotary leather punch

2 lightweight cowhide leather strips (⅝ inch wide) cut to desired length

1. Using strong thread, sew two buckles each to top edge of bag front and back, spacing as desired. Stitch around each buckle's center bar several times to secure attachment.

2. Punch holes 1 inch apart in leather strips, starting about 2 inches from ends. (The holes here were made with the ⅛-inch tube.) Slide ends through buckles and fasten.

GROMMET TOTE

SUPPLIES

Handleless tote

Pencil

Craft knife

Grommet kit

Mallet or hammer

Ribbon, or cord strips, cut to desired length

Sewing supplies

1. Trace inside grommet opening with pencil onto bag. Using craft knife, cut an X in marked circles. Set two grommets each on front and back of bag, using a mallet or a hammer following kit instructions.

2. Slide ribbon through grommets at bag front. Fold ends under ¼ inch twice; pin to other side of ribbon at bag top. Sew to secure. Repeat at bag back. (For cord handle, thread through grommets; knot to secure.)

HOW TO
SEW FABRIC FLOWERS

These dahlias and pansies can be crafted from nearly any kind of cloth—the looser the fabric weave, the more the edges will fray, creating beautiful imperfections. Attach the blossoms to brooches or pins for an instant clothing, accessory, or hairstyle update.

HOW-TO

When rolling the fabric into shape in step 3, making a few small, random stitches will help to keep the fabric from twisting, so you end up with prettier petals.

PANSY

SUPPLIES

Embroidery scissors

Fabric

Fabric-marking pen

Sewing supplies

Pin (see Pin Picks, opposite)

1. See template (page 379). Cut a 2-by-36-inch strip of fabric (or for a smaller version, a 1½-by-30-inch strip) with embroidery scissors. Use pen to trace template on fabric, covering length. Cut out. (Use a damp cloth to wipe off any pen markings.)

2. Sew a running stitch several inches along bottom, ¼ inch from edge. Every 3 to 4 inches, pull thread to gather; secure with another running stitch closer to edge.

3. Spiral strip tightly to create flower shape, securing with random stitches. When it's completely rolled, stitch through all layers to secure.

4. Cover stitched back with a small disk of fabric. Sew to desired pin.

DAHLIA

SUPPLIES

Linen and organza fabric, in similar shades

Detail scissors

Sewing supplies

Pin (see Pin Picks, opposite)

1. Cut one 2-by-36-inch strip from each type of fabric with detail scissors. (For a smaller version, cut 1½-by-30-inch strips.) Snip V shapes into each strip, about ½ inch from edge. Place one strip on top of other.

2. Sew a running stitch several inches along bottom, through both layers, ¼ inch from edge. Every 3 to 4 inches, pull thread to gather; secure with another running stitch closer to edge.

3. Spiral strip tightly to create flower shape, securing with random stitches. When it's completely rolled, stitch through all layers to secure.

4. Cover stitched back with a small disk of fabric. Sew to desired pin.

PIN PICKS

The type of pin you choose will depend on the desired target—sweater, scarf, hat, or French twist, for example.

SHAWL PIN Simply slide the pin's point through the flower's back (no sewing required), then use to keep a wrapped scarf intact.

BROOCH With its safety-pin enclosure, a brooch is the classic backing and can be fastened to any type of garment (or throw pillow).

BOBBY PIN This updated pin's perforated end is easy to sew through when attaching the flower.

HAT PIN This old-fashioned pin can be used with its catch at the top (for a lapel) or without (for a hat).

BUN PIN Slide one end of pin through flower's back, or sew to attach, before pinning hair.

TIP

To give your pinned flower a finished look, glue on a piece of fabric to the center, such as the round cutout on the pansy (middle left) and dahlia (upper right).

SHAWL PIN

BROOCH

BUN PIN

BOBBY PIN

HAT PIN

HOW TO
SEW A DUVET COVER

Protect your duvet—and spruce up your bedding—with a DIY cover made from two flat sheets in the corresponding size. Go for a matching pair, or partner sheets with contrasting shades or patterns, like the solid-and-striped duo shown opposite. Ribbon-ties are easier to make than the usual button closures (though feel free to stitch those using the technique on page 145, spacing them equally), plus they add welcome color and texture. For even more flair, tie on tassels or pom-poms (see pages 164 and 165, respectively).

SUPPLIES

Duvet comforter

Flat sheets (in same size as duvet)

Sewing scissors

Pins

Thread (in same color as sheets)

Sewing machine and supplies

Iron and ironing board

Ribbon

HOW-TO

1. Measure duvet comforter, as manufacturers' sizes vary; if necessary, cut sheets so they are each 2 inches wider than duvet and 3 inches longer (to accommodate seams).

2. Align sheets with finished top edges matching up and wrong sides facing in. This will allow you to sew a French seam. Pin and stitch (using a ¼-inch seam allowance) around three edges, 1 inch from edge of sheets, leaving finished top edge unstitched to serve as the opening.

3. Turn duvet cover inside out (now wrong sides of fabric are outside), press with iron, pin, and sew a 1-inch seam, just covering allowance of your first seam. Turn duvet cover right side out; press again. (This is a French seam; see page 163.)

4. To hem the opening, if desired, turn a 1-inch width under once, then again, making one complete fold. Sew top and bottom together at each corner of opening, leaving a gap large enough for the duvet to fit through.

5. Cut 10-inch lengths of ribbon. Pin one piece of ribbon to top and bottom sheets, at approximately 5-inch increments, inside flaps of opening. Sew on ribbons; remove pins. Insert duvet and tie ribbons.

TIP

To keep the duvet from slipping in the cover, sew two pieces of fabric tape to the inside of each of the cover's four corners, then tie tape around each corner of the duvet when inserting (start with cover inside out for easier maneuvering).

KNIT

Knitting can be habit-forming—in the best way. It's blissfully portable and wonderfully relaxing. If you're already an avid knitter, this isn't news—and yet you may still have a trunk stashed with half-made cardigans and other projects. If you're a beginner or due for a refresher course, review the fundamentals and then try your hand at one of the simple projects that follow—all of which rely on the most basic stitches, explained on the following pages.

STOCK UP ON SUPPLIES

Any knitter will agree: A big part of the fun of this productive pastime is gathering the essentials, especially the yarn. Take pleasure in buying the provisions. But before buying, consult your pattern: It's the pattern that tells you the ideal yarn weight and amount, needle sizes, and other notions such as buttons or trim. Other than these items, your knitting stash should include small scissors (embroidery ones work great), a crochet hook (for picking up drop stitches), and a yarn needle (for finishing).

KNITTING NEEDLES

A knitting needle's size is based on its diameter and is indicated with a number (in the United States), or in millimeters (in Europe). See chart for conversions. In general, needles that are neither too long nor too short—so somewhere in the mid-range for the number of stitches required (as suggested in the pattern)—will be the easiest to handle.

Of the three basic types—straight, circular, and double-pointed—straight needles are a wise first pair. These have stoppers at the ends for using in so-called flat knitting, the most fundamental technique (and the one used for the projects here).

You can find needles in metal, wood, bamboo, and plastic. Wood and bamboo needles are good for beginners—they're more flexible, comfortable to use, and less slippery (so stitches aren't as likely to slip off).

YARN

There's so much more to yarn than meets the eye. For one, it can be made of either animal-based fibers (sheep's wool, mohair, angora), plant-based fibers (cotton, hemp, silk), or synthetic fibers (polyester, nylon, rayon). These interlocked fibers (referred to as plies) are spun together into thicker strands. The number of plies (single-ply, two-ply) will affect the drape, stitch definition, and general feel of the yarn.

Finally, each ball of yarn has a ball band (a label) stating the fiber content, weight, amount (in yards and ounces), care instructions, suggested needle size, gauge, and dye-lot number. To ensure that all your yarn for a project is exactly the same color, buy it all at once and check that the dye-lot numbers match.

NEEDLE SIZE CONVERSIONS

U.S. size range to millimeter range

000	1.5 mm	7	4.5 mm
00	1.75 mm	8	5 mm
0	2 mm	9	5.5 mm
1	2.25 mm	10	6 mm
2	2.75 mm	10.5	6.5 mm
3	3.25 mm	11	8 mm
4	3.5 mm	13	9 mm
5	3.75 mm	15	10 mm
6	4 mm	17	12.75 mm

YARN 101

Choose a yarn that's suitable for your project (wool for mittens, for example, or silk for a scarf) and in the correct weight, as dictated in your pattern's instructions. From lightest to heaviest, yarn is referred to as: fingering, sport, double-knitting, worsted, aran, and bulky.

WOOL

Wool is rightly one of the most popular yarns, for being natural, traditional, accessibly priced, and easy to handle (even for beginners). It is also utterly beautiful in so many different iterations. Its one weakness is durability, so if that's a concern, look for a wool blended with other fibers.

MOHAIR

Despite being one of the warmest animal fibers, mohair is known for its lightness, soft sheen, and fluffy texture. It is also extremely elastic—stretching and springing back to shape so it resists wrinkling and sagging. It can be hard to knit, however, and will not give you defined stitches.

COTTON

Natural, inexpensive, and smooth: These are the qualities that recommend cotton for knitting. While this material has great drape, it is inelastic and prone to splitting in the middle of your knitting. Consider yourself warned—but cotton is worth the trouble.

CASHMERE

Due to its superb quality, cashmere—so lovely but prone to pilling—is a true luxury yarn. The softness actually improves with wear, though you'll end up with that trademark, cloudlike halo. It is typically blended with other fibers to make the cost more accessible.

ANGORA

This rabbit fur is light, silky-soft, and incredibly warm—even warmer than wool. Similar to mohair, angora isn't great for knitting ornate stitches and tends to be slippery, so choose a textured set of needles for grip, and look for yarns blended with an acrylic fiber to counter its elasticity (and make it more affordable).

ALPACA

As a hypoallergenic fiber, alpaca is a good choice for baby knitwear. Because it has a strong tendency to over-drape, it's usually blended with other natural fibers to strengthen the tension.

SILK

This smooth, lustrous fiber costs more than others, though it's still the standard-bearer for knitting lace. Because it is susceptible to static cling and catching, look for silk that's spun tightly with a higher ply, or is blended with other fibers.

RAYON

This man-made fiber has the ability to imitate natural fibers. It is also cool, comfortable, and wicks heat from the body, making it a good choice for summer knitwear. Nylon yarn, a similar synthetic fiber, is more durable against wear and tear.

KNIT

While not essential, a Knit Kit sure comes in handy. I discovered the crafter cult favorite after spotting an employee using the all-in-one accessory case to work on knitting projects while traveling. Holding eight essential knitting tools in one compact container, the Knit Kit is a TSA-approved "Swiss Army knife for knitters" that fits easily in purses or knitting bags.

FIRST THINGS FIRST

As mentioned on page 174, the knitting pattern is your road map, and you will need to follow the directions meticulously to avoid getting lost (the most common reason people abandon projects). Be forewarned: It will take time and practice to learn how to decode the pattern's language, but with perseverance comes mastery—and confidence.

HOW TO READ A KNITTING PATTERN

Knitting patterns often have a series of steps that are repeated several times across a row, as indicated by symbols such as asterisks (*) and abbreviations, to save space. (See chart on page 178–179 for a helpful guide.) When you pause in your knitting project, always make a note of where you are in the pattern so that you don't lose track of your stitches.

> **TIP**
>
> Stay organized with knit gauge cards: write color, gauge, pattern, and other relevant information, then attach a swatch of your project and store cards together. Or use one of many apps that help you keep track of your projects.

HOW (AND WHY) TO MAKE A GAUGE SWATCH

A gauge swatch helps ensure the finished project will be correct. Each 6-by-8-inch swatch allows you to gauge the number of stitches to be worked over 1 inch of knitting, using a particular stitch, weight of yarn, and needle size (all dictated by the pattern).

To determine the number of stitches to cast on for 6 inches of knitting length, multiply the number of stitches in 1 inch of knitting (from the pattern's instructions) by 6. Then cast off loosely, and lay the swatch flat.

Check your gauge by measuring the swatch. Since stitches at the edges tend to curl inward or become misshapen, measure just the inner 4 inches of the swatch. Place a tape measure parallel to a row of stitches, and count how many stitches (how many Vs) fall within these inner 4 inches, including half stitches. Divide this number by 4, and compare it with the specified gauge. In the example of a 4-stitch gauge, if there are fewer than 4 stitches per inch, your knitting is too loose; use needles a size smaller. If there are more than 4 stitches per inch, you are knitting too tightly; use needles a size larger.

HOW TO CAST ON

No matter the project, this is always your first step: By casting on, you are creating a foundation row of stitches on your needle. The following instructions are for right-handed readers; reverse if you are left-handed.

1. Make a slipknot by looping yarn into a pretzel shape, leaving a tail end at least three times the width of what you are knitting (if your scarf is 8 inches wide, you'll need a 24-inch-long tail). Slip knitting needle through pretzel shape as shown, and pull yarn ends to tighten.

2. Drape tail of yarn over left thumb and working yarn (ball end) over left index finger. Use your other fingers to catch yarn lengths in left palm.

3. Insert needle upward through loop on thumb. With needle, catch the working yarn that's on your index finger, and pull it through the loop on your thumb. Remove thumb from loop. Keeping yarn ends secured in palm, reposition thumb, and tighten new stitch on right-hand needle. Repeat these steps until you've cast on the required number of stitches.

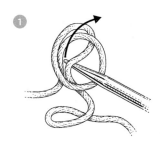

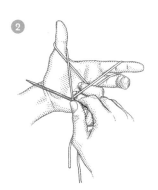

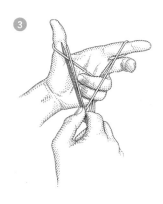

HOW TO KNIT A STITCH

To make your first stitch, hold the needle with cast-on stitches in your left hand. Wrap the working yarn around your left index finger, and hold it in back of the left-hand needle.

1. Insert point of right-hand needle from front to back into the first cast-on stitch on the left-hand needle, opening up a stitch.

2. Catch working yarn with right-hand needle.

3. Pull yarn through opened stitch.

4. Slip cast-on stitch off left-hand needle and onto the right-hand needle while holding middle finger against second cast-on stitch to ensure it does not also slip off. The stitch on the right-hand needle is the newly formed knit stitch. Continue knitting across the cast-on row. When you have emptied the last stitch from the left-hand needle (completing a row), exchange needles, moving the needle with stitching to your left hand.

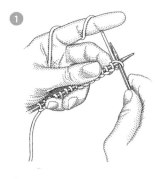

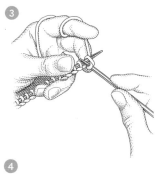

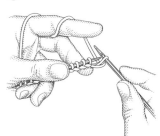

COMMON KNITTING ABBREVIATIONS

The most common abbreviations for knitting patterns are included here, in a convenient one-stop resource. It's a good idea to keep a copy in your knitting basket (or snap a photo of the chart) for quick reference—at least until you've mastered the shorthand and it becomes second nature (which it will, so keep at it). And remember, when you see an asterisk (*), that means to repeat that step or series of steps across a row.

ALT
Alternate

APPROX
Approximately

BEG
Begin or beginning

BET
Between

BO
Bind off

CC
Contrast color

CM
Centimeter

CN
Cable needle

CO
Cast on

CONT
Continue

DEC
Decrease

DK
Double knit

DPN OR DPNS
Double-pointed needle or needles

FL
Frontloop

FOLL
Follow

FROGGING
The act of unraveling or tearing out knitting

G
Garter stitch (created from knitting every single row, resulting in a ridged surface)

INC
Increase

K
Knit

K2TOG
Knit two stitches together

KTBL
Knit through back loop

KWISE
Knitwise (which indicates the side from which you will hold your needle)

LH
Left hand

LP OR LPS
Loop(s)

M
Meter

M1
Make one stitch

MC
Main color

NDL OR NDLS
Needle(s)

P UP
Pick up and purl

P
Purl

P2TOG
Purl two together (which indicates purling two stitches together as though they were one stitch)

PAT OR PATT
Pattern

PM
Place marker

PR
Previous row or previous round

PREV
Previous

PSSO
Pass slipped stitch over (which indicates that you slipped a stitch and then worked one or more stitches following that slipped stitch)

PTBL
Purl through back loop (which indicates that you pass your right needle through the back side of the next stitch from left to right)

PWISE
Purlwise

R & R
Row rem (which means remaining)

REP
Repeat

REV ST ST
Reverse stockinette stitch (which is created by beginning with a purl row and then alternating knit and purl rows)

RH
Right hand or righthand

RND OR RNDS
Round(s)

RS
Right side

SK
Skip

SK2P
Slip 1 knitwise, knit 2 together, pass slipped stitch over, decrease, knit 2 together; double left-leaning

SKP
Slip, knit, pass slipped stitch over

SL
Slip

SL ST
Slip stitch (which means to move it from the left needle to the right without working it)

SL1K
Slip 1 knitwise

SL1P
Slip 1 purlwise

SSK
Slip, slip, knit

SSSK
Slip, slip, slip, knit

ST OR STS
Stitch(es)

ST ST
Stockinette stitch

TBL
Through back loop

TFL
Through front loop

TOG
Together

WS
Wrong side (which indicates the side of the project that will face inward or may not be seen)

WYIB
With yarn in back (which indicates that working yarn should hang down the backside of your knitting)

WYIF
With yarn in front

YB
Yarn back (which indicates that working yarn should be brought from the front of the work to the back, passing under needle tips)

YFWD
Yarn forward (which indicates that working yarn should be brought from the back of the work to the front, passing under the needle tips)

YO
Yarn over (which indicates to bring your yarn from back to front—if it was initially in the back—or from front to back—if it was initially in the front—under needle tips. After doing so, continue to knit as the pattern indicates)

YO2
Yarn over twice

YON
Yarn over needle (which indicates to pass the yarn from the back of the work to the front—or from the front to the back—and lay it across the top of the needle as opposed to between/under needle tips as in a yarn forward)

YRN
Yarn round needle (which indicates the same instruction as yarn over)

KNIT

HOW TO PURL

The purl stitch differs from the knit stitch in two fundamental ways: The working yarn is held in the front of the project instead of the back, and the needle is inserted from the back to the front instead of from front to back. Hold the needle with cast-on stitches in your left hand. Wrap the working yarn (ball end) around your left index finger, and hold it in front of the work.

1. Insert point of right-hand needle, from back to front, into the first cast-on stitch on the left-hand needle, opening up a stitch.

2. Lay working yarn over needle from front to back by moving left index finger downward.

3. Push working yarn from front to back through cast-on stitch. Slip cast-on stitch off left-hand needle and onto the right-hand needle while holding middle finger against second cast-on stitch to ensure it does not also slip off. The stitch on the right-hand needle is the newly formed purl stitch. As a purl stitch faces you, it looks like a grain of rice; its reverse side looks like a V.

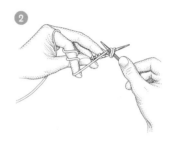

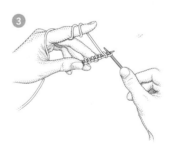

HOW TO PICK UP A DROPPED STITCH

 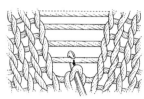

Don't panic if you drop a stitch (meaning the yarn slips off your needle) while knitting. This all-too-common mistake is simple to remedy with a crochet hook. You'll know you've dropped a stitch when you see a hole or any unusual nubs of stitches hanging out—or an entire row of "ladders" (which look just like they sound). You can help avoid dropped stitches in the first place by keeping close count on the stitches as you go, and by always finishing each row before pausing (and stuffing the project into your tote bag).

 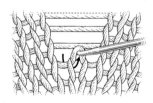

1. With the knit side facing you, insert crochet hook, front to back, into loop of dropped stitch.

2. Use hook to catch the first horizontal "ladder," and pull it through loop to the front.

 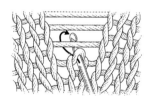

3. Repeat until all ladders have been pulled through loop. Place the stitch back onto left-hand needle, with the right side of the loop on the front of the needle.

To pick up a stitch dropped on a purl row, turn your work around, and follow the directions above.

HOW TO CAST OFF

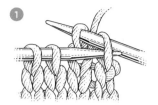

These steps, also called "binding off," keep stitches from unraveling once removed from the needle.

1. Knit two stitches. Insert left-hand needle into first stitch; lift stitch up over second stitch and …

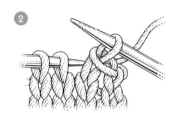

2. … off the needle. Continue knitting stitches in this manner until all stitches have been cast off. Cut working yarn, leaving a 6-inch-long tail. Pull tail through last stitch to secure.

3. Use a yarn needle to weave tail ends of yarn through backs of several stitches, picking up only surface loops.

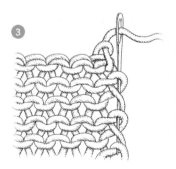

181

KNIT

HOW TO KNIT IN THE ROUND

You will need four double-pointed needles to do this elemental stitch, so named for the motion you use.

1. Cast your stitches onto one needle, then divide them by slipping them onto two more, until each needle has the same number of stitches.

2. Lay the needles flat on a table, lined up end to end, with the working yarn on the rightmost needle and all stitches facing the same direction (make sure none are twisted).

3. Take the left needle in your left hand and the right needle in your right hand, then bring the needles together to form a triangle with middle needle.

4. Pick up your fourth needle. With the working yarn still on the right needle and the needles in a triangle, knit the stitches onto the left needle, pulling working yarn tightly to join (see figure A). You are now "knitting in the round."

HOW TO MAKE SLIP STITCHES

To slip a stitch, such as when "decreasing" or dividing knitting, is to pass it from one needle to the other without working it. When slipping "knitwise," the stitch is twisted; "purlwise" slip stitches are not.

TO SLIP KNITWISE

Insert the right needle into the next stitch on the left needle, as if making a knit stitch, then slip this off the left needle, so it is only on the right one.

TO SLIP PURLWISE

Insert the right needle into the next stitch on the left needle as if you were making a purl stitch, then slip this off the left needle, so it is only on the right one.

HOW TO GIVE SHAPE TO KNITTING

Unless you are knitting basic scarves or other straight items, you'll need to know how to give your knitwear shape—as with hats, mittens, and sweaters. That's where an increase or decrease in the number of stitches per row comes into play, as indicated in the pattern's instructions. Dividing is essential when you are making items where one part (the thumb in mittens, a sleeve in a sweater) separates from the rest.

HOW TO DECREASE

The "knit 2 together" (and its wrong-side equivalent, "purl 2 together") is the usual method of reducing the number of stitches.

Slip needle knitwise through two loops, not one (see figure B); knit both stitches together.

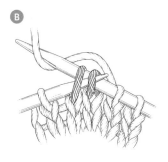

TIP

One of the most common complaints when knitting in the round is that "ladders" form in the spaces where two needles join, between stitches. Avoid that by knitting the first and last stitches of each needle tightly; pulling the first and second stitch on the new needle also helps.

HOW TO INCREASE

The classic technique is to knit in the front and back of a stitch, as follows. Note that the following instruction is the equivalent of "make 1 left," working from front to back. Do the opposite when a pattern says to "make 1 right," working the right needle from back to front.

1. Insert left needle, from front to back (see figure C), below the horizontal strand between the two stitches.

2. Knit picked-up stitch through the back of the loop, crossing your right-hand needle behind the left (see figure D).

HOW TO DIVIDE

There are different ways to divide knitting, but here is the most common:

Slip first stitch purlwise off the left-hand needle and onto a double-pointed needle. Slip second stitch purlwise onto other working needle. Repeat, alternating (see figure E) until stitches are divided equally between needles.

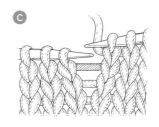

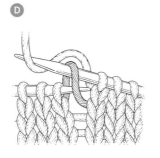

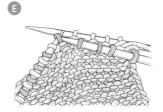

HOW TO FINGER KNIT

The simplicity of this no-needle technique belies its many applications—from necklaces to garlands. Teach it to a child and you'll be rewarded with gifts galore.

1. Slip the end of a ball of yarn between your thumb and index finger. Pinch to anchor the yarn as you knit. Then loop the yarn around your pinkie and weave it through your fingers.

2. Loop yarn around your index finger completely, and weave it toward your pinkie.

3. Make a full loop around your four fingers.

4. Slip the bottom (woven) row over the top (unwoven) row, from pinkie to index finger. Repeat steps 2 through 4 as the knitted side flows down the back of your hand to the desired length. To cast off, cut the yarn, leaving about a 10-inch tail. Pull the yarn through all four loops, then pull the loops off your fingers. Tie the tail to the closest loop; trim.

HOW TO
KNIT MITTENS

With their playfully mismatched color-block patterns, these row-by-row mittens are easier to knit than you might think. Buy at least two skeins of yarn in coordinating colors (two skeins are enough to make one pair of women's and one pair of kids' mittens), or use leftover yarn from your own collection.

SUPPLIES

4 double-pointed needles, U.S. #4

2 skeins worsted weight yarn, in different colors

4 single-pointed needles, U.S. #6

Darning needle (optional)

HOW-TO

The first number of stitches is for a women's pair, the second (in parentheses) is for a kids'. Start counting rounds anew at base of each section.

1. KNIT CUFF

Using #4 needles, cast on 36 (26) stitches. Join for working in the round, being careful not to twist stitches. Work in a knit 1, purl 1 rib until cuff measures 2¾ (1¼) inches.

2. SWITCH TO #6 NEEDLES

Change colors if desired (as shown, A; for details, see tip at right). Work 10 (4) rounds in stockinette stitch.

3. START THUMB

Round 1: Knit 1, make 1 right, knit 1, make 1 left, knit to end of round = 38 (28) stitches on needles. Rounds 2 and 3: Knit. Round 4: Knit 1, make 1 right, knit 3, make 1 left, knit to end of round = 40 (30) stitches. Round 5: Knit. Round 6: Knit 1, make 1 right, knit 5, make 1 left, knit to end of round = 42 (32) stitches. Continue in pattern as set, increasing 2 stitches (see How to Increase, page 183) every third round 7 (5) times before and after the increases from the round before, until you have 15 (11) stitches between increases. Round 15 (11): Knit 50 (40) stitches. Round 16 (12): Knit 1, slip 15 (11) stitches onto waste yarn (as shown, B), knit to end of round = 35 (25) stitches. Pull working yarn tight over held stitches when continuing to work rest of round (to prevent a gap when picking up stitches for the thumb).

4. KNIT HANDS

Work in stockinette stitch for 24 (12) rows, or until hand measures 1¾ inches (1 inch) from desired finished length.

5. ROUNDS 25 (12), 27 (14), 29 (16), 31, 33, 35

Knit all stitches. Round 26 (13): *Knit 5 (3), knit 2 together, repeat from * around = 30 (20) stitches. Round 28 (15): *Knit 4 (2), knit 2 together, repeat from * around = 25 (15) stitches. Round 30 (17): *Knit 3 (1), knit 2 together, repeat from * around = 20 (10) stitches. Round 32 (women's size only): *Knit 2, knit 2 together, repeat from * around = 15 stitches. Round 34 (18): *Knit 1 (0), knit 2 together, repeat from * around = 10 (5) stitches. All sizes: Trim yarn, leaving a 5-inch tail. Using darning needle, thread tail through remaining stitches and pull together tightly. Weave in and trim ends.

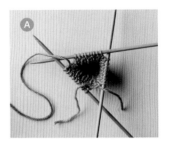

TIP

To make stripes, switch colors: Drop the old yarn, leaving a 5-inch tail, then begin knitting with new yarn, leaving a 5-inch tail. Knit a couple of stitches with the new yarn; tie a loose half-knot with both tails on wrong side of knitting. Adjust tension of stitches and continue knitting as directed.

6. COMPLETE THUMB

Place the 15 (11) held stitches from waste yarn onto 3 double-pointed needles. Round 1: Knit 15 (11), pick up 2 stitches in space between thumb and hand = 17 (13) stitches. Round 2: Knit 15 (11), knit 2 together = 16 (12) stitches. Rounds 3 through 12 (5), 14 (7), 16 (9): Knit all stitches. Round 13 (6): *Knit 2 (1), knit 2 together, repeat from * around = 12 (8) stitches. Round 15 (8): *Knit 1 (0), knit 2 together, repeat from * around = 8 (4) stitches. Round 17 (women's size only): Knit 2 together all around = 4 stitches. All sizes: Trim yarn, leaving a 5-inch tail. Using darning needle, thread tail through remaining stitches and pull together tightly. Weave in; trim ends.

7. FINISH

Undo half-knots or bows created when changing colors, and cross tails over each other. Using darning needle, thread tails through same-color fabric section; trim ends (as shown, C).

HOW TO
KNIT HATS AND SCARVES

With just two stitches and a basic rectangle, you can stitch up multiple pieces to keep you snug this winter. A child's hat is a rectangle folded in half and stitched at the sides; the cowl is a longer rectangle, sewn end to end.

HOW-TO

For each square and rectangle you knit, the measurement in inches is more important to the final size or fit than the number of stitches or rows, so adjust those counts accordingly. The general method follows; see specific instructions for each project.

1. Cast on the number of required stitches.

2. To create a garter stitch, which appears bumpy on both sides, knit each row.

3. To create a stockinette stitch, which appears smooth on one side and bumpy on the other, knit one row, then purl the next. Continue alternating rows.

4. To knit one "yarn over," you simply bring the yarn you are knitting (the "over" strand) over the needle between two existing stitches.

CHILD'S HAT

SUPPLIES

Size 6 needles

1 skein merino-wool yarn

Yarn needle

This is sized to fit a child who is 5 to 10 years old. Adjust as needed.

1. Cast on 72 stitches (12 inches) with two strands of yarn. Knit every row (garter stitch; see left) for 104 rows, until the piece is 10½ inches long.

2. Cast off, weaving in ends.

3. Fold rectangle in half. Sew sides together with basic running stitch (see page 158).

PURSE-STITCH SCARF

SUPPLIES

Size 9 needles

5 skeins merino-wool yarn

1. Cast on 50 stitches (or 16 inches).

2. Row 1: Slip 1 stitch purlwise with yarn in front. Move yarn to the back between the needles. Knit 1 *yarn over, decrease (by purling 2 together), and repeat from * until the end of the row.

3. Repeat step 2 until scarf is 72 inches long.

4. Cast off loosely, using a larger needle if necessary to retain stretch in the fabric. (Steam lightly, if needed.)

HOW TO
KNIT A BLANKET

Rather than stitching one big blanket, follow this method to make one out of multiple mix-and-match pieces. Use a contrasting-colored yarn to crochet them together, as shown at right.

SUPPLIES

Size 11 needles

38 skeins bulky yarn

3 skeins merino-wool yarn

Yarn needle

HOW-TO

Adapt this process to make a smaller throw or baby blanket, or a generous-size shawl.

1. See page 380 for the diagram and measurements. For the 10-inch-wide pieces, using bulky yarn, cast on 30 stitches; for 15-inch pieces, cast on 45 stitches; and for 20-inch pieces, cast on 60 stitches. Knit all pieces in garter stitch.

2. Cast off when you reach the lengths indicated on the diagram. Weave in ends.

3. Following the diagram, sew pieces together with the merino yarn, using a loose mattress stitch: With pieces aligned, insert threaded yarn needle through next-to-last stitched hole in one piece, then go behind two horizontal bars and back up to the front. Insert needle in same position on other piece, again going behind two bars and back up again. Continue sewing from one piece to the next in this manner until next-to-last hole on other side is reached.

4. Optional: Crochet around edge of blanket with a single crochet (see page 380 for instructions).

EMBROIDER

Perhaps the simplest of needlecrafts, embroidery is also among the oldest—but that doesn't mean it is old-fashioned. There are many ways to use a needle and thread to give fabric a fresh, modern appeal. Familiarize yourself with the essentials and you'll soon be stitching up samplers—or shirts and lampshades and bracelets.

THE SUPPLIES
Gather these essentials.

EMBROIDERY HOOP
This holds fabric taut, allowing for even stitches. Hoops come in a variety of shapes and sizes, but round ones ranging from 4 to 12 inches are the most common. (Note that stiffer fabric can be embroidered without a hoop.)

EMBROIDERY NEEDLES
Also called crewel or millinery needles, these come in different sizes for use with different weights of thread and fabric. For example, a thicker needle with a larger eye and blunter tip uses thicker thread on heavyweight fabric.

EMBROIDERY SCISSORS
Their small size and sharp blades let you snip even the finest floss.

EMBROIDERY THREAD, OR FLOSS
The standard thread is cotton floss, made of six separate strands (silk and rayon threads also come in divisible strands); use two strands for most woven fabrics.

FABRIC OR OTHER MATERIAL
Linen fabrics are easiest to work with, but woven cotton, wool, and felt are also suitable, as are tea towels. Embroidery fabrics are sold in different thread counts; match the right weight fabric to the technique you will be using. Aida cloth, designed for cross-stitching, can also be used for embroidery.

TRANSFER METHOD
Use a heat-transfer pencil and tracing paper or an iron-on design. Rubber stamps and fabric ink also work.

THE STITCHES

BACKSTITCH

Use this simple stitch to make the classic "dotted line." Insert needle from wrong side to right, coming out at 1. Reinsert nearby (2), pull back out (3), and tighten thread. Repeat, making stitches and spaces even in size.

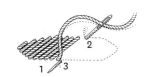

SATIN STITCH

When filling in the outlines of a design that incorporates shape or width, these side-by-side stitches are the ones to use, and are either made at an angle or straight across. Insert needle from wrong to right side, coming out at 1. Insert needle at 2, and pull it back through at 3, right next to 1. Keep the stitches tight and flat for a smooth finish.

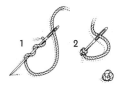

FRENCH KNOT

Use the French knot to create a raised point in a pattern. Insert needle from wrong to right side. Holding thread taut with one hand, wrap it twice around the needle close to fabric (1). Reinsert needle, as close as possible to where it first emerged (2), keeping thread taut. Pull needle through to back, continuing to hold thread tight until you have a 3- to 4-inch loop, then let go and finish the knot.

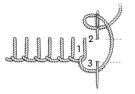

BLANKET STITCH

As its name implies, the blanket stitch is most often used to finish blanket edges. It can also create a decorative edge when you keep the base of the U along the fabric's edge. For lightweight fabrics, stitch along the finished edge. Insert the needle from wrong to right side, coming out at 1. Insert at 2. Come out again at 3; hold the thread under the needle with your thumb as you pull tight.

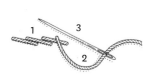

STEM STITCH

The stem stitch, which is similar to the running stitch, creates a ropelike effect. Insert needle from wrong to right side, coming out at 1. Insert the needle at 2 at a slight diagonal, and pull through at 3 (halfway between 1 and 2). Repeat stitching, keeping thread on the left side of the needle and making sure stitches are all the same length.

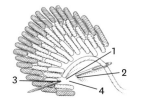

LONG AND SHORT STITCH

This is the stitch to use when you want to blend colors or create a feathery texture. Insert needle from wrong to right side, coming out at 1, insert at 2, come out at 3, and insert again at 4. Repeat for next tier. If desired, change colors and use the same technique for the following tiers, piercing the stitches in the previous tier.

CHAIN STITCH

The chain stitch is an open-loop stitch that can be worked on straight or curved lines. Insert needle from wrong to right side, coming out at 1. Making a loop, insert next to 1. Come out again at 2, holding thread under needle as you pull tight. Insert needle again next to 2 (inside new link), and continue.

TIP

Self-adhesive embroidery backing (or stabilizers) lends temporary structure to supple fabrics while stitching them; the tear-away kind can be cut to size, adhered to back of fabric, and peeled away after embroidering.

HOW TO
EMBROIDER
A PILLOW

Rather than embroidering a design from scratch, use stitches to punctuate a pattern on a piece of fabric. Here, wool-and-silk thread in shades of blue and red transforms an otherwise subtle large-scale botanical, for a pillow cover with panache.

SUPPLIES

Tear-away embroidery backing (optional)

Patterned fabric

Embroidery hoop, 8-inch

Wool-and-silk thread in red and blue-gray (or desired color scheme)

Embroidery needle

HOW-TO

No matter which fabric you choose to embroider, the following steps will apply (see page 189 for stitching how-tos).

1. ADHERE BACKING, IF NEEDED: Depending on the type of fabric being used, you may want to adhere backing to prevent it from puckering or shifting while you work; cut backing into appropriate size, and adhere to wrong side (back) of fabric, behind area of pattern you will be embroidering over.

2. ATTACH HOOP: Place patterned area of fabric over hoop's inner ring, then press the outer hoop ring over the fabric; tighten screw until fabric is taut and smooth.

3. SATIN STITCH: Thread red floss onto needle. Use the satin stitch (see page 189) to outline or fill in some of the petals, or to highlight other details. Here, blue-gray thread is also used to outline some petals.

4. CHAIN STITCH: Use the chain stitch and blue thread to embroider along the stems.

TIP

The beauty of wool-and-silk thread is its soft sheen as well as how the strands can be divided to be a lighter weight.

HOW TO
EMBROIDER
A BLOUSE

A plain button-front shirt is instantly personalized when embroidered with a subdued "hi," as in this back-to-school icebreaker. Or skip the salutation and stitch your child's first initial instead.

SUPPLIES

Pencil

Embroidery transfer paper

Button-front shirt

Tear-away embroidery back-ing (optional)

Embroidery hoop (4-inch)

Embroidery floss in light pink, light blue, and "pen" color of choice

Embroidery needle

HOW-TO

A dotted-line fuchsia makes the letters pop.

1. See template (page 381). Using a pencil and transfer paper, transfer it onto front of shirt.

2. Cut a 3-inch piece of backing (if using), and adhere to inside of shirt, behind tracing. Attach hoop to shirt.

3. Thread two strands of pink embroidery floss onto needle. Sew a running stitch across middle line. With four strands of blue floss, backstitch thicker top and bottom lines.

4. Using four strands of "pen"-color floss, backstitch to sew letters.

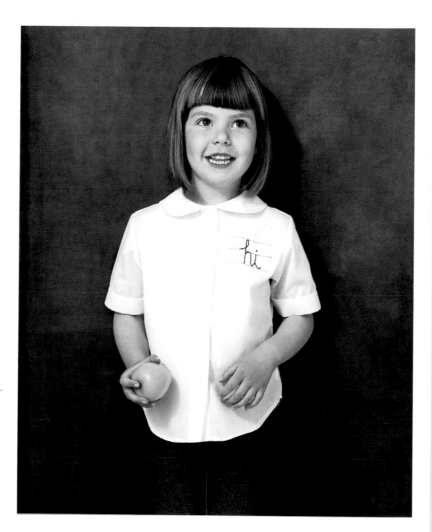

HOW TO
EMBROIDER SAMPLERS

A classic craft featuring fresh designs—here, cute critters (great for kids), but also personal passions (cooking, gardening, and more)—feels fresh and modern. Frame your menagerie in 4- and 5-inch wooden embroidery hoops, painted for added polish (using enamel spray paint).

SUPPLIES

Aida cloth

Embroidery hoop (4-inch)

Embroidery scissors

Embroidery floss

Embroidery needle

HOW-TO

Use Aida cloth to make X-shaped stitches in neat rows. See templates (pages 382–383) to make these animals. Or turn any design into a cross-stitch pattern by printing a grid onto acetate and placing it over the design.

CROSS-STITCH: Center fabric in an embroidery hoop. Count the stitches in each row of the template. Using the fabric's weave as a grid, make that number of stitches; first, create a row of evenly spaced diagonal lines, then stitch back over the row, creating Xs. To make a half cross-stitch (for a diagonal line in your design), make the first stitch from the corner to the grid's middle, and then the second stitch as normal. When the design is complete, trim excess cloth.

BACKSTITCH: Use this stitch to create thin lines (see page 189).

TIP

If you're stitching single-color designs like these, you'll find it easier to make the outline first and then fill it in.

HOW TO
EMBROIDER FRIENDSHIP BRACELETS

A childhood favorite takes on grown-up glitz thanks to arresting color combinations and luxurious embroidery floss and other threads (some with metallic accents). Start each of the following patterns by anchoring the strings with tape or a straight pin.

REFRESHER COURSE

Each string represents a stripe in the bracelet; arrange and tie them in the order in which you want them to appear.

For wider stripes, place same-color strings next to each other (you can also go monochromatic). Start with much longer pieces than you think you'll need—all the knotting significantly shortens each strand, and it's easier to trim to fit than to start over.

For a diagonal pattern, cut a little more than 35 inches and knot one end to start (or cut 70 inches, then fold in half and tie a loop). For a chevron, start with 70 inches, fold in half, and tie a loop.

SUPPLIES

String, yarn, or embroidery floss

Embroidery scissors

Tape (or a safety pin)

DIAGONAL PATTERN

Loop string 1 around string 2 as shown below, pulling tight toward top. Repeat. Use string 1 to make 2 knots each on strings 3, 4, 5, and 6. String 2 will be on the end. Repeat process with all 5 remaining strings.

1 2 3 4 5 6

CHEVRON PATTERN

Loop strings and arrange them so colors mirror one another. Starting from left side, follow instructions for diagonal pattern, left, for half of the strings. Repeat from right side. Double-knot the two strings in the middle. Repeat for next row.

CHINESE STAIRCASE

For this pattern, one string needs to be much longer than the others. Loop the longer string around all others, as shown below, running end up through the loop you made. Pull knot taut, up toward the top. Repeat to create the spiral pattern.

MORE IDEAS
AND INSPIRATION

If you are looking to ease into embroidery before embarking on a bigger needlework project, try your hand at one of these small wonders. They all involve the basic stitches on page 189.

STITCHED SACHETS

When it comes to making presents by the dozen, these scented sachets are a quick solution (meaning you can keep a few to tuck into your own drawers). If you have a pretty pattern, use that as your design and choose floss in the same or contrasting color. Rubber stamps are used for the solid sachets (and tea towels, above, right).

TRANSFER-FREE TOWELS

Use a rubber stamp and fabric ink in desired color to imprint a pretty bloom (or other design, as desired) on a hand towel or tea towel—or a plain scarf or blouse. Then stitch over part of the stamped design (outlining some blooms, as above) so the ink shows through in the other areas.

EMBROIDERED NOTE CARDS

Give friends and family a "handwritten" card like no other. To create your pattern, use a pencil to lightly write out the desired word on front of card. Then open card, place a piece of felt behind the word, and use a pushpin to make holes along the letters. Remove felt, erase pencil, and embroider the word with a backstitch.

NAPKIN PLACE CARDS

Linens make lovely place settings. Embroider one for each member of the family (or give them as party favors for dinner-party guests). Write each name on a piece of paper; stack tracing paper, then name paper, on napkin. Trace name with a ballpoint pen; remove papers. Use a stem stitch (see page 189) to embroider name, starting on wrong side of napkin.

QUILT

Patching together scraps of fabric to make a blanket may have been born out of necessity, but it is the act of quilting—gathering the materials, plotting the pattern, and stitching them together—that continues to make this needlecraft so compelling. Here's to stitching a new spin on tradition.

GETTING STARTED

No matter the pattern you opt to create, you'll be starting with the same basic steps.

CONSIDER YOUR FABRICS: Raid your fabric samples and scraps for ideas; outdated clothing (a too-small dress or men's shirt) is also fair game. Think about the placement of striped or patterned fabric amidst solids. Note that a monochromatic palette lets the seaming be the star, while contrasting colors can be used to accentuate a particular feature (rings, for example). Prewash and iron fabric that will need laundering before cutting and sewing.

DECIDE ON THE PATTERN: To create your own pattern—or to customize an existing one (such as the log cabin motif, see right)—plot the desired size and shape of your finished project on graph paper. Determine the number and size of fabric strips needed to achieve that shape (this may take a little trial and error). You can experiment with pieces of various widths for a freer design, or keep them uniform for a more traditional look.

GATHER THE MATERIALS: Quilting is essentially stacking three layers of material in a "quilt sandwich" involving the fabric facing, or top layer; the filling, or batting; and the backing. Batting is made of cotton (flatter) or wool (more lofty); you can also find polyester batting, which falls somewhere in between those (but tends to flatten out over time). Flat sheets make natural choices for backing, especially if you are making a coverlet for a bed. You can also buy extra-wide, seam-free cotton backing at fabric stores.

LOG CABIN PATTERN

Of all the traditional motifs, the log cabin—with a center square (the heart of the home) surrounded by concentric strips (the "logs")—captures quilting's past while also being among the easiest patterns to master. Indeed, the clean geometry of this frontier favorite still suits modern tastes, and the pattern is as variable as the person making it. Switch the color of the fabric, for example, and the outcome is entirely changed. Here are other ways to inject some ingenuity.

PLAY WITH RATIO: Because the center piece is typically double the width of the outer strips, it's easy to tweak those dimensions to alter the outcome. Keeping the strips all the same size produces a graphic result; more random-size pieces combine in a more abstract, contemporary way.

CHANGE DIRECTIONS: To spiral the strips in a different direction (see top right and middle framed squares opposite), start by ironing the first seam toward the center, rotating the piece to the left as you add other pieces.

LOG CABIN HOW-TO

To make a log cabin pattern, start with a small square and add strips in increasing lengths around it. The final 8-inch square, opposite, can be framed as is or used as the start of a bigger quilt.

SUPPLIES

Rotary cutter

Quilting ruler

Fabric

Basic sewing supplies

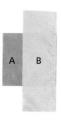

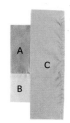

1. Using a rotary cutter and a quilting ruler, cut a 4-inch square of fabric (A). Cut a strip that's 2½ inches wide and about 6 inches long (B). Place strip on top of square, front sides facing; align edges, and stitch together with a ¼-inch seam allowance.

2. Open the two pieces of fabric. Keep the seams closed, and press the face of the fabric, ironing seam allowances out from the center. Use a quilting ruler and a rotary cutter to trim the strip (B) to the same length as the center square.

3. Cut a 2½-inch-wide strip (C) about 8 inches long. Rotate the sewn piece a quarter turn to the right. Place the strip on top of the sewn piece, front sides facing; align the right edges, and stitch together.

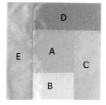

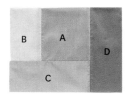

4. Repeat the opening, pressing, and trimming to size.

5. Cut a 2½-inch-wide strip about 8 inches long (D). Rotate the sewn piece a quarter turn to the right. Place the strip on top of the sewn piece, front sides facing; align the right edges, and stitch together.

6. Open the 2 pieces of fabric, and press the seams—toward the center this time. Trim strip (D) to size.

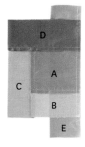

7. Cut a 2½-inch-wide strip about 11 inches long (E). Place sewn piece on top of strip to ensure all parallel seams lie in the same direction. Align right edges, and stitch.

8. Repeat the opening, pressing, and trimming to size.

9. Examine the back of the fabric, ensuring that all parallel seams lie in the same direction. Repeat steps 2 to 8 to add a second layer of longer strips around your original square.

BINDING A QUILT

This technique involves attaching the layers of a quilt—front, batting, and back—with a strip of fabric around the edge.

1. To make binding, use a rotary cutter to cut strips of 2¼-inch-wide fabric on the bias. Stitch strips together to make a piece a few inches longer than the quilt's perimeter.

2. Fold the binding strip in half lengthwise, wrong sides together; do not press. Beginning in the middle of one long side on the quilt front, align and pin the binding's raw edges to the quilt's raw edges. Start sewing the binding to the quilt with a ¼-inch seam allowance. Fold the fabric at the corners. When you get all the way around the quilt, fold the end of the binding under for a neat look.

3. Finish the binding by folding it over the edge of the back of the quilt and hand-stitching it in place, as shown above: Holding the binding against the back of the quilt, secure it by blind stitching its folded edge every ⅛ inch, picking up just a couple of threads of the quilt back beyond the seam allowance with each stitch, so no stitches are visible.

INSIDE-OUT QUILTING

Here's one basic way to sew fabric to a backing.

1. Place front and back fabrics, right sides together, on work surface, with front fabric on the bottom; top with batting. For larger pieces, pin edges in place.

2. Machine-sew around edges of the three layers with a ¼- to ½-inch seam allowance, leaving an opening on one side. Clip corners on the diagonal. Turn the piece right side out. Use a point turner or other blunt tool to push corners into shape from the inside.

3. Hand-stitch the opening closed, using a running stitch. If you are making a pot holder, insert a ribbon loop first.

STITCH IN THE DITCH

While binding attaches the three layers at the edges, this method connects the different pieces along the seams (aka "the ditch"). Make a running stitch along the seams, stitching through all the layers of fabric (or use a sewing machine). You can use a contrasting color, such as the bold yellow shown opposite, or one that blends in.

TIP

Seven types of seersucker in different directions give the spiraling pattern, opposite, a tactile quality. For a 40-inch-square quilt, surround a 10½-inch center square with 5¼-inch-wide strips.

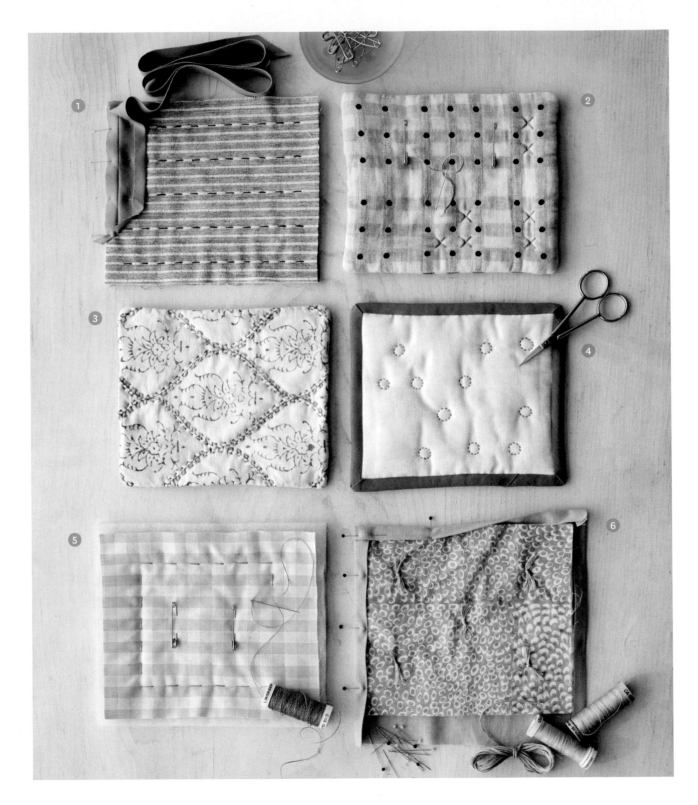

HAND-QUILTING MADE EASY

Rather than stitching together separate pieces of fabric, as in traditional quilting, so-called hand-quilting is a freehand method for embellishing one large piece of fabric after tacking together the layers and closing up the edges. Some favorite designs are shown opposite and described below. Use them to come up with your own creations, letting the fabric's pattern or palette be your guide.

1. STRIPES AND LINES: Have fun with striped fabric, such as the men's shirting material shown here, by stitching your way down every fourth stripe (or pick your own interval). First draw the dotted lines with a disappearing-ink fabric marker, then follow that with needle and thread. Also shown here (and in swatch 4): To create a contrasting border, you can sew raw edges closed using bias tape, a narrow strip of fabric that's been cut on the bias.

2. CRISSCROSS STITCHES: A checkered pattern invites a connect-the-dot approach. Start by sewing down through the center of a square, leaving a 2-inch tail on top; bring needle back up through the upper right corner, down through the bottom left corner, up through the center, down through the bottom right, up through the center, down through the upper left, and up through the center again. Repeat in other squares. When finished, tie off the excess thread and the initial tail together.

3. TRACED MOTIF: To play up a subtle fabric pattern, trace a design that "frames" the repeat in the fabric. Then stitch over the traced pattern for a puffed-up effect. Using lightweight (fine-gauge) thread will emphasize the fabric's repeat, while thicker thread (such as multistrand embroidery floss, shown here) makes the topstitching more prominent. Play around to get the desired effect.

4. STIPPLED CIRCLES: Perk up a solid fabric with dotted-stitch polka dots in a random pattern. For the finest "lines," use a thinner embroidery floss; here, the plies were pulled apart and only three strands of six were used. Imperfections add interest, but for uniform rings, stencil on templates using a disappearing-ink fabric marker and a small round object as a guide.

5. RUNNING DASHES: To punctuate a gingham pattern, sew a running stitch about an inch inside the square's edge, with each stitch the same width as the alternating stripes. You could repeat this to make more concentric squares inside that one. First baste the layers to keep them in place while you work; curved safety pins designed for quilting grab the batting and keep your project flat. Also, for easier edge binding (as layers may shift as you sew), make the batting and bottom fabric slightly wider than the top piece.

6. QUILT KNOTS: Even beginners can handle this project, as the tassel-like knots are simply stitched into place. To keep the batting from shifting inside the quilt, secure with quilting safety pins every 5 to 7 inches. To create the knots, measure and mark where to tack quilt together with ties, making sure the knots are no more than 7 inches apart (check your batting's packaging for specific guidelines). Thread needle with three strands of embroidery floss. Insert, pull through all layers, and then bring back up ⅛ inch from insertion point. Tie a square knot—cross left strand over right and pull tight, then cross right strand over left and pull tight again. Snip ties to desired length, and fluff. Remove pins.

MARTHA MUST

Once you've made a beautiful quilt, you'll want to keep it out where you can see it. To hang lightweight quilts, sew a muslin pocket sleeve about an inch from the top, on the back, then insert a wooden rod and rest rod on mounted brackets. I prefer to display a heavier quilt in a guestroom, laying it horizontally across the bed, without folding it.

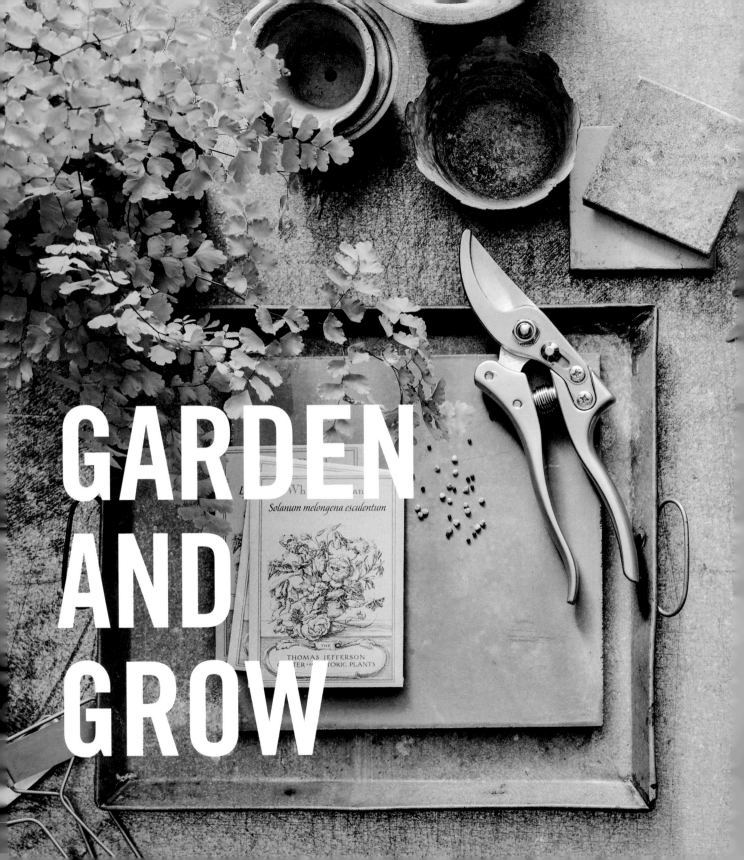

GARDEN AND GROW

Solanum melongena esculentum

THOMAS JEFFERSON
...TER ...TORIC PLANTS

Of all the chapters in this book, and of all the how-to guidance I have learned and shared in my work and personal life, gardening is what I think I am most proficient at—and the most sought-after for as an "expert."

It is surely the biggest mystery to the most people, who did not grow up, as I did, in a family that spent many hours of many weekends planting and tending and harvesting the vegetables—something that really anyone can and should do for the freshest-tasting meals. As an adult, I have practiced backyard farmsteading, first at our rustic cabin in the Berkshires and now on my more cultivated estate in Bedford.

I've also had great fun overhauling the property in Bedford by planting thousands of trees and creating vast cutting gardens that keep my home filled with fresh flowers spring, summer, and into fall. Having fallen in love with tree peonies as a burgeoning gardener, I now have peonies in a great many varieties and that create a riot of blooms each May. I am also proud of my thriving rosebushes, which keep producing prodigious blooms year in and year out.

Of course, all this gorgeousness is the result of years and years of discovering and rediscovering what types of plants grow best in my zone and in my soil, and in different locations depending on the plants' exposure to sunlight, wind, rainfall, and other conditions. I always consider time in the garden to be time well spent.

THE GARDEN TOOLKIT

A selection of reliable tools makes gardening tasks easier and more likely to reap favorable results. Invest in sturdy, well-made models that will hold up to regular use. Stainless steel is a rust-free option, though it will still need regular cleaning.

BEDDING RAKE

Also known as a hard rake, this tool levels garden beds, moves soil, and removes large debris. It's also great for spreading mulch or compost over a bed that already exists.

JAPANESE WEEDER

Use this underrated favorite whenever you need to do some light weeding or to aerate the soil around the root systems of your plants.

HAND CULTIVATOR

Designed to loosen and rough up the soil in preparation for planting, this tool's three sharp prongs also allow you to remove strong weeds.

HEDGE SHEARS

In addition to maintaining boxwood and topiaries, these are ideal for clipping grass around trees, walls, and fences. The Japanese model shown here has very sharp, rust-proof steel blades.

LOPPERS

Reach for this when you want to remove branches that are too large to be cut with pruners. Loppers with long but lightweight aluminum handles provide leverage to slice through branches up to 2 inches thick.

SECATEUR

This essential tool (also known as pruning shears or hand pruners) is excellent for deadheading, pruning, cutting flowers and small branches, and cutting back annuals and perennials. Try to purchase "bypass" shears, which cut with a scissorlike action.

SHOVEL

A long handle is best for heavy digging and lifting, such as when you break new ground. A shovel also comes in handy when transporting coarse mulch, leaf mold, or compost.

SPADE

Cut and loosen soil first with a spade, then lift it with a shovel. Or use the spade to edge beds, cut and lift sod, or turn over a new garden bed. Buy one with metal straps that reinforce the handle.

SPRING RAKE

While its primary use—gathering fallen leaves from lawns and garden beds—is apparent, a rake can also be used during the final grading of a fresh garden bed. Metal tines are more durable; bamboo ones are lighter and easier to wield.

GARDEN FORK

This tool levels garden beds, moves soil, removes large debris, and spreads mulch or compost. It's also used to loosen and lift perennials when dividing. Never use this on grass or around shrubs.

TROWEL

This tool is just right for planting small container plants, seedlings, and bulbs. Keep one indoors for houseplants, and another in the potting shed.

WATERING WAND

A wand allows easy watering of hanging baskets or any other plants that require an extended reach. The rose (at top, also called a water breaker) functions like a showerhead. Look for a model with adjustable flow settings and multiple nozzles.

HORI HORI

This special "knife" is used to slice easily through weeds, roots (when transplanting or dividing), and root-balls (such as when planting a tree). The model above even doubles as a bulb planter, the concave stainless-steel blade etched with digging marks to use a guide.

HAND SAW

A hand saw is a must for pruning shrubs, rosebushes, and even smaller tree branches. Buy a foldable model where the blade tucks into the handle, for safety and storing as well as portability; then you can carry it with you (in a pocket, for example) as you work.

HOW TO
GET THE MOST
OUT OF YOUR YARD

The first step to horticultural know-how is gaining an understanding of your soil as well as your "hardiness zone." These factors will determine what you can grow and how best to go about doing it.

KNOW YOUR SOIL

Soil is a blend of mineral (or rock) particles in different sizes—ranging from coarse sands to finer silts and clays—combined with an amount of organic matter. The soil in each garden is unique, and it determines how moisture is absorbed and retained, how easily roots can grow into the earth, and the supply of vital plant nutrients present.

The composition and texture of soil is one of many factors to consider. For example:

- Extremely sandy soil will not hold water or nutrients well.

- If soil is dense in clay, it will be difficult to work and your plants will struggle.

- A loamy mix (roughly equal amounts of sand, clay, and silt) is the best environment for growing most plants (and also vegetables).

TEST

A soil test will pinpoint any deficiencies and indicate which nutrients will turn the soil into a good growing medium (called fertile). It can also tell you the soil's pH. You can perform a test yourself using an inexpensive kit, or contact your local cooperative extension for assistance or to find a service to do it for you (sometimes for free).

The ideal pH for your soil depends on your plants:

- Most vegetables, flowers, and turfs prefer slightly acidic to neutral soils (pH 6 to 7).

- Rhododendrons, azaleas, hollies, and magnolias flourish in moderately acidic soil (pH 5 to 6).

- Soils in rainy areas tend to be acidic, while those in arid regions are sometimes more alkaline, or basic. Applying lime is one way to raise the pH (making the soil less acidic); applying sulfur lowers the pH.

REMEDY DEFICIENCIES

Adding organic matter generally makes the soil looser and airier, which enhances its ability to absorb water. As a result, the soil will retain necessary nutrients as well as moisture between waterings. While organic matter occurs naturally in soil, you can supplement that by adding compost, available at garden supply stores and nurseries—or by making your own (see pages 208–209).

FEED

Fertilizers are used to boost the soil's nutrient content. Overfeeding or supplying the wrong balance of nutrients can be more harmful than not fertilizing at all.

- When shopping, check the three-number ratio on the label, such as 5-10-5 or 10-10-10. This describes the content by percentage of the three principal plant nutrients: nitrogen, phosphorus, and potassium (often abbreviated as NPK).

- Use liquid fertilizers for a quick boost; granular ones break down more slowly, providing a more gradual, long-lasting release.

PROTECT

Mulch is a porous layer of material that, when spread a couple inches thick on soil, keeps weeds at bay, locks in moisture, prevents erosion, and boosts the quality of the soil (without the need for harsh chemicals). It also keeps the soil cool and moist in warm weather, cutting down on the need for watering. Mulch comes in many forms, including shredded bark, pine needles, and gravel—all sold at garden centers. Larger-grade mulch works best under trees and shrubs, finer grades for perennial and vegetable beds.

KNOW YOUR ZONE

Professional and home gardeners alike rely on the USDA's plant hardiness zone map (available online) to identify which plants thrive in their locations. The zones on the map indicate temperature. Generally, you can confidently grow plants that are hardy in your zone. In protected spots of the yard, you may push the limits to a zone or so less hardy, but you chance that the plants may not survive the winter.

HOW TO
COMPOST IN (AND FOR) THE GARDEN

Compost is one of the best ways to increase your garden's growing power. Producing it yourself will save you money at the nursery—especially if you have a sizable amount of ground to cover—and provide a way to utilize all of those kitchen scraps and gardening castoffs. Plus, having an endless supply of "black gold" will do your plants (and the planet) a tremendous amount of good.

WHAT TO COMPOST

A diverse mix of ingredients creates the most nutrient-rich compost. To obtain an optimal bacterial decomposition, aim for a proportion of one-third nitrogen (moist green materials) to two-thirds carbon (paper or dried brown materials). Adding livestock manure will enrich the compost, especially recommended when using in vegetable gardens.

AUTUMN LEAVES: These are the cheapest, most plentiful form of brown matter. Stockpile them after raking to use throughout the winter.

PAPER, NEWSPAPER, AND HAY: These items make good brown matter when dry leaves are in short supply. Shred newspaper so it doesn't form a mat (and feel free to use the contents of your security shredder). Do not compost glossy or colored paper.

FRUIT AND VEGETABLE DISCARDS: Wilted vegetables from the refrigerator and overripe fruit, as well as cores, rinds, and stems, are good additions.

KITCHEN WASTE: Rinds, peelings, leftovers, and bread are very active decomposers. Eggshells will also degrade, but not as completely. Avoid adding dairy, animal fat, fish, oils, fatty foods (such as peanut butter), or meat (no bones, either) to the pile, since they will attract vermin.

COFFEE AND TEA: Grounds from the morning coffeepot or tea bags add important nitrogen to the mix.

PLANTS: Use only healthy dried leaves and stems from the garden. Discard any diseased leaves or those near plants infested with pests; they may carry insect eggs. Add unwanted but healthy cuttings from houseplants and vegetable plants from the garden, as well as grass clippings.

TIP
Never compost cooking oil, butter, or fish bones; these create odor problems that attract pests. Also, black-walnut-tree leaves and twigs release a toxic chemical called juglone that will compromise a compost pile.

WAYS TO COMPOST

While you can certainly pile up materials on the ground and let nature take its course, many composters prefer to contain the compost in a bin instead.

SINGLE BINS: These simple, compact solutions are easy to find or to construct and come in a range of sizes to suit most any need.

THREE-BIN SYSTEM: Active gardeners might want to consider this classic setup: one pile to add to, one pile that is decomposing, and one pile that's finished for use in the garden. Check with your local garden center or cooperative extension for where to buy these as well as blueprints for building your own.

HOW TO COMPOST

Your role is to create the ideal conditions so science can do its magic, turning scraps into sustenance for plants.

1. SETTLE ON THE LOCATION: You'll need a spot with good drainage and at least partial sunlight (full sun will require frequent watering; full shade slows decomposition). Make sure it's out of harm's way for your pets (dogs especially find the smell of decomposing matter irresistible); erect fencing or even chicken wire as a protective barrier, or use a bin.

2. BUILD THE BASE: Begin your pile with an airy layer of brown matter (preferably leaves for the best circulation). Aim for about a 6-inch base. Top with a few inches of green matter, then twice as much brown matter.

3. SCOOP IN SOIL: A handful (or shovelful, depending on the size of your pile) of garden soil in the middle of the pile promotes the necessary microorganisms. Some experts recommend fertilizer, though a well-built pile will have enough nutrients (namely nitrogen) on its own.

4. CONTINUE LAYERING: Repeat adding brown and green matter in a 2 to 1 ratio, ending with brown (never leave food scraps exposed). Cut down large pieces to speed up decomposition. Poke holes for aeration and keep the top of the pile slightly concave to catch rain.

5. TURN AND REPEAT: After about a week, you'll notice the pile start to heat up. Now is the time to start turning it with a compost fork (or pitchfork) to mix the layers. As it continues to "cook" and reduce, turn the pile every few days, and keep adding more layers, ending with brown. The more frequently you turn, the sooner the compost will be ready.

6. WATCH FOR WETNESS: The pile should always be about as moist as a wrung-out sponge. Too much or too little water can slow down or even stop the composting process. Water the pile with a hose when weather is dry, or cover with a tarp during heavy rain, as necessary.

7. HARVEST WHEN READY: Once the compost is dark brown and free of recognizable ingredients (and has no offending smell), it's ready. This could take up to a full year. Use it as a mulch or top dressing, dig it into any problematic soil, or rake it directly onto the lawn for greener grass.

MARTHA MUST

I have devoted a field at the farm in Bedford to composting: Useless boughs, branches, and stumps are collected and professionally ground in a rented tub grinder, along with livestock manure, plants, and other green matter (weeds are discarded).

HOW TO
PLANT FLOWERS

Even budding gardeners can create a patch—or multiple pots—of paradise, with the right sun and soil. Whether you choose to purchase bulbs or established plants from a nursery or start from seeds, the following primer will walk you through the essential steps to success.

ANNUALS, BIENNIALS, AND PERENNIALS

Choose flowers based not only on which ones you love but also on the time and budget you have for planting and tending.

- Annuals, such as marigolds, sprout from seed, bloom, bear seed, and die within a single growing season. If allowed to set seed (indicating to the plant's energy reserves that bloom season is over), they will stop flowering and soon expire. Because of this, deadheading—pinching off blossoms as they fade—is an essential part of their care.

- Biennials, such as foxglove and forget-me-nots, live two years, but show only their foliage the first year and make you wait until the next year to reward you with a display of flowers. After flowering, they die. To have a steady supply of blossoms, plant new seeds each year; this way you'll get foliage and flowers at the same time.

- Perennials survive from year to year. Some, such as daffodils, retreat underground when faced with harsh conditions such as drought or cold weather. In warm regions, some perennials, such as sedum and phlox, grow and remain green year-round. There are also evergreen perennials, such as hellebores, that flourish in cold climates.

- Tender perennials, such as impatiens, are considered perennial in their native warm-climate habitats but cannot tolerate winter cold. They are grown as annuals in more frigid parts of North America.

HOW TO PLANT BULBS

These steps are for planting flowers that start as bulbs, such as tulips, daffodils, hyacinths, anemones, and crocuses—all excellent for beginners. Aim for a mix of spring-blooming flowers and those that bloom in summer and into early fall; the planting times will vary, too.

1. SELECT THE FLOWERS

Start by choosing plants that can thrive in your zone. But since flowers are a relatively low-cost endeavor, you may want to experiment on a small scale with other varieties. Order your bulbs from a reputable supplier, and save the tags for planting instructions.

2. TIME IT RIGHT

When you plant bulbs is key to their longevity. There are general guidelines for planting in different zones, though you can be sure you are timing it right by following these tips.

- Fall is the best time to plant spring blooms, such as tulips and hyacinth, allowing them ample time to get established over the winter. The ground should be cool, however, so don't plant until you've had a week or more of below-50-degree temperatures (and well before the first expected frost date)—and the ground feels cool at about 6 inches deep.

MARTHA'S PICKS

If you enjoy having beautiful bouquets in your home, be sure to choose flowers that grow well in your zone, selecting ones that bloom at different times.

Allium (bulb)

Daffodil (bulb)

Dahlia (perennial)

Foxglove (biennial)

Hydrangea (shrub)

Lilac (shrub)

Lily (bulb)

Peony (perennial)

Poppy (annual/perennial)

Rose (shrub)

Snapdragon (perennial*)

Sunflower (annual)

Sweet Pea (annual)

Tulip (bulb)

This is technically a tender perennial and is generally treated as an annual (see further explanation at left).

■ For summer flowers such as gladioli and dahlias, it's essential to wait until after the last frost in spring to plant (and better late than early, in case of unexpected temperature drops). A good rule of thumb is to wait until after at least two weeks of above-50-degree nighttime temperatures to check the ground, which should feel warm at about 6 inches deep.

■ Plant the bulbs as soon after buying as possible, to keep them from withering or growing moldy. If you must wait, keep them in a cool place away from direct sunlight, such as in a potting shed, garage, or basement.

3. PLANT PROPERLY
Plant bulbs (and seeds, right) on a cool day when the earth is slightly damp but still friable, meaning just moist enough to clump together. Bulbs need soil that drains well; don't try to plant in mud or ultra-dry earth. (Same goes for planting in containers, in which case you create the friable potting mix yourself; see page 230.) To ensure a unified look, try to plant all bulbs in an area at the same time.

■ Before digging, arrange the bulbs on the ground as desired, or simply scatter the bulbs, for a more natural look.

■ Dig each hole to a depth that is roughly three times the diameter of the bulb, and just wide enough to hold it snugly. (Plant small bulbs 3 to 5 inches deep, larger bulbs 6 to 8 inches deep.)

■ Place the bulb, tapered side up, in the hole, then backfill hole with soil, pressing to eliminate air pockets and secure bulbs upright.

■ To nourish bulbs, prevent weeds, and trap in moisture, top bed with a thin layer of rich compost, cover surrounding soil with 1 to 2 inches of mulch, and water well.

HOW TO SOW SEEDS
Growing flowers from seeds can be much more affordable than buying potted plants.

■ While some specimens require germinating indoors first, there are many hardy types—sunflowers, marigolds, poppies, nasturtiums, pansies, sweet peas—that will thrive when direct-sown in a garden bed. Always wait to sow seeds until after the last frost in spring.

■ Start by checking seed size: Put very fine seeds in a clean saltshaker and mix with enough gelatin powder or fine sand to coat. Some small seeds are sold as "pelleted" and already coated (check the package); others are large enough to sow on their own.

■ Follow the seed-package instructions for depth and spacing. The general rule is to sow the seed at a depth that's three times the seed's width. So a ¼-inch-wide seed would go ¾ inch deep, and so on. For tiny seeds, you simply sprinkle them over the base and tap the container to let the seeds settle.

■ Water well after sowing and then when needed after that (the soil should always remain clumpy when pinched).

MARTHA MUST

Turn your garden rake into a two-in-one tool for planting and evenly spacing bulbs or seedlings. Use a black marker and a ruler to delineate inches along the handle, and the fork of the rake to make indentations for the seed holes.

FEEDING AND WEEDING

Both will boost the power of all your flowers—annuals, perennials, and shrubs alike.

- Feed perennials monthly (spring through summer) with a low-nitrogen, high-phosphorus fertilizer. Feed annuals every three weeks with a balanced (5-10-5) organic fertilizer.

- Weed out any unwanted plants so flowers won't compete for nutrients. To keep weeds at bay, add a couple inches of mulch at the beginning of spring and replenish as needed.

SUPPORTING

Certain flowers need support to help encourage upright stems as they grow and when blooming; even those with sturdy enough stems can be undermined by a heavy wind or rainfall.

SINGLE STAKES: For tall, heavy flowers that grow in singles (delphinium, foxgloves, hollyhocks, lilies, and sunflowers): Place a tall wood or bamboo stake (or tree branch) next to a single stem, then loosely tie twine around stake and stem in a figure eight.

GROW-THROUGH STAKES: For annuals and perennials that grow in clumps (peonies, asters, garden phlox, helenium, goldenrod): Use "peony rings," placing the stakes in a circle around groups of flowers when planting. Once shoots appear, secure the grow-through ring about 1 foot above ground. As plants grow, raise ring as needed. Tomato cages can also be used.

LINKING STAKES: For less sturdy flowers (Japanese anemones, Shasta daisies, ladybells, and crocosmia) that tend to lean after blooming, or have been trampled by rain: Insert upright stakes in a line in front of the flowers, in regular intervals, then link the arms between each one, bending the joints to secure.

DEADHEADING

To extend the life of blooms (and the plants themselves), remove spent flowers (aka "dead heads").

- Some flowers can simply be pinched, and you'll know this by trying—they should fall off without any effort.

- Others need to be cut with secateurs. For the most part, follow the shape of the flower and its connection to the stem as your guide, cutting where stalk meets leaves. For shrubs with tiny flowers, you can use grass shears to snip off a bunch at a time, leaving buds behind.

- Roses require more precision (see page 214).

HOW TO
GROW ROSES

Caring for a rose garden isn't nearly as challenging as many gardeners assume. Here's how to enjoy an abundance of fragrant blooms all season long—and for decades to come.

FIRST THINGS FIRST

Growing roses starts with the selection; you will have the greatest success with those suited for your zone. You'll also need to plant them correctly and prune them properly.

PLANTING

Bare-root roses, which are dormant plants that have no soil around their roots, come in a much greater variety than container-grown (or grafted) roses, but they must be planted right away. Beginners may prefer the appearance of grafted roses, however, which can be kept in their containers, in a semi-sunny spot, until you are ready to plant them in the soil.

BARE-ROOT ROSES: Open the package right away and inspect the plant's condition. Prune any damaged canes or roots immediately to deter any infection from setting in.

- Before planting, soak the roots in water overnight, adding a root-stimulating solution (found at any quality gardening center) to the water.

- Dig a hole about two times as deep and wide as the length of the root system. Work a slow-release organic granular fertilizer and some compost into the soil at the back of the hole (do not let fertilizer touch roots directly).

- Make a mound of soil in the center of the hole such that the plant's bud union (the swollen point above the roots where the canes emerge) is 1 inch above the soil line in

warm climates and 1 inch below the surface in cooler climates. Place the plant in the hole; spread the roots evenly around it.

- Backfill hole two-thirds full with soil; fill with water, and allow to drain. Fill hole with more soil, and water again.

GRAFTED ROSES: When shopping for container-grown roses, look for a well-established root system (test by tugging on the main stem; if it comes out easily, don't buy that plant).

- Trim off any blooms before planting (put them in a vase); this will ensure the plant's energy is focused on root development.

- Follow same method as above when planting, loosening roots before placing in hole.

PRUNING

It is very important to properly prune roses, which requires a bit of know-how.

- A simple rule is to remove any crossing canes and those with inward-facing buds. More refined nuances will depend on rose type. It's important to know the form of your plant, and whether it is repeat blooming.

- Prune heavily in winter to stimulate growth and prevent disease; prune lightly throughout the season to maintain an attractive shape.

- Deadhead stems after blooms fade: Cut toward center of bush at a 45-degree angle, just below the first pair of leaves and directly above an outward-facing stem.

MARTHA MUST

Here's a little-known secret for growing bountiful roses: Every spring and fall, sprinkle one cup of Epsom salts (magnesium sulfate) around the perimeter of each established rosebush to add important nutrients, then work it into soil with a hand cultivator. You can find Epsom salts in bulk at farm-supply stores or at your local pharmacy.

HOW TO
WINTERIZE YOUR PLANTS

Most varieties can survive winter on their own, without any interference from you—indeed, many gardening experts encourage people to leave eye-catching flower stalks and seed heads alone, as the latter provides food for wildlife. That said, here are some general guidelines for how to prepare common plants for the cold.

PREPARING THE GARDEN

Putting the garden to bed each fall both marks the end of the growing season and presents a wonderful opportunity to get a head start on the next season. How you prepare your garden for winter depends on your region, but here are some general tips:

- Schedule the work over several weekends so it doesn't become overwhelming.

- Start with a cleanup: Cut down and remove the past season's annuals and vegetables, and add them to the compost pile. Cut back faded or dead foliage on perennials after the first hard frost and compost. Never compost diseased or pest-infested plants.

- Rake up and compost fallen leaves on the lawn, and pull weeds before mowing for the last time.

- Before the ground freezes, water evergreens (especially broad-leaved ones) deeply, and spray them with antidesiccants if they are planted in exposed, windy areas.

- Cover containers that will remain outdoors to prevent them from filling with water, freezing, and cracking. Clean terra-cotta pots and concrete containers; store in a potting shed to protect them from the elements.

- After the ground freezes, mulch perennials, evergreens, and newly planted trees; if necessary, protect them with burlap screens to minimize heaving, desiccation, scalding from intense sun, and other winter damage.

- Once the garden has been put to bed, bring in garden hoses, turn off taps, and take some time to tune up tools before storing.

PRUNING THE PLANTS

Remember to clean your pruners when switching between different plants.

HERBACEOUS PERENNIALS (CONEFLOWER, GLOBE THISTLE, PEONY): Cut back leaves and stems to 1 to 2 inches above the ground in the fall, generally after the first frost (and before a heavier snowfall causes them to collapse).

WOODY SHRUBS (FORSYTHIA, LILAC, SMOKE BUSH): Don't prune spring bloomers (better to do this after blooms fade in the spring). Shape branches of other shrubs as desired, but be careful—cutting too much can weaken the plant.

ORNAMENTAL GRASSES (MISCANTHUS, PENNISETUM): Leave the seed heads through winter. Before the plant leafs out in spring, cut to 2 to 3 inches above the ground.

VINES (CLEMATIS, HONEYSUCKLE): Lightly trim perennial vines. Leave major pruning until spring. Remove dead annual vines entirely and compost them.

ANNUALS AND VEGETABLES: Pull dead plants after the hard frost, once they've withered or turned brown, then compost them.

MARTHA MUST

Burlap covers protect the tender branches of my boxwood shrubs (above) from splaying and breaking from the weight of snow, while shielding the foliage from freezing windburn. It is a practice I've followed for years, and I think it also provides a cozy and pretty look to the winter landscape.

PROTECTING THE PLANTS

Frigid temperatures, gusty winds, heavy snowfalls, icy conditions—these can all take their toll on your exposed plants. Stock up on burlap, garden jute, and other supplies, described below, all available at garden centers and many hardware stores.

POTTED PLANTS

The freeze-and-thaw cycle that root-balls face this time of year can damage plants. If you can, consider moving potted plants indoors for the winter. If your planters are too heavy to move indoors, wrap the pots in cushioned packaging material for insulation. To hide the plastic and give further protection, cover with burlap.

BOXWOOD

To protect against winter storms and wind damage, boxwoods (and other broadleaf evergreen shrubs, including azaleas, holly, and rhododendron) can be wrapped in burlap. While frost is commonly considered the most destructive force in effect during the winter, acute winds can prove equally if not more detrimental to these ornamental shrubs.

To cover your shrubs, make a framework around the plants with bamboo stakes or lumber; secure burlap to the structure using a staple gun, jute twine, or wood screws, as appropriate. The wrapping should not lie directly on the foliage. Remove it when the ground begins to thaw. Also, keep shrubs strong year-round by covering roots with mulch and watering during dry periods, right up until the ground freezes.

1. Drive long pieces (about 8 feet long) of bamboo into the ground, just outside the plants' roots, in crosswise pairs.

2. Secure each pair with garden twine and one screw. Lay more bamboo across the top of the pairs to create a teepee "roof."

3. Hammer wooden stakes into the ground, then sandwich bottom of long sheets of burlap (using one on either side that's about the same length as your bamboo) with a shim screwed into the wood stake.

4. Pull burlap up over the teepee, making it taut; sew seams together at the top and wherever needed using a 4-inch upholstery needle and jute twine.

TIP

Keep in mind that the first and last frost dates for a particular zone are only estimates; err on the side of caution and push out those dates by two weeks or more (later in spring, earlier in fall). If the temperature rises above freezing after an initial frost, remove any coverings in the morning to allow the ground to heat up during the day.

HOW TO
ATTRACT BIRDS, BEES, AND BUTTERFLIES

A carefully selected variety of plants should beckon invaluable pollinators, and other winged visitors, to your garden. Offer shady spots and a steady source of clean water. Don't expect to see immediate results, especially for bees and butterflies. Once your sanctuary is established, though, it will be buzzing for years.

FOR BEES AND BUTTERFLIES

These creatures are drawn to nectar-producing flowers that bloom throughout the summer. Note that butterflies tend to like flat blossoms, such as daisies, while bees are more universal in their attractions.

- Some favorites include black-eyed Susans, purple coneflower, oxeye daisy, valerian, bee balm, and butterfly bush.

- Extend the season with asters and goldenrods that bloom in the fall.

- Create a woodsy section of your garden for host plants such as wild blue lupine and wild spice bush, for butterflies to lay their eggs on—and for caterpillars to feast on as they develop into butterflies.

> **TIP**
>
> Monarch butterflies are in decline. Help in the repopulation effort by planting two of their primary food sources: wild milkweed and butterfly weed.

FOR BIRDS

Birds are generally more finicky than bees and butterflies, and are most often attracted to native plants.

- Take walks in your neighborhood and note which plants attract them.

- Some of the same plants will attract all three flying creatures at different stages of development. Purple coneflower, for example, produces nectar for bees and butterflies (and hummingbirds) when it flowers in summer and early fall, and then seeds for birds from late summer to mid-fall.

- Many birds stick around for winter, when food is especially scarce. Members of the rose family, such as mountain ash, are relished by songbirds, as are crab apple, hawthorn, and serviceberry. Winterberry, a native holly, is another bird favorite.

- Plant evergreen trees or shrubs around the edge of your yard to provide perches. You can also create layers of small trees and shrubs that mimic the forest and bring in the birds.

- Hummingbirds are drawn to tubular or throated nectar-bearing flowers, such as aloes or salvias.

NATIVE PLANTS

Besides attracting pollinators, incorporating native plants into your landscape will ensure your garden thrives year in and year out—and with significantly less upkeep than non-native species. Start by checking with your local cooperative extension to discover the best native plants for your own backyard; nearby botanical gardens, nurseries, and garden centers are other excellent resources.

REDUCE TIME AND EFFORT: What's "native" to different regions will vary (by definition), as this category will include plants that have evolved over the years to survive in their local climates, an especially valuable quality in areas with recurring droughts, harsh winters, or other extreme conditions. As a result, these sturdy, low-maintenance plants will save you time, effort, and money by requiring less water, fertilizer, and pest control (and you won't end up having to replace the plant when it withers, as can often happen with non-natives).

GET HEALTHIER SOIL: What's more, these plants contribute to the overall health of your soil, thereby supporting the other plants in your very own ecosystem; they can also help prevent the spread of invasive plants.

SAVE POLLINATOR POPULATIONS: By creating a natural, sustainable habitat for butterflies and bees, you will help stem the alarming decline in these and other pollinator populations.

MARTHA MUST

To attract a wide variety of birds, feeders filled with different seeds hang from the rafters of my garage in Bedford. I look for well-built feeders that are easy to fill and clean. When purchasing, keep in mind that certain seeds call for specific feeders so that birds can extract them.

HOW TO
GROW TREES

A riot of colorful blooms may steal the spotlight, but trees tend to woo you in more subtle ways, with their scale and steadfastness. Unlike those fleeting flowers, trees offer a year-round opportunity to boost your home's curb appeal.

BEFORE YOU BUY

Trees represent big investments in money, time, and space. That's why you'll want to plant them for the long haul, minding these preliminary steps.

MEASURE YOUR SPACE: Plan for the largest potential size of the mature tree (as in height, width or crown spread, and root space, all stated on the tag) when plotting where it will go, lest it end up too close to your house or other structures on your property. You'll want to make sure the trees will not extend into a neighbor's property (or be prepared for them to prune those branches), and there may be ordinances prohibiting trees from extending over public streets. Think safety, too; you wouldn't want a large tree to end up hitting electrical wires when it is at its full height.

KEEP VIEWS IN MIND: Do you long to wake up to the sight of treetops (and the sound of birds) from your second-story bedroom window? Or to gaze upon the distant landscape from the dining room table? Picture how you want the tree to be viewed from inside as well as outside, using it to hide a not-so-pretty fence rather than your prized porch, for example.

CONSIDER ALL SEASONS: If trees will drop acorns, berries, or other fruits at different times of the year, you may not want to plant them near a driveway or exposed patio. Likewise, you may want to avoid planting a sprawling shade tree that could impact your sun-loving perennials—or darken your sun-filled living room or home office.

WEIGH YOUR OPTIONS: Start with trees that grow in your zone (native species are always recommended), then decide whether you want fruit trees or ornamentals, flowering trees or those with glorious fall foliage (or all the above, planting as many trees as you can). For privacy, nothing beats a row or allée of trees, either along a street or your entire property. If this is your goal, you'll want to look for fast-growing varieties that provide year-round foliage, such as evergreens. Note that planting trees close together will create a lower canopy (for more privacy) and will require more pruning than those planted farther apart.

MARTHA MUST

I feel strongly about reforestation and giving back to the earth, so every year I plant thousands of seedlings. Trees provide habitat and food for birds and other animals, they absorb carbon dioxide and potentially harmful gases, and they release oxygen.

	SPACING		
SIZE OF TREE	SPACING BETWEEN PLANTS	MIN. SPACING FROM WALL OF 1-STORY BUILDING	MIN. SPACING FROM CORNER OF 1-STORY BUILDING
SMALL TREES (30' OR LESS)	6-15'	8-10'	6-8'
MEDIUM TREES (30-70')	30-40'	15'	12'
LARGE TREES (70' OR MORE)	40-50'	20'	15'

GENERAL GUIDELINES

Consider these factors before you head to the garden center or nursery, for plantings that will last generations.

- Select trees that will thrive in local conditions and, when possible, are grown locally.

- Rather than choosing large, mature trees, go with young, well-grown, freshly dug specimens with 2- to 4-inch calipers (the diameter of the tree's trunk).

- A container-grown tree is much smaller and lighter (and thus easier to plant) than a traditional ball-and-burlap one.

- Plant at the right moment to ensure the roots have enough time to become established before winter's chill; this is typically spring in cooler regions, fall where it's warmer longer.

- To create a rich, fertile, homogenous growing medium, thoroughly incorporate a bit of compost into the site's soil for both planting and backfilling.

- Feed young trees with a fertilizer designed for use at planting time; avoid mixing it into the soil for backfilling, though, as it can cause the tree's roots to burn.

- Water well when planted, as well as several times a week for its first season.

STAKING TIPS

You can often eliminate the need for staking by following a few guidelines, though in some instances this extra support is unavoidable.

- Shop at a reputable nursery and choose a shorter tree with healthy roots: They should not be soft, black, or decayed; if in burlap, roots should feel solid and heavy.

- Secure the tree by planting it at the proper depth—just cover the top of the root-ball—

and tamping down the soil well to eliminate air (overdoing it, however, can cause compaction).

- Don't water the hole before the tree is placed, but water immediately after planting and give the tree at least 1 inch of water per week thereafter.

- Conifers planted in late fall should generally be staked, as their shallow root systems won't anchor them sufficiently before winter sets in.

- The same is true of trees planted in windy areas, such as near the ocean or at high altitudes.

- Professionals will usually stake mature trees (and ones with large, leafy crowns) that have been moved to a new site.

MARTHA MUST

I've discovered the vast financial rewards of planting seedling trees. Because they are much more affordable than mature specimens, seedlings allow you to grow many more trees than you ever thought possible.

PLANTING HOW-TO

Read through the following steps carefully before you begin, as you will want to arm yourself with the right tools and employ the proper techniques.

1. Using a sharp spade, dig a hole roughly three times the diameter of the container and just deep enough to let the tree's buttress (the swelling at the base of the trunk) sit about 1 inch above the surface of the soil. The hole should have sloping sides to allow the roots to grow properly. Mix a few shovels of compost into the soil.

2. To remove the tree from the container, grasp the trunk and slide off the plastic pot; firmly tap on the container to release any stubborn areas.

3. Container-grown trees must have their roots scarified and teased apart to prevent them from continuing to grow in circles. Use a tool or your hands to gently remove the soil and separate the roots.

4. Position the tree in the hole, taking time to place the plant's most attractive side outward. Backfill the hole using the same soil you dug out. For ball-and-burlap specimens, slide the still-wrapped tree into the hole, cut away as much of the wire basket around the root as you can, and push the burlap down to the bottom of the hole.

5. Add a starter fertilizer (such as Bio-tone Starter by Espoma, available at nurseries) when planting a new tree; sprinkle it around the edge of the root-ball according to the package directions.

6. Water thoroughly right after planting, then apply a 2- to 3-inch layer of mulch to slow evaporation and keep roots cool, leaving a 2-inch buffer around the trunk. Sculpting a "water well" helps prevent runoff so water drains directly into the plant. Give the new tree 1 inch of water a week through its first season.

TIP

If you decide to relocate a tree, you will have much greater success transplanting younger ones (those up to four years of age) than established specimens.

HOW TO GROW A VEGETABLE GARDEN

The path to homegrown is worth every ounce of time and effort. Just imagine trading in the trip to the store for a saunter out to your backyard. Vegetables are surprisingly forgiving, too, so long as you lay the foundation with fertile soil and provide sufficient sunshine.

FIRST THINGS FIRST

More than any other type of plantings, vegetable gardens require the most planning and preparation to be fruitful. If you are visited often by deer, rabbits, or other wildlife, you'll also want to erect a fence, ideally at least 6 feet tall.

DETERMINE THE BEST SPOT

Must-haves for a vegetable garden are a level or gently sloping site and eight hours of sun daily. Fertile soil is also needed, as well as regular watering.

MAKE A PLAN

Planting without a plan is too risky. Use graph paper to sketch your designs, bearing in mind each plant's potential size and customary habit. Make sure to place larger plants where they won't overshadow shorter ones, and choose compact varieties if you have limited space. You can always dig more beds or enlarge pre-existing ones in subsequent years.

PREPARE THE SOIL

Loamy, well-drained, nutrient-rich and slightly acidic soil (6 to 6.8 pH) is the ideal environment for most vegetables. Start by taking a soil pH test (see page 206).

WHAT TO PLANT

Give due consideration to the following when deciding on the produce.

PALATE: Concentrate on your favorite vegetables, especially those unusual varieties (such as heirloom tomatoes or dwarf cucumbers) that are hard to find at the grocery store.

TIME COMMITMENT: Don't bite off more than you can chew. Good vegetables for beginners include carrots, zucchini, cucumbers, herbs, and salad greens.

GARDEN ZONE: Where you live will determine what grows best in your region (and, importantly, when to plant).

AVAILABLE SPACE: For a small yard, choose compact, high-yielding crops such as tomatoes and pole beans (which grow vertically) and lettuces; avoid sprawlers such as melons and squashes (winter and summer varieties).

TIP

There's no need to struggle with what nature gave you; raised beds allow you to create the ideal growing conditions, with better sunlight and soil that warms up more quickly than in-ground beds. Note that because these boxes are self-contained, you will need to water them more frequently.

GUIDE TO GROWING VEGETABLES

Timing is everything when it comes to growing your own. Check your hardiness zone and plant accordingly, usually no sooner than two to three weeks after the average last frost. Note that if you want to start your seeds indoors, do so about eight weeks before the average last frost. (Check seed package.)

	BEETS, CARROTS, RADISHES	BROCCOLI, CAULIFLOWER	CORN	CUCUMBERS	EGGPLANTS
PREFERRED TEMPERATURE & TOLERATED RANGE	60–65° (40–75° range)	60–65° (40–75° range)	65–75° (65–90° range)	65–75° (65–90° range)	70–85° (65–90° range)
WHEN TO HARVEST	These can be gently pulled or dug as soon as the tops are large enough to handle. Consult your seed packet for the recommended time to harvest for optimum flavor and texture.	The heads should be densely packed; broccoli should be green. If petals appear, harvest heads right away.	You'll know it's ready when the silks turn brown and the ears feel full through the husk from end to end.	Cut these from the vines when they are young, small, and softly spined. As they grow large, the seeds develop and are best removed before eating.	Pick them at any size, but the larger they get, the more seeds they'll have.
MORE TIPS	Once you've harvested the roots, immediately remove the green tops; beet and radish greens can be washed and dried, then used in salads or for cooking, similar to other greens.	Cut the heads from the plant at an angle, taking 4 to 6 inches of stem and leaving behind side shoots for more heads to develop.	To harvest, grab the ear firmly, then twist at the base and pull downward to separate it from the stalk.	While staking is not essential, it does help keep the fruit off the soil in a raised bed or container garden; you can even grow cucumber vines up a trellis or fence.	Stake eggplants as soon as the bushes are visible, placing bamboo or metal posts about 2 inches from the plant, so it will grow around the stakes and support the heavy fruit.

KALE, CHARD, LEAFY GREENS	LETTUCES	MELONS	PEPPERS	SUMMER SQUASHES	TOMATOES
60–65° (40–75° range)	60–65° (40–75° range)	70–85° (50–90° range)	70–85° (65–90° range)	65–75° (50–90° range)	70–85° (65–90° range)
Snip the outer leaves once they are the size of your hand above the stalk (or at the base of the stalk for chard), leaving enough intact to allow the plant to keep growing.	Once the leaves are about 4 inches long, snip only the outer leaves about an inch above the crown so the plant can continue to grow.	When the fruit is ripe, it will slip easily from the vine, and, in the case of cantaloupe, the netting on its surface will turn beige.	These can be harvested green or ripe (in various colors), depending on the taste you want. They have their best flavor during periods of high heat.	These become tough and seedy when large, so harvest the small ones for the best flavor and texture.	Tomatoes continue to ripen after picking, but develop the best flavor when left to reach their full color outdoors on the vine (or pick when green and nicely tart).
These greens are ideal for succession planting, where you stagger the time of planting so they aren't all ready for harvesting at once.	Tender lettuces can be particularly prone to pests; plant rows of chives or garlic between them to help control aphids.	Melons, especially watermelons, do best when grown in raised rows, or hills, mounding the soil about 12 inches above ground to allow for greater drainage and sun exposure.	When harvesting, never pull a pepper from the stem; cut it with pruners instead, leaving a 1-inch stub for other fruit to grow on.	To keep these prolific growers from taking over, cut some blossoms for eating, too; just be sure to leave behind the females (the ones with the tiny swollen bulge at their base).	Whether grown in a container or the ground, tomato vines require staking to support the weight of the fruit; do this when planting, using bamboo posts or metal tomato cages.

HOW TO
GROW CONTAINER PLANTS

You don't need a sprawling expanse in the country (or even a yard in the suburbs) to grow a wealth of beautiful plants—just a small sunny outdoor space will do. Or perhaps you do have either of the above and still want to create an outdoor oasis on a porch or patio. Follow these steps to potted-plant perfection.

HOW-TO

For most plants, the process for prepping and nurturing is the same.

1. PICK THE POT: Almost any type will do, so long as it has drainage holes, preferably on bottom and sides. To protect the surfaces they sit on, raise pots on wooden panels or bricks.

2. SELECT THE SPOT: For optimum growth for plants that require full sun, put plants in a spot that receives six to eight hours of direct sunlight a day. Lighter pots can move with the sun; heavier ones can be placed on a rolling cart, if needed.

3. PREP THE SOIL: Potted plants need potting mix, a nutrient-rich type of soil specially designed for containers. You can find potting mix at any garden center or nursery, or make your own (see page 230). First cover drainage holes with fabric or broken ceramic (to keep soil from falling out), then moisten the mix before adding a layer to the pot, covering the bottom only.

4. POT THE PLANT: Check the tag to find out how much space is needed between seedlings. Loosen up the roots of the plant and suspend them in your pot to figure out how much more dirt you'll need to cover the roots; the leaves should appear just above the surface. Add enough soil so it's level and an inch shy of the container's rim. Pat down the soil firmly, then add enough water that it starts to drain through the holes.

5. FERTILIZE FREQUENTLY: Unlike in-ground plants, those in pots have fewer nutrients to draw on (because of the limited amount of soil). Add a slow-release fertilizer after planting, and then a diluted liquid organic fertilizer every two weeks during the growing season (or as recommended on the plant's tag).

6. WATER WELL: You'll know the plant is thirsty when the soil feels dry an inch below the surface. Add enough so that the water starts to drain through the holes, but don't overdo it (or you'll also drain out nutrients). Never let the soil fully dry out.

7. PRUNE AS NEEDED: Some flowering plants require deadheading to encourage new growth; pinch or snip off dead blooms during the season. Those that are covered in small flowers, or that begin to wilt in late summer, should be cut back to one-third the size when the blooms are spent; don't worry, the plant will grow back in no time.

TIP

Plants may look a bit wilted during the hottest part of the day; this is their way of protecting themselves from excessive moisture loss. Don't allow plants to sit in water; empty their saucers after each watering and rainfall, or rest the pots on stands.

MIX YOUR OWN POTTING SOIL

Container gardening calls for a bit of alchemy in imitating nature in a pot. That's why potting mix is essential to any success, providing three key materials: for drainage, water retention, and nutrition.

You would do fine by purchasing a quality organic mix from a garden center, but making your own potting soil will give your potted plants a leg up. The all-purpose mix is a good place to start, or try the custom formulas to make your container garden flourish.

FOR WOODY PLANTS AND PERENNIALS

Longevity is the goal when you're making a mix for long-term plants in pots. This blend uses compost and composted bark to release nutrients slowly over the course of several seasons, allowing plants to thrive over time.

1 part coarse sand

1 part perlite

1 part ground coir (coconut husks)

1 part composted bark

1 part compost

ALL-PURPOSE POTTING MIX

This basic blend suits most flowers, vegetables, and small shrubs—and is a starting point for customization.

1 part garden soil (store-bought or from a well-amended bed)

1 part compost (for nutrients)

1 part perlite (for drainage)

1 part ground coir (for water retention)

FOR TROPICALS

Continually moist and always fertile soil is best for tropical plants, so bark and compost are the primary ingredients in this recipe. They hold moisture and release nutrients as they biodegrade, creating the perfect environment for jungle species.

FIRST, MIX:

2 parts composted bark

1 part compost

1/50 part charcoal

THEN COMBINE:

3 parts compost-bark-charcoal mixture

1 part perlite

1 part calcined clay

1 part shredded coir

FOR ANNUALS

The extra fertility this recipe offers keeps flowers blooming all season long. It's ideal for annuals, which are heavy feeders.

2 parts coarse sand or poultry grit

2 parts composted bark

2 parts compost

½ part organic fertilizer (or mix in ¼ part bone meal and ¼ part kelp meal)

FOR SUCCULENTS

The mantra is "drainage, drainage, drainage" when you're growing succulents. These desert and dry-climate natives never want to be soggy, so a healthy amount of ingredients that help water flow through is a must.

4 parts All-Purpose Potting Mix

3 parts perlite

2 parts coarse sand

1 part vermiculite

GROW A POTTED PRODUCE GARDEN

Growing produce in pots requires a bit more thought than raised-bed gardening when selecting and pairing plants.

CHOOSE PRODUCTIVE SPECIES: Tomatoes are among the most popular for growing in pots, though you'll need a large vessel to hold them. Rather than wait all season for huge slicing ones, opt for early-bearing cherry tomatoes, such as Sun Gold.

BUY SPACE-SAVING PLANTS: You can find an ever-growing selection of dwarf varieties bred just for container gardening, including the 'Diamant' cucumber, 'Thumbelina' carrot, 'Fairytale' eggplant, or 'Tom Thumb' butter lettuce.

ADD EDIBLE FLOWERS: Sowing some easy-to-grow nasturtiums and calendulas into any produce garden adds welcome color to pots and salads alike.

COMBINE LIKE WITH LIKE: An 18-inch pot will hold a wide selection of plants, such as habanero, lemon chiles, and purple-leaved peppers for a colorful mix.

DO COMPANION PLANTING: Beets and kale, carrots and tomatoes (the classic), pole beans (staked) and zucchini; certain plants grow better when sharing the soil with compatible neighbors. Try these pairings, then research others.

- Parsley and basil: Both of these leafy herbs enjoy more water than woody herbs. Chives, nasturtiums, hot peppers, and cherry tomatoes make great container mates with these, too.

- Rosemary and sage: These woody herbs prefer more sun and drier soil than leafier varieties. If you live in a warm zone, they may continue growing until the following year.

- Oregano and thyme: These and other semi-woody varieties keep good company with each other. Both will stop growing in fall, even in warm zones; keep the herbs in the pot, as they should sprout again next spring.

HOW TO
GROW HOUSEPLANTS

Houseplants bring life—by way of delightful foliage—to every room (even one without a lot of sunlight). The options are varied, with as many distinctive shapes and textures and shades as what you see out your window. Follow the instructions on pages 229–230 to prepare the pots and do the planting. Then use the tips provided here to help them thrive.

TYPES AND TEMPERAMENTS

There's an indoor plant to suit every space. Generally speaking, kitchens and baths are more humid (so are better for thirstier plants); hallways and bedrooms are cooler and drier. Ultimately, though, it's the amount of light that matters most.

LOW LIGHT

These plants can even grow in a dark corner or a basement with some natural light coming in.

BAMBOO PALM

Also known as butterfly palm, this popular plant has long, feathery fronds and is among the easiest to care for, requiring little in the way of light or water.

CAST-IRON PLANT

This tropical understory plant—in nature it grows on the forest floor—can take a lot of neglect (hence its name) and thrives in even dark spaces.

JAPANESE FATSIA

In the South, this shade-loving, big-leaved plant is a shrub. In the North, it makes a dramatic foliage plant in a dimly lit corner of a house.

PHILODENDRON

Easy to grow—and to love, with its draping foliage—this plant is highly adaptable, needing little light to thrive. It is, however, potentially toxic to pets (and people) if ingested.

SANSEVIERIA

With its tall, thick, spiky leaves, this striking architectural succulent (known as the snake plant) is among the most forgiving, prospering in dry air and with minimal direct light.

BRIGHT INDIRECT LIGHT

Grow these in rooms that get lots of filtered sunlight (ones with windows that face east, west, and north).

BEGONIA COLLECTION

The easy-to-care-for rhizomatous varieties thrive in high humidity, but need to dry between waterings.

CLIVIA

When these South African natives bloom in midwinter, they're ready to take center stage. For best bloom, give them a dry period from late October to late November.

DIEFFENBACHIA

Large, marbled (usually) tropical leaves make this a favorite houseplant, either alone or as part of a mix. Its English name, dumb cane, is a reference to its toxic sap that, when chewed by humans or pets, can cause numbness or swelling in the tongue (consider yourself duly cautioned).

GESNERIAD

Many in this group of plants, which includes African violets, can bloom on and off all year if given bright filtered light and allowed to dry out slightly between waterings.

Remember to keep water off the leaves, lest they end up spotted. A regular dose of African violet fertilizer will increase the bloom.

FERN

This frilly plant adds a breezy, casual feel to your interiors. Like begonias, ferns benefit from high humidity, so set them on pebble-lined trays that have been filled with water to just below the surface of the stones.

FICUS

With its glossy green leaves, this upright woody plant is usually sold as a single-trunk tree, though you can also find it in a more expansive shrub form. It prefers constant conditions, so keep it in its happy place.

IVY TOPIARY

Trained ivy grows well in filtered light. Small-leaved varieties make the best topiaries. For a dash of color, try a variegated form.

TIP

To combat dry winter air indoors, invest in a few houseplants. Their moist soil is a natural humidifier.

ORCHID

While you can always count on orchids to do well in southern exposures, many collectors cultivate them entirely under grow lights.

PEACE LILY

This plant produces pretty white flowers—and, according to NASA, tops the list of plants that reduce indoor volatile organic compounds (VOCs). However, it is also potentially toxic if ingested by pets. It prefers constantly moist soil (so water frequently and lightly).

POTHOS

Here's another climbing, cascading plant that looks like philodendron, but with larger, thicker leaves that tend to be variegated. Caution: It's also potentially toxic to pets and children.

BRIGHTEST LIGHT

Southern exposure is a must for these sun-seekers.

MYRTLE TOPIARY

During winter, myrtle topiaries can live near a sunny south-facing window. To encourage vigorous growth, move them outdoors during summer months.

SUCCULENT

See page 236 for more about succulents.

ROUTINE CARE

Growing plants indoors requires its own kind of TLC.

ROTATE

Potted plants living along a windowsill will become disproportionately leafy on the side facing a window. A quarter turn each week will prevent this. Simplify the task by placing the pots atop lazy Susans, available in hardware and garden centers. The rotating platforms come in sizes that range from 3 to 18 inches in diameter; larger sizes are useful for pots on the floor. (Add surface protectors, such as rubber bumpers, to the undersides of the lazy Susans.)

DUST

Like everything else in your home, plants will collect dust—and this can prevent essential light from reaching the leaves. Be sure to dust them gently with a microfiber cloth, or try this neat trick: Swipe an envelope moistener, sold at office-supply stores, filled with water, over the surface.

WATER

Give your housemates a healthy diet: Fill plastic jugs with water and leave the cap off for 48 hours; the chlorine in the liquid will evaporate, leaving cleaner water behind. As a result, plants will get nutrients more easily. It's also important to use water that's at room temperature—more extreme temperatures can damage roots.

ADD HUMIDITY

Plants are most susceptible to insect infestation and other problems when the air is too dry. Create a humid environment to help them thrive: Fill the bottom of a watertight, rustproof metal tray (available at garden-supply stores) with pebbles. Arrange pots, and add water almost to the top of the pebbles. Water plants as usual. (This is a great setup for myrtle topiaries.)

PREP FOR SPRING

After months of winter dryness, your indoor (and outdoor) plants may need a boost in the spring. Combine a few teaspoons of compost with water in a spray bottle and spritz the leaves with the mixture. The nutritious liquid fertilizer will breathe new life into tired plants.

MARTHA MUST

When warm weather arrives, many houseplants deserve a vacation outdoors. Move them to a semi-shady spot, don't forget to water them, and mist or sprinkle their leaves on a regular basis.

PROPAGATION

There are different methods depending on the type of plant, all described below.

STEM CUTTINGS

Vining plants such as philodendron and pothos.

1. With a clean, sharp knife (or clippers), cut the stems or vines close to the soil.

2. Cut the main vines into small sections including a leaf, stem, and part of the main vine.

3. Submerge the cut ends in water (use small vases, jars, glasses, etc.) and place in indirect sunlight. New roots should appear within a couple weeks.

4. The cuttings will actually survive just fine in water, for the ultimate in ease; to repot, wait until the roots are at least an inch long and then bury the roots in well-watered soil and keep out of direct sunlight.

ROOT DIVISION

Bushy plants such as ferns, peace lillies, and snake plants.

1. Gently remove the entire plant from its pot and shake to loosen the soil from roots.

2. With a clean, sharp hori hori or knife, cut the root-ball in half and replant each half into separate pots.

3. Water and keep the plants moist in a spot with bright indirect light.

LEAF CUTTINGS

For all types of succulents and cacti.

1. Break off leaves from a small branch, exposing a short stem. Dry, or "callus," both stem and leaves for several days (out of direct sunlight) before rooting.

2. Mix equal parts sand, perlite, and vermiculite; water well and use to fill paper-towel-lined seed flats.

3. Push the stems or ends of the leaves into the mixture, and tamp around them to set them in place.

4. Water and keep the succulents moist in a sunny spot. Watch for new growth in four to six weeks, then repot as needed.

OFFSHOOTS

Self-propagating plants such as dieffenbachia and snake plants as well as some types of succulents.

1. Allow the new shoots, or "pups," to grow to at least 3 inches, then use clean, sharp clippers or scissors to cut them as close to the parent plant as possible (it's fine if you lose some leaves).

2. Pot the new plants and keep moist and in bright but indirect light.

WHILE YOU'RE AWAY

Instead of asking a neighbor to water your plants while you're on a trip, use one of these methods to keep them hydrated for at least a week.

- On the day of your departure, give each plant a good watering. Then snugly arrange the plants in a small tub that's deep enough for the pots. Next, crumple up old newspaper and wet it. Arrange the newspaper around the pots, filling in all the gaps—it will keep the plants moist while you're gone.

- Cut a piece of nylon clothesline long enough to connect a water source to the plant; soak the rope for 30 minutes. Meanwhile, water and then drain the plant thoroughly. Bury one end of the wick deep in the soil and drop the other end in a container of water. (Use a water container that is taller or set higher than the potted plant.) For extra-large pots, use more than one wick.

HOW TO
GROW SUCCULENTS

Succulents require little mainte-nance—as long as they get ample sun and not too much water. They can thrive indoors and out, but are often happiest as houseplants.

GROWING BASICS

While simple to grow, succulents do have some basic needs:

- Let the soil dry between waterings, then drench them; it is very important for the container to have proper drainage, too.

- Packing plants too tightly together will encourage mold and also deprive the plants of essential nutrients; pluck out some to grow in their own pots.

SUCCULENT VARIETIES

JADE (A): The bonsai-like appearance of jade makes it among the most popular of succulents; given plenty of full sun, mature plants will sport small blooms in the winter.

STONECROP (B): One of numerous stonecrop variet-ies, this plant has pointed green leaves covered in soft, bristly "hairs"—and loves a south-facing window.

LACE ALOE (C): A dwarf mem-ber of the vast aloe family, this stemless plant has dark grayish-green leaves spiked with white thorns. Aloe can thrive in only partial sunlight.

PERLE VON NÜRNBERG (D): This striking succulent ranges from silvery green to purplish-brown; the tight rosettes eventually sprout up on a stem. Keep in full sun for the best color.

MOLDED WAX (E): The plump, smooth leaves look as if formed out of wax, with sharp red points as tips. Like other echeveria, it can toler-ate partial sunlight.

ELEPHANT BUSH (F): Named for the elephants who like to nibble on it, this leggy suc-culent has small glossy leaves and offers wonderful contrast to the more compact, spikier specimen. Put in a window with indirect sunlight.

MARTHA MUST

If you like growing plants but don't have time to care for them properly, I encourage you to consider growing succulents or cacti. Succulents are so easy to maintain and are able to survive prolonged dryness because they store moisture in their fleshy stems, roots, and leaves.

HOW TO CARE FOR A LAWN

Learn the ins and outs of tending to your turf and the grass will forever be greener on your side of the fence. Rule number one: Avoid cutting the grass too short, as this welcomes more weeds as well as damage from drought and soaring temperatures.

LAWN BASICS

As a ground rule, never cut more than one-third the height of grass at any time. Read on for more tips.

MOW LATE
The best time to cut your grass is in the evening, before the dew settles. Wet grass from the morning dew clogs up blades, and midday heat can rob turf of moisture.

AIM HIGH
Keep your mower blades set at least 3 inches high for all grass species except Bermuda, seashore paspalum, and bent grass—these should be mowed closer to the ground, at 1½ to 2 inches.

KEEP IT GREEN
To help your lawn stay green, use a blend of turfgrasses and clover. Clover also supports healthy soil by taking nitrogen from the atmosphere and fixing it into the ground.

SOAK INSTEAD OF SPRINKLE
Water deeply once a week. This method trains the roots to grow downward toward the moisture rather than rise to the surface.

FEED WITH CAUTION
Never apply fertilizers during droughts or in high summer, particularly when the temperature is 90°F or above. Nitrogen encourages lush new growth, which is more vulnerable during hot spells.

DON'T FIGHT NATURE
It's normal for cool-season turfgrasses to go dormant and turn brown to make it through droughts. The plant will resume growth once the cooler weather returns.

TROUBLESHOOTING TIPS

If your grass has seen better days, devote an afternoon in early fall to this eco-friendly (pesticide-free) rejuvenation. Come spring, you'll be rewarded with a lawn that's lush and green and wonderful for bare feet (and paws).

1. Rake the lawn to remove leaves and dead grass (save for composting) and create good seed-to-soil contact.

2. Apply grass seed; don't skimp. Using a rotary seed dispenser (available at hardware stores) ensures the most even distribution.

3. Cover with a ½-inch-thick layer of compost; this helps retain moisture and keep birds away from tasty seeds.

MOWER MAINTENANCE

Always park the mower under shelter and follow the manufacturer's instructions for adding oil and gas (and for siphoning off gas before the winter). Also, remove caked-on grass from the underside; this allows airflow beneath the mower to lift the grass, for a better cut.

TO CLEAN: Disconnect the spark plug, then tilt the mower on its side, and scrape down the underside of the mower with a putty knife.

TO SHARPEN: A finely honed blade will provide the most consistent cuts, but you'll need to take it to a garden shop equipped with a professional grinder for the best results. You can either take the entire mower to the shop, or remove the blade yourself with a wrench (first remove the spark plug, and wear safety gloves).

HOST AND ENTERTAIN

I wrote my first book, *Entertaining,* in 1982, when I was 41 years old. I had much to share about hosting parties, both big and small—but I was clearly just getting started.

These days, I host regularly at my four homes, and often have guests stay for a few days. And I've learned quite a bit more that I can pass along to you.

Granted, planning weekends with houseguests is perhaps the biggest challenge a host can face. There are many factors that go into making a weekend fun, interesting, and stimulating, not the least of which is planning menus, shopping for ingredients, and cooking dishes so that meals are served on time and guests and family are satisfied. I personally find such a challenge highly enjoyable, and have compiled a file of recipes that can be prepared easily and that make use of locally available foodstuffs and produce.

Hosting a brunch, dinner, or cocktail party requires fewer logistics (no sheets to change or excursions to plan!) but equal attention to the details—the guest list, the date and timing, the food and drinks, the table settings and décor, the conversation, even the cleanup. Brunch may involve more casual, boisterous meals around the large kitchen table, while formal dinners, with great wines and well-prepared food, typically will be held in the dining room—with a big fire going in cooler months. Summer calls for inviting large groups for cocktails and finger foods by the pool or on the patio.

The effort expended for any of these events is worth it—my guests always leaved sated, happy, and having made new friends.

SET UP A HOME BAR

Whether you're having guests over for drinks, dinner, or the weekend, well-thought-out attention to all the details will make the experience more enjoyable for them—and you. For starters, a help-yourself bar makes everyone feel welcome (and impromptu gatherings all the easier to pull off). With just a half-dozen base spirits and a few mixers, you can turn out a great number of cocktail classics along with your own signature sips.

WHAT TO STOCK

Pick and choose according to what you and your frequent guests like to drink.

WINE: Always have at least one red and one white wine on hand, plus a sparkling wine; and rosé during warmer months. See page 243 for more tips.

BEER: Although beer can be purchased as needed, it's worth keeping some good bottles around. IPAs, pilsners, and lagers are universal favorites; wheat beers and stouts are nice for summer and winter, respectively.

LIQUOR: Start with three or four types of liquor and build from there:

- Vodka, the mainstay of any liquor cabinet, is used for tonics, gimlets, screwdrivers, Bloody Marys, Moscow mules, and vodka martinis.

- Gin is the traditional choice for martinis and other drinks, such as Negronis, French 75s, Tom Collinses, and Singapore slings. It's also a more herbal alternative to vodka in martinis, tonics, gimlets, and rickeys.

- Tequila is a must for margaritas, sunrises, and palomas—or for drinking straight, preferably followed by lime and salt. Blanco (silver) tequila is the most versatile, while a reposado (aged) one is worth exploring, too.

- Rum makes tropical drinks possible. Dark rum goes into tiki-style drinks, including hurricanes and mai tais (as well as dark and stormys); white rum is the classic choice for daiquiris and mojitos.

- Whiskey is for sipping and mixing into Manhattans, old-fashioneds, juleps, sours, Sazeracs, and milk punches. Types include rye (the most versatile choice), bourbon (often slightly sweeter), and scotch (with more intense and complex flavors). You may want to save top-shelf liquors, such as a fine scotch or bourbon, for a swankier soiree.

- Specialty liqueurs, such as cachaça for caipirinhas and pisco for pisco sours expand your cocktail-making options.

- Aperitifs—notably vermouth, Aperol, Campari, and St-Germain—double as ingredients for making cocktails (martinis and negronis, for example).

- Cognac, a staple of sidecars and milk punches, is also nice for sipping after a meal, as are other types of brandy.

- Sherry, port, and similar fortified wines are equally appropriate before (such as with tapas) or after dinner.

MIXERS: Keep club soda, seltzer, and tonic in steady supply. Fresh fruit juices are easy to make and better than anything from a bottle.

GARNISHES: Lemons, limes, and other citrus are the most versatile, for wedges and twists; fresh mint, basil, and other herbs brighten summer drinks. Olives, cocktail onions, pickled items (cucumbers, dilly beans, okra), and other salty goods are also worth having on hand.

WHERE TO STORE

There are many ways to create a home bar, and to suit any space. Keep in mind that spirits should be kept in a cool place, away from direct sunlight; vermouth and other fortified wines need refrigeration.

- Traditional bar carts offer portability and style, as do other rolling carts with shelves (think stainless steel ones meant for the kitchen).

- An armoire or credenza offers more storage (and doors to hide the goods). Convert a standard piece with a few alterations, such as adjustable shelves and stemware racks.

- Wall-mounted shelves and wine-bottle racks are great space-saving options (see page 86 for one idea).

- If space is really tight, simply set out everything on attractive trays and rest on top of a credenza, coffee table, or other accessible surface.

MUST-HAVE TOOLS

MUDDLER (A): This wooden tool is essential for making proper mojitos, juleps, and other drinks where fresh herbs and citrus are key.

CUTTING BOARD AND PARING KNIFE (B): A small board is just right for prepping garnishes.

ICE BUCKET AND TONGS (C): Stainless steel ones keep in the cold. You can also improvise with a galvanized tin tub.

JULEP STRAINER (D): Rest it on the serving glass when pouring in a stirred cocktail—not just juleps—to strain out muddled mint or other solids.

BOTTLE OPENER AND CORKSCREW (E): The classic "waiter's key" is still the go-to choice.

SHAKER (F): The two-part kind (without the spout on top) is the favorite of pros; the one here has convenient measurements for common cocktails marked on the glass canister.

COCKTAIL SPOON (G): They come in a range of sizes; the long-handled one shown here lets you stir pitcher drinks with ease.

HAWTHORNE STRAINER (H): The coil does the straining and won't clog; use it when pouring drinks from a shaker.

JIGGER (I): Look for one that has both a quarter-ounce and half-ounce measure on either end, or with levels marked inside.

HONORARY MENTION

- Skewers and/or toothpicks
- Stirrers and/or swizzle sticks
- Peeler or zester, for citrus
- Vacuum stoppers, including for champagne
- Bartender's guide, recipe book, or both

HOW TO
SERVE WINE

When choosing wine for entertaining, personal preferences are a good place to start. Odds are, if you are fond of a particular Pinot Noir, your guests will appreciate drinking it, too. Serving it at the right temperature is also key to maximum enjoyment.

WINE BASICS

Great wines for special gatherings can be found at all price points. Spend a bit more on selections for more formal or intimate dinner parties, when everyone will be able to savor the wine.

KNOW YOUR MENU: This is the best way to ensure you select wines that will pair well with the food being served, and you can always ask your wine merchant for help. It can even be helpful to bring your recipes with you to the store, so that the vendor can suggest wines to complement all the dishes.

MIX IT UP: A variety of red and white wines will accommodate guests who may have a preference, and will provide an interesting selection. Try serving a white wine with the first course, then offer a red wine with the rest of the meal. Or pour one balanced, medium-bodied red and a similarly food-friendly white throughout the meal, depending on your menu.

THINK SEASONALLY: For lighter, warm-weather sipping, you might lean toward lighter whites and reds—and rosé, the summer staple. That said, jammy Zinfandel is pretty fantastic at a summer barbecue. Full-bodied whites and reds have the stamina for heartier cold-weather braises and stews that would overpower lighter options.

GO REGIONAL: What grows together, goes together. That means pairing Italian dishes with wine from the same region (such as ribollita and Montepulciano, boeuf bourguignon with Burgundy, and tapas or paella with a Rioja red or other Spanish wine).

HOW MUCH TO BUY

Depending on your pour, a standard (750 ml) bottle of wine has 4 to 6 glasses—but generally 5 five-ounce glasses. Plan on two-thirds of a bottle per guest, more if you'll be serving wine before dinner and/or are having a multiple-course meal.

STORING

If you're stocking up on wine and storing it for any longer than a few days, heed the following tips:

- Keep the bottles away from direct sunlight (and fluorescent lights) as well as any heat-transmitting devices, such as an oven.

- The ideal conditions are a cool room temperature (preferably around 60 degrees), which is typically what's found in a basement or cellar, if you have one.

SERVING

- Wine (and beer) will be perfectly chilled after one hour in the refrigerator. The ideal temperature for white wine is 45 to 50 degrees. If it's too warm, the flavors can be muddled; too cold, they're harder to detect.

- While red wines are usually served at room temperature, their ideal range is a slightly cooler 50 to 65 degrees (lighter reds at the lower end and robust ones at the higher). So you might want to give them a brief chill on especially warm days.

GLASSWARE

Most people are fine with basic red (deeper) and white (slimmer) glasses—plus flutes or coupes for sparklers. It's also perfectly appropriate to serve wine in tumblers, trattoria-style, at casual gatherings.

ALL-PURPOSE WINES

FULL-BODIED REDS

Barolo, Bordeaux, Cabernet Sauvignon, Carménère, Malbec, Syrah (or Shiraz), Zinfandel

LIGHT-TO-MEDIUM-BODIED REDS

Barbera, Beaujolais, Chianti, Côtes du Rhône, Montepulciano, Pinot Noir (or Burgundy), Tempranillo, Sangiovese

FULL-BODIED WHITES

Chardonnay (oaked), Gewürztraminer, Grüner Veltliner, Viognier, Riesling (dry), Pinot Blanc

LIGHT-TO-MEDIUM-BODIED WHITES

Albariño, Chablis, Chenin Blanc, Gavi, Pinot Grigio (or Pinot Gris), Sauvignon Blanc, Verdicchio

HOW TO
CREATE A CHEESE BOARD

There are many reasons cheese boards are a popular choice for entertaining: They work as starters or even as entire meals, are easy to get right (even on the first try), and offer guests a chance to sample many different flavors.

CHOOSING THE CHEESES

Some combinations work better than others, so pay attention to the following factors.

BUY THE RIGHT AMOUNT: Aim for three to five cheeses, or up to seven for a larger group. Plan on about 3½ ounces of cheese (total) per guest, or 1 pound per five guests. If the cheese board is the main part of a meal, up the per-person amount to 5 ounces.

VARY THE TASTES: The selections should include different ages, textures, and types of milk (cow, goat, sheep). Remember, cheeses that look different usually taste different.

MIX THE TEXTURES: Try one fresh, smooth cheese, such as mild goat or mozzarella, and a buttery one with a soft, edible rind, like Brie or Camembert. Then add one or two semi-hard or hard cheeses: Go for a milder one, like Gruyère or Manchego, or a dry, sharp variety, such as Pecorino Romano or Parmigiano-Reggiano. If you like, include a blue cheese (creamy Roquefort or pungent Stilton both work).

LOOK FOR DIFFERENT SHAPES: Opt for one or two wedges, a small round, a single-wheel cheese, and a pyramid. If using multiple wedges, cut them in different sizes.

STICK TO ONE REGION: Whether Italian, French, or Spanish, staying within one region helps unify the spread. Or keep it local by visiting your farmers' market to pick up artisanal cheeses.

SERVING SUGGESTIONS

Here's how to get the most out of the cheese.

TEMPERATURE: Most types of cheese will taste best after resting for about an hour at room temperature, softer ones (especially fresh goat cheese) about half that time.

SLICING: Cut larger ones (wheels and blocks) just before serving to keep them from drying out. Provide a table knife or cheese spreader for each soft cheese, and sharper knives or slicers for harder varieties.

ROUNDING OUT THE PLATTER

Cheese may be the star attraction, but the accoutrements help highlight its qualities.

- Aim to tick off all the tastes (salty, sweet, bitter, sour, and umami) plus provide crunchy contrast to the creamy cheeses. Add chutneys, jams, and fruit pastes; fresh and dried fruits; roasted nuts and chickpeas; olives and caper berries; and cornichons and other pickles.

- For the bases, a baguette and water crackers are classic components, but crostini, flatbreads, and rustic breads are other good options. It's nice to offer a gluten-free option, too.

- Regional cheeses, such as a Spanish trio of Manchego, Cabrales, and Idiazábal, go best with regional specialties, such as serrano ham, quince paste, Marcona almonds, blood oranges, and piquillo peppers.

MARTHA MUST

When I was growing up, a picnic was often a board of freshly picked cucumbers, sliced tomatoes, blocks of farmer's cheese, and cold stuffed cabbage (*golumpki*) with sour cream. I love to recreate those displays as cheese boards, with artisanal black bread and ricotta, plus homemade cottage cheese and my own backyard honey.

HOW TO
HOST A WEEKEND BRUNCH

Because of the midmorning timing, you can serve breakfast favorites, lunch to-go's, or a combination of the two. To keep it appropriately low-key, lean into dishes that can be made in advance and scale up if you need to serve a crowd.

PLAN THE MENU

Start by having at least one egg dish and one hearty dish, then build around those with baked goods and a salad of sorts. You'll want coffee and tea, of course, plus fresh fruit and juices. A cocktail or mocktail is also in order.

EGG DISHES

When deciding what egg dish to make, consider those that can be prepared in advance.

- Instead of individual omelets, you can make one big one by pouring the beaten eggs in a rimmed baking sheet, baking until just set, then layering with the filling of choice and rolling up into a log. This makes a lovely centerpiece that can be sliced and served at the table. Or skip the rolling and sprinkle fresh herbs onto the eggs halfway through baking, then cut into squares to serve.

- Stratas can be assembled the night before, refrigerated, and cooked just before serving.

- Even poached eggs can be held for a couple hours, so you can stack them on toasts with other toppings to serve. Or, make them a day before, cool quickly in an ice bath, and then store covered with cold water in the refrigerator; to serve, place the eggs briefly in a pan of barely simmering water, just until warmed through.

HEARTY DISHES

Eggs aren't the only dish with enough heft to see your guests through to dinner. There are many others to choose from:

- Guest-worthy sandwiches include croque monsieurs (or madames), Cubanos, panini (the classic Caprese, for example), and tartines or other toasts (try avocado and Manchego)—all great for brunch.

- Homemade gravlax is simple to prepare and impressive to serve, atop potato cakes or galettes, or the classic way: with bagels, cream cheese, thinly sliced red onion, and capers.

- Sprinkle thick bacon slices with brown sugar and bake on a rack set in a foil-lined baking sheet until crisp and browned—and your kitchen is smelling amazing.

MARTHA MUST

Bloody Marys are still one of my favorite brunch cocktails. I prepare my own spicy base from fresh tomato juice a day ahead. To serve, I set out pitchers of the base along with chilled vodka and assorted garnishes, such as pickled vegetables from my garden.

BREADS AND SWEETS

These are the crux of the meal, according to many a brunchgoer. The more guests you are having, the more you should look into make-aheads. Include at least one gluten-free option, too; almond, chickpea, quinoa, and other alternative flours, as well as packaged blends that can be substituted for regular flour in equal measure, will let you bake those with ease.

■ Pancakes and waffles can be cooked before guests arrive and then kept warm in the oven until ready to serve. Consider the go-withs, too, offering peak-of-season fruit along with whipped mascarpone or crème fraîche—or just creamy butter and warmed maple syrup.

■ For an easy take on French toast, layer thickly sliced bread with the egg mixture in a casserole dish the night before, cover and refrigerate, then bake in the morning before guests arrive.

■ You can't go wrong with coffee cakes, muffins, quick breads, and scones—all of which you can make the day before.

TIP

If you're having families over for brunch, skip the tablecloth and roll out a length of kraft paper at the kids' table. Stamp or draw a design down the center for them to color in, and then set out a cup of crayons or colored pencils.

SALADS AND SIDES

The key is to balance the richer, sweeter options with fresh and lively flavors.

■ Frisée, escarole, and kale make great salads for chilly mornings; baby greens and fresh herbs for warmer days. Toss with a sherry vinaigrette, adding thinly sliced fennel or radishes, chopped toasted nuts, fresh or dried fruit, and other elements for more flavor and textural contrast.

■ Or opt for asparagus, leeks, or haricots verts with a vinaigrette in the spring; fresh sliced heirloom tomatoes drizzled with pesto in the summer; roasted root vegetables in the fall; and wilted kale or other hearty greens with bacon in the winter.

FRUIT AND GRAINS

The freshest peak-of-season fruit speaks for itself, without any further embellishing. When you want a little extra substance, consider these options as well.

■ Instead of individual parfaits, make a larger shareable dish: Layering yogurt and granola in a glass compote lets the fare double as a centerpiece. For a winter spin, try warm pineapple; first heat the fruit with sugar and oats until soft and caramelized before layering over yogurt and topping with chopped and toasted hazelnuts.

■ For mix-and-match bowls, you can prepare a big batch of oatmeal, quinoa, or barley, then set out fresh, dried, or roasted fruit, creamy yogurt or ricotta, toasted nuts and seeds, and other desired toppings that guests can pick and choose from.

DIY TOAST BAR

A fun and carefree way to entertain at brunch is to set out trays of toasted bread—whole grain, sourdough, and rye, for example—along with assorted mix-and-match (and make-ahead) toppings, such as the ones shown opposite. Then let guests help themselves. This way there's sure to be something to please every palate (and people can skip the bread, if they prefer).

SUGGESTED TOPPINGS

■ Cured meats and smoked fish

■ Boiled or poached eggs

■ Fresh or cooked vegetables

■ Fresh or dried fruit

■ Jams, mustard, labneh, and other spreads

■ Honey and maple syrup, for drizzling

■ Chopped nuts, seeds, and other sprinkles

HOW TO
THROW A
COCKTAIL PARTY

Entertaining on a budget? Prefer to
snack as you sip and chat? Then skip
the seated dinner and have a drink-
focused fete instead.

PLAN THE DRINKS

There's no right or wrong way to serve drinks,
so choose a method that suits the occasion.

SELF-SERVE BAR: For a casual gathering, a rea-
sonably priced selection of spirits and mixers
(see page 240) set on a table or counter will
allow guests to serve themselves.

SIGNATURE DRINKS: Consider mixing one of your
own favorites or something that's a bit unexpected, so guests can experience a new drink.
Then send everyone home with the recipe.

BIG-BATCH COCKTAILS: Rather than mixing
individual drinks, prepare multiple servings
in pitchers, carafes, or punch bowls ahead
of time. Sangria and margaritas are just the
beginning. Hold off on adding ice until the
party gets going.

NONALCOHOLIC OPTIONS: No matter which
way you go with the cocktails, always make
sure to have ample nonalcoholic refreshers
on hand, too, both for mixing and sipping.
Choose among flavored seltzers, small-batch
sodas, sparkling water, lemonade, and fresh
fruit juices—or create a signature mocktail.

TIP

For double-duty drinks, prepare nonalcoholic
punches for all to enjoy, setting out a bottle or
two of liquor so any of your guests can spike
their own beverages.

DRINK CALCULATOR

The average guest will have two drinks per hour. See the chart below to determine how many bottles to buy.

1 liter alcohol (33.8 ounces)	=	22 drinks (each 1.5 ounces)
1 750-milliliter bottle wine	=	5 five-ounce glasses
1.5 liter bottle wine	=	10 five-ounce glasses
1 bottle Champagne	=	5 flute or 6 coupe glasses
1 case Champagne or wine	=	60 five-ounce glasses

PLAN THE MENU

In general, the earlier the party, the lighter the fare can be. Then again, cocktails fuel appetites, and it is better to err on the side of having too much food rather than not enough—and you can always send your guests off with any extras for the ride home.

- For a two-hour party that begins around 6 p.m., aim for five or six different appetizers, each yielding two to three servings per guest.

- If the party starts and/or ends later and lasts longer, you'll need more sustenance. Plan on 8 to 10 options, each with at least three servings per guest. Choose options with a bit more heft, including cheese platters (see page 245) and charcuterie.

- Be sure to load up on make-aheads and room-temperature offerings as well as dishes that can easily be replenished throughout the evening, without much effort on your part.

TIP

If guests will be standing, you'll want to serve only finger foods; likewise, if you plan to serve anything requiring a fork (and knife), be sure to provide enough seating.

HOW TO GIVE A TOAST

Whether thanking the host of a party or congratulating the happy couple, the goal as a toast giver is to be entertaining while keeping the spotlight on the person being toasted.

BE SPECIFIC

Share one-of-a-kind anecdotes that bring that person and your relationship to life. In other words, no one else but you should be able to give that toast.

SHOW RESPECT

That said, don't get too personal. Ask yourself if the honoree will appreciate having that memory shared with everyone in the room. There's also nothing wrong with running something you plan to say by the person, assuming it won't spoil a surprise.

KNOW THE AUDIENCE

Make sure jokes are appropriate (in terms of ages and sensibilities) to the situation. A group of 20 close acquaintances is much different from a room of 100 mere acquaintances. Also, it's fine to poke fun so long as you know the person is also in on the joke.

BE IN THE MOMENT

Practice, to banish any butterflies, but keep your delivery natural, not stilted—nobody wants a robotic memorized speech.

TELL A STORY

Any good toast should have a beginning, middle, and end. And don't go on for too long—three to five minutes, tops.

HOW TO
PLAN A DINNER PARTY

Having guests over for dinner involves some proper planning and preparation. If it's your first time, the magic number of guests is six—it's enough people to feel festive without too many to cook for. But even if it's your fiftieth party, you'll benefit by reading the following tips.

PLAN THE MENU

Dinner parties require their own planning protocol, including a considered menu.

- The best appetizers serve to stimulate your guests' appetites—not fill them up. Think vegetables and dips, nuts, and light cheeses.

- Pair dinner items with seasonal produce (asparagus in spring, tomatoes in summer, root vegetables in autumn).

- Aim for items that can be made in advance rather than those requiring last-minute attention.

- Don't overcrowd your oven or stovetop with too many dishes.

- Now is not the time to tackle a brand-new recipe without giving it a test run; better to stick with something that's tried-and-true.

- Do consider special diets, but don't let them rule the day. Provide enough meatless options for vegetarians, and include some gluten-free, nut-free, and dairy-free items.

ESTABLISH A TIMELINE

This step should be done at the outset—allowing you time to adjust the offerings to incorporate more make-aheads, or dishes that can be cooked at the same time (one on the stove, another in the oven).

- Plan the order in which you'll make each recipe by starting with the serving time, then working backward.

- Be sure to include any special information for make-aheads, noting storage and heating instructions; some frozen items, for example, can go straight into the oven, while others require thawing first.

- Take inventory of the serving pieces, glasses, flatware, and table linens you'll need; it's a good idea to gather these together and put a note inside each one to mark what you plan to serve in it.

- Devise a schedule that includes all the other elements of the event, too (see right).

STRATEGIZE YOUR SHOPPING

Read through all recipes as soon as you've finalized the menu. Do this early enough that you can buy, rent, or borrow any necessary items.

- List all ingredients, organizing them into three categories: those you already have, those that can be bought in advance, and those that should be purchased closer to the event (fresh produce, bread, and fish).

- Note anything that requires advance ordering, such as a rack of lamb that the butcher will clean for you, or your favorite oysters from Maine.

- Be sure to include beer, wine, and non-alcoholic options, as well as ice.

DINNER PARTY TIMELINE

THE MONTH BEFORE

- Make your guest list and send invitations.

THREE WEEKS BEFORE

- Choose the menu and make shopping lists.
- Stock up on pantry items, such as sugar, flour, and other non-perishables.

TWO WEEKS BEFORE

- Buy wine and liquor.

A WEEK BEFORE

- Follow up with guests who have not RSVP'd.

TWO TO THREE DAYS BEFORE

- Set out all serving pieces.
- Prep centerpieces and make-ahead dishes.

THE NIGHT BEFORE

- Set the table.
- Prep all produce for remaining dishes.

THE DAY OF

- Chill wine.
- Follow your cooking timeline.

SET AN INVITING SCENE

You could do nothing more than clear the clutter and set the table for a low-key, weeknight get-together. But it doesn't take much time, effort, or know-how to improve the ambience.

- Dim the lights and set out candles for that soft, warm glow.

- Music is a must. Create a playlist or let your favorite music app do its thing.

- For the table itself, just let your style and the season guide the settings, striving for harmony over hodgepodge (see page 257 for more tips on setting an informal table).

- Layer on the comfort. Bring out extra pillows, floor cushions, and throws for nestling on the sofa before or after dinner.

- Don't forget the bathroom(s). Special soaps and hand towels are nice touches, as are scented candles.

CHOOSE A STYLE

Consider your space and budget constraints when determining the type of party.

- Factor in liquor, food, and flowers or decorations to establish your initial budget. Think drinks first, as alcohol can be a major expense.

- For a sit-down meal, you must have dishes, flatware, glassware, linens, seating, and serving pieces (plus enough chairs!).

- For a family-style buffet, you'll still need serveware but can forgo more formal place settings.

TIP

Make a plan for clearing the table and holding dirty dishes during the party. Start the evening with an empty dishwasher and sink. Designate a spot in the kitchen to store dirty plates and glasses; soak flatware and serving spoons in a large bowl. Use cooling racks for additional drying.

BUFFET BASICS

Menus for buffets and open houses easily lend themselves to advance preparation, as the dishes must be able to sit for an hour or so at room temperature (or to be reheated and replenished as needed). Also, the food should be easy to handle, since guests will serve themselves. This may simply mean slicing steak into thinner-than-usual pieces, or cutting pies into wedges and placing on individual plates.

QUANTITY

- When calculating the amount of food to serve, use the five-servings-per-guest formula for lighter appetizers: If you are having a party for 20, look at the yield for each dish and make sure you have a total of 100 servings (5 times 20).

- Serve at least two entrée choices, making one vegetarian if some of your guests don't eat meat.

- Plan on one main-dish serving per guest, with an extra portion for every fourth guest; that means you would need 12 to 13 servings of each entrée for a party of 20.

PRESENTATION

There are no rules governing the layout of a buffet, though common sense suggests a certain order of the day. Start by placing the table so guests can access food from both sides, especially if serving a sizable crowd.

- Stack plates at the head of the table and silverware and napkins at the other end.

- The main courses go first, with accompanying condiments in separate bowls on each side of the serving dish.

- The sides come next; make sure to provide a large serving spoon or fork (or nice-looking tongs) for each dish.

- Before plating hot foods, heat the platters in the oven.

- Place cold foods on ice, keeping extra servings in the refrigerator.

- Keep desserts in the kitchen until after the main meal, or set them all out on their own table.

MARTHA MUST

Buffets are one of my favorite ways to entertain year-round, including in the summer, when much of the food can be cooked on the grill throughout the party and I can grill the meat to order for my guests. This also lets me share vegetables from my garden, as they hold up well when seasoned ahead of time, and taste equally good served hot or at room temperature.

HOW TO
SET A TABLE

A well-planned and -executed meal deserves a well-considered table. How you go about setting the table depends on the style of the dinner. Below are the two most common scenarios, explained.

INFORMAL

For more casual dinner parties, many people tend to forgo the fuss and stick with the standard five-piece setting: dinner plate, wine glass, and fork, knife, spoon. But even that "rule" is open to interpretation. What matters most is that the table is welcoming.

MIX AND MATCH: Varying dishes, flatware, glasses—even chairs—creates interest, so long as you have some unifying element (be it color or pattern or decorating detail). Even if you're not using your fine china for the full setting, a few pieces here and there add elegance.

RETHINK THE CENTERPIECE: While an oversize arrangement makes a striking statement, you can get just as much impact with a mix of smaller items, such as sweet bouquets (as shown opposite), potted plants, foliage and other garden clippings (as on page 252), or hurricane lanterns. There's power in multiples.

DESIGNATE SEATS: This will help any dinner party run more smoothly—especially when there are eight or more guests. Plus, place cards add to the décor.

EMPLOY SERVING DISHES: Use cutting boards, platters, trays, baskets (for bread), bins, jars, and other vessels to house the odds and ends and keep the table tidy, not jumbled.

FORMAL

Time was when kids would be taught table-setting techniques in school (or by their diligent grandparents). Nowadays even many grown-ups are unfamiliar with the proper arrangement of plates, glasses, and flatware. But it's never too late, and it's easy to pick up.

THE BASIC BLUEPRINT
Although these guidelines might seem arbitrary, they are based on a certain logic. (See page 258 for a visual guide.)

- Because most people are right-handed, knives and glasses are placed on that side and forks are on the left, where they can be used to steady the meat while the stronger hand does the cutting.

- The flatware is placed, left to right, in the order in which it will be used.

- Glasses for water and white wine are placed closer to guests than those for red wine because they are traditionally provided first. (The water glass should be filled before guests are seated, and white wine is typically served next, to complement the lighter dishes in the first few courses.)

- The dinner plate usually rests on a charger, which is meant to keep the tablecloth free of crumbs and spills and is usually removed along with the plate, before dessert is served.

SPOTLESS SILVER

Protect your investment with the following steps.

POLISH

- Start by inspecting the piece for past polish marks and polish in that pattern, using a light touch.

- Use only liquids or creams specifically made for silver; acidic silver dips are too harsh.

- Work near a sink so you can rinse the pieces as you go.

MAINTAIN

- Wash heirloom silverware by hand, never in the dishwasher.

- Keep new pieces apart in the dishwasher, so they don't damage one another (and don't mix silver and stainless steel).

STORE

- Keep silver in a chest lined with tarnish-resistant fabric.

HOW TO SET A FORMAL TABLE

Note the symmetry in the setting below, which both keeps things orderly and appeals to the eye.

MARTHA MUST

A no-sew table "silencer" or liner mutes the clanking of plates and cutlery, and shields the table's surface from spills and heat. Purchase heavyweight felt or baize (woven wool that's napped like felt) at fabric stores, measure the size of your tabletop, and cut the fabric to fit (felt doesn't fray, so no hemming is needed). Place it under the tablecloth and, if you like, attach ties to the corners (using safety pins) to secure it to table legs.

1. The bread plate and the butter knife sit above the forks.

2. Above the dinner plate are a dessert fork and spoon.

3. The stemware forms a triangle. The water glass sits above the knife, the white-wine glass is to its lower right, and the red-wine glass is above them.

4. From left, the forks are for the salad and main course.

5. The napkin is placed on the center plate or charger, but it can also be placed to the left of the plate under the forks or to the left of the forks.

6. To the right of the plate, from left, are the dinner knife and the soup spoon.

TIP

If you plan to provide individual saltcellars, set them anywhere above the dessert utensils.

THE DESSERT COURSE

Whisk away most of the dinner-course dishes, leaving the water glass and dessert utensils on the table.

- Replace the dinner plate with the dessert plate.

- Position the coffee cup or teacup and saucer to the right of the dessert plate, with a teaspoon, which goes on the saucer or the table.

- After-dinner drinks, such as brandy or dessert wine, are served when dessert is finished.

THE TABLE LINENS

Formal need not be fussy when it comes to layering on the linens. A crisp white tablecloth is still the standard-bearer—and provides a soothing backdrop for china in all shades and styles.

- The four most common shapes and sizes of tablecloths are 54 inches square, 70 inches round, and rectangles in 60 inches by 90 inches or 70 inches by 108 inches.

> **TIP**
>
> If you will have candles on a formal table, brand-new white taper candles are the most traditional option. Light them before everyone is seated and extinguish (preferably with a candle snuffer) after they leave the table.

- Bear in mind the desired drop is 10 to 15 inches—so the cloth hangs around lap level—for a formal table, and a little less for a more informal occasion, such as brunch or lunch.

- That said, if you have a beautiful hand-stitched tablecloth with a shorter drop, you should feel free to use that piece, as long as it covers your view of the underside of the table.

- Be sure the drop is even and level on all sides, and that it looks proportional to your table.

- For the napkins, there is no hard-and-fast rule to the way they are folded, only that they be folded—neatly and uniformly across the table (see Napkin and Flatware Etiquette, at right, for more guidelines).

NAPKIN AND FLATWARE ETIQUETTE

Follow these rules during formal dinners.

NAPKINS

- Wait for the host to place her napkin in her lap before following suit. If there is no host at the table, place the napkin in your lap as soon as you are seated.

- Keep the napkin on your lap until after dessert.

- If you leave the table during the meal, rest the napkin, soiled side up, on the seat.

- When finished eating, place the napkin to the left of the plate setting—unless the plate has been cleared, in which case put the napkin in that spot.

FLATWARE

- To show you're still eating, place the fork at eight o'clock, tines facing down, and the knife at four o'clock, blade facing in.

- To show you're done, set your knife and fork at four o'clock, fork tines facing up.

HOW TO
HOST HOUSEGUESTS

Whomever you'll be hosting, whether it's for just one night or an extended holiday weekend (or even longer), you'll want to make your home hospitable—and your company as comfortable as can be. That's not at all difficult to do: Pay attention to the little details that add up to a welcoming environment.

PLAN AND PREPARE

Take the time to put your home in good order before your guests arrive.

REFILL SUPPLIES: Put toilet paper and other bathroom essentials (hand soap, Q-tips, cotton balls) in plain view so guests don't have to go searching for them. Replace any missing or limited items in your first-aid kit. Purchase everyday medicines in case anyone catches a cold or has other common complaints.

EQUIP THE HOUSE: Keep extra phone and tablet chargers on hand. Outfit bathrooms and hallways with nightlights. Check batteries in smoke and carbon-monoxide alarms. Replace any burned-out light bulbs. Order more firewood and gather kindling.

STOCK UP ON FOOD AND REFRESHMENTS: Find out ahead of time if there are any special dietary needs. It's a good idea to have ample snacks and breakfast items so your guests can fend for themselves, especially for families and early risers. Now's the time to restock your home bar, too (see page 240).

TIP

Include refillable water bottles or carafes for guests' bedsides. If you're short on tables, substitute a chair, which doubles as extra seating.

CHILDPROOF (OR PET-PROOF) YOUR HOME: If there will be little ones in tow (of the two- or four-legged variety), you may need to put safety gates at the top or bottom of stairs and to make sure any potentially hazardous items are well out of reach, indoors and out.

THINK SEASONALLY: Provide extra blankets in the winter and a small fan in summer; Turkish cotton robes are appreciated all year round. Bonus points for blackout blinds (or temporary shields) in a sunny guest room. Don't forget about extra beach towels and picnic blankets for warmer months, woolens (hats, gloves, and scarves) during the cold season.

GREET AND GET SITUATED

Starting off on the right foot will help set the tone for the rest of the stay. The goal? Letting them feel free to explore on their own.

MAKE A CARE PACKAGE: Prepare a "make yourself at home" basket filled with toiletries and snacks. Have a toothbrush, hair dryer, and other bath basics on standby in case they forgot their own. Include brochures for local attractions, and a local magazine if there is one, to get them acquainted with the area.

BE AN ENTERTAINMENT ENVOY: Share brochures and websites for local sights, restaurants, kid-friendly activities, parks, museums, and other attractions. Offer up your membership cards (or numbers) for discounts and deals.

CREATE AN INFORMATION STATION: Provide Wi-Fi and other passwords, home-security alarm codes, and the location of fire extinguishers.

DO A WALK-THROUGH: Demonstrate how to use the TV and remotes (and provide passwords for streaming their favorite shows). Ditto the fireplace and any special kitchen gear.

ENGAGE AND ENTERTAIN

Some guests are more self-sufficient than others. Either way, make the most of their stay by providing enjoyable diversions.

PLAN AT-HOME AMUSEMENT: Include a reading light and a selection of books and magazines for bedtime reading. Board games and puzzles are good rainy-day pastimes, and lawn games are welcome warm-weather activities. Movie nights with popcorn are great for kids.

PLAN GROUP ACTIVITIES: While you are not expected to go on all outings with your guests, you'll want to plan at least one or two for the whole group. Attend an outdoor concert in the summer, go apple picking in the fall, or hit the slopes in the winter. Or visit a museum anytime of the year.

COOK A MEAL: It's fine to treat your guests to lunch or dinner at a local hot spot, but you'll want to spend an enjoyable evening at home at least one night during their stay—preferably the day they arrive, when they may be tired from traveling.

SEND OFF IN STYLE: Make a point of gathering any souvenirs and photos each day, so you can present them with a going-away scrapbook or other remembrance of their visit.

HOUSEGUEST ETIQUETTE

Just as important as being a generous host is being a gracious guest.

1. Let the host know of any special accommodations (dietary or otherwise) upon accepting the invitation, not on arrival.

2. Offer to help out—but never insist. Do, however, always pick up after yourself.

3. Respect your host's privacy; don't be intrusive. If your host skipped a couple doors on your initial tour, consider those off-limits.

4. Silence your phone. If you must make any calls, do so outside or in your own room. Same rules apply for your kids.

5. If you're an early riser and your host isn't, use this time to check emails and texts, or slip out for a run.

6. Be sure to offer to pick up the tab, for grocery-store runs as well as when eating out.

7. Don't arrive empty-handed. Pick a gift that shows you appreciate being invited.

ENJOY

I have always found the most enjoyment from learning and doing. Even when I'm not working, I am always active, hiking the extensive trails near my home in Maine, riding my horses in Bedford, biking at the beach, traveling around the world, or practicing yoga.

And when I discover a new activity that I love, I want to learn everything about it. I encourage you to do the same. Determine what brings you joy and pursue it wholeheartedly.

This chapter includes a selection of activities, like lawn games, that are really wonderful diversions. When I was growing up, many of my friends had horseshoe courts or croquet on their lawns; several even had bocce, though it wasn't as common as it is today. You needed that perfect spot—rectangular and level. I still enjoy croquet and even have a regulation-size court on my lawn in Bedford.

In this chapter, we go through the rules of these games and more. We also instruct you how to maintain your bike, so you can ride confidently with the knowledge that you can fix a flat tire. (And always, always wear a helmet!) You can finally learn how to do a sun salutation to start your day, and how to build a fire, either inside or out.

Whatever you do, keep discovering new activities. Never stop learning and doing—and enjoy every minute.

PACK FOR
A PICNIC

Any time is a good time to load the hamper and revel in a picnic—even if it's in your own backyard. Just as when packing for a trip, *compact* and *lightweight* are the watchwords, as is *organized*. Keep the food simple, and take care when putting all the essentials into your carryall. Remember: Heavy items go first, lighter items on top.

WHAT TO PACK

It all starts with the carrier. For traditionalists, there's the classic woven hamper with the double-sided, flip-up wooden top, which can also serve as a "table." If storage (and weight, as the old-fashioned style can be cumbersome) is an issue, consider a collapsible market tote, which has a rigid frame on top (for stability) and is lightweight by design. Bonus: Many market totes are insulated. Some people choose to go with two large canvas totes, one for chilled items and the other for everything else. Look for one with pockets to provide storage for all the inevitable odds and ends, including the following.

BLANKET: There's no one-size-fits-all when it comes to picnic blankets. Repurpose an old quilt or coverlet, use a generously sized Turkish towel (or two), or unfurl a large tablecloth, first throwing down a canvas drop cloth as a shield from damp grass. You can also buy waterproof blankets made from oilcloth or nylon ripstop, which are equally impervious to mud and food stains, and clean up easily. Whichever you use, roll them up and tie with sturdy cotton clothesline, forming a loop for an over-the-shoulder sling.

PLATES AND BOWLS: Choose stackable melamine or enamelware dishes, as these are washable and chip-proof. Eco-friendly (reusable or disposable) bamboo and compostable paper plates are other good options; both are available at many supermarkets.

FLATWARE: Reusable stainless steel is the best choice, and you can pick up inexpensive sets just for this purpose (or hunt some down at flea markets). As with plates, eco-friendly options exist. Be sure to tuck in as many large serving spoons as you need.

DRINKWARE: Acrylic wineglasses (look for stackable ones) are a leap forward from the flimsy plastic variety and come with or without stems; plus, they are dishwasher-safe. Ditto for tumblers.

CUTTING BOARD: Besides providing a surface for cutting cheese, fruit, and other picnic fare, a board makes a nifty serving tray for drinks and appetizers. Choose slender, lightweight bamboo or wood boards that look nice and are also functional. Bring along parchment to line the board, for easy cleanup.

SHARP KNIFE: Look for serrated blades that are sharp enough to slice cleanly through tomatoes and bread, as well as smooth blades sturdy enough for hard cheeses and salami. Foldable models (and there are many) offer storage, as do knives that come in protective sheaths. There are even "picnic knives" with a corkscrew in the handle.

CORKSCREW AND BOTTLE OPENER: If you are packing wine and beer, these are likely a must (and better safe than sorry).

PACKING TIPS

Organize your carrier according to when you will use the items, from bottom (later) to top (immediately).

- Corral flatware in a tall jar, or fold each set in a napkin and roll up in a washable or bamboo placemat (A).

- Stackable, reusable storage containers work best (B). Take-out cartons (sold at party or crafts stores) are another fun option (C).

- Wrap sandwiches using food-safe paper in cheery patterns (D).

- Put your lemonade and iced tea in large sealable pitchers (E) or jars; when making those items, replace some of the water with ice—or frozen fruit—to keep them cold (without diluting).

- Frozen water bottles (F) help keep food cold during transport and later offer refreshment; otherwise, use frozen gel packs to keep food from spoiling.

- Keep salads fresh in a sealed container (G); pack vinaigrette separately and toss just before serving to avoid sogginess.

OTHER TIPS

- If you are bringing along the makings of a cheese board (see page 245), you can prearrange everything on the board, wrapping it tightly in plastic.

- Bring along biodegradable trash bags and wet wipes for cleanup.

- If necessary (such as when bringing raw meat for grilling on site), pack extra food containers for cooked leftovers; discard any perishable items left out in the sun for more than an hour.

HOW TO
HANG A HAMMOCK

One trip to the hardware store, and you're just a few basic sewing stitches away from an outdoor hammock. Secure it between two well-positioned trees or two poles planted firmly in the ground. Toss in a pillow, and relaxation awaits.

SUPPLIES

6-by-9-foot canvas drop cloth (8- to 10-ounce weight)

Sewing machine and sewing supplies

36 $7/16$-inch grommets and grommet-setting kit

Hammer or mallet

¼-inch cotton rope, 70 feet, cut into two equal lengths

2 O-rings

⅜-inch cotton rope (see step 5 for determining length)

Scissors or punch

MARTHA MUST

Use the gentle cycle on a front-loading machine to wash a hammock. Put macramé ones in a mesh laundry bag. Tie the ends of canvas ones to avoid tangling.

MAKE THE HAMMOCK

Be sure to use only drop cloths made of canvas, and in a sturdy enough weight.

1. Reinforce each 6-foot end of drop cloth by folding over 2 inches and stitching across.

2. Set 18 grommets along each sewn-down end, spaced equally, starting 1 inch in from edge (see Set the Grommets, right.)

3. Tie an end of one 35 foot length of ¼-inch rope into a knot. Thread unknotted end through back of first grommet, then through an O-ring, leaving 32 inches between O-ring and grommet. Run rope through front of next grommet, then over and under next two grommets before threading rope back through O-ring. Repeat pattern as shown until you have woven through all grommets. Knot rope at opposite end. You may need to adjust slack on rope to achieve even tension. (This is easiest when O-ring is being tugged in opposite direction.)

4. Repeat above on other end of drop cloth.

5. To hang, cut two pieces of ⅜-inch-thick rope at least twice as long as needed (double the distance to anchoring post, plus an additional 2 feet for tying). Fold each piece in half, and slip loop under an O-ring, then thread ends through loop to secure it. Hammock will hang lower when occupied, so secure it 12 to 18 inches above desired height, wrapping rope on either end around the tree and tying in a figure-8 knot or even a basic double knot.

SET THE GROMMETS

Grommets come in two pieces—a shank and a flat washer. Set grommets on a surface that won't bend when hammered, like a piece of scrap wood.

1. Cut or punch hole in drop cloth, slightly smaller than inside hole of grommet shank.

2. Place shank through hole in drop cloth (with right side facing grommet).

3. Place shank and drop cloth (shank side down) on round metal setting disk. Shank should rest in circular groove found on top of disk.

4. Place washer over shank, so metal sandwiches drop cloth.

5. Place setting tool with pointed end inside shank. Hammer to set.

HOW TO
PRACTICE MEDITATION AND YOGA

When it comes to slowing down and getting centered, yoga and its partners in peacefulness, meditation, and deep breathing are hard to beat. These age-old practices also improve your overall health and well-being, immeasurably boosting mind, body, and spirit.

TRY MEDITATION

Take a breath and hold for two or three seconds, observe your surroundings, identify how you feel, then exhale and proceed with your life. That's all meditation is—easy and accessible to everyone, with impressive mind-body benefits, including clearer focus, reduced stress, and possibly even long-term mental acuity.

Better yet, you can reap some of these benefits by meditating during spare minutes throughout your day—as you're waiting for the subway, walking the dog, or prepping the family dinner.

IF YOU JUST CAN'T FOCUS, try guided meditation. An instructor talks you through the exercise of clearing and centering your mind. Find a class at a gym or yoga studio, or listen to sessions—some as brief as five minutes—by downloading meditation apps.

IF YOU CAN'T BE STILL, try moving meditation. This popular practice says that if you can brush your teeth and sweep the floor, you can meditate. Indeed, a series of books by Vietnamese Buddhist monk Thich Nhat Hanh—including *How to Walk* and *How to Eat*—provides instruction on how to meditate while engaging in these and other everyday activities. Or see Sun Salutations, page 270, for another option.

IF YOU DON'T HAVE TIME, try building in the deep-breathing exercises that follow throughout the day. Take one or two minutes out of every hour—it all adds up.

PRACTICE DEEP BREATHING

Breathing deeply lifts your mood and calms the mind—and helps ease headaches, backaches, and muscle tension, too.

BASIC TECHNIQUE
Conscious breathing is a two-part process: Breathe in, then breathe out. Long, slow inhalation creates energy and lifts the lungs, heart, and upper body, stimulating the nervous system and giving your body a needed boost. Similarly, taking time when exhaling—while keeping your tongue, throat, and jaw relaxed—will quiet your thoughts and alleviate stress.

Breathing exercises can restore calm or energize the body, depending on the technique.

FOR RELAXATION
- Sit with your back against a wall and your legs crossed comfortably. Inhale slowly through your nose for six seconds, hold your breath for six, and then slowly exhale through your mouth for another six. Repeat this exercise 20 times. You'll feel your body unwind and your heart rate decrease.

- Another technique: Lie on your back with a rolled-up towel or a bolster pillow positioned lengthwise beneath your spine. Prop up your head with a folded pillow so that your forehead is just higher than your chin. Keep your arms out to your sides and your legs relaxed. This position opens your chest to maximize inhalation. Take smooth, slow breaths in through your nose and out through your mouth.

FOR ENERGY
- Sit with your back against a wall and your legs together and extended in front of you. Take 50 short, deep breaths from your belly, exhaling more slowly through your nose. Repeat this exercise three times.

- This technique can sharpen focus and help with circulation—it's a good exercise to practice before diving into an important task or starting an endurance workout.

INTRODUCTION TO YOGA

Most yoga classes draw upon one of the traditional disciplines. Depending on your goal—building strength, taking a mental break—some styles might be a better fit than others.

HATHA: A slower pace and basic moves make this class perfect for beginners. As a bonus, all modern forms of yoga stem from Hatha (the practice of physical asanas, or poses)—so the class can serve as an introduction to the practice as a whole.

IYENGAR: A meticulous style that focuses on achieving exact alignment. Props, such as blocks, rolls, or mats, can be used to help students refine their positioning and hold poses for longer.

BIKRAM: This style is practiced in intense heat (100-degrees-plus) to allow the muscles and ligaments in the body to stretch. Bring a water bottle and towel, and take frequent breaks if you're just starting out.

VINYASA: This discipline centers on Sun Salutations (see page 270), with an added aerobic element. Postures can flow at a challenging pace based on the teacher. (Power yoga classes can be similar and often tend to focus more on strength training.)

MARTHA MUST

My favorite time to practice Iyengar yoga is from 5 to 6 p.m., when I am limber and relaxed after work.

THE BASICS:
SUN SALUTATIONS

This energizing series of basic positions is designed to be performed at the beginning of the day (ideally sunrise)—or as a wonderful warm-up for other yoga routines and other types of exercise. Sync your movements to your breath (using your nose for breathing) to increase the physical benefits and reduce mental stress; repeat the sequence two to three times and work your way up to six or more.

MOUNTAIN (TADASANA)

Stand with big toes touching, heels slightly apart. Bring your hands together in front of your heart, keeping your shoulders relaxed. Lift the crown of the head upward, while taking deep breaths in and out through your nose.

UPWARD HAND
(URDHVA HASTASANA)

On an inhalation, sweep your arms out to your sides and bring the palms to touch up above your head, keeping your shoulders down. Lengthen your torso and gently bring your gaze to your hands.

STANDING FORWARD BEND
(UTTANASANA)

As you exhale, sweep your arms out to the sides and bend at the hips to come into a forward bend. Bring your fingertips to the floor alongside your feet. Let your head release downward.

UPWARD-FACING DOG
(URDHVA MUKHA SVANASANA)

As you inhale, straighten your arms and roll forward over your toes, lifting your hips, thighs, and shins off the floor. Press into the tops of your feet and palms while you gaze straight ahead.

DOWNWARD-FACING DOG
(ADHO MUKHA SVANASANA)

As you exhale, roll back over the toes and lift the hips to come into an inverted V shape, reaching the thighs back to lengthen the spine. Keep your shoulders down and release the weight of your head.

LUNGE

As you inhale, step forward with the leg you initially stepped back with, coming back into lunge pose. Keep your front knee bent at a 90-degree angle and your fingertips on the ground, on either side of the front foot.

LUNGE

Keeping your fingertips on the ground, inhale and take a giant step back with the right foot. The left knee bends at a 90-degree angle. (**NOTE:** *In your subsequent rounds of Sun Salutations, alternate the lunging leg to keep both sides of the body balanced.*)

PLANK

As you exhale, place your palms flat on the floor and step the left foot back to meet the right to reach a starting push-up position. Engage the hips and abdominal muscles to come into one straight line from head to feet.

FOUR-LIMBED STAFF (CHATURANGA DANDASANA)

At the end of an exhalation, bend your elbows straight back and lower your body down to the bottom of a push-up. Keep elbows close to your sides and your entire body long and engaged as you activate your core.

STANDING FORWARD BEND

Exhale and step your back foot forward; straighten your legs and fold your body over them, keeping your fingertips on the floor.

UPWARD HAND

With an inhale, rise up to a standing position. As you rise, reach your arms out and up over your head.

MOUNTAIN

Exhale and float your arms back into prayer position. Enjoy the stillness of this pose. Keep the chest broad, the legs engaged, and the spine long. You can choose to end your session here or go for another round.

HOW TO
PLAY LAWN GAMES

These traditional pastimes never go out of style. Learn the playbook for marshaling some matches on your home turf.

CROQUET

Don't let this sport's heritage as a court game fool you—croquet can get downright competitive. It's also easy for all ages and perfect for team play at a party.

EQUIPMENT

Nine wickets, two stakes, and four or more colored balls (blue, red, black, and yellow; some sets have green and orange, too), plus one mallet per player (or teams can share).

OBJECT OF THE GAME

In nine-wicket croquet, two sides (single players or teams of two) play through a course of arched metal-wire wickets and a pair of stakes. The first side to finish the course in the correct order wins.

COURT SETUP

A standard court is 50 by 100 feet, but the size can be scaled to fit your yard. Wickets are placed in two diamonds, with an extra wicket and a stake at each end. Backyard players can set up the court to work around trees and other fixed objects.

BASIC PLAY

These are the basic rules; variations can be found online at *croquetamerica.com/croquet/rules*.

■ The winner of a coin toss chooses his colors: either blue and black, or red and yellow. In singles, one person plays two balls; in doubles, it's one player per ball.

■ The balls are played in the sequence of blue, red, black, yellow. Players take turns striking the appropriate-color ball (the "striker ball") with a mallet.

■ One strike counts as a turn, unless the ball passes cleanly through a wicket, which earns the player one bonus stroke, or hits another ball (a "roquet"), which earns the player two bonus strokes.

■ In the case of a roquet, the player can pick up the striker ball, move it next to the ball that was roqueted, and hit the striker ball again (a "croquet shot"); after this, the roqueted ball is out of play until a wicket is run or the next turn begins.

TIPS AND TECHNIQUES

There is no wrong way to hold a mallet; you just have to swing at the ball instead of pushing it. The classic between-the-legs swing offers the most accuracy. The side stroke, similar to a golf swing, packs more power.

SCORING

The first team to maneuver both balls through the entire course (running all wickets and hitting both stakes) wins. When a ball finishes the course, it is removed; the game continues to be played without it.

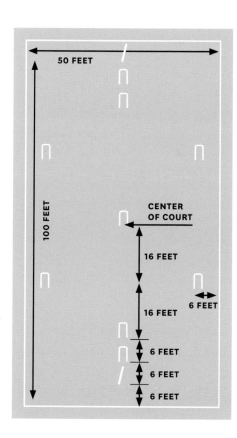

50 FEET

100 FEET

CENTER OF COURT

16 FEET

16 FEET

6 FEET

6 FEET

6 FEET

6 FEET

HORSESHOES

Test your luck with this ancient and easy-going family game.

EQUIPMENT

Two 3-foot iron stakes and four steel shoes.

OBJECT OF THE GAME

Ring a horseshoe around a stake (known as "tossing a ringer").

COURT SETUP

Official courts are usually clay or sand, but grass works for at-home play. The field includes two stakes that stand 40 feet apart, 14 inches high, and lean about 10 degrees in toward each other. A 6-foot-square pitcher's box is marked around each stake.

BASIC PLAY

In a two-person game, players start at the same stake. In the first inning, one player (standing inside the pitcher's box) pitches two shoes, followed by the opponent. The score is tallied. For inning two, the players aim at the opposite stake. They alternate stakes for 25 innings (or you can also play to 40 points). In doubles, partners separate and pitch from opposite sides of the court.

TIPS AND TECHNIQUES

Types of throws are identified by the number of turns in the air before landing. For a flip, hold the shoe from the top, at the middle. For a one-and-a-quarter and a one-and-three-quarter, grip along one shank.

SCORING

Any shoe landing less than 6 inches from the stake scores a point. A ringer scores three (you should be able to draw a line between the shoe shanks without touching the stake).

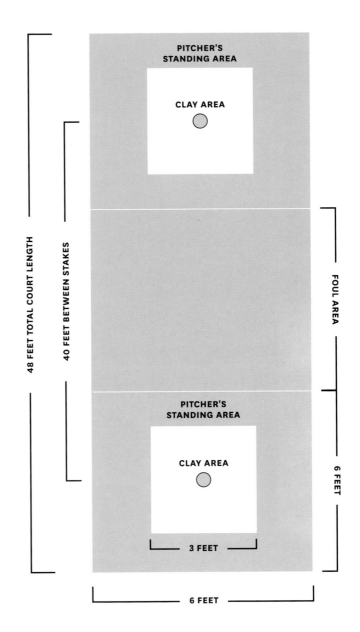

NOTE: *Diagrams are not drawn to scale.*

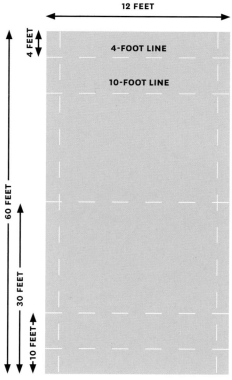

12 FEET

4 FEET

4-FOOT LINE

10-FOOT LINE

60 FEET

30 FEET

10 FEET

MARTHA MUST

Croquet is one of my favorite pastimes. At my home in Bedford, I dedicated a regulation-size portion of the lawn just for croquet or badminton.

BOCCE

Bocce (BOTCH-ee) is the Italian iteration of French pétanque and British lawn bowling. Portable sets are ideal for games on the go—especially on a sandy beach.

EQUIPMENT

Eight large balls (made of resin, in two colors) and one small *pallino*, or "jack," the target ball.

OBJECT OF THE GAME

Toss the large balls so they land as close as possible to the *pallino*.

COURT SETUP

An official court is 60 to 90 feet long and roughly 12 feet wide, on a level surface (gravel, dirt, clay, or grass can be used). A center line is marked, as are foul lines, at 4 and 10 feet from each end and one foot in from each side. Unofficially, a level patch of grass or sand works just fine.

BASIC PLAY

Each player (or team) has four balls. Standing at the 4-foot line, a player tosses the *pallino* past the center line and then tosses a bocce ball. Next, the opponent tosses, trying to get closer to the *pallino* than the first player. This player keeps tossing until a ball has landed closer or no balls remain. The game continues until both teams have thrown all four balls. The winner begins the next frame at the other end of the court.

SCORING

A player (or team) scores one point for each ball that is closer to the *pallino* than any of the opponent's. Thus, only one side scores (up to four points) per frame. The game ends when a player (or team) earns 12 points.

HOW TO
HANG A TIRE SWING

A good-size tire, some simple hardware, and a sturdy, well-positioned tree can offer you hours of old-fashioned swinging enjoyment.

SUPPLIES

Tire

Cordless power drill with ½-inch bit and ⅜-inch bit

One ⅜-inch-diameter eyebolt long enough to go through the branch and extend a little, plus a washer and locknut

½-inch-thick nylon rope, long enough to reach the branch plus 10 feet

Garden twine

Quick-link hook

TIP

To provide a soft landing in case of a fall, you may want to include a 6-inch layer of double-shredded bark mulch under and around the swing, spreading it equal to the height of the swing in all directions.

FIRST THINGS FIRST

Take your time scoping out the best place for the swing, keeping safety in mind.

FIND A TREE: A hardwood, such as oak, sugar maple, or ash, will safely hold a swing on a branch that's 8 or more inches in diameter; the farther out you hang your swing, the thicker the branch should be. The branch should be at least 9 feet high and shoot pretty much straight out, parallel to the ground, as it leaves the trunk. You'll also want at least 3 feet of open space in every direction.

OBTAIN A TIRE: One from a light truck, such as a pickup or SUV, is best. You can get a castoff from an auto shop; avoid steel-belted tires, so you won't have to worry about the metal working its way through the surface. To avoid standing water, drill ½-inch-wide holes in the bottom of the tire every 4 inches.

GET A LENGTH OF NYLON ROPE: Nylon is softer on hands than natural rope. Also make sure you have the right hardware to hang it from the tree following the instructions below.

HOW TO HANG THE SWING

Screwing a bolt through the branch is safest for the tree (a rope tossed over the bark will cut off nutrients). A trip to the hardware store will net you all you need to hang the tire.

1. Drill a ⅜-inch hole through the limb. Attach eyebolt with washer and locknut.

2. Loop rope around tire; tie knot (see right). Loop other end around quick-link hook, adjusting length (tire should hang high enough that feet won't drag but low enough so kids can stop themselves); cut off excess and knot. Fasten to eyebolt.

NOTE: *Make sure all of the hardware is grade 5 or higher and has an appropriate working load limit, which is determined by the total weight of the entire assembled swing (tire and eyebolts) and the estimated weight of the children using it. Always supervise children when swinging.*

HOW TO TIE THE KNOT

The three-strand eye splice knot is a loop, with one end woven back into the rope.

1. Wrap the rope tightly with twine, 12 inches from one end. Unravel rope's strands up to twine. Tape the end of each strand to make a tip.

2. With the unraveled strands, or "end strands," on your left, form a loop with the intact portion of the rope. Grasp right-hand side of loop—or "standing part." Slightly untwist below loop so there is a space between its threads.

3. Weave innermost end strand (A) from back to front under the leftmost thread of the standing part, then over the thread to its immediate right, and under the next thread.

4. Weave middle end strand (B) under the thread of the standing part that A just passed over. Pull taut.

5. Rotate knot so remaining end strand (C) is on your right. There should now be only one thread of the standing part with no end strand under it. Weave C from right to left under it. All three end strands should now exit the same tier or level of the standing part. Pull taut.

6. Continue weaving end strands, one at a time, into standing part in a downward spiral that twists in the opposite direction from the rope's natural twist. Weave at least six rows. Trim end strands ½ inch from rope; remove twine. Roll the knot on the floor with your foot to tighten it.

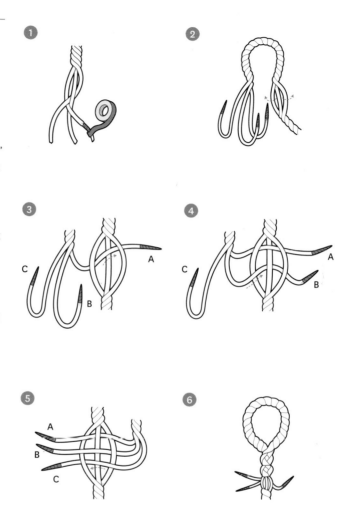

HOW TO
RIDE A BIKE

Whether it's your daily commute or a recreational pastime, cycling is one of the more enjoyable ways to take in the outdoors. Don't overlook the importance of routine maintenance, however, something even regular riders can use a refresher course in.

ROUTINE TUNE-UP

Keeping the bike clean, lubricated, well-adjusted, and with inflated tires is the goal. The good news is you probably have some of the necessary supplies in your arsenal, so you'll only need to pick up a few special ones.

CLEAN YOUR BIKE: Keeping to a schedule is key. Once a month is recommended for frequent riders, two or three times a year for recreational. Of course, if you ride through a puddle, you'll want to clean up any grime right away. Here's how to do it:

First, wipe down the frame with warm, soapy water. Then use an old toothbrush to remove dirt from the moving parts (chain, derailleurs, and cogs), spraying with soapy water or an all-natural solvent (such as Simple Green), when necessary, and then lubricate, as below.

LUBRICATE THE CHAIN: If you hear a persistent whirring noise coming from the chain as you ride, clean it as above, then add a drop of bike-chain lubricant to each link while backpedaling slowly with your free hand; thoroughly wipe off excess with a rag (oil attracts dirt).

ADJUST THE SEAT: For proper leg extension, your knee should be slightly bent when the pedal is at the bottom of the cycle. Some bikes have a quick-release lever that allows you to move the seat up and down; others require an Allen key to loosen a bolt. Either way, be sure to properly retighten when seat is in desired position. Also, make sure you cannot see the "maximum height" indicator on the post. Note that if the seat ever starts slipping or rotating from side to side, you'll need to tighten the lever or the bolt that holds it in place.

ADJUST THE HANDLEBARS: You can also raise or lower the handlebars. Have someone hold the bike from the front while you sit on it and test it for comfort. To adjust the height, loosen the bolt on the stem cap with an Allen key, then lift or lower as desired; tighten the bolt securely once you are finished. Repeat these steps whenever the stem of the handlebar is no longer squared with the front wheel.

TIRE MAINTENANCE

If you do nothing else, you'll want to check your tires before each ride, especially for long outings. Fully inflated tires allow for more speed and stability, protect the rim and spokes, and are less likely to pick up debris that can cause punctures.

TO INFLATE: Use a standing floor pump with an air-pressure gauge, which is the only way to be sure your tires are inflated to the recommended pressure (indicated on the side of the tube). Be sure to always take a portable pump with you, too, as air can seep out of tires even when there's no hole.

SAFETY MATTERS

Heed these simple rules whenever you or your family are heading out for a ride.

- Wear a helmet at all times.
- Wear bright clothing during the day and reflective gear whenever it is dark out.
- Equip your bike with reflectors on the rear, front, pedals, and spokes.
- Use a bright (and flashing) headlight for night riding.
- A horn or bell is also recommended, to alert pedestrians and other riders.
- Use appropriate hand signals when turning.
- Follow traffic laws (cyclists are like other motorists).
- Use bike paths whenever available.

TO REPLACE A FLAT TIRE: See "Bike Repair Kit" below for a description of the tools needed.

1. Remove the tire from the rim, using a tire lever to pry it off if necessary; work around one side before loosening the other. Pull out the inner tube and check for damage; patch it if possible, following instructions on the patch kit, or use a spare tube.

2. Run your hand along the tire to find the source of the problem, and remove it.

3. Insert one side of the tire into the rim. Starting at the valve hole, begin tucking the partially inflated tube into the tire. Then roll the other side of the tire into the rim, using the palms of your hands. Make sure not to pinch the tube and that the tire is properly seated in the rim.

4. Attach the pump to the valve stem and inflate the tire to recommended tire pressure.

BIKE REPAIR KIT

For on-the-go repairs, tuck these tools in a pack that straps to the bike's frame or fits inside your carrier of choice:

BIKE LOCK: As a last resort, if you simply cannot fix whatever is broken, you'll want to lock up your bike before heading off for help.

MINIPUMP: For inflating flat or underfilled tires; some models also come with gauges.

MULTITOOL: Look for ones (such as Swiss Army knives) with assorted hex keys and screwdriver heads for adjusting hardware.

PATCH KIT: This contains an adhesive fluid that you apply to the hole and patches to cover it.

SPARE TUBES: Always have at least two of these in case a patch won't do the trick.

TIRE LEVER: This is especially helpful when replacing tubes on road bikes, as their skinnier tires are harder to remove from the rim.

HOW TO
BUILD A FIRE
(INSIDE AND OUT)

The art and science of fire-building is easy to master with some basic skills and tricks. Start with the appropriate provisions and take the time to lay the groundwork according to the following diagrams.

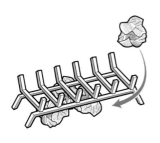  

HOW TO BUILD A FIRE IN A FIREPLACE

Before you light the tinder, open the chimney's damper all the way to allow sufficient air circulation. Follow the steps at right to get the fire started, and once you've got it going steadily, add more wood, Lincoln-log fashion, in increments; do not over-crowd lest you smother the blaze. When the fire has died out, make sure there are no embers in the remaining ash before discarding it.

1. START WITH TINDER

Place tinder between the andirons or under the grate, if you have one. Otherwise, just form a layer of tinder in the middle of the fireplace.

- Black-and-white newspaper is the go-to fire starter; avoid anything with colored ink, which contains metals that give off toxic fumes when burned.

- Crumple or wad the newspaper into a fairly tight ball, to help the paper catch quickly and burn longer.

- If you aren't a reader of print newspapers, hemlock twigs, birch bark, and the tips of dead pine branches also make good tinder.

2. ADD KINDLING

Rest pieces of kindling on top of the grate (or directly over tinder), arranging them in a crosshatch fashion. Light the tinder in multiple spots with a long match or ignition lighter, and let the flame then spread to the kindling above.

- Too-thin kindling will not stay ablaze long enough to do its job. Instead, look for pine or birch sticks that are ½ to 2 inches thick; those that are about 12 inches long will fit most fireplaces, inserts, and pits.

- If gathering your own sticks is not an option, look for fatwood, highly flammable resin-laden sticks from coniferous trees, at supermarkets and hardware stores.

3. LAYER LOGS

Add two logs, side by side, lengthwise atop the burning kindling. Then place another log crosswise on top. If the wood smokes rather than catches fire, move it around a bit to allow air to circulate.

- All logs must be split and aged before using; green, or young, wood—and any wood that is not completely dry—will either burn unevenly or put the fire out.

- Choose among the many hardwood logs: maple, ash, beech, oak, and birch.

- Avoid softwood logs, such as from pines and spruces; they leave behind resin that collects on chimney walls. Save these for kindling.

HOW TO BUILD A CAMPFIRE

Where there's a campfire, there's sure to be crackling conversation—it's irresistible fun. Seat guests in a circle on haystacks, blankets, or camping chairs, and enjoy. If it's been a while since you earned your merit badge, here's a quick lesson in building a teepee-style campfire, courtesy of the Girl Scouts of the USA.

Always choose a cleared area that's well away from trees.

1. Gather three types of firewood. Tinder: pine needles, bark, and matchstick-width sticks. Kindling: thumb-size twigs. Fuel: large sticks and small logs. Aged logs will catch fire faster than greener ones.

2. Arrange three pieces of kindling in an A shape. Set a handful of tinder near the A's crossbar. Light tinder from underneath, and let it burn until you have a healthy flame.

3. Use kindling to build out the teepee, adding it over tinder; wait for each piece to catch fire before adding a new one. As the fire grows stronger, begin adding "fuel to the fire," one piece at a time, as above. Finish off with the biggest logs.

PRACTICE FIRE SAFETY

Don't take chances when it comes to fire—and that goes for putting it out, too. Remember: If it's too hot to touch, it's too hot to leave unattended.

- Allow the wood to burn completely to ash, if possible.

- Pour lots of water on the fire. Drown *all* embers, not just the red ones. Pour until hissing sound stops.

- If you do not have water, stir dirt or sand into the embers with a shovel to bury the fire.

- With your shovel, scrape any remaining sticks and logs to remove any embers. Make sure that no embers are exposed and still smoldering.

- Continue adding water, dirt, or sand and stirring with a shovel until all material is cool.

TIP

When planning a firepit for your home, make sure it is at least 10 feet away from any structure (including on your neighboring properties). Set it on a fireproof surface (bricks, stone, or concrete). Also, never build an outside fire on a blustery day.

COOK

Whether you cook only once in a while or are proficient in the kitchen, you should continue to sharpen your cooking and baking skills.

Knowing which types of basic ingredients (what we like to call the building blocks) to keep on hand so you can create a wide array of dishes, and knowing how to buy and store those ingredients, is the first step.

Always reading through a recipe, prepping everything before you begin cooking—practicing mise en place—and learning to rely on visual cues over specified cooking times is another.

The latter is even more important in baking than other types of cooking: If a recipe says to cook a pie for an hour, but after that time the crust is not yet "golden brown" and the filling is not yet "bubbling," keep cooking until they are. Same for cakes that should be "springy to the touch" and custards that should still "jiggle in the center." We've pulled together these and other "good things for the kitchen" to help you gain confidence as you go about the daily task of putting meals on the table. There is also a chart to help you master different cooking techniques. Read through them, and then I suggest you put them to practice: Braise some chicken legs and poach some pears.

In addition to being a great advocate for sharpening one's cooking and baking skills, I'm also a big proponent of composting all the vegetable scraps or peels (or even spent coffee grinds) from the kitchen. I don't want any food to go to waste. So composting tools are included, too. It's an integral part of food preparation, and a practice that will do you, your garden, and the planet good.

PUT OLD TOOLS TO NEW USES

You may already have all the essential equipment in your kitchen, but are you making the most of those tools? They're taking up valuable space in your kitchen drawers and cabinets, so let them work for you in ways other than their intended purpose. Included here are many test-kitchen favorites and their secondary features.

MARTHA MUST

Originally used in cheesemaking, cheesecloth is how I "baste" turkey (see page 343). I also line a sieve with cheesecloth for straining the solids from homemade stock, and when draining yogurt to make yogurt cheese.

1. Garlic press

It may seem like a single-use tool, but a press is also the easiest way to mince fresh ginger (peeled easily with a spoon); plus, you get the flavorful juice.

2. Coffee grinder

Freshly ground whole spices pack more punch than anything from a jar; toast them in a dry skillet until fragrant, shaking the pan, then let cool before grinding. Have a separate grinder for coffee beans, or use this neat trick: Grind uncooked rice in the grinder to clean out aromatic oils, so your coffee doesn't taste like mustard seed, and vice versa.

3. Mortar and pestle

Another way to grind those toasted spices by hand is in one of these devices, which are also excellent for mud-dling fresh herbs, mashing garlic and salt to a paste, or even making aioli.

4. Pastry cutter

This tool is better than a fork, two knives, or your fingertips for working cold butter into dough, and will help you make the flakiest biscuits and pie crusts around. It's an efficient chopper, too, for softer foods such as boiled eggs (for egg salad), avocado (for chunky guacamole), and chickpeas (for hummus).

5. Meat mallet

When making cutlets, a fast and great dinner any day of the week, use this tool to pound meat thinly—and to crush bread into crumbs, for coating, or cookies for press-in crusts, or chocolate for melting. Give texture to cookie-dough shapes with the mallet's toothed side, or crack a bag of ice with the smooth side.

KITCHEN KNIFE MAINTENANCE

Follow these four easy steps to make your knives last.

 USE

Always work on a (preferably wood) cutting board; marble, stone, and other hard surfaces will ruin the blades.

 WASH

Leaving knives in the kitchen sink can damage the blades (and cause injuries); wash by hand and dry thoroughly (not in the drying rack).

6. Tongs

The tool of choice for all your flipping (meats and vegetables), tossing (salads), and twirling (pasta) tasks. Tongs can also get at hard-to-reach items in your upper cabinets (wrap the pinchers in rubber bands for extra grip).

7. Fine sieve

Grab this when straining and draining, of course, but also for sifting flour with dry ingredients, dusting desserts with confectioners' sugar, and removing bitter skins from toasted nuts. Metal ones can also stand in for a steamer basket—as well as a splatter guard (just turn the sieve upside down and rest the handle over the skillet's).

8. Pastry brush

This is a great multitasker: Besides brushing pastries with egg wash or melted butter, or cakes with flavorful syrups, it helps wash down the sides of the pan when making caramel, sweeps away excess flour from bread doughs, and bastes meat with glazes during cooking. Just be sure to designate brushes for either sweet or savory cooking.

9. Blender

A must for smoothies and shakes, margaritas and other frosty drinks—and also for no-churn frozen desserts (see page 307). Plus, you can whiz coffee beans in a blender for coarsely ground coffee (ideal for a French press).

10. Skillet

Think beyond the stovetop and use the bottom of this essential to crack whole peppercorns (when your pepper mill would make too fine a powder), or to "chop" nuts (between parchment to keep them from flying). A heavy skillet is a handy weight when draining tofu (lined with paper towels) or other foods.

11. Parchment paper

Besides keeping cakes and cookies (and roasted vegetables) from sticking to the pans, roll parchment up into a funnel for filling your pepper grinder; cut in a round and place atop fruit as it poaches, to keep it submerged; fold into a cone for piping melted-chocolate details; wrap around fish, chicken, or vegetables to cook "en papillote." Also, sift flour or grate cheese or chocolate on a piece of parchment, then use paper as a sleeve for mess-free moving.

12. Ice-cream scoop

Those with a release mechanism do more than just form perfect balls of ice cream; they create uniform meatballs, dumplings, and cookies, and offer drip-free dispensing of muffin and cupcake batters into tins.

13. Microplane

Not just for grating cheese, the tiny holes work wonders on garlic, fresh ginger or horseradish, chocolate, and whole nutmeg.

14. Box grater

It's got four sides and countless uses as a way to shred vegetables, cheese, bread (for breadcrumbs), and whole spices; use it, too, for grating chilled butter into pieces that will incorporate more quickly into pastry and biscuit doughs.

15. Y-shaped peeler

The preferred way to peel carrots and potatoes—and also to shave cheese, chocolate, or coconut.

STORE

Protect blades (and fingers) by keeping your knives in wooden blocks or drawer inserts, or on a wall-mounted magnetic strip.

SHARPEN

Sharper blades are safer to use (less slipping); use a knife stone or honing steel, or take to a professional.

HOW TO
BUY AND STORE FRESH PRODUCE

When purchasing produce, be sure to shop the season, choosing fruits and vegetables that are at their peak in your own region of the country. It will make eating the rainbow all the easier.

BUYING

You'll get the best flavor when you follow these simple steps.

- Buy locally as much as possible—either at farmers' markets or at the many supermarkets that sell local produce (look for the labels in the produce aisle). This will also ensure that you are buying what's in season.

- Skip the prepackaged (clamshell or bagged) greens and buy them in bunches; same for fruits and vegetables sold bundled in bags. For the most part, you'll want to hand-pick each specimen for the freshest results.

- Don't buy more than you think you will be able to consume (except for storage vegetables like potatoes and onions); better to shop frequently for these items.

- Learn what to look for when picking your produce: Lettuces should have close heads and, similar to kale and other greens, no signs of wilting; fruit should be free of soft or bruised spots (melons and stone fruit should also smell sweet); avoid broccoli and cauliflower with any dark spots.

STORING

Many fruits and vegetables will stay fresher longer in the refrigerator (see right for exceptions). Wait until just before using to wash produce—delicate herbs and leafy greens can quickly wilt if damp.

- Most refrigerated vegetables do best in a perforated resealable plastic bag (make six to eight holes in a one-gallon bag). The bag holds in moisture; the holes help release compounds that produce spoilage while letting the vegetables "breathe."

- If vegetables were sprayed with water at the market, lining the plastic bag with paper towels will help absorb excess moisture.

- Keep mushrooms in a breathable brown paper bag (to avoid slime or spots) in the refrigerator's vegetable bin for up to a week.

- Fruit can be stored at room temperature, or in the refrigerator to slow ripening. Keep in a separate drawer from vegetables, preferably one set at low humidity, while the latter should generally be set at high humidity.

- For faster ripening, put stone fruit—peaches, nectarines, apricots, and plums—in brown paper bags. Same goes for avocados, or keep these on a sunny windowsill.

TIP

After buying a bunch of basil, trim the stems and stand them in a tall glass of water. Loosely cover the basil with the plastic bag it came in, cinching it around at the base; this will extend its life for a couple of days.

NO REFRIGERATION REQUIRED

Those flabby, flaccid tomatoes? Most likely they were improperly stored. Those and other fruits and vegetables can take on unsavory textures and flavors when kept in the cold.

KEEP THESE ON THE COUNTER, AWAY FROM DIRECT SUNLIGHT (UNLESS RIPENING, SEE LEFT):

Avocados

Eggplants

Tomatoes

STORE THESE SEPARATELY IN A COOL, DARK PLACE:

Garlic

Onions

Potatoes

Shallots

Sweet Potatoes

HOW TO
MAKE THE MOST OF YOUR FREEZER

Besides big-batch leftovers, there are a number of fresh ingredients you can store in your freezer—extending the life of bought-in-bulk items as well as anything at risk of getting spoiled before you can consume it. Of course, homemade doughs (pizza, pie, and cookie) take well to being frozen, as do many baked goods, from biscuits and quick breads to all sorts of cakes and cookies—even some pies.

WHAT TO FREEZE

Here are the most common items that can be kept fresher longer by freezing.

- Staples such as nuts and seeds, whole-grain flours, butter, hard cheese, bread and breadcrumbs, bacon and sausage, vanilla beans, fresh ginger, and grated coconut.

- Seasonal berries and sliced fruits such as peaches and plums, grapes, and (peeled) bananas.

- Fresh woody, stemmed herbs such as rosemary, thyme, oregano, marjoram, sage, and bay leaves.

- Even milk (yes, milk!) can be frozen before its best-by date to avoid spoilage, though its taste and texture might be affected (in which case use it for cooking or baking, not drinking).

- Egg whites and/or yolks left over from a cake, custard, or other dessert recipe; note the number on the container for future reference (see page 309 for more information). Do not freeze eggs in the shell.

- Do not freeze soft cheeses, mayonnaise, sour cream, and cream-laden soups and sauces.

HOW TO FREEZE

In general, the best way to freeze things quickly is to ensure you do it in a very cold (0°F) freezer that isn't overpacked—the frosty air needs to circulate. (Think of this as the home version of the food industry's flash-freezing, which exposes foods to seconds of cryogenic temperatures.) A good way to tell if your freezer isn't cold enough? You can easily scoop ice cream right out of the icebox. Here are some tips to help ensure food tastes its best after thawing.

- Let cooked foods cool before storing; still-warm dishes can raise freezer temperatures and tend not to freeze uniformly. For fast cooling, add a few ice cubes to soups and stews; set a container of hot leftovers in a bowl filled with ice water. Dividing food into shallower containers can also help.

- When freezing liquids, leave at least 2 inches of space between surface and lid—liquid expands a lot when frozen, which is why regular glass jars are not the best option (they can crack).

- Otherwise, pack the containers to the brim, leaving as little headroom as possible—that's where ice crystals are allowed to develop. The smaller (and fewer) the ice crystals, the less dehydrated the food will be when thawed.

- When adding new packages or containers to freezer, leave several inches of space between them to allow air to circulate and lower internal temperatures; once frozen, you can store items more tightly. Place newest things in the back, and pull older foods to the front.

- Meat, poultry, bread, hard (but not soft) cheese, and fish can be tightly swaddled in butcher paper (waxy side in) and then in plastic wrap or aluminum foil.

- Slow thawing in the refrigerator is best for meats and cheese (and milk), since it allows much of the moisture to reabsorb, which prevents dryness. Place wrapped meats on a plate or in a tray to catch any juicy drippings. Smaller items might thaw as quickly as overnight, but most will require more time—give them a day or two. Be sure that your refrigerator is kept at about 36°F.

- Briefly blanching vegetables, then shocking them in an ice-water bath, can help preserve their color, flavor, texture, and nutrients; drain well before storing in separate resealable bags.

- To freeze berries and sliced stone fruits, place them on a baking sheet in a single layer and freeze until hard, then transfer to a sealed container. A little sprinkling of sugar (raw, brown, or white) or of honey can help the water freeze in the fruit's tissue without affecting texture.

HOW TO
SAVE THE SCRAPS

Using up the odds and ends that might otherwise be tossed into the trash (or down the disposal) will do more than save you cash and shrink your carbon footprint. It will also make your cooking more creative—and very possibly more delicious. Try these repurposing tricks for some common kitchen castoffs.

KEEP VS. COMPOST

If you do nothing else, save the vegetable scraps for making stock. Many of the peels, stems, and other trimmings that you've been throwing away are full of flavor—though some make a better stock than others. Here's what to save and what to toss in the compost bin (see page 208 for more on composting).

KEEPERS	COMPOSTERS
▪ Asparagus	▪ Artichokes
▪ Carrots	▪ Beets
▪ Celery	▪ Broccoli
▪ Corncobs	▪ Brussels sprouts
▪ Fennel	▪ Cabbage
▪ Garlic	▪ Cauliflower
▪ Herbs	▪ Mushrooms
▪ Leeks	▪ Turnips
▪ Onions	
▪ Summer squashes	

USE, DON'T LOSE

Many food-centric cultures—Italy and India both come to mind—prize frugality as a sign of being a good cook. In that spirit, here are ways to put scraps and trimmings and other remnants to another delicious use.

VEGETABLE PEELS AND SCRAPS = STOCK

Freeze vegetable peels and produce trimmings in a gallon-size resealable plastic bag. When it's full, use the contents to make stock. Aromatic vegetables (carrots, celery, garlic, onions, shallots) work best. Cover the trimmings with water, and simmer for 2 hours, skimming the surface frequently. Strain, and let cool completely before freezing in single-serve airtight containers.

SOAKING LIQUID FOR DRIED MUSHROOMS = RISOTTO

Next time you reconstitute dried mushrooms, save the soaking liquid for using in place of broth when making mushroom or other types of risotto (and also for using in cooking soft polenta, in place of water). Strain out the solids in a cheesecloth before using.

TIP

Get in the habit of planning for leftover ingredients. Extra meat and potatoes are the beginnings of a delicious hash, fish or shrimp a lovely risotto. Tacos and sandwiches can be made from most leftover dinners, as can stir-fries, noodle dishes, and anything-goes salads and stews. Once you're accustomed to shopping your refrigerator, you just might find that "making do" can be as rewarding as starting from scratch.

NUTS = NUT BUTTERS

If you bought more nuts than you need (or
want to freeze), turn them into nut butter.
Use raw or toasted nuts of one type or any
combination—throw whatever you have on
hand into a food processor with a sprinkling
of salt (and some oil, if desired), and blend
for a few minutes, just until smooth. Refrigerate, covered, for up to 2 weeks.

PARMESAN CHEESE RIND = MINESTRONE

Save the rind from a wedge of Parmesan
cheese; it will keep, well wrapped, in the
freezer for months. As a source of umami, the
cheese rind will impart incredible depth and
richness to minestrone—and other soups
and stews. Add it during the last 15 minutes
of cooking.

CORNCOBS = CHOWDER

When you shave kernels from ears of corn,
take this extra step: Holding the ear of corn
upright in a shallow bowl, use a paring knife
to slice off the kernels. Then scrape the cob
with the back of the blade to extract the
creamy liquid, which can be stirred into the
broth for corn (or other) chowders, along
with the cobs, for deeper corn flavor. You can
also make a delicate broth by boiling the cobs
with water to cover.

TIP

For easy shucking, place whole ears
of corn—husks and all—directly
on the racks of a 400°F oven. Thirty
minutes later, the peels will slip right
off—silk and all—and the kernels
will be perfectly tender and ready to
eat or slice into salads, salsas, and
pasta dishes.

DIJON MUSTARD = VINAIGRETTE

Avoid the hassle of getting the last bit of
mustard out of the bottom of jars. Instead,
add the makings for a tangy vinaigrette. Start
with a crushed garlic clove or minced shallot
and some chopped fresh herbs (tarragon or
thyme are good choices), then add enough
vinegar of choice to fill jar about a quarter of
the way. Season with salt and pepper, then
close the lid and shake vigorously. Add extra-
virgin olive oil (following a 3:1 oil to vinegar
ratio); shake again to emulsify the dressing.
It will keep in the refrigerator for up to one
week; shake to combine again before serving.

MARTHA MUST

Because I often
start the day with
a fresh juice made
from spinach, kale,
or other greens,
I end up with a lot
of nutrient-rich
pulp. In addition
to composting the
pulp, I save it for
making stocks, stir-
ring into soups and
stews, and feeding
to my dogs, horses,
and chickens.

PICKLE BRINE = COCKTAILS

The next time you hit the bottom of the pickle jar, reserve the leftover brine for adding to a dirty martini, instead of the usual splash of olive juice. Any kind of pickle works this way: dill, bread-and-butter, sour—even dilly beans or pickled okra. You can also put the vinegary brine to use in a salad dressing or as a flavor booster in potato or tuna salad.

CILANTRO STEMS = CURRIES

When a recipe calls for just the leaves of cilantro, save the stems; they add depth and complexity to Southeast Asian and Indian curries and other dishes, including salads, stir-fries, and soups.

VANILLA-BEAN PODS = VANILLA SUGAR

Vanilla beans are expensive, so you'll want to save the pods once the seeds have been scraped. Just pop the pod in a container of sugar, seal the lid, and keep at room temperature for at least a week. Or add the pod to a decanted bottle of vodka—it's especially tasty in White Russians.

LEFTOVER CHEESE + WINE = FROMAGE FORT (A FRENCH CHEESE SPREAD)

We have the French to thank for excellent cheese and wine—and a way to use up the remains of both from a party. *Fromage fort*, which translates to "strong cheese," is made

by mixing leftover cheeses and wine with a little optional garlic (whether or how much depends on the cheeses) in a food processor. You can combine almost any type of cheese: a piquant goat cheese, rich Gorgonzola dolce, buttery Brie, nutty Gruyère—anything goes. Serve the spread with crackers or atop slices of baguette (run them under the broiler for toasts to serve with cocktails); or place a hefty dollop on a grilled steak or burger, or steamed green beans or asparagus, for an instant sauce.

TIP

Here are some other delicious ways to savor those cheese remnants: Grate and add to doughs for slice-and-bake crackers, savory drop biscuits (spiked with cayenne or cracked black pepper), or fruit pies (apple, pear, or quince); or break out the fondue pot and add them to the melting cheeses.

HOW TO
PREP
INGREDIENTS

If all the slicing and dicing keeps you from cooking meals more often, you'll appreciate these time-saving strategies and solutions. Because being your own sous chef can be part of the pleasure—not the pain—of getting dinner on the table.

BASIC KNIFE SKILLS

A supersharp knife makes fast work of prepping produce and more. You'll also need to use the right knife for the job.

- A chef's knife is your multitasking workhorse for mincing, chopping, and slicing fruits and vegetables; a paring knife offers more precision in trimming, coring, and peeling; the jagged teeth of a serrated knife cuts through soft items such as bread, cake, tomatoes, and peaches (without squishing them) and chops nuts and chocolate with ease.

- To use a chef's knife properly, hold the base of the blade between your thumb and forefinger—what the pros call "choking up." With the other hand, secure food to be cut, curling fingers back so they're safely out of the way.

- When chopping or slicing, keep the tip of the knife in place while rocking the blade back and forth in a fluid down-and-back motion, moving your curled hand away with each chop to expose a portion of the food to cut. Cutting same-size pieces will allow ingredients to heat, soften, and brown at the same pace, for even texture and flavor.

PREPPING PRODUCE

To avoid cross-contamination, designate different cutting boards—whether wood or plastic—for raw meat and fish and another for fresh produce (and even a small one just for garlic and onions). Place a damp kitchen towel (or paper towel) under the cutting board for skid-free slicing.

ONIONS

Recipes call for onions cut in specific ways—minced, chopped finely, chopped coarsely, sliced—because it affects both flavor development and cook time. For instance, minced onions soften and cook more quickly than larger coarsely chopped ones, while whole slices or half-moons can hold up to long, slow caramelization (see page 294). Same goes for other aromatics (garlic, celery, carrots).

HOW TO CHOP AN ONION:

1. Cut the stem end off, then peel back the skin by grasping it between your thumb and the blade of a paring knife.

2. Halve the onion vertically; then place each side cut side down. Slice vertically lengthwise at even intervals, being careful not to cut through the root end.

3. Then slice horizontally in even intervals, again leaving root end intact.

4. Lastly, make perpendicular cuts, letting the pieces fall as you go.

KNIFE-SHARPENING KNOW-HOW

You can take your knives to a professional to be sharpened every three to six months. Or you can invest in a whetstone, found at kitchen-supply stores. Lubricate it according to the manufacturer's instructions (usually with food-grade mineral oil), then place the stone on a damp towel for traction. Use the coarse side of the stone first, pushing the knife blade away from you at a 20-degree angle. Repeat with firm strokes over the stone, from the tip to the base of the blade. Do this on each side of the blade 10 to 20 times, then repeat on the fine side of the whetstone, and clean the blade once you're finished.

GARLIC

Dealing with this allium's papery skins and sticky nature can be frustrating.

- No need to peel individual cloves—simply smash the cloves with the flat side of a chef's knife blade and they will slip right out. To peel a whole head of garlic, place garlic in a metal prep bowl. Top with another bowl and shake vigorously for about 15 seconds. The cloves will separate and most of the papery skins will be removed; pull off the rest.

- While crushing cloves makes them easier to peel—it also releases a sticky oil. Once you've chopped the garlic into a little pile (wipe down the blade to remove stray bits), sprinkle with a tiny pinch of salt to expedite mincing. If the recipe calls for making a garlic paste, increase the salt and continue mincing until the mixture is smooth.

CITRUS

When zesting and juicing citrus, such as lemons, limes, and oranges, zest first, then juice. It's a good idea to remove the zest even if you only need the juice, so it doesn't go to waste; it will keep fresh for months in an airtight bag in the freezer.

- When zesting, use this trick: Hold the microplane upside down, with the opening facing up, right on top of the fruit. As you grate, the zest will collect for easy measuring and cleanup.

- For the rest of the juice, roll a room-temperature piece of citrus firmly between your palm and a work surface before squeezing.

FRESH HERBS

There's no need to pluck individual leaves from fresh herbs such as parsley or thyme. Instead, use one of these easy methods.

FOR LEAFY HERBS: Holding the bunch at an angle, shave off the bulk of the leaves with a sharp chef's knife, turning the bunch as necessary. Reserve the stems for flavoring soups or sauces—or to use in juicing.

FOR WOODY HERBS: Grasp the tip of a stem to hold steady, then run your fingers along the stem, from top to bottom, against the direction of the leaves.

SALAD GREENS

The key to crisp, clean greens? An ice bath. The ice will crisp them up—especially any that have been refrigerated for more than a couple of days.

1. Discard discolored leaves and root ends; chop or tear the leaves, if necessary.

2. Fill a bowl with ice and cold water. Throw prepped greens into the ice bath in batches, stirring them periodically; swishing the greens around will loosen any dirt.

3. Remove the greens from the water and spin or towel them dry; serve within a few hours.

BUTTERNUT SQUASH

Armed with a sharp chef's knife, you can cut any tough squash—such as butternut, acorn, pumpkin, kabocha—with ease; just follow these simple steps.

1. Cut off the top, halve squash lengthwise, then scoop out seeds and pulpy flesh.

2. Slice crosswise into desired thickness, remove peel with a paring knife, and cut into cubes or as directed in a recipe. (Or leave in

CARAMELIZED ONIONS

Want flavor to spare? Make a big batch of golden-brown, meltingly soft onions to use in omelets and frittatas, sandwiches and burgers, and tacos and quesadillas.

1. Melt a generous amount of butter in a pot (about a tablespoon of butter per onion).

2. Add lots of sliced onions and toss to coat.

3. Cook, stirring occasionally, until onions are very soft and nicely browned, about an hour; start on high heat and reduce to medium-low once onions begin to wilt. (Adjust heat as needed to keep onions from scorching on the bottom.)

4. Onions will keep, covered, in the refrigerator for at least a week.

halves, and the squash is ready for roasting, cut-side down on a parchment-lined baking sheet, until tender.)

STURDY GREENS

- To remove tough stems from kale, collards, and other such vegetables: Fold each leaf around the stem and, holding the base of the stem in one hand, strip off the leaf with your hand—or place on a cutting board and slice off folded leaf with a knife.

- These vegetables often taste best (and cook faster) when first cut into chiffonade: Remove the stems (reserve them for soup), stack and roll up the leaves, and cut them into thin strips, as shown at right. Then toss in a salad, try a quick sauté or steam, or throw some raw into your soup or smoothie mix.

FRESH GINGER

This knobby root adds its own brand of spicy heat to savory and sweet preparations.

- To peel, reach for a spoon: It removes the thin skin in quick fashion and can reach those nooks and crannies. Pull the spoon toward you with the concave side facing you as you go.

- For easier grating, freeze the ginger; it will keep, well wrapped, for several months. Then just cut or break off what you need. The frozen ginger will grate more easily, without separating into fibers.

CARROTS

When a recipe calls for carrots to be cut into julienne, or matchsticks, here's a quick way to do just that. Note the same method works for other vegetables, such as parsnips and turnips.

1. Peel carrot and trim off ends, then cut into thirds or quarters lengthwise, depending on size of carrot.

2. Slice off a thin piece from one side of each piece to keep it from rolling, then rest on flat side while thinly slicing lengthwise with a sharp chef's knife.

3. Then stack slices and cut lengthwise again into thin strips.

TIP

Practice the art of *mise en place* by cutting up and pre-measuring ingredients before you start cooking. Prep all the produce and put it in separate vessels (a great reason to stock up on inexpensive restaurant-supply metal bowls), wash and dry the greens, measure out and soften the butter, toast the nuts, bone the chicken—whatever your recipe calls for.

ARTICHOKES

Look for vibrant green artichokes that are compact, not with leaves splayed out. Before you prep the artichokes for steaming, squeeze one lemon into a cold bowl of water; it will keep them from discoloring while you work.

1. Trim off top quarter with a serrated knife, then snip off sharp tips from all leaves with kitchen shears.

2. Remove any smaller leaves from bottom of artichoke, then trim stem flush with bottom, so the artichoke can stand upright.

3. Submerge each artichoke in the prepared lemon water right away.

CABBAGE

Whether you are cutting cabbage into wedges, for roasting or braising, or slicing thinly, for salads and slaws, always begin by removing any damaged or wilted outer leaves, then cut head in half through the core.

- For wedges, trim off tough outer stem. Turn each half cut side down and slice into desired-width wedges through the core, to help leaves stay intact during cooking.

- For shredding, remove core from each half by cutting into cabbage around core, in a triangle shape. Then place cut side down and slice thinly from top to bottom with a sharp chef's knife; the layers will naturally separate.

BELL PEPPERS

How you go about prepping peppers depends on the end goal: slicing or stuffing.

- When slicing, use a chef's knife to cut off pepper in sections to remove flesh from the seeds. Cut off bottom as well. Hold each

section skin side down on cutting board, then run tip of knife along the raised rib to remove. Slice or dice as directed in a recipe.

- For stuffing, rest pepper stem side up on cutting board, then run a paring knife around stem to remove. Lift stem and slice off ribs and seeds that are attached; also trim away ribs from inside pepper and shake out any remaining seeds. Now you have a pepper with a top, ready for filling.

CHILE PEPPERS

Most of the heat resides in the seeds, so you may want to remove those for a less spicy result. You may also want to wear rubber gloves when working with spicy chiles.

1. Trim off the stem end of the chile, then halve chile lengthwise.

2. Use a paring knife to scrape out ribs and seeds, if desired.

3. Slice chile lengthwise into thin strips, then stack those and cut crosswise into small dice.

TIP

If the idea of pitting cherries prevents you from making pie, try this: Unbend (halfway) a paper clip, insert it in stem end, then twist it around (be patient at first; you'll eventually get it) until the pit comes right out. Plan B: Poke the tip of a small pastry tip into stem end to push out pit.

BROCCOLI AND CAULIFLOWER

Be sure to save the stalk for cooking, too.

1. Cut off and discard bottom of stem, then slice off any small branches.

2. Use a vegetable peeler or paring knife to peel off outer layer of stem to reveal the tender, lighter stalk.

3. Cut florets from stalk, then slice stalk thinly crosswise.

4. Cut head into florets, from top to bottom.

TOMATOES

When a recipe calls for peeling a tomato—or a peach, nectarine, or apricot—here's how.

1. Use a paring knife to score an X in the bottom of the fruit.

2. Using a spider or slotted spoon, lower fruit into a pot of boiling water and let remain until skin begins to split, about 30 to 60 seconds.

3. Plunge into a bowl of ice water to stop the cooking. Once cool, peel off the loosened skins with a paring knife, beginning at the X.

LEEKS

Of all the alliums, leeks win for being the grittiest. Clean thoroughly every time.

1. Cut off the dark-green top of the leek at the point where it meets the pale-green part, then trim the roots, leaving the bulb intact.

2. Slice leek lengthwise in half through the root so leaves stay intact. If braising whole leeks, loosen leaves and rinse well under cold running water.

If a recipe calls for leeks to be thinly sliced, do this first, then submerge in a bowl of cold water and swish to remove grit, changing water as needed.

FENNEL BULBS

Reserve the frilly fennel fronds for garnishing dishes, adding to greens, or topping pasta. Finely chop it, then add it to egg, tuna, or potato salads, in place of dill.

1. Cut off stalks as close to bulb as possible, then halve fennel bulb from top to bottom.

2. Insert tip of knife along the line where the core meets the bulb to remove the core in a wedge shape.

3. Place each bulb half cut side down and slice either crosswise or lengthwise, as desired.

If not using right away, toss fennel pieces with lemon juice to prevent discoloration.

MANGOES

The goal is to get every last bit of flesh from the pit, and without it being at all stringy.

1. Begin by holding mango on your cutting board, narrow side down; use a sharp chef's knife to slice off both large sides of the fruit, leaving the oblong pit in the center.

2. Stand fruit upright and cut to remove small remaining sections on either side of pit.

3. Working with one large side of the fruit at a time, and holding it skin side down in the palm of your hand, cut through flesh (leaving skin intact) in a crosshatch pattern. Doing this cuts through the fibers of the mango.

4. Gently push up in center of piece to turn it inside out, then use a paring knife to remove the scored sections from the skin.

5. Run paring knife between skin and flesh of the remaining two small sections and cut those into pieces.

MARTHA MUSTS

I've tried many different methods for extracting pomegranate seeds, but this one is still my favorite: Score the perimeter of the fruit with a chef's knife, to avoid cutting into any of the seeds, then pry pomegranate open with your hands. Hold each half cut side down over a bowl and whack the back of the fruit with a large spoon—the seeds should fall right out (pry out any stubborn ones with the spoon).

HOW TO
MASTER THE METHODS

Even if you have the kitchen basics down pat, there's always something more to learn, a new method to try. Refer to this chart for the classic cooking techniques, plus some general how-tos to help you master them.

METHOD SAUTÉING

PROS
Sautéing yields tender, lightly browned food in relatively short order—and with only a small amount of fat. It is also the starting point for making soups, sauces, and many other dishes.

HOW-TO
The meaning of *sauté* is "to jump," which describes what the food being cooked does when it hits the hot pan.

1. Heat pan over medium-high heat for 2 to 3 minutes. Add oil or butter to coat bottom of pan, swirling to cover.

2. When pan is hot but not smoking, add food and cook over medium heat, turning until light brown all over. Remove from pan.

BEST FOR
Tender steaks and chops; chicken breasts; fish and seafood; fruit; vegetables

TIPS
- Butter will create more browning than oil.
- Cut food into portions of the same size for quicker, more even cooking.
- Dredge proteins in flour to encourage a delicate crust to form; Wondra flour, which dissolves easily, is considered the chef's secret.

BONUS TECHNIQUE
Stir-frying is basically sautéing over higher heat, with the need for more frequent stirring to prevent the food from scorching before it is cooked through.

1. Cut each type of food into uniform pieces.

2. Cook items first separately (for example, chicken or steak, followed by vegetables).

3. Combine everything at the end and coat with desired sauce.

4. Serve with rice.

METHOD **FRYING**

PROS

Frying garners the crispiest crust on the outside while keeping food juicy on the inside. When done correctly, very little of the oil is absorbed by the food.

HOW-TO

You don't need a deep fryer to cook foods according to this method, just a heavy-bottom pot or deep-sided skillet.

1. Heat as much oil as directed in recipe (or enough to reach top of foods, generally 2 to 3 inches) until it reaches between 350°F and 375°F on a deep-fry or candy thermometer.

2. Add food carefully and cook, turning as needed, until crisp and browned.

3. Adjust the heat of the burner as needed to maintain a steady temperature, returning it to 350°F before adding the next batch.

4. Remove food from oil and drain briefly on a paper-towel-lined plate before serving.

BEST FOR

Chicken parts (for classic fried chicken); fish fillets; shrimp; vegetables (such as potatoes, green beans, and okra)

TIPS

- Use oil with a high smoke point, such as canola, grapeseed, safflower, sunflower, or peanut. Or use lard.

- A deep-fry or candy thermometer helps monitor the oil between batches. If the oil is not hot enough, the food will be greasy; too high, and it will burn.

- Food should be patted dry before coating or frying; if adding a batter, do so just before cooking.

- Cook food in batches to keep from crowding pan; adding too much food at once lowers oil temperature and keeps the food from remaining separate in the oil, essential for achieving a crisp crust.

- Use a spider or skimmer to lower smaller items into the oil—and then leave it there, so the food doesn't wind up burning while you try to fish it out.

- Keep fried foods warm while you finish batches: Spread on a paper-towel-lined baking sheet and place in a 275°F oven.

BONUS TECHNIQUE

For the classic batter that fries to a golden-brown and crispy coating:

1. In a shallow bowl, whisk flour with salt and pepper and any other desired seasonings (cayenne, for example). Add baking powder for a lighter yet thicker crust; cornstarch to help the batter adhere.

2. Put a beaten egg in another shallow bowl.

3. First dredge food in dry ingredients (with one hand, keeping other free), tap off excess, and then dredge in the wet (with other hand), allowing excess to drip off.

METHOD **BROILING**

PROS

Broiling uses direct heat to cook food quickly, sealing in juices and browning the surface. Think of it as the indoor, year-round alternative to grilling (with no special tools required).

HOW-TO

Some broilers are in a lower drawer, others in the main oven. Either way, be sure to preheat the broiler before you begin; that blast of heat ensures food gets the requisite sear.

1. Preheat the broiler, positioning the rack as suggested in a recipe (or use 4 to 6 inches from the heat source as the default).

2. Season food and place on the broiler pan (or a broiler-proof baking sheet), leaving space between for even browning.

3. Watch food carefully when broiling, as it can scorch in a flash; lower the rack away from the broiler's heat source if food is cooking too quickly.

BEST FOR

Thin, tender steaks, boneless chops (beef, pork, and lamb); chicken cutlets and wings; fish fillets; shrimp and scallops; fruit; vegetables

TIPS

- Bring food to room temperature before broiling, for more even cooking.

- Get to know your broiler; they can take from 5 to 10 minutes to heat up.

- Remove all excess marinade and moisture from foods before broiling, to prevent flare-ups.

- When broiling kebabs or satays, soak bamboo skewers in water for 30 minutes before cooking.

- You can sear larger cuts of meat under the broiler as a first step before roasting or braising, instead of doing this on the stove.

- Or finish things off under the broiler, such as gratins and casseroles, for a final boost in browning.

- As soon as the broiler has cooled down, wipe away any food spatters.

BONUS TECHNIQUE

To have the broiler most successfully approximate a grill:

1. Preheat a lightly oiled cast-iron grill pan on the rack before adding the food, putting it as close to the heat source as possible (but not closer than 3 inches).

2. Add steaks, chops, fish fillets, and even thick slices of onion or other vegetables (or halved stone fruit, as on the grill, with cut side down) to the heated grill pan.

3. Once the underside gets those desirable grill marks (watch carefully, as food can scorch quickly), rotate food 90 degrees if a crosshatch is desired.

4. There's no need to flip the food; just serve it with the marked side up.

METHOD **ROASTING**

PROS

Cooking at higher oven temperatures (typically 400°F and above) promotes even caramelization, for richer flavor (especially for vegetables). Also good for cooking large cuts evenly.

BEST FOR

Roasts and chops (beef, pork, and lamb); poultry (whole birds or parts, especially breast meat); fish (whole or filleted); fruit (apples, pears, figs, strawberries, plums); vegetables (all kinds, but especially starchy roots and tubers)

BONUS TECHNIQUE

When roasting a whole chicken or a turkey breast, make an edible "rack" in lieu of the wire one:

1. Cut or tear a leftover baguette into pieces and spread evenly in the center of the roasting pan.

2. Rest bird on top; similar to a wire rack, the bread lets hot air circulate, so the meat cooks evenly and the skin gets browned and crisp—as do the bread pieces, which soak up the flavorful juices in the oven.

3. Serve the bread alongside the chicken, or toss it, crouton-style, in a salad or atop soups and stews.

NOTE: *Instead of bread, this same method works for waxy potatoes, whole carrots, parsnips, or turnips.*

HOW-TO

The precise process will vary depending on whether you are cooking a large roast or cut-up vegetables (or a combination), but the basic steps are essentially the same.

1. Preheat oven to temperature, according to recipe.

2. Rub or toss food with extra-virgin olive oil or melted butter, and season with salt and pepper.

3. Place in a roasting pan (or on a rimmed baking sheet); rest meat on a wire rack fitted in pan to allow fat to drip off; spread smaller items in a single layer.

4. Roast, tossing or turning as needed, until evenly browned and cooked through.

5. Allow roasts to rest for about 10 minutes before serving.

TIPS

▪ Smaller roasts (such as pork tenderloin) are often first seared on the stovetop to get browned all over before moving to the oven; larger roasts can develop their color over their longer cooking time.

▪ Whole birds and other larger roasts need to cook on racks set in the roasting pan; otherwise they will steam in their juices rather than form the desired sear on the surface.

▪ Use an instant-read thermometer to check pork and poultry for doneness. Remember that meat and poultry will continue to cook outside the oven.

▪ If desired, make a sauce right in the roasting pan: Remove food and deglaze pan with wine, stock, or water, bringing it to a simmer (place large pans over two burners), and cook, stirring up the flavorful browned bits, until thickened and reduced.

METHOD **POACHING**

PROS

This method yields tender, juicy results, with subtle flavor from the poaching liquid. It's great for leaner cuts prone to drying out. To preserve the food's shape, cook gently over low heat.

HOW-TO

The key to poaching is to keep the liquid almost at a simmer, meaning you shouldn't see any bubbles (the temperature should hover between 160°F and 185°F).

1. Start large whole fish and pieces of meat and poultry in cold liquid, and bring up to a simmer.

2. Smaller, quicker-cooking foods (fish fillets, chicken breasts, shrimp) should be added to simmering liquid.

3. Add aromatics (onion wedges, carrots, celery, and/or fennel) along with herbs and spices (bundle in cheesecloth).

4. Poach gently until food is tender and cooked through.

5. Remove food from liquid; serve as is, or reduce poaching liquid to a sauce, for serving.

BEST FOR

Whole chicken or chicken breast; firm-fleshed fish such as salmon, halibut, and cod; lobster; eggs; fruit (pears, peaches and other stone fruit, citrus, and dried figs)

TIPS

- Poaching-liquid options include stock, dashi, brewed tea, wine (great for pears) or beer, buttermilk (great for chicken), or even water.

- When poaching a whole chicken, keep it submerged by weighting it with a plate; use the meat in salads, sandwiches, and Asian-style noodle dishes.

- When poaching fish, tie delicate fillets in cheesecloth to prevent breakage; set large, whole fish on a wire rack in a large pot or deep-sided roasting pan (and poach over two burners).

- When poaching fruit, cut a round of parchment and place on top to keep it submerged during cooking; or cover with cheesecloth and a plate to weigh down.

- For lean, flaky white fish or boneless, skinless chicken breasts, try "shallow poaching," where the food is only partially covered with the poaching liquid (kept at the barest simmer).

BONUS TECHNIQUE

When poaching eggs, the method differs slightly:

1. Bring a couple inches of water to a simmer in a sauté pan and add a generous pinch of salt (to help egg float in water).

2. For each egg, crack into a cup or small bowl; add a tablespoon of vinegar to the pan; stir to create a vortex, then slide egg into simmering water.

3. Let cook for 3 to 4 minutes until white is just set and yolk is still runny, then remove with a slotted spoon and let drain on a paper towel, trimming edges of white if desired.

METHOD **STEAMING**

PROS

Indirect moist heat cooks food gently, without much (if any) added fat needed, and with minimal loss of nutrients; vegetables also retain their color.

BEST FOR

Chicken breasts; firm-fleshed fish such as salmon, halibut, and cod; shellfish; dumplings; vegetables

BONUS TECHNIQUE

Cooking *en papillote* (in parchment packets) lets you steam chicken, fish, or vegetables in the oven. Each parcel is meant to be a meal-in-one; herbs and spices, a drizzle of oil, and a splash of wine or spritz of lemon juice are the usual flavor enhancers.

1. Place all ingredients off-center on a sheet of parchment, then fold it over and begin crimping the edges to seal completely.

2. Place on a rimmed baking sheet (in case of leaks) and steam in a 350°F oven until parcel is puffed up and browned in spots, or according to recipe.

3. Carefully snip open parcel with kitchen scissors to serve.

HOW-TO

The following steps are the same whether you use a collapsible metal basket or stackable bamboo baskets (the latter traditionally set in a wok).

1. Bring about 2 inches of water to a boil in a pot fitted with the basket (make sure it is not touching the water).

2. Arrange food in a single layer in basket; if cooking foods with different times, add them to basket at different stages.

3. Cover with a tight-fitting lid and cook just until food is done, using caution when removing lid (as steam can burn).

4. Season as desired, and drizzle with a bit of olive oil (or sesame oil for Asian-style dishes) before serving.

TIPS

- Cut food into same-size pieces for even cooking.

- Line bamboo baskets with parchment to keep them from picking up strong flavors; or line with cabbage or banana leaves.

- When using stackable baskets, place the food with the longest cooking time in bottom basket and then progress up from there; remove the top basket(s) when the food is ready.

- Don't have a metal or bamboo basket? Use a heatproof colander.

METHOD BRAISING

PROS

The path to meltingly tender meat (even tough, inexpensive cuts) and other food is braising—simmering food in liquid, which then doubles as the sauce.

HOW-TO

This method involves "low and slow" cooking in the oven.

1. Brown the meat in a little fat (butter or oil), turning with tongs to get color on all sides. Remove.

2. Sauté aromatics (onion is key), herbs and spices, and other vegetables as desired.

3. Deglaze the pot with wine, beer, stock, or water, stirring up the browned bits.

4. Return meat to pot and add enough liquid to just cover.

5. Cover pot tightly and braise in a 300°F oven until meat is fork-tender, anywhere from 30 minutes for fish to as long as 3 hours for briskets and other larger cuts.

6. Serve everything together, as is, or remove the meat and vegetables and reduce the liquid to desired consistency.

BEST FOR

Brisket and chuck roast; picnic shoulder and Boston butt; lamb shanks and shoulder; chicken legs and thighs; whole or filleted fish (such as monkfish, sea bass, and red snapper)

TIPS

- A good-quality Dutch oven is optimal, but any sturdy pot with a tight-fitting lid will do.

- Use bone-in meat for maximum flavor, and be sure to brown it well on all sides, and in batches if necessary.

- Vary the aromatics to create different flavor profiles: fresh ginger and lemongrass for Thai-style braises; fennel and tomato paste for Italian; chiles and harissa for North African-style tagines.

- Add more or less liquid depending on how long the meat will need to cook and how saucy you want the final dish to be.

- Cooking liquid plays an important factor in the flavor; wine, beer, vermouth, stock, even water all work well for deglazing.

- Use bright garnishes and finishing touches, such as fresh herbs or vinegar or lemon juice, to offset the richness.

BONUS TECHNIQUE

Braising doesn't always take hours to do, especially when it involves fish. To achieve the same richness in short order, however, it helps to infuse the cooking liquid with flavor before combining.

1. Follow the general formula—sear the fish, sauté the aromatics, deglaze the pot—and then add the cooking liquid.

2. Let this simmer away (covered) for 10 to 15 minutes to allow the flavors to meld before returning the fish (whole or fillets) in a single layer and braising just until opaque throughout.

HOW TO
SOLVE KITCHEN CONUNDRUMS

This roundup of ten common cooking dilemmas will ease your day-to-day meal prep—and provide you with the confidence to tackle the more uncommon ones. Think of them as problems, solved.

1. FOOLPROOF OMELET

The test of a true chef? A neatly folded omelet that's the proper degree of cooked and without a speck of browning on the surface. Follow these steps to success, every time.

- Crack three eggs into a bowl and gently whisk with a fork or whisk. Season with salt and add finely chopped fresh herbs, if desired. Cut 3 teaspoons of unsalted butter into small pieces and add them to the eggs.

- Use a 10-inch nonstick skillet to cook the eggs; the larger pan will allow the eggs to spread out in a thin, crepe-like manner for faster, more even cooking without taking on any color.

- Heat the pan for 30 seconds over medium heat before coating it with a tablespoon of butter.

- Pour eggs into center of pan, then immediately start to swirl the pan to coat evenly with one hand while running the fork in a figure-eight motion with the other, for about 30 seconds. The omelet should be just set around the edges but still slightly wet in the middle (it will continue to cook off heat).

- Run a heatproof flexible spatula around edge of omelet to loosen, then, with side of pan closest to you tilted up, gently use spatula to fold omelet over by one-third onto itself, then fold other side into the middle.

- Invert omelet onto serving plate, so the seam side is down. Sprinkle with more fresh herbs, if desired.

2. EASY-PEEL BOILED EGGS

It seems simple enough to do, but if you've ever ended up with an under- or over-cooked egg that's impossible to peel, you'll appreciate a couple of helpful hints.

TO COOK: Cover eggs with about an inch of water in a saucepan. Add ¼ teaspoon white vinegar (this will soften the shells, making them easier to peel). Bring to a gentle boil; take off heat. Cover pan and set timer for 6 minutes for soft yolks that are still runny, and up to 11 minutes for drier yolks.

TO PEEL: Cold eggs are easier to peel than hot. Shock the cooked eggs in an ice-water bath to cool quickly; let stand for at least 2 minutes, as the eggs will shrink back slightly from their shells, making them easier to peel—preferably right away. Eggs are also harder to peel after storing, so do so once they are cool enough to handle. First, tap egg all over (on the counter), then roll it around under your palm. Start peeling from the broad end to remove shell; you can do this under running water, if that helps.

3. SPATTER-FREE BACON

Frying bacon can be a messy endeavor; try this method instead. Lay bacon strips flat (do not overlap) on rimmed baking sheets lined with parchment paper. Bake, rotating the sheets once, until crisp and browned, 15 to 18 minutes, or to desired doneness. Transfer strips to a paper-towel-lined plate to drain.

4. QUICKER (AND TASTIER) OATS

Steel-cut oats make a heartier, tastier oatmeal, but they are admittedly more time-consuming than the quick-cooking variety. A few tweaks to your regular routine will increase the flavor and decrease the time.

- Cut the cooking time in half by fully submerging oats in tepid water, at room temperature, overnight or up to 24 hours. Thoroughly drain before cooking.

- To bring out the oats' flavor and texture, sauté them with a pat of butter and a pinch of salt until fragrant and golden before adding water to the pot and cooking until thick and creamy. (This same toasting trick can be used when adding oats to cookies and other baked goods.)

5. FLUFFIER PANCAKES

If your pancakes turn out too thin, there are several tricks you can try.

- First, bring your wet ingredients to room temperature before using them; cold liquids and eggs produce soggy pancakes. Also check that your baking powder is not outdated.

- Make sure not to overwork the batter when whisking wet and dry together—that develops the gluten in the flour, giving the pancakes a flat, gummy consistency. Instead, don't be bothered if there are some lumps of dry ingredients remaining (they will cook out).

- You can create more loft by folding a few whipped egg whites into the batter. This is yet another reason to save extra whites when baking (see page 309).

- Finally, and importantly, make sure your griddle is properly heated before you begin, as you need the heat to give the batter a boost so it puffs up. A drop of water should immediately sizzle and disappear. Also, don't over-grease the griddle; a thin film of oil or butter will suffice.

6. CLUMP-FREE RICE

If your rice tends to stick together, use the boiling method (similar to cooking pasta). You can also start by toasting the grains in a little oil before adding the water, for deeper flavor.

- Season a pot of boiling water generously with salt, then slowly stream in 1 cup long-grain rice, such as basmati or jasmine (for 3 cups cooked); give it a good stir, and return water to a boil.

- Cook (uncovered) for about 10 minutes, then test the grains; they should be tender but with a bit of bite. Drain in a fine-mesh sieve, shaking to remove excess liquid.

7. NEW-AND-IMPROVED PASTA

Here are three ways to put pasta's natural starchiness to use in creating a more harmonious dish.

- If you plan to top the pasta with something other than a cooked sauce, reserve about half a cup of cooking water at the end, before draining the pasta. Use this to help bind the pasta and toppings, adding a little at a time.

- If you are serving the pasta with a marinara or other cooked sauce, don't drain the pasta; instead, use kitchen tongs to transfer the pasta from the water to the pan with the sauce; let that simmer for a minute or so. This allows flavors to meld and adds a little hearty starchiness to the sauce.

- For one-pan pasta, combine all the ingredients—pasta, fresh or canned tomatoes, basil, chopped garlic and onion, and enough water to cover—in a deep-sided skillet, add a generous drizzle of olive oil, and bring to a boil. Simmer, uncovered, until pasta is al dente, the water has evaporated, and everything is wonderfully combined, tossing in fresh mozzarella or ricotta at the last minute for added creaminess.

ICED-COFFEE UPDATE

For a smoother, more flavorful iced coffee, start with a homemade cold-brew concentrate: Stir together 1 pound ground coffee and 8 cups cool water. Cover; let stand at room temperature for 24 hours. Strain through a coffee filter or cheesecloth-lined sieve into a container, pressing on solids to remove as much liquid as possible. Store in the refrigerator, covered. One batch makes a week's supply. To use, dilute one part concentrate with one to two parts cold water or milk; sweeten as desired and serve over ice. For full-strength enjoyment, freeze coffee in ice-cube trays and add to iced coffee.

8. NO-FUSS "REFRIGERATOR" PICKLES

You don't need to sterilize jars to "put up" these easy pickles. In a mere 60 minutes, you can have crispy, crunchy sidekicks for all your grilled meats and cheese platters.

- To make, combine white vinegar with a little coarse salt and sugar (white, brown, or raw). You will need about 1 cup vinegar per 2 cups of vegetables. Stir to dissolve.

- Add thinly sliced or whole vegetables, including radish, red onion, cucumber, green beans, okra, fennel bulb, and carrot, and let sit for an hour before serving. Refrigerate, tightly covered, for up to a month.

9. NO-CHURN FROZEN SWEETS

For the best texture, you need an ice-cream maker (and often a cooked and cooled custard). But you can skip some steps and get a similar payoff by making frozen treats in a food processor, or by scraping with a fork.

SHERBET: Peel and slice 6 large, ripe peaches, then freeze until firm. Blend with 1 cup sweetened condensed milk (in batches, if necessary) until creamy and smooth. Serve immediately for soft-serve consistency, or freeze in a covered loaf pan for up to one week.

SORBET: Follow steps above, leaving out sweetened condensed milk. Instead, dissolve ¾ cup sugar into ¾ cup water and blend with frozen peaches, along with 1 teaspoon lemon juice and a pinch of salt.

GRANITA: Stir together 2 cups fresh fruit juice with 1 cup simple syrup. Pour into a shallow dish, and freeze, uncovered, for 4 hours; every hour, scrape the mixture with tines of a fork, breaking up the ice crystals. Before serving, fluff the granita up with a fork. Transfer leftovers to an airtight container and freeze up to one month.

10. SHORTCUT CARAMEL

Making caramel from scratch can seem intimidating, but it doesn't have to be. Here are two ways to cheat on time and technique—no candy thermometer or "washing down the sides of the pan with a pastry brush" required.

- Employ the microwave: Stir together a half-cup of sugar and two tablespoons corn syrup in a microwave-proof bowl. Microwave on high 3 minutes, stirring after each minute. Stir again, then microwave just until golden and caramelized, about 15 seconds more. Then you can stir in enough cream to achieve your desired color (carefully, it will spatter) for a sauce, or leave as is.

- Or, make dulce de leche, a similarly smooth sauce: Place an unopened can of sweetened condensed milk (with the label removed) on its side in the bottom of a stockpot filled with water. Gently boil for 2 hours, replenishing the water as necessary to keep the pot full and the can submerged. (This is important! It prevents the can from bursting.) Using tongs, transfer the can to a wire rack and let cool completely before opening.

HOW TO BRUSH UP ON BAKING SKILLS

Baking is as much about kitchen science as it is your own skill set. Pay attention to the recipe and use precision from start to finish: Measuring, oven temperature, techniques, and gauging doneness all add up to achieving delicious baked cookies, cakes, and pies, time after time.

PREPPING INGREDIENTS

Measuring is just one part of the process; you'll also need to heed temperature requirements for ingredients (cold versus room temperature butter or eggs, for example) and other essentials.

FLOUR

When flour is to be sifted, skip the traditional sifter and use a whisk instead; it does an equally good job of breaking up clumps and incorporating air. Know that a cup of sifted (or whisked) flour and a cup of unsifted flour are not the same, so read recipe instructions carefully to determine which is being measured:

- For "1 cup sifted flour," sift first, then measure.

- For "1 cup flour, sifted," measure first, then sift.

- For cake flour, always sift before measuring—even when not specified in a recipe.

- To measure properly, practice the scoop-and-level method, using a straight edge like a ruler or large knife to scrape the flour flush with the rim of the measuring cup. Packing or tapping the measuring cup will change the results.

- Whisking together dry ingredients before adding to wet ensures the leavener (if there is any) is evenly distributed. It also helps to aerate the flour, for a smoother (lump-free) batter.

BAKING SODA VS. POWDER

While these two staples are both leaveners, they work differently, so they are not interchangeable. Baking soda requires an acidic ingredient, such as sour cream, chocolate, or molasses, to release carbon dioxide and cause dough or batter to rise, yielding fluffy muffins or cake. Baking powder, on the other hand, consists of baking soda, cream of tartar, and cornstarch—and can be used in

MARTHA MUST

Butter temperature is key in making tender, flaky pie crusts and biscuits. Grated frozen butter is quicker to distribute in the flour than chilled cubes, without overworking the dough.

recipes without an acidic ingredient because it already contains one (cream of tartar).

Both come in containers that make them easy to measure; scoop up with a measuring spoon, then scrape against the lid or perforated opening so the extra falls back in.

BUTTER

Using softened, not cold, butter is essential when creaming it to make cookies and cakes. Usually it takes about 30 minutes in a normal room temperature to soften sufficiently.

- When that's simply too long to wait, here's a shortcut: Microwave the butter up to 20 seconds, or until evenly softened, flipping it a quarter turn every 5 seconds. You can tell it's ready when it just holds an impression when pressed.

- No microwave? Slice it into thin pads, lay flat, and it should be ready in half the time.

EGGS

Eggs act as both leavener and binder—when separated, different aspects of each become more pronounced. Beaten whites incorporate air into angel food cake, while yolks add rich texture to custards and pastry creams. Eggs are easiest to separate when cold, but many recipes call for eggs at room temperature—so separate as soon as you take them out of the refrigerator and note these other tips. If you are using whole eggs, and need them to reach room temperature more quickly, soak them in a bowl of warm (not hot) water for about 10 minutes.

SEPARATING EGGS

Cracking eggs over a single bowl can lead to broken yolks in the whites—a no-no when beating egg whites for airy meringues and soufflés, as even the slightest bit of fat can impede the process.

- Instead, use three bowls and follow these steps: First crack an egg and separate white into one bowl, then drop yolk into another. Transfer egg white to third bowl. Repeat with remaining eggs, transferring each separated white to the third bowl before cracking the next egg.

- Or rest a colander over a bowl and get cracking, breaking each egg into a cup before adding to the rest; the whites will seep through, leaving the yolks in tip-top shape.

- Also, crack eggs on the kitchen counter instead of on the rim of your dish; that way, if bits of shell break off, they won't fall into the rest of the ingredients.

BEATING EGGS

Whites and yolks don't behave the same way when whisked and whipped. Here's how to handle each successfully.

- Whipped whites: Start with room temperature whites and a pristine bowl. Beat whites with a mixer on low speed and gradually increase speed to medium-high until soft peaks form (peak falls over when whisk is held straight up); if you are adding sugar, do it now. Beat until firm or stiff peaks form (peaks stand up straight).

- Beaten yolks: When a recipe calls for beating egg yolks (or whole eggs) with sugar "until a ribbon forms," that means the mixture should be thick and aerated enough to hold its shape—in the form of a ribbon—on its own

TIP

Unused yolks and whites can be refrigerated in airtight containers for up to three days, or frozen for up to three months and thawed overnight in the fridge; to keep the yolks from gelling, add a pinch of salt or sugar for every four yolks. Use whites to make meringues, cocktails, and egg-white omelets. Yolks can be used for curds, custards, hollandaise, and mayonnaise. Both can be brushed on pie dough and other pastry as egg washes (whites add sheen, yolks promote browning).

SUBSTITUTING EGGS

For vegan baking, you can replace each egg in a recipe with the following (and replace any butter with an equal amount of vegetable oil, in ounces).

- ¼ cup applesauce (or other unsweetened fruit puree)

- ¼ cup pureed silken tofu

- 1 tablespoon ground flaxseed plus 3 tablespoons water

surface for a few seconds when allowed to drip down from a whisk or spoon. A too-thin yolk mixture will not provide the necessary structure. If the mixture quickly disappears, keep beating and test again.

FOLDING EGGS

When folding in beaten egg whites, there's just one goal: Don't let them deflate. To accomplish that, cut the spatula down through the center of the batter, then make a sweeping motion up the side of the bowl—like making the letter *J*. Next, turn spatula over and repeat until just combined, rotating bowl as you go. It's also generally a good idea to fold in eggs in three batches.

VANILLA

Almost as common as flour, sugar, and butter in baking, vanilla lends subtle depth to all types of batters (as well as frostings, fillings, custards, frozen desserts, and other sweets). Many recipes call for vanilla beans, which offer a more pronounced, concentrated flavor, though good-quality vanilla extract (look for "pure" on the label) packs enough punch on its own.

- If using vanilla beans, split the pod lengthwise with the tip of a paring knife, then use the dull side of the knife to scrape out the seeds. Save the pods for other uses (see page 291).

- Vanilla beans can be expensive and hard to find; you can use 2½ teaspoons pure vanilla extract instead of each bean called for.

CHOCOLATE

Many of the best desserts wouldn't be the same without chocolate as an ingredient. Dark, bittersweet, semisweet, or milk—they're all delicious, especially when you start with a good-quality bar.

MELTING

Chocolate can seize, or harden, if any water gets in during or after melting. Here's how to avoid that (and fix any errors).

- Chop chocolate into fine shards using a serrated knife (as shown at right), so it melts quickly and evenly.

- To melt, put the shards in a heatproof bowl set over (not in) a pan of barely simmering water, making sure bottom of bowl is not touching the water; heat until halfway melted, then remove from heat and stir until smooth.

- If it still manages to seize, try adding boiling water, a teaspoon at a time, and whisk until chocolate is satiny smooth again.

SHAVING

Curls and shavings make any dessert instantly more impressive. Use a vegetable peeler and a slightly warm block of chocolate.

- To produce nice, tight curls, start from the far edge of the chocolate and move a regular peeler toward you, making short swipes.

- Or, spread melted chocolate in a thin layer on the back of a rimmed baking sheet; let stand until set, then use a bench scraper (held at a 45-degree angle) to scrape into curls, chilling the chocolate as needed if it gets too warm.

TIP

An even easier way to melt chocolate is in the microwave. Use 20-second intervals, and stir after each, just until three-quarters of the chocolate is melted; then let sit for a few minutes to allow residual heat to melt the rest before stirring until smooth.

BAKING TIPS

Your oven is your partner in any baking endeavor, so you will want to make the most of its capacities. If you've ever noticed uneven browning or that food took much longer to reach the desired state of doneness than the recipe called for, odds are it's due to oven hot spots or because its actual temperature is not matching what it says on the dial.

■ Calibration is key: Set an oven thermometer on the middle rack, in the center. Preheat the oven; if the temps don't match up, you'll need to adjust up or down until they do. Take note so you can use these adjusted temperatures going forward (or have your oven repaired).

■ Pay attention to the recipe: If it calls for baking something on the upper, middle, or lower rack, there's a good reason. In general, if you are using more than one rack, you should switch the positions halfway through baking—it's also a good practice to rotate the pans from front to back when you do this (in case of hot spots).

■ Finally, while baking times are helpful, they aren't the final word on when something is at its ideal state. Pay attention to the visual cues—"golden brown on top" or "no longer jiggles in the center" are just some of the stop signs.

SUBSTITUTIONS

When you're up to your elbows in flour and find that you're short on brown sugar, the substitutions in this chart will come in handy.

INSTEAD OF 1 CUP	YOU CAN USE
Self-rising flour	1 cup all-purpose flour plus 1½ teaspoons baking powder and ½ teaspoon salt
Cake flour	1 cup minus 2 tablespoons all-purpose flour
Light-brown sugar	1 cup white sugar plus 1 tablespoon molasses
Molasses	¾ cup dark-brown sugar plus ¼ cup water
All-purpose flour	¾ cup whole wheat flour
Buttermilk	1 cup regular milk plus 1 tablespoon of fresh lemon juice or white vinegar (let mixture stand 5 minutes before using)

HOW TO
FROST A CAKE

Birthdays, anniversaries, graduations, showers, bake sales—all are made more special with a beautifully frosted and filled cake. Follow these tips to ensure yours is a triumph.

PREP THE PAN

A well-prepped pan ensures the cake layers cook evenly and won't stick.

- First grease the pans with softened butter; a pastry brush lets you reach into the nooks and spread it evenly. When buttering muffin tins, be sure to brush the surface between each cup to make unmolding easier.

- Then line the bottom of the pan with parchment. Parchment that's too big can produce a wrinkly cake. To cut a liner for a round cake pan, fold a square in half horizontally, and then vertically. Fold so the two creased sides meet to form a triangle. Fold the same way again; repeat until the narrowest side is 1 inch long. Place the sharpest point at the pan's center; use scissors to cut to size. Butter the pan, unfold paper, place in pan, and butter the parchment.

- Finally, dust the pan with flour—or cocoa, if making chocolate cakes—and tap out the excess before pouring in the batter.

TIP

To create the layers shown opposite, bake two genoise cakes in rimmed baking sheets; roll each into a log, let cool, then unroll; spread with filling and freeze until firm. Halve cakes lengthwise; starting with a short end, roll up one strip and place in center of turntable; starting at the end, wrap another strip around first, and so on. Spread more filling over top. Freeze until firm (8 hours).

LEVEL AND LAYER

After cakes are baked and before assembling, they often need to be split into layers, or leveled to make even. Either way, cakes are easier to handle after being chilled overnight (wrap tightly in plastic once they cool completely). The jagged edges of a serrated knife slice cleanly through cakes, without tearing; one that's long enough to extend all the way through is the easiest to maneuver.

- Besides helping the layers to stack up nice and straight, leveled tops provide a smooth surface for piping on decorations (this goes for cupcakes, too). Holding the cake steady with one hand, use a long serrated knife and a gentle sawing motion to trim off just the top.

- When splitting a cake into two layers, instead of trying to eyeball it, measure the height of the cake, then insert toothpicks at the halfway point at intervals around the circumference. Keep the top steady with one hand, and slice through the cake (using the same sawing motion) just above toothpicks.

- To help lift and move the cake layers, use cardboard cake rounds (sold at baking supply shops); slide the layers on and off the rounds as you work.

MARTHA MUST

A rotating cake stand, or turntable, makes decorating cakes all the easier to do; many can also double as a serving piece. Before decorating, tuck strips of parchment paper underneath the cake's edges—that way the stand will be frosting-free (remove paper before serving).

FILL AND FROST

Two coats of frosting add up to one beautifully frosted cake. A turntable is useful when
applying both coats and when piping a design
onto the cake ("glue" cake to turntable with a
dab of frosting before you begin). Remember
to chill the cake until the frosting is firm after
each step.

■ When filling between layers, learn from the
experts: Put the filling in a pastry bag—or a
plastic bag with a corner snipped off—and
pipe to form a "dam" around the perimeter,
then fill in by piping a loose spiral to the
center. Smooth lightly with an offset spatula.
You'll end up with a more even result.

■ Crumb coating ensures seemingly flawless
results: Spread a very thin layer of frosting over the assembled cake to seal in stray
crumbs; use a bench scraper to smooth it
and wipe off the excess. Chilling is essential;
an hour at the minimum, longer is even better. Then add a second, final coat to finish.

■ For an ultrasmooth surface—ideal for piping
on details—spread the frosting with a large
offset spatula. Use it to spread more frosting
on top of the crumb coat; for cake sides, hold
the spatula at a 45-degree angle while rotating
the cake. Wipe off the blade with a hot kitchen
towel (or dip the knife in hot water and dry off)
as you go, for seamless results.

MEASURING EQUIVALENTS
1 tablespoon = 3 teaspoons
⅛ cup = 2 tablespoons
¼ cup = 4 tablespoons
⅓ cup = 5 tablespoons + 1 teaspoon
½ cup = 8 tablespoons
⅔ cup = 10 tablespoons + 2 teaspoons
¾ cup = 12 tablespoons
1 cup = 48 teaspoons
1 cup = 16 tablespoons
8 fluid ounces = 1 cup
1 pint = 2 cups
1 quart = 2 pints
1 quart = 4 cups
1 gallon = 4 quarts

MARTHA MUST

When you will be
transporting a
decorated cake
to a party and it's
too big for a cake
carrier, place it in
a box that's large
enough on all
sides and taller
than the cake; line
the bottom of the
box with a nonskid
mat to keep the
cake from sliding.
Be sure to bring
extra frosting and
other embellish-
ments, along with
piping tools and
offset spatulas, for
any last-minute
repairs.

TIPS FOR BETTER BUTTER CAKES

The quintessential birthday cakes, butter cakes have a tender crumb and rich flavor that make them perennial favorites. They are also among the easiest of cakes to prepare, but that doesn't mean you can't improve the odds by following these simple steps.

1. PLAN AHEAD: Butter, eggs, and dairy (such as buttermilk or sour cream) should be at room temperature to ensure they combine evenly and thoroughly. Butter is soft enough when it holds an impression from your fingertip while keeping its shape.

2. DON'T RUSH: Start by beating the softened butter with the sugar. Called creaming, this important step aerates the batter for a light and fluffy texture. The fluffier the mixture, the airier the finished cake. If you are using a stand mixer, this can take about 5 minutes; a hand-held one may take double that time.

3. ADD AS DIRECTED: Recipes often instruct to add one egg at a time. This allows the egg to emulsify with the butter (just like oil and water, these two ingredients don't readily combine); beat well after each addition. Alternating dry and wet ingredients when beating them into the batter is also important in helping prevent toughness (beating all the flour at once causes the proteins in the gluten to develop). Always begin and end with the dry ingredients.

4. STOP AS NEEDED: Scrape down the sides of the bowl with a flexible spatula every now and then, especially when adding the dry ingredients; this is the surest way to achieve a smooth, lump-free batter. And here's a nifty tip: Use the mixer's paddle attachment to scrape across the bottom of the bowl at the end, to make sure there are no bits of dry ingredients lingering there.

CELEBRATE

I'm an unabashed fan of the holidays—all of them. I love decorating Easter eggs and hiding them for children to hunt, I love carving pumpkins and dressing up for Halloween, I love hosting the Thanksgiving feast for family and friends, and I love making wreaths and trimming the tree for Christmas.

There are simply not enough pages in this book to cover every aspect of every holiday. But we hope that most everyone can find—from this curated selection of tips and techniques— useful, inspiring ideas to bring to their family traditions and occasions, and make them their own.

Of course, celebrations aren't just for holidays. There are anniversaries, college graduations, and birthdays, too. I have had so much fun inventing clever ways to celebrate my grandchildren's birthdays over the past several years, each party and theme better than the year before. And so, we've shared some fun ideas on these pages to surprise the special kids in your life.

Finally, for me, the most joyful part of any occasion is giving thoughtfully chosen, beautifully wrapped, handcrafted presents. This chapter starts with gift-giving, and making tags and toppers that are worthy of what's wrapped inside. Celebrating is all in the details, after all.

CREATE FESTIVE TAGS, TIES, AND TOPPERS

Wrap gifts that bear your own personal stamp—and are almost too gorgeous to open. The presents will likely contribute to your holiday décor, parked under the tree or otherwise arranged around the home, so that's a good place to start when looking for inspiration. If you have a sparkly metallic theme with ornaments and wreaths, for example, carry that out with the gift toppers, too. See the following for how to create festive packages galore.

THREE FESTIVE IDEAS

For easy embellishments, upcycle baking cups, pipe cleaners, and other simple supplies, all available at your local party-supply store (or well-stocked craft cabinet).

1. BAKING CUPS

Paper liners for cupcakes and candies come in different sizes, colors, and patterns—and no cutting is needed.

TASSELS: Wrap a piece of waxed twine around a wrapped box as shown. Pinch a paper liner at its center to form a conical shape, then knot one end of twine around pinched end to close. Repeat to make another tassel on other twine end.

CIRCLES: Use a glue stick to attach flattened liners onto a wrapped box or envelope, folding over edges, and layering smaller ones over larger ones.

TAGS: Flatten six or so liners in different sizes and colors; fold a few, for a staggered look. Then layer them and glue them together. Using a craft knife, cut two slits in center, and thread a ribbon through, wrapping it around box to secure.

2. SILVER ACCENTS

All that glitters is not gold, at least when it comes to these metallic accents—all made with inexpensive materials.

GARLAND: Wrap shiny, starry wire garland around box, then secure with silver tape.

BAND: Center a strip of paper-fringe garland on top of a long gift; tie down with silver ribbon. Or stick a line of self-adhesive mini bows on a ribbon tied around center of box.

STARS: Glue the bottom of a small gift on top of a store-bought star-shaped tag. Then glue another star tag on top of gift.

BOW: Rather than sticking a smaller bow on a larger package, nestle a tiny box inside an oversize metallic bow.

TASSELS: First adhere two mini bows, flat sides together, with one end of a length of bakers' twine in between. Wrap around gift box, then add two mini bows around other end of twine in the same manner.

GIFT-WRAPPING BASICS

How to make a beautifully wrapped present? Gather your supplies (double-sided tape is a must), clear a large work surface, and follow these simple steps.

MEASURE PAPER

Center box on paper and wrap paper around box—the ends should overlap by a couple of inches. Cut with sharp scissors.

SECURE SIDES

Bring one side of paper halfway across the top; affix with double-sided tape. Repeat with opposite side, just overlapping the first; tape in place.

3. CONFETTI

Brightly colored paper cutouts are practically a dime a dozen at the dollar store. Use them to dress up your holiday presents.

GLITTER GIFT TAGS: With a small hole punch, punch out even tinier bits of confetti in different colors. Adhere double-sided tape to an envelope flap and trim to fit; cover with confetti. Or simply place one strip of double-sided tape on a gift tag, then cover with confetti.

SEE-THROUGH WRAPPING: Put a handful of store-bought and mini DIY confetti in a small cellophane bag (trim as needed to turn it into an envelope) and slip a gift card inside. Or cover a wrapped box with cellophane and toss in confetti before taping up final flap.

BAND OF CIRCLES: Adhere a strip of double-sided tape down the side of a gift box, and cover with confetti in different sizes and colors.

FOLD ENDS

Starting on one end, fold down top flap, creating wings on either side; push in and flatten those wings against box. Then fold remaining flap up against box, folding it under itself if it extends too far; tape in place. Repeat with other end.

ADD EMBELLISHMENTS

Wrap boxes with a ribbon or twine, embellish with toppers, such as those described above, and don't forget to include a tag with the recipient's name.

HOW TO CELEBRATE A KID'S BIRTHDAY

Whether someone is turning 1 or 101 years old, they deserve a party that reflects their personality. Kids really take the cake, though, in celebrating their special day. Following are six steps for throwing a successful party.

1. CHOOSE THE THEME

Having a theme helps to unify all the details, from the invitations and party favors to the cake and decorations. When settling on one, take a cue from the birthday boy or girl.

STICK WITH NUMBERS AND LETTERS: Kids are proud to be turning another year older, so tap into that excitement by putting their brand-new digit on all the details. Or use their initials (first and/or last) as the organizing motif.

PLAY UP THEIR PASSIONS: Same goes for a favorite color, toy, or hobby—a tiny tot's beloved stuffed animal, a preschooler's delight in the circus, or a school-age kid's fascination with outer space, just for some examples.

GO WITH THE SEASON: Summer opens the door to beach-themed bashes and stargazing, while winter has its share of snowflakes and other snowy scenes. Think colorful leaves and campfires for fall, baby animals, bugs, and blossoms for spring.

PICK A PATTERN: Polka-dots, stars and stripes, anchors, arrows, checkerboard, confetti, even doodles—whatever the motif, it will make a striking statement when replicated across all elements of the party.

2. SETTLE ON THE LOCATION

The choice of location will depend on the guest count, season, and desired activities. Here are some options to keep in mind.

- Many kids experience pride of place when it comes to celebrating their birthdays in their own homes. For the party thrower, hosting a home party allows for more improvisation on the theme, though you will be handling everything yourself, start to finish.

- On the other hand, a venue (such as an indoor trampoline park or a private pool) can often help you with at least some of the preparations and on-site supervision. Check the policies on group pricing and other restrictions (minimum ages, parental waivers, and maximum guest count) at the outset.

- Don't overlook nearby parks and recreation centers, bowling alleys, family-friendly restaurants, skating rinks, amusement parks, and other destinations where you can take a smaller group without prior arrangements.

3. PREPARE THE GUEST LIST

Unless the guest of honor is a preschooler, you will need to consult with him or her in determining who should be invited; if it's a surprise party, try coordinating with the best friend (if they can keep a secret)—or just ask your child, hypothetically speaking.

- To avoid letting fickle affections create problems come party time, some hosts invite the whole class, so no one is left out.

- Otherwise, one helpful rule of thumb is to ask as many kids as the child's age plus one: That works out to eight guests for a seventh birthday, 13 for a 12-year-old.

MARTHA MUST

When developing my grandchildren's outer-space-themed birthday party, we found many important elements online, including giant inflatable planets that we hung from the ceiling, and a portable planetarium show. The children made soft-foam planets, which doubled as party favors.

- The planned activities can also help determine the right number of guests. A larger, even number of kids—at least eight or 10—may be best for team games at a 5-year-old's party, but you may want just three guests for a 9-year-old's sleepover.

- Allow siblings to invite a friend—and then let them help with activities if they are old enough. Or find a place for siblings to spend time elsewhere if that's what they prefer.

- Importantly, decide whether the party will be drop-off, or if adults will be included.

4. SEND OUT INVITATIONS

It's best to send out invitations—either by e-vite or mail—about a month before the date. If you haven't yet nailed down all the particulars, at least send a "save the date" e-vite to put it on families' calendars, and then follow up with the official invite no fewer than two weeks before the party. Be sure to include the following information:

DATE AND TIMEFRAME: Be sure to provide both start and end times.

- Some venues limit the time to just two hours; for other parties, tailor the duration to the age group (the younger, the shorter; no more than two hours for preschoolers).

- If the party will take place during regular mealtimes, indicate whether lunch or dinner will be served.

- Even slumber parties should have an end time. Some hosts prefer to be straightforward: "Drop-off: Friday at 5 p.m./Pickup: Saturday by 10 a.m." Others take a more subtle approach: "Morning-after activity: Sleep late, have a pillow fight, and eat pancakes."

WHO IS INVITED: Specify whether adults are dropping off or encouraged to stay, or if it's up to each family. You can also indicate this by asking for the number of attendees on the RSVP.

LOCATION AND DIRECTIONS: This might not be necessary if everyone knows where you live; otherwise you'll need to be proactive.

- Providing a map is easy to do with e-vites—simply plug in a link (and check to make sure that link takes you to the actual address, not the one in the next town over).

- For mailed invitations, be sure to include the GPS address (and a landmark for hard-to-find locations).

RSVP INFORMATION: Specify your preferred mode of responding, whether that's via text, email, or phone call, along with the desired date for replying.

- Venues that require a precise head count have cutoff dates for refunds, so allow yourself some wiggle room; it's entirely appropriate to call anyone who hasn't replied in a timely fashion for a final confirmation.

- For at-home parties, a week should allow sufficient time for you to plan accordingly, but don't expect the RSVPs to arrive mere days after people receive their invitations.

- Ask people to indicate any allergies (to food or other substances) or other medical conditions when they respond, too.

SPECIAL INSTRUCTIONS: Include any items guests should bring, such as a swimsuit and towel; snowsuit, hat, and gloves; or sleeping bag and pillow.

- If it is a surprise party, tell guests to keep it a secret! For younger kids, it's probably better to send the invitations to the adults only.

THE TIMELINE

6 WEEKS BEFORE

Choose the theme; make a guest list; confirm the date; reserve off-site space (if needed).

4 WEEKS BEFORE

Get updated class list; prep invitations; decide on activities and food.

3 WEEKS BEFORE

Send invitations; purchase party goods; start decorations and favors, if making by hand.

1 TO 2 WEEKS BEFORE

Purchase craft supplies and favors; finalize party schedule; make samples of planned crafts; call guests who have not yet responded; confirm guest count with venue.

3 DAYS BEFORE

Buy food and refreshments along with any serving supplies.

1 TO 2 DAYS BEFORE

Bake the cake; decorate your home or be sure off-site supplies are gathered; prepare make-ahead foods.

THE DAY OF

Add last-minute decorations to the cake.

5. DECIDE ON THE FOOD

While most kids would be happy with cake and ice cream, you'll want to tailor the menu to the timing of the party.

■ For the birthday cake, let the honoree help with picking out flavors, frostings, and the overall design, which should tie into the theme of the day. You don't have to make an elaborate cake for it to be memorable; often just seeing his name in icing and getting to blow out the requisite number of candles is special enough.

■ For a party at midday or early evening, more substantial fare will often be expected (even if you didn't say as much on the invitation). You could let the theme of the party guide you in planning the menu, whether it's a "concession stand" (with hot dogs, nachos, and popcorn) for a movie-night motif, or sandwiches cut into space-themed (or other appropriate) shapes with cookie cutters.

■ For an all-purpose, all-age crowd-pleaser, provide a build-your-own-pizza station— older kids can even help with the cooking. Set out prebaked individual pizza crusts along with sauce, cheese, and a variety of toppings.

■ For a similar fun, hands-on idea, offer a taco bar with all the fixings; this is especially good for picky eaters who can choose among the options, while letting more adventure-some appetites have their fill.

■ No matter the time of the party, plan on snacks: fresh fruit and vegetable platters, tortilla chips and (mild) salsa or guacamole, pita chips and hummus, even a bowl of pretzels.

■ For drinks, fill pitchers and bottles ahead of time with water and decorate them to match the theme, then set them at a help-yourself drink station (for all but the youngest kids).

Juice boxes are a great spillproof (almost) option for the youngest children. For an outside party, fill a cooler with ice and bottled drinks.

6. PLAN THE ACTIVITIES

The beauty of having a party at a venue is that the activities are built into the event. For at-home parties, or those at a nearby park, you'll want to keep the kids busy. Also, consider crafts that double as party favors, for the guests to take home.

■ Here again, the theme can suggest certain games or crafts, such as making cardboard rockets or papier mâché planets for a space party, or doing experiments (baking soda volcanoes) for a mad-science theme.

■ For outside parties, the sky's the limit on what you could do. Consider lawn games (see page 273) for older kids, water slides and balloons for younger ones, and scavenger hunts for any and all ages (with adults supervising the very young). Or have all the materials for tie-dyeing or kite-making.

■ For indoor events, set up a crafts table (or tables) with the necessary supplies and a premade example of the project. Make sure the craft is age-appropriate—no sharp scissors for preschoolers, for example. Origami and paper punches are safe bets, as are pipe-cleaner projects, finger knitting (see page 183), friendship bracelets (see page 193), jewelry beading, duct-tape creations, and embellishing picture frames.

■ Seasonal projects, such as snow globes— or iced sugar cookies—in the winter, pressed flowers in the spring, rock crafts in the summer, and leaf arts and crafts in the fall, are other options.

TIP

For an at-home event, replenish your first-aid kit, make arrangements for your pets (in case of allergies or fears), and, when younger children will be attending, do a careful once-over to make sure all potential toxins are out of reach.

HOW TO CELEBRATE
VALENTINE'S DAY

If ever you needed a cause to create a card from scratch, it's Valentine's Day—and not just for kids' classroom parties. There are a great many fun techniques that let you customize the sentiments, two of which are included here. Adapt the techniques to put your own stamp on the cards, for February 14 and throughout the year (e.g., for birthdays, anniversaries, and other special occasions).

CARD-MAKING BASICS

No matter what kind of Valentine you decide to produce, doing it in assembly-line fashion will help you make multiples in very little time.

1. GATHER THE MATERIALS: You likely have most of the supplies to make a variety of cards.

- Use sturdy card stock or scrapbook paper for the card itself as well as for creating templates and to use as backing.

- There are many types of paper, plain and patterned (including origami), that you can use for inserts and embellishments.

- Sharp scissors and a craft knife are needed to cut the card and embellishments, aided by a self-healing cutting mat and a ruler.

- A bone folder makes the crispest folds.

- Double-sided tape affixes things invisibly.

- Paper punches can provide pretty edges or other flourishes.

- Assorted pens, pencils, and markers let you put your sentiments in writing.

2. DECIDE ON DIMENSIONS: If you plan to present the card in an envelope (a must if mailing), measure envelope first and size card about ¼ inch smaller all around. Otherwise, the card can be any size you like.

3. CUT AND FOLD: For the cleanest results, cut the paper with a craft knife on a self-healing mat, using a ruler for a straightedge. If folding, score paper with a bone folder.

4. ADD BACKING: Some cards need additional backing to conceal cuts or add weight: Create a border by cutting the back piece slightly larger than the front, and layer with patterned and solid papers (as shown opposite, left).

5. INCLUDE THE MESSAGE: Write out by hand, or use rubber stamps and ink, stickers, paper cutouts, or pop-ups.

TIP

Invite friends over for a V-Day "crafternoon," setting out a variety of plain and patterned papers; twine, tape, and glue adhesives; and assorted writing implements.

MORE IDEAS AND INSPIRATION

While you can certainly express your emotions with a simple open-and-shut greeting, a card that delivers an element of surprise inside will really capture the heart and attention of its recipient(s).

POP-UP CARDS

A quick photocopy, cut, and crease is all it takes to craft these sweet-talking cards. Make one design or all three. Copy the template (see page 384) onto card stock, then cut out and trace onto desired paper for the folded piece. (If making just one card, you can print the template directly onto desired paper.) Use bone folder to fold paper along score marks. Then unfold, cut out, and refold. Position the folded piece inside the base of the card so it pops when opened. Secure with double-sided tape.

GARLAND CARDS

These cards start by folding desired paper embellishments in half, then cutting along the fold or making doubles to sandwich cord between. Copy the template (see pages 385–386) onto card stock, then cut out and trace onto desired paper. For lovebirds, position template so that the beak's point is right at paper's folded edge. For heart lock, cut two lock bases, one lock front, and two keys. Sandwich the cord's ends between duplicates, and secure with double-sided tape. For airplane, cut two fuselages and six heart clouds. Sandwich ribbon between duplicates; tape to secure.

HOW TO CELEBRATE
PASSOVER

The Passover seder (from the Hebrew word for "order") is a symbolic celebration where family and friends gather at the table—and where certain foods bring the story of Passover to life. Matzo, an unleavened bread that represents ancient Israelites' hurried escape from slavery in Egypt, when there wasn't time to wait for dough to rise, is perhaps the most familiar of those foods. But every item on the seder table holds some special meaning.

THE SEDER PLATE

The focal point of any Passover table, the seder plate, features five ceremonial foods:

- *Karpas*, a vegetable or herb, such as celery or parsley, is dipped in salt water to suggest the tears shed by the slaves.

- *Maror*, a bitter herb, typically horseradish and/or romaine lettuce, represents the bitterness of slavery.

- *Haroset*, a mixture of apples, nuts, and spices, signifies both the hard labor they endured and the sweetness of liberation.

- *Z'roa*, a roasted lamb-shank bone, represents the *paschal* (lamb) sacrifice the Israelites made on their exodus from Egypt.

- *Beitzah*, a roasted egg, symbolizes spring, renewal, and fertility.

- Plus, the four glasses of kosher wine prescribed for every adult symbolize the four stages of their journey: freedom, deliverance, redemption, and release.

PASSOVER DESSERTS

When it comes to baking, matzo meal is often employed to replace standard flours for cakes, cookies, pie doughs, and pastries. Nut flours are another option—and are classic ingredients in European-style tortes (and many modern gluten-free recipes). Since dairy products often contain additives (and so are not kosher), some people avoid those, too. Instead, use coconut oil, non-dairy creamers, or "kosher-for-Passover" chocolate and other ingredients.

FLOURLESS OPTIONS: More often, flour-free treats are in order, and there are a surprising number to choose from.

- Meringues—basically, beaten egg whites with sugar and vanilla or other flavorings—can be baked into disks and then layered with kosher curd or coconut cream and fresh fruit.

- All sorts of cookies can be prepared, including coconut or almond macaroons.

- Flourless chocolate cake is perhaps the most classic holiday dessert, substituting butter with coconut oil.

MATZO CRACKERS: These make dessert even easier—and very delicious.

- For matzo bark, cover two whole crackers (side by side in a rimmed baking sheet) with melted dark chocolate; before it sets, sprinkle with chopped toasted nuts and flaky sea salt; chopped candied ginger and grated orange zest; or toasted flaked coconut.

- Stack the crackers, icebox-cake-style, with whipped "cream" and coat with chocolate ganache (both made with coconut cream or non-dairy cream of choice); top with fresh raspberries and shaved dark chocolate.

- Make matzo s'mores, sandwiching toasted marshmallows (under the broiler, if preferred) and chocolate-bar squares between crackers.

TIP

Rather than having a communal seder plate, create one for each individual at the table; this one features the five symbolic foods, with both romaine and horseradish representing *maror*.

MORE IDEAS
AND INSPIRATION

As a food-centered holiday that takes place at the table, Passover calls for personalized gifts (below, left) and settings (below, right) that can be enjoyed during the meal.

GIFT FOR THE HOST

If you're invited to a seder and are unfamiliar with the host's traditions, kosher wine is always appreciated. Wrap the bottle in decorative paper with a matching tag (punch out a circle to hang over the bottle's neck); colorful crepe paper cinched with twine; or a large handwritten note secured with a ribbon, as shown above.

MATZO PLACE CARDS

Matzo crackers with piped-chocolate names perform double duty as lovely, symbolic, and edible place cards. To make them, fill a re-sealable plastic bag with melted and cooled dark chocolate, snip off the corner, and write each guest's name across a short side of a cracker. Let set before tucking into a folded napkin, allowing the name to show.

PROJECT
BOOKMARK PLACE CARDS

This pretty place card doubles as a take-home bookmark for the Haggadah. Watercolor paper has a nubby texture (or "tooth") that is designed to be painted on; it is also durable and sturdy, both good qualities for a gift that's meant to be used again and again.

SUPPLIES

Watercolor paper

Craft paints or watercolors

Paintbrush

Scissors or craft knife

Hole punch

Thin ribbon

Pen or pencil

1. Start by painting a whole piece of watercolor paper with watered-down craft paint or watercolors in the desired color (test your paint on scrap paper until it is the right opacity). Let dry.

2. Cut paper into bookmarks. You should be able to get three per sheet by cutting crosswise, to match the one shown here.

3. Punch a hole near the top, in the center, and run a ribbon through it; tie ribbon.

4. Write each person's name near the top, so it will show when tucked inside napkin.

HOW TO CELEBRATE
EASTER

Whether or not the Easter bunny is a fanciful figment in your child's mind, egg decorating—and hunting—can still be a much-anticipated tradition. Dip-dyeing eggs is great old-fashioned fun for the whole family, and even "mistakes" can be magical.

EGG-DYEING BASICS

Keep it super-simple with only primary colors, or strive for the spectacular—and be sure to enlist the little ones to help. For a more interesting display, use eggs in a variety of sizes (besides medium, large, and extra-large, you can sometimes find small and jumbo eggs at supermarkets and farmers' markets). White eggs will yield the cleanest results; brown eggs require more coloring.

TIP

To make speckled eggs, fill paper cups halfway with either dried beans, popcorn kernels, uncooked rice, or peanuts in the shell; mix in desired food coloring, then add boiled egg. Gently shake and swirl to create the splatter effect.

EGG-DYEING HOW-TO

No matter the technique, the steps are basically the same:

1. BLOW OUT EGGS: Pierce top and bottom of each egg with a craft knife, turning the knife in one hole to widen it slightly. Poke a paper clip through one hole; stir to break up the yolk. Hold the egg over a bowl, with the larger hole facing down, and blow the contents out with a rubber syringe. (Alternately, hard-boil the eggs as described on page 305.)

2. MAKE A DRYING RACK: Cut ½ inch of foam core into roughly a 10-inch square. With a pencil and ruler, draw a grid. Where the lines cross, insert straight pins.

3. PREP YOUR SPACE AND DYE: Cover the area with paper towels or newspaper. Mix 1 teaspoon vinegar and 20 drops food coloring (use more to intensify color) in 1 cup hot water in a heat-proof bowl, cup, or jar deep enough to let you submerge an egg completely. Or consult the Egg-Dyeing Color Chart (see page 332) for the specific shades shown.

4. DIP TO DECORATE: Place eggs in bowl, spooning dye over egg and/or turning to coat completely. To create different tints of the same color, consult the Egg-Dyeing Color Chart (see page 332) for exact dyeing times.

- To make a two-color egg, dye the whole egg first in a light color, let dry 15 minutes, and then dip half in a darker color. Stick with colors that are near each other on the color chart; those opposite each other tend to look muddy if they overlap.

- To marbleize, dye the whole egg, then prepare a second batch of dye using a darker shade or a different color. Add 1 tablespoon olive oil, swirl to create curlicues of oil on the surface, and add dyed egg; roll it once around bowl, and remove to dry.

MARTHA MUST

My Araucana hens lay eggs in the most beautiful colors, which take on dye in an interesting way (or you can leave them as they are). I also like to dye smaller quail eggs and larger duck or goose eggs, for a variety of shapes and sizes. Always wipe these specialty eggs with distilled white vinegar before dyeing them, so they take the color more evenly.

EGG-DYEING
COLOR CHART

Follow the formulas in the chart to achieve the bright hues in the color wheel below (darker shades are shown; dipping time is also provided for lighter shades of the same color).

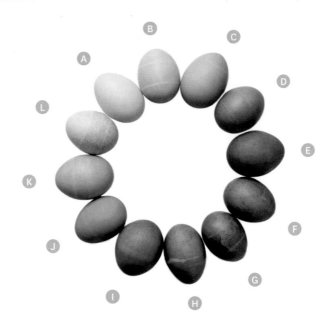

DESIRED COLOR	DROPS OF FOOD COLORING (PER CUP OF WATER)	DIPPING TIME FOR LIGHTER SHADE (MINUTES)	DIPPING TIME FOR DARKER SHADE (MINUTES)
Yellow (A)	20 Yellow	½	15
Yellow-Orange (B)	19 Yellow + 1 Red	2	12
Orange (C)	17 Yellow + 3 Red	2½	12
Pink-Orange (D)	6 Red + 14 Yellow	2	12
Pink (E)	20 Red	1	4
Pink-Violet (F)	10 Blue + 10 Red	1	5
Violet (G)	15 Blue + 5 Red	1	7
Blue-Violet (H)	18 Blue + 2 Red	1	5
Blue (I)	20 Blue	½	5
Blue-Green (J)	6 Blue + 14 Green	1½	8
Green (K)	20 Green	½	8
Yellow-Green (L)	15 Yellow + 5 Green	½	10

MORE IDEAS AND INSPIRATION

Easter eggs are not just for hunting; they also make stunning decorations. Dye dozens in complementary colors (i.e., next to each other on the wheel), or give them metallic accents.

GILDED EGGS

To make these opulent ovals, first dye the eggs in bright colors (see page 331), and then use a fine paintbrush to apply copper or gold leaf, available at craft-supply stores. Here, some of the eggs have a few or more blurry blotches; others are coated completely in a smoother sheen.

DYED-EGG CENTERPIECE

This impressive basket is filled with finely shredded brown paper and 110 dyed eggs, arranged in concentric ovals. For the deepest shades, start with dark-brown eggs (if using white eggs, you'll need to double dip). Dye kids' Easter baskets, and tie them with ribbons, in the same shades as the eggs.

HOW TO CELEBRATE
INDEPENDENCE DAY

Between the parades and jaw-dropping fireworks displays, July Fourth means backyard barbecues or other down-home celebrations. Make yours a spectacular salute to the nation—right down to the table settings and menu offerings. Don't forget to hang the real Old Glory, too. See right for how to fold it properly post-festivities.

A FRESH FOURTH

▪ With its patriotic palette, Independence Day parties are as easy as red, white, and blue—or flag motifs. Light the grill, string the party lights, and chill the drinks—plus see the following ideas.

CREATE A COMMON MOTIF: Stars-and-stripes is an appropriate theme, of course, but that doesn't mean going overboard. Buy striped linens, or DIY with the embellishments:

▪ Use craft paint and stamps (rubber or made from a potato) or stencils to decorate a table-cloth, runner, and/or napkins.

▪ Inexpensive glass tumblers, carafes, and pitchers can also be easily painted or stamped; same for serving trays.

▪ Fill mason jars with bands of red, white, and blue sand to hold votive or taper candles.

▪ A drop cloth from a hardware store makes a durable outdoor table covering; hang curtain clips, each strung with two or three fishing sinkers, from the corners (use pliers to pry clips open and closed).

UPGRADE THE FOOD: Aim for ease over effort, especially if you'll be serving a range of ages.

▪ Update burgers and hot dogs by serving them with not-the-usual toppings, such as

kimchi or chutney, chipotle or Sriracha mayonnaise, and house-cured pickles (see page 307), for just a few examples.

▪ Give grilled corn different toppings, such as chile powder, lime zest and juice, and chopped cilantro or softened butter flavored with fresh herbs or spices.

▪ Tweak potato salad by tossing grilled fingerling potatoes and scallions with olive oil, sherry vinegar, and copious fresh herbs.

▪ For an easy striped dessert, layer raspberry, coconut, and blueberry sorbets in a loaf pan (lined with plastic wrap for easy unmolding), freeze until set, then slice to serve.

▪ Or make a berry pie, cutting stars out of the top crust with a cookie cutter before baking (see opposite for another dessert).

RETHINK THE DRINKS: Besides beer and wine, which can be chilling in several coolers around the yard, consider offering a signature cocktail.

▪ Red-wine sangria with sliced citrus, firecracker punch made with watermelon and vodka, Aperol spritzers, and Negronis are all aptly hued offerings. Margaritas and mojitos are always surefire crowd-pleasers.

KEEP PESKY INTRUDERS AT BAY: Make sure flying pests don't spoil all the fun.

▪ Run fans near where food is served and eaten; keep food and sugary beverages covered until they are served.

▪ Bees are attracted to sweet-smelling flowers (such as peonies and roses); best to avoid having these blooms as centerpieces.

▪ Place pots of peppermint, lavender, and lemon balm (all natural insect repellents) on the table, or combine in bouquets.

▪ Offer guests DEET-free insect-repellent bracelets, sprays, and wipes.

FLAG FOLDING HOW-TO

It takes two people to fold the flag properly, as it should never touch the ground.

1. Both people should hold out the flag waist-high, right side up, with its surface parallel to the ground. Fold the flag in half lengthwise, bringing the striped lower section over the canton (the blue field of stars).

2. Fold it again lengthwise, bringing the canton to the outside.

3. Start a triangular fold by bringing the striped corner of the folded edge up to meet the open edge. The outer point is then turned inward to form a second triangle. Continue folding the flag in this manner eight more times. These triangular folds bring the red and white stripes into the star-strewn blue field, symbolizing the day's light vanishing into the darkness of the night.

MORE IDEAS AND INSPIRATION

No fireworks on your holiday horizon? Get creative. Paper-crafted pom-poms or a "whirling" dessert can light up any Independence Day event, day or night.

"SPINNER" FIREWORKS PIE

Skip the pyrotechnics and wow your guests with this fantastic finale instead. It's made by topping your favorite cherry-pie filling (sour cherries are especially delicious) with twisted strips of rolled-out pie dough arranged in a pinwheel fashion. Use a pastry cutter and straightedge to cut dough ½-inch wide; when arranging on pie, work from center out, pinching ends of strips together to adhere. Brush the dough with an egg wash so it turns wonderfully golden brown as the pie bakes— and the juices from the filling bubble up.

POM-POM NAPKIN RINGS

Easier-than-ever pom-poms make pretty and patriotic napkin rings for blue-and-white striped linens. For each one, wrap colored matte raffia ribbon around a pom-pom maker (see page 165; a large Clover maker was used on these) or a credit card; cinch the raffia at center on one side with floral wire, slide it off, and cut raffia loop in half with craft scissors. Fluff the ends to open up pom-pom. Form the wire into a circle and twist it closed; slide ring around napkin.

HOW TO CELEBRATE
HALLOWEEN

It wouldn't be Halloween without jack-o'-lanterns. Even if you forgo other decorations or disguises, it's unlikely that you'll want to let a pumpkin-carving opportunity pass you by. The tools and techniques to get you started are on these pages; use your own imagination to come up with more creepy creations.

PUMPKIN-CARVING BASICS

A variety of blades (serrated, looped, and curved) make carving a proper jack-o'-lantern easy and accurate (and much less likely to end in injury). Assemble a set of tools to remove the pumpkin's insides quickly and sculpt intricate details on the rind.

Remember that these carving tools are sharp: All cutting should be done by adults. For pumpkins that will rest outside your home, use outdoor holiday lights or battery-operated "candles" that have a label indicating they've been tested for safety. Pumpkins should be well ventilated with holes so they don't overheat and become a fire hazard.

You can find all of the following tools at art-supply stores:

FLESHING TOOL: A serrated loop easily scrapes away the skin, thinning the walls and allowing light to shine through.

LINOLEUM CUTTER: Make skin-deep outlines and patterns with V- and U-shaped blades in a few sizes.

MINIATURE SAW: To cut out areas with lots of detail, such as facial features, use an easy-to-maneuver blade, like #2- and #3-sized.

KEYHOLE SAW: This tool's sharp teeth cut through the rind to make the large hole, either on the top or the bottom.

TIP

Pumpkins come in all shapes and sizes, and in different shades of orange and green, and even cream and black. Head to the nearest patch to pick an assortment for an arresting display, as above.

HOW-TO

Draw a design freehand, or find a premade template online.

1. Hollow out pumpkin: Using keyhole saw, cut a hole in pumpkin. If using a candle for illumination, cut hole in the top (always put candle in a high-sided glass, and never leave it unattended). If using electric or battery-powered light, make hole in bottom or side so you can hide the cord. Using fleshing tool or scraper, remove flesh, pulp, and seeds.

2. Cut out your custom design or premade template and tape to pumpkin.

3. Trace design onto pumpkin or poke holes with awl, needle tool, or T pin.

4. Remove template and carve along traced pattern. Use miniature saw to cut all the way through and linoleum cutter to carve details into just the surface of pumpkin (generally #2 and #3 blades for finer details and #5 blades to remove larger sections of skin). Apply petroleum jelly to exposed areas of pumpkin's flesh to prevent them from turning brown.

LIGHTING TIPS

If lighting a large pumpkin, string or battery-operated lights will provide greater (and more even) illumination than a traditional candle ever could (and they won't blow out in a breeze):

■ Wrap a glass jar with a strand of mini lights, securing one end to the jar with masking tape. To light a small pumpkin, arrange strand's bulbs into a bouquet-like bundle and place wires in a glass jar or ramekin.

■ Use a 25-light strand for small and medium pumpkins, and a 50-light strand for larger pumpkins.

■ If using larger lights, start by cutting out the base of the pumpkin (rather than the top) to remove the flesh, reserving the base. Then place light-strung jar or battery-operated candle on the base, and place pumpkin over lights. (Make sure the lights don't touch the inside surface; this can be a fire hazard.) Secure base cutout with T pins.

■ Once the pumpkin is lit, you may want to do a few touch-ups: If the light shines unevenly through the cutouts, the flesh may be thicker in some spots; simply scrape away a little more wherever it appears darker.

MARTHA MUST

I grow many types of pumpkins at my farm and love to incorporate them into my Halloween decorations. When it comes to jack-o'-lanterns, I've become fond of "funkins," made from polyurethane foam. They are much easier to carve, without all the seeds and pulp, and can be brought out again in future years.

TIP

Employ kitchen implements: Cookie cutters make uncommon designs; place cutter on pumpkin shell, and tap with a mallet. A melon baller takes decorative scoops out of the shell too, and can be used to hollow out small pumpkins.

MORE IDEAS
AND INSPIRATION

Expand your pumpkin-carving possibilities with the ideas below (lights off, lights on), and round out the spooky scene with other Halloween icons.

UN-HOLLOWED PUMPKIN

Here's proof that not all pumpkins need to be lit from within to shine. The flesh of this hefty specimen (it weighs in at 90 pounds; the little one is a mere 5 pounds) is carved with a linoleum cutter to replicate a famous fabric design. Open the door to other patterns by looking to your own favorite textiles (or wallpaper) for a template. To preserve the pumpkin for a longer display, don't gut it.

PUMPKIN PROJECTOR

One side of this two-faced pumpkin greets unsuspecting visitors with a friendly "Boo!" scraped into the flesh with a narrow linoleum cutter; the other side casts a sinister sneer on the wall behind it, with the facial features cut out with a miniature saw. To achieve the spectral effect, you may need to try it at different proximities to the wall; it will, of course, work best in a dimly lit room or front porch.

PAPER-BAT MOBILE

You'll need to head outside and look for a fallen tree limb with spindly branches to dangle multiple bats from; painting it black is optional. Trace bat template (see page 387) onto black card stock; cut out and fold according to instructions. Make a small hole in center of each bat, then thread and knot. Tie bats to branch. Hang the mobile from two pieces of thread or microfilament secured to the ceiling or top of the window with thumbtacks.

HOT-GLUE COBWEBS

Make it look like your home has gone to the spiders in no time. Place hot-glue pads around area to be covered, about 3 inches from object. With glue gun on low heat, squeeze out a dime-size dot on one pad; dip gun's tip in glue, quickly loop over object, and rest tip on another pad. Squeeze more glue on this pad; go back over same object. Repeat until sufficiently spidery. Let harden before carefully loosening webs from pads.

HOW TO CELEBRATE
THANKSGIVING

Whether it's your very first or the umpteenth time hosting, anti-stress strategies and solutions are always invited for Thanksgiving dinner. Read on for prep secrets, time-savers, modern updates, personal favorites, and other holiday surprises.

THREE SIMPLE STRATEGIES

Adopt these approaches when hosting any dinner party, but especially when pulling off the most multifaceted meal of all.

1. MAKE SMART MENU SELECTIONS

Choose a balance of dishes that cook on the stove and in the oven; oven dishes should cook or be reheated at compatible temperatures. Avoid too many items that require same-day cooking. Select sides and desserts that can be prepared at least a day or two in advance.

2. BE A SAVVY FOOD SHOPPER

Order your turkey before they sell out and with enough time for proper thawing. Rely on careful lists when heading to the supermarket, so you don't end up realizing you forgot the eggs or butcher's twine in the middle of cooking.

3. FRONT-LOAD THE WORK

With the right dishes in mind, plan to tackle as much as you can as soon as it's reasonable. Get all the greens washed and dried at least the night before, and the chopping and dicing done.

THE TURKEY

When it comes to the bird, observe the three Cs: choosing, cooking, and carving.

1. CHOOSE

Plan for 2 pounds for each guest, less if you don't want any leftovers. There are many types to choose from, even at supermarkets. All turkeys in the United States are raised without hormones. When possible, buy organic, pasture-raised turkeys from a local breeder or farmers' market, or a supermarket. Avoid self-basting turkeys, which will not taste the way you want them to.

FRESH VERSUS FROZEN
The regular commercial, conventionally raised supermarket turkey is the most affordable option, and is available both fresh or frozen—with frozen often being the fresher option, given the way fresh birds can end up sitting in the refrigerated section for weeks (check the sell-by date). Frozen turkeys, on the other hand, are flash-frozen (below 0°F) and can last up to a year; some are sold defrosted and labeled "previously frozen," which should be purchased within two days of cooking.

ORGANIC: While organic turkeys vary in quality, they all have to meet minimum requirements in terms of getting only organic feed and being raised without antibiotics; unless otherwise labeled, the birds are also free-range. Natural turkeys must be minimally processed and have no artificial preservatives or coloring (and no brine injections), though so-called natural colorings can be used, and there's no indication of how the bird was raised (free-range or conventionally).

PASTURE-RAISED: For a turkey to be labeled free-range, it must have access to the outdoors for more than half of each day, though there's no requirement the bird actually spend time in a field as opposed to having access to a door that leads outside. If you want a turkey that was free to roam, look for "pastured" or "pasture-raised" on the label—or seek out a local farm or breeder.

KOSHER: These usually free-range birds are processed in accordance with Jewish dietary law. They're salted, which improves flavor and texture, then rinsed in cold water, which tightens the skin; that's the reason some quills remain. Allow time to remove them with needle-nose pliers. Don't brine a kosher bird, as it will be too salty.

THANKSGIVING TIMELINE

A FEW WEEKS BEFORE

CHART OUT THE MENU

Once you've decided on your recipes, gather those together—copy any from books and magazines and print those from websites; this way you won't have to juggle or toggle your way through cooking. (Tip: Put them in a binder.) Then give the recipes the once-over, noting the temperatures and times required, and think about how you'll strategize the cooking.

PLOT A POTLUCK

Potlucks have the potential to become a free-for-all. Avoid that fate by telling your guests that you plan to make the turkey, stuffing, and mashed potatoes (the most common scenario), and then ask if they would mind bringing a green vegetable or a dessert.

MAKE THE PIE CRUSTS

Prepare all pie dough and store it in the freezer, wrapping the disks well in plastic and then tucking into sealable freezer bags. (It will keep for as long as three months, in case you want to make it that far in advance.)

UP TO A WEEK BEFORE

THAW THE TURKEY

Depending on its size, a frozen turkey can take anywhere from one to six days to thaw in the refrigerator. Keep the bird on a rimmed baking sheet, covered in plastic wrap, to keep juices from spilling over.

PREP VEGETABLES

Blanch or sauté vegetables that need to be precooked before going into stuffings or casseroles.

PURGE THE REFRIGERATOR

Maximize space by getting rid of leftover takeout, dregs of condiments, and anything you don't use anymore. Consider moving any unneeded items to a cooler.

DOUBLE-CHECK SUPPLIES

Now's a good time to sharpen your carving knife. Also, use an oven thermometer to test your oven's temperature; if it is low or high, you'll know to adjust the heat setting accordingly. You'll also need an instant-read thermometer to know when the turkey is ready; do not rely on the pop-up gauge that comes with many birds.

THE DAY BEFORE

CLEAN THE GREENS

Rinse herbs and last-minute vegetables, shake dry, and store in plastic bags in the refrigerator's drawer.

MASH THE POTATOES

You can prepare this dish entirely the day before without compromising on creaminess. To serve, heat the dish in a heatproof bowl set over a pot of simmering water, stirring and adding milk or cream (or broth) as needed to moisten.

PREPARE THE CRANBERRY RELISH

Cooked or raw, this is an easy make-ahead to scratch off your list. Plus, it will always be better the next day.

ASSEMBLE THE STUFFING

It has to be cooled before putting it in the bird, so it's worth getting that step out of the way. If you plan to bake it outside the bird, you can either do so now or wait to bake it before the bird goes into the oven.

BAKE THE PIES

Most need sufficient cooling time before they're ready to eat; others may need chilling. Either way, having these ready and waiting will do much to ease your mind.

THANKSGIVING DAY

BRING ITEMS TO ROOM TEMPERATURE

Let any pre- or partially cooked casseroles sit out at room temperature for about a half hour before putting them in the oven.

PREP DESSERTS

Designate a pie slicer and server for each pie (same for other types of desserts). If you need to whip cream, put the bowl and beaters in the refrigerator or freezer so it fluffs up faster. Get a pot of coffee ready (but wait to brew until after dinner).

MAKE THE GRAVY

For the best taste and texture, the gravy should be the last thing to leave the stove.

2. COOK

Cooking a whole turkey presents its conundrums: There's the space the bird takes up in your refrigerator and oven, as well as the length of time it takes to cook through. Then there's the dilemma of too-dry, tasteless white meat—mostly because it cooks more quickly than darker meat. Finally, if you're serving a small group, you end up with more leftovers than you can handle. Read on for ways to offset these concerns, along with general tips, no matter the cooking method.

CHOOSE THE PAN: If you cook turkey and other roasts frequently, invest in a sturdy stainless steel pan that will last a lifetime.

Skip nonstick pans, which will not allow foods and meat juices to brown and caramelize. Most pans come with racks; if not, buy one.

DEFROST: Thaw turkey in the refrigerator, where it's too cold for harmful bacteria to grow.

Place the turkey, breast side up, in its original wrapper, on a rimmed baking sheet (to catch any drips). Allow a full day for every 4 to 5 pounds of turkey being thawed.

PREP: Remove neck and packet of giblets (heart, liver, gizzard) from cavity. (You can use them in the stuffing, or add all of them, except for the liver, to gravy or stock.)

Before cooking, let turkey come to room temperature, 1 to 2 hours (depending on size). Kitchen hygiene is especially important when handling raw poultry.

TRUSS: Place turkey on rack in the roasting pan and tie the legs together with kitchen twine; finish with a bow that will be easy to undo later.

If stuffing the bird, do this before trussing, and secure the neck flap by pulling down the skin and fastening it with skewers or trussing needles (see page 345 for more stuffing tips).

Tuck wing tips under the body. Rub the bird inside and out with oil or butter, and season as desired.

BASTE: Begin basting with pan juices (or melted butter) after the first hour of cooking; then baste every 30 minutes or so, up to the end.

Don't be tempted to skip this step, as it will contribute much moisture to the meat and also promote browning of the surface.

FINISH: The bird is ready when an instant-read thermometer inserted into the thickest part of the thigh (avoiding the bone) reads 165°F (do not rely on pop-up thermometers).

Once out of the oven, tent turkey loosely with foil, and let it rest for 20 minutes before carving to allow the bird to keep cooking and the juices to be redistributed.

MARTHA MUST

Though more expensive, heritage birds have incredible flavor, and the skin gets wonderfully crisp. By choosing a heritage bird, you are also helping to protect the cultural legacy of the old breeds and to keep genetic diversity for the future. You can find them at certain farms and specialty purveyors, or ask your local butcher.

3. CARVE

A whole turkey glistening on a platter certainly does make a stunning centerpiece, but a carved bird presented just so makes an equally grand statement. Fan out the meat slices; add the wings and drumsticks. Then garnish with fruits and herbs for a platter that's both pretty and practical.

This simple four-step technique yields neatly sliced portions of meat.

1. Pull each leg away from the body and slice through skin between breast and drumstick. Bend leg back until thighbone pops out of socket. Cut through joint and skin to detach leg completely.

2. Keeping the blade close to rib cage and using it as your guide, slice along each side of the breastbone to remove breasts. Cut wings off at joint.

3. Cut between joint to separate thigh from drumstick. Both pieces can now be cut off the bone into slices.

4. Slice breasts crosswise, skin side up, and arrange on a platter with dark meat and wings. If bird is stuffed, scoop stuffing from cavity.

TIP

Use a very sharp, flexible slicing knife with a blade that's at least 10 inches long; never use a serrated knife, which will tear the meat. Save the carving fork for slicing the breast meat and serving, and use your hand (and a clean towel if bird is too hot to touch) to hold the bird in place otherwise.

CRANBERRY SAUCE UPDATES

Update a cranberry sauce by mixing any of the following two-ingredient options into it before it cools. Start with 2¼ cups of cranberry sauce.

- ¾ cup finely chopped dried figs and ¾ teaspoon balsamic vinegar
- ¾ cup grated peeled, cored apple and ¾ cup chopped toasted walnuts
- 1 tablespoon finely grated orange zest plus a pinch of ground cinnamon

THE STUFFING (OR DRESSING)

Stuffing cooks inside the bird; dressing bakes in a dish. Stuffed birds take longer to cook but will have more flavor from the stuffing. Dressing develops a crispy topping during baking—and there's none of the worry about food safety; you can also make it ahead.

CLASSIC OPTIONS: Here are just three of the most traditional versions to try.

- Sausage stuffing: A great all-purpose option that's made with day-old bread (sandwich bread, baguette, challah) and chock-full of sausage, herbs, and apples or pears (and sometimes chestnuts). This is the one to cook in the bird, as it gets very moist and flavorful.

- Cornbread dressing: This Southern staple is typically baked outside the bird. Bake the cornbread with nuts and dried fruit mixed right in, then freeze it up to a month. The day of, toss with aromatics and bake in a buttery dish. (Vegetarians will thank you.)

- Oyster dressing: For the characteristic crunch, cook this in a shallow layer, never inside the bird. It's traditionally made with saltines—and a must-have on many tables throughout the Northeast and New England.

FOOD-SAFETY CONCERNS: Because you are starting the stuffing in a raw turkey, you must heed certain steps to ensure proper cooking.

- Always allow stuffing to come to room temperature before putting inside cavity, and do so right before putting the turkey in the oven.

- Avoid overstuffing. A 12- to 15-pound turkey can hold 8 to 10 cups of stuffing; a 16- to 20-pound bird can hold up to 12 cups.

- The stuffing needs to reach 165°F; if doing so means the bird will be overcooked, remove the bird from the oven when it is ready, then scoop stuffing right away into a greased baking dish to cook until it is a safe temperature.

- If you cook the stuffing inside the turkey for the duration, wait 20 minutes before removing it from the bird; this will allow the temperature to continue rising.

THE SIDES

Lean toward ease and contrasting tastes, textures, and colors—and seasonal flavors.

A good formula to follow is one or two of each of the following: green vegetables (Brussels sprouts and green beans, for example); starchy vegetables (such as mashed potatoes and roasted squash wedges); and sweet-tart cranberry relishes and other fruit chutneys.

THE PIES

For many people, the pies are what they are most thankful for. Here are some easy ways to tweak the all-time favorites.

CRUST: Instead of a rolled-out pie dough, make a less fussy press-in-the-pan crumb crust with crushed gingersnaps for pumpkin pie, chocolate wafers or pecan sandies for pecan pie, and buttery shortbread for apple.

FILLING: For pumpkin pie, use pureed flesh from a roasted pumpkin or other squash (butternut or kabocha) in place of the canned variety. For apple pie, line the pie shell with sea-salted caramel before adding the fruit; use melted dark chocolate to line pecan pie.

TOPPING: Infuse heavy cream with cinnamon sticks, cardamom pods, or star anise; chill before whipping. Or sweeten the cream with maple syrup in place of sugar while beating.

GRAVY 101

1. While turkey is resting, pour pan drippings into a fat separator; let stand until fat rises to surface. (Or use a large glass measuring cup and skim fat from top with a spoon.)

2. Bring 1½ cups stock to a boil in roasting pan over two burners, scraping up browned bits from bottom of pan with a wooden spoon. Whisk together another 1 cup stock and 3 tablespoons flour; stir into pan. Boil until thickened and reduced, about 5 minutes.

3. Stir in defatted pan juices; cook until heated through. Season with salt and pepper. Serve hot, in a gravy boat.

HOW TO CELEBRATE
CHRISTMAS

The glittering tree rightly gets all the attention, but not without some thoughtful planning on your part. Plus you can make wreaths and other adornments to help create a festive scene. Even if you stick with your own perfected-over-time traditions, there are always new things to try.

DECORATE THE TREE

No matter how lovely the adornments, the success of this holiday harbinger starts with the tree itself.

BUYING CONSIDERATIONS

When looking for your ideal tree, consider these features: height, silhouette, density (important for decorating), and aroma.

■ See the chart on page 348 for a description of the more common types. Always measure the designated space (away from fireplaces and heaters) for height (leaving room for the topper!) and girth.

■ Visit a farm to cut the tree yourself if possible. The National Christmas Tree Association lets you search by ZIP code for tree farms in your area. The first trees to get picked over tend to be the ones near the parking lot, so head to more remote spots; as you browse, tie same-colored ribbons on those you like so you can find them again.

TREE-TRIMMING TIPS AND TECHNIQUES

Now that you've procured your tree, you'll want to decorate it to the nines. There is a method to making it as beautiful as can be.

1. Leave a good stump on the tree you buy or cut, and trim a half inch at home before putting it in the stand; this will allow the tree to drink up water (and replenish as needed).

2. Prune any small protrusions that jut straight out from the top and bottom of the branches; these make it hard to decorate.

3. String the lights on the tree (see page 349 for the how-to). Stop every so often to make sure your spacing is even.

4. Start by laying your ornaments out before you begin hanging them. Sort them by color or shape or motif so you can achieve the proper balance on the tree.

5. Hang your primary ornaments (or those more simple ones that you have multiples of, such as dozens of shiny teal balls or silvery snowflakes) first to establish a rhythm, then use others to fill in the gaps. Or just start by hanging all of one assortment around the tree before starting on another type, and so on. Place antique and fragile ornaments near the top of the tree, where they will be less likely to get knocked off by pets and passersby.

6. Continually take a step back while decorating to see which areas need filling. Hang ornaments inside the tree—not just near its edges—for added dimension, and don't neglect the back of the tree if it's visible from any part of the room or outside a window.

MARTHA MUST

Each year, I love creating a different theme for my grandchildren's Christmas tree, mixing old and new ornaments and carrying the motif (woodland, for example) into the wreaths, stockings, and gift-wrapping.

TYPES OF CHRISTMAS TREES			
FRASER FIR (*ABIES FRASERI*)		Region(s): Midwest, Northeast, Southern Appalachians	This tree is known for its singular scent and lovely shape, with short, durable needles and open, well-spaced branches—perfect for holding lots of dangling ornaments, even heavier ones.
SCOTCH PINE (*PINUS SYLVESTRIS*)		Region(s): Northwest, Midwest, Great Lakes, Northeast	Thanks to its sturdy, tightly spaced branches, this tree has ample room for holding ornaments of all weights and sizes—plus it tends to hold on to its (very sharp) needles and earthy scent through the holidays, even when dry.
DOUGLAS FIR (*PSEUDOTSUGA MENZIESII*)		Region(s): Northwest, Midwest, Great Lakes, Northeast	If you are looking to fill your home with a wonderful sweet scent, a Douglas is your tree. The blue-green foliage is fuller and thicker than a Fraser, though its needles are softer and tend to fall off sooner.
WHITE PINE (*PINUS STROBUS*)		Region(s): United States-Canada border	This large, unscented blue-green often has a more narrow silhouette and dense, flexible branches that can obscure ornaments and sag under bulky garlands or lights. That said, it's also the tallest of the bunch (great for cathedral ceilings and lofty spaces).
LEYLAND CYPRESS (*CUPRESSUS LEYLANDII*)		Region(s): Southeast	A favorite in the South for its longevity and feathery forest- or bluish-green branches, Leylands need to be watered as often as several times a day, depending on your home environment.
CONCOLOR FIR (*ABIES CONCOLOR*)		Region(s): West, Great Lakes, Northeast	Also called white fir, Concolor has a tall, narrow profile and a faint citrus aroma. Full, bushy branches support heavier ornaments and have silvery, loosely spaced needles that tend to last.

LIGHT THE TREE

This all-important element of Christmas-tree decorating tends to stump people more than anything else. A little patience and planning will help you achieve the result you want.

LIGHTING HOW-TO

If you've always wrapped the strings of light around the tree's perimeter, you may want to give this method a go. Wrapping strings around individual branches creates a brighter, denser twinkle, but requires more effort.

1. Starting at the bottom bough, string lights along the underside of each branch. When you get near the end, loop the string around the top of the branch.

2. Work back to the tree trunk, winding around the branch and light strand. Continue in this manner around the entire tree.

CALCULATING THE LIGHTS NEEDED

If you've ever run out of lights halfway up the tree, or ended up with extra strings and a less-than-stunning result, use these equations to calculate the number of bulbs required. Then divide the number by the number of bulbs per string.

Surface-winding (the usual way):
Number of lights =
height × diameter of tree × 20

Branch-weaving (above):
Number of lights =
height × radius × radius × 50

STORING THE LIGHTS

Here's how to avoid tangled-up strings the next year.

1. Test each strand before putting it away. (Replace dead bulbs; discard any nonworking strands.)

2. Keep extra bulbs and fuses in a kit.

3. Make a loop with each strand and wrap the ends around the loop, or loop strands around a piece of cardboard cut to fit the storage container.

4. Store each strand in its own sealed one-gallon freezer bag. Leave some air in the bag to act as a cushion that will protect the bulbs.

5. Stack the bags in a large storage container.

TIP

You can also use the branch-weaving how-to (left) for lighting an outdoor tree, making sure to use only lights that are approved for outdoor use (check the package); use different-size bulbs for a more natural effect. A tall tree like the one shown above requires a sturdy extension ladder (or a qualified professional).

MAKE A WREATH

Adorn your front door with one of these classic symbols of the season—or put one on a wall, mantel, or window. Starting with basic craft supplies and greenery and/or other natural elements, such as pine cones and acorns, you can create statement pieces to last many seasons.

SUPPLIES

Floral wire

Double-rail metal wreath form

Pine cones in various sizes

Acorns, nutmeg, and sweet-gum seed pods

Drill and 1/32-inch bit

Hot-glue gun

White spray paint

About 30 millinery or silk leaves

Metallic craft paint and paintbrush (optional)

HOW-TO

1. Zigzag floral wire between rails of form as shown (A) to stabilize pine cones when attaching them.

2. Cut a 12-inch piece of wire and loop it around a pine cone (at the base for a shorter one, in the middle for a longer one); twist to secure. Press both ends of wire together,

creating one thick tail. Wrap tail around wreath form to connect pine cone to wreath. Repeat with more pine cones until wreath is mostly covered, placing smaller ones where needed to fill in gaps.

3. Make decorative picks (B): Remove an acorn cap, drill a small hole on either side of stem, thread wire through, and glue cap back onto acorn. Drill through nutmeg and thread same wire through, then thread through natural holes of sweet gum. Spray-paint white. Repeat to form as many picks as desired.

4. Optional: Cover leaves with metallic paint or gold leaf.

5. Twist wire picks onto stems of leaves. Place leaves on wreath as desired and glue to secure.

MORE IDEAS
AND INSPIRATION

When making festive wreaths, there are many ways to tweak tradition, either with some basic craft supplies or by forgoing greenery altogether.

BAY LEAF WREATH

To make this classic laurel (aka bay leaf) wreath with a twist: Spray-paint eucalyptus leaves silver and gold, and add them to a base of fragrant bay leaves fashioned into a U shape. Finish with a champagne-colored satin ribbon knotted at the base and clusters of silver and gold balls wired to picks. Hang indoors or out.

CARD PINUP WREATH

What to do with an abundance of holiday cards? Arrange them into a wreath shape, for a novel spin on the holiday motif. First attach wooden clothespins to a large wooden embroidery hoop, spacing them about 2 inches apart, with wood glue, then hang it up with a pretty ribbon (using a nail or adhesive hook). Slip in the desired cards, rotating them as desired.

HOW TO CELEBRATE HANUKKAH

The Festival of Lights is all about family, friends, and traditions. The menorah may be the most symbolic element, but there are others (including the white-and-light-blue palette) that also shine bright. Here, some twists on traditions that may add a new glow to your celebration.

THE MENORAH

Hebrew for "candelabrum," the menorah is central to any Hanukkah celebration. The legend is thus: In ancient Israel, when the Jews reclaimed their temple and won religious freedom, a candelabrum miraculously burned for eight days, fueled by an amount of olive oil that should have lasted only one.

- Rather than buying a menorah, many families prefer to create their own; see two examples, opposite. Just make sure it holds nine candles, one for each night of the eight-day celebration, plus one for the shammes, the candle used to light all the others.

- As the holiday progresses, the candles are placed from right to left, and then lit from left to right. The new light is always lit first (after the shammes).

TRADITIONAL FOODS

Holiday meals revolve around fried foods such as latkes and doughnuts, which, in their preparation, refer to the miracle of the oil. You can stick with classic versions or give them a few thoughtful updates.

- Latkes can be tweaked to include other roots in addition to regular or sweet potatoes. Try adding grated carrots, beets, parsnips, turnips, or rutabaga, for example.

- Instead of the standard applesauce topping, swap in pear or quince, and add fresh ginger, ground toasted cardamom, or pure maple syrup in lieu of other sweeteners.

- Additional sweet and savory topping ideas include smoked salmon and horseradish sauce; crème fraîche with sliced pear and cinnamon; and honey-drizzled pomegranate seeds.

- Sugar-dusted *sufganiyot*, or jelly-filled doughnuts, are the usual dessert. For a yeast-free alternative, make apple or pear fritters.

GIFTS AND GAMES

No celebration would be complete without dreidels and gelt, at least for younger guests.

- Derived from a German word for "to turn," dreidels are also fun for kids to fold out of paper, origami-style; then have them write the four Hebrew letters—*nun*, *gimel*, *hey*, and *shin* ("a great miracle happened there")—on each of the spinning toy's four sides.

- Gelt, chocolate coins wrapped in foil, are a must for giving as gifts to children—and they make appropriate party favors for all ages.

TIP

To make the place cards above, cut out two dreidel shapes from card stock (see template on page 387), making a slit in pointed end of each. Write name on one cutout, then slip pieces together at slits. For the gelt favors, embellish small cellophane envelopes with a menorah stamp (both found at craft supply stores or online) before filling with treats.

MORE IDEAS AND INSPIRATION

The only prerequisite for creating your own menorah is that it have the correct number of candleholders; below are two variations on the theme, each one as inviting and easy to make as the next.

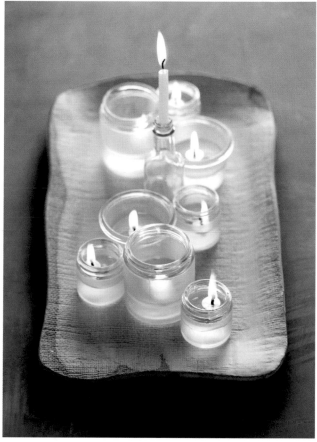

SILVERED BRANCH

For a festive spin on nature, find a fallen branch at least 16 inches long, with a raised knot for the shammes. Mark nine evenly spaced dots with a pencil, one on top of the knot; drill holes with a ⅜-inch bit. (Hole size depends on candle size.) Paint with silvery craft paint. Let dry and affix self-adhesive bumpers to the bottom if desired. Be sure to never leave the menorah unattended while candles are burning.

OLIVE OIL LIGHTS

This modern menorah sets an appropriately reflective mood, and olive oil is a nod to the Hanukkah miracle. Cover top halves of eight small jars (use a variety) with masking tape. Using etching cream, etch bottom halves according to product directions. Remove tape. Fill jars halfway with water. Add ⅛ inch olive oil. Drop a floating wick into each jar, cork side down. Use a birthday candle in a small, narrow-necked bottle for the shammes.

HOW TO CELEBRATE
NEW YEAR'S EVE

Come December 31, skip the crowds and host a celebration at home, such as the bubble-themed party described below—the details of which can be tailored to suit your own space and style. Think about new ways to entertain to start the new year.

BUBBLE-THEMED BASH

What could be more appropriate for New Year's Eve than an elegantly effervescent party? Stock up on sparkling wine and pick and choose among the following suggested elements.

If you don't have the same (or even similar) punch bowl or glasses shown opposite, scour your home or party-supply store for other ways to implement the theme. Even balloons and bubble wands can make any party a blast.

TIP

To replicate the dessert stand shown above right, rest different-size Lucite cubes, sold at organizing stores, atop a beribboned or painted board.

THE DRINKS

Carry out the theme on the help-yourself drink station.

- Coupe glasses have a more fitting profile than flutes for serving sparkling wine.

- For chilling cocktails, swap out regular ice cubes with round ones molded in special trays (see those in ice bucket at left); to give them similar pastel hues, tint the water with different liqueurs such as Aperol, Campari, or Limoncello before freezing.

- Punches (like the rum punch at left) are even more festive with frozen melon balls to keep them cold.

- For nonalcoholic options, serve bubble tea (with tapioca pearls), or pour sparkling water over the tinted ice balls or frozen melon balls.

THE HORS D'OEUVRES

Once you start looking for bubble-shaped food, you'll discover lots of options. Take these as inspiration:

- Caviar (and its less expensive cousin, salmon roe) can be scooped onto canapés spread with sour cream or crème fraîche.

- Roll miniature goat-cheese balls in chopped pistachios, pink peppercorns, or finely chopped fresh herbs.

- Gougères, or cheese puffs, are delicious freeze-aheads; bake just before serving.

THE DESSERTS

Fluffy frosted cupcakes look as light as air—these are coconut, but any flavor will do, as long as the frosting is billowy and pastel.

- Cream-filled pastry puffs are also bubble-shaped options; dust the pastries liberally with confectioners' sugar for the same ethereal effect.

- You can never go wrong with truffles; coat them in white chocolate or roll in chopped coconut.

CLASSIC PARTY STARTERS

Consider incorporating three common symbols—coins, confetti, and crackers (the British kind made from a cardboard tube), all of which portend good fortune—into your fête.

FOR EDIBLE COINS: Prepare logs of icebox cookies that you can make ahead, store in the freezer (wrapped well), and then slice and bake the day of the party. Serve them along with other sweet treats, and wrap up extras in festive packaging (inexpensive plastic tubes are sold at party supply stores) and give out as party favors.

FOR NO-TOSS CONFETTI: Punch out shiny paper into circles or other shapes and then string those on twine for confetti streamers that you can suspend from the ceiling with adhesive hooks. Or cut gold or silver tissue paper with a fringe cutter or scissors, tie into bundles with twine, and hand out to the kids.

FOR FESTIVE CRACKERS: Wrap cardboard tubes in tissue paper, securing with double-sided tape; perforating the paper at the folds keeps the gathered ends loose enough to break. Tie one end with ribbon or twine, then fill with trinkets and a paper crown (according to tradition); tie off the other end and then wrap middle part with decorative paper, stickers, or other embellishments. Use as place cards, give out as midnight markers, or send home as party favors.

NEW YEAR'S FOOD TRADITIONS

As the single most celebrated holiday around the globe, there are many New Year's traditions thought to bring happiness, health, and prosperity in the year ahead.

THE AMERICAN SOUTH

Black-eyed peas are credited with the ability to summon good luck; wilted greens such as collards also promise riches.

CHINA

For the fabulously festive Chinese New Year, which falls in January or February depending on the lunar calendar, family and friends enjoy an extravagant feast of dishes including whole fish, dumplings, citrus fruit, and *nian gao* (a sticky rice cake).

COLOMBIA

Here the locals tote empty suitcases around the block (or throughout the day, for some)—all in the hopes of a travel-filled New Year.

DENMARK

Two traditions to try: Smash old dishes against your friends' front doors to keep away evil spirits, and jump off chairs at midnight to "leap" into the New Year.

HOLLAND

Hot spiced wine is used to toast in Holland, wassail in certain parts of England.

ISRAEL

Honey-coated apples are traditional Rosh Hashanah (Jewish New Year) treats.

ITALY

An abundance of lentils—tiny edible seeds—symbolizes wealth.

JAPAN

In addition to smiling as the clock strikes midnight, denizens ring their town bells exactly 108 times according to the Buddhist prescription for cleanliness.

PHILIPPINES

Customs include piling round fruit on the table and wearing polka-dots (anything round symbolizes coins and prosperity), opening all doors, windows, and drawers (to let good fortune in), or turning on all lights (for a bright New Year).

SCOTLAND

During Hogmanay, locals practice "first-footing," where the first person to cross a home's threshold in the New Year must carry a gift for luck. Also, to purify the year ahead, Scots parade while swinging poles with fireballs at bonfire ceremonies.

SOUTH ASIA

Rice promises prosperity in India and Pakistan.

SPAIN

Revelers in Spain eat a dozen grapes at midnight, one with each stroke of the clock.

MORE IDEAS AND INSPIRATION

Decorating on a budget—or in minimal time? Just customize some simple party supplies to create adornments worthy of any New Year's Eve bash.

BUOYANT BALLOONS

Here's an easy ornamentation that instantly says "party." Start with some preinflated silver Mylar balloons, then replace the attached string with ribbon in desired widths and colors (whatever matches your party palette). Attach a shiny gift-wrap pom-pom bow at the base of each balloon, for a flourish. The balloons will stay inflated for days, meaning you can buy them in advance—and/or give them to your guests when the party's over.

GLITTERING VOTIVES

These sparkling table decorations feature a neat trick: First you blow up small balloons in assorted sizes, then brush the tops with a glittery glue mixture (you can buy glittered glue or make your own, using craft glue such as Mod Podge and coarse glitter). Once it dries, pop and discard balloons—leaving behind shells you can paint on the inside with craft paint in desired color (gold coarse-glitter paint was used here). Add more glitz with pillar candles that get dusted with fine glitter after being coated with transfer adhesive. The dip-dyed napkins are fashioned from metallic linen (use a T pin to unravel threads for a selvage edge).

CARE
FOR PETS

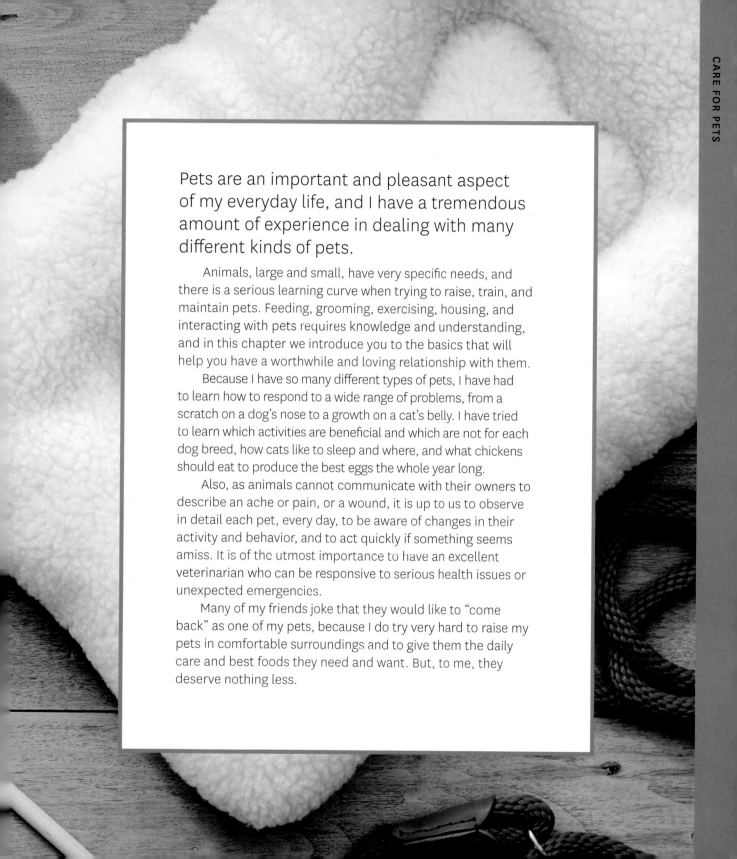

Pets are an important and pleasant aspect of my everyday life, and I have a tremendous amount of experience in dealing with many different kinds of pets.

Animals, large and small, have very specific needs, and there is a serious learning curve when trying to raise, train, and maintain pets. Feeding, grooming, exercising, housing, and interacting with pets requires knowledge and understanding, and in this chapter we introduce you to the basics that will help you have a worthwhile and loving relationship with them.

Because I have so many different types of pets, I have had to learn how to respond to a wide range of problems, from a scratch on a dog's nose to a growth on a cat's belly. I have tried to learn which activities are beneficial and which are not for each dog breed, how cats like to sleep and where, and what chickens should eat to produce the best eggs the whole year long.

Also, as animals cannot communicate with their owners to describe an ache or pain, or a wound, it is up to us to observe in detail each pet, every day, to be aware of changes in their activity and behavior, and to act quickly if something seems amiss. It is of the utmost importance to have an excellent veterinarian who can be responsive to serious health issues or unexpected emergencies.

Many of my friends joke that they would like to "come back" as one of my pets, because I do try very hard to raise my pets in comfortable surroundings and to give them the daily care and best foods they need and want. But, to me, they deserve nothing less.

WELCOME A NEW PET

Getting a new pet is always exciting—and not just for you and your family. Your four-legged friends will be experiencing many unfamiliar smells and sights, so you'll want to take the time to consider the following before bringing them home.

GIVE PETS THEIR OWN PLACE

Just like people, pets will feel more at home if they have a spot that's designated just for them.

- Most dogs will feel safe in a right-sized crate with a soft liner. Bigger, older dogs can be kept in a small room, or a larger one that's been closed off with a gate.

- Cats also appreciate having soft beds here and there to curl up on, along with a window perch or tiered "cat condo" for climbing and snoozing.

- Avoid alienating a pet by putting "unsightly" crates or beds in the garage, or even in unused rooms. This will only serve to isolate the dog, and loneliness can create behavior problems. Instead, place the crate away from high-traffic areas but near the family—for example, in a mudroom just off the kitchen.

- It's also nice to provide pet beds and perches in areas where people like to hang out, such as in the kitchen or den—even on a front porch (buy an indoor/outdoor model).

- Besides a bed, you'll want to outfit the spot with a water bowl and some favorite toys. You could even place the toys in an open bin or basket on the floor so pets can get them at will—and some dogs can be trained to put the toys away at the end of each day. Never leave unattended any toys with parts that can become dislodged or with strings that can strangle.

- Both dogs and cats may also discover their own hiding spots (under a sofa or bed, for example), for healthy self-soothing. Whenever they make use of those spots, leave them be until they are ready to come back out on their own. Resist the urge to draw them out with treats, lest you "reward" them for being afraid or anxious.

- Choose a bed that suits your dog's sleeping style: fluffy round beds for dogs who like to curl up; longer, flatter beds for dogs who stretch out. A bolster bed allows a dog to rest its head up, while the removable cushion provides a place to "bury" their toys.

ALLOW TIME FOR ADJUSTMENT

Don't expect a new pet to feel immediately at home, or to bond with you from the get-go.

- To get your new pet acclimated to her habitat, begin by leaving her there for only brief periods each day for the first few days. Load it with positive associations each time: Provide treats and toys, engage in playtime, and show ample love and affection.

- Gradually leave the pet there for longer periods of time each day, working up from an hour to overnight. Unless your puppy is hurt, you'll need to use tough love in ignoring the whimpers and pleas.

- Avoid using your high-pitched, reassuring voice if your dog is begging to get out; this sends the message that you approve of her behavior. Instead, use a firm but gentle command to "be quiet" before walking away.

- Once she's adjusted, you can start leaving the door open to her crate so she can decide when she wants to come and go.

INTRODUCE NEW AND EXISTING PETS

Expect to spend some time and effort in getting new and old pets adjusted to each other.

INTRODUCING CATS: Cats can be fiercely territorial, so it's a good idea to clip—but not declaw—both cats' nails before they meet to reduce the risk of scratching each other, and also you. (Do this even if there is a dog but no other cat in the home.)

- To prevent turf wars, keep cats in separate rooms for one or two weeks, letting them peek at each other through a screen or play with each other's paws under a door.

- During this time, switch the cats' rooms each day but keep the other's water bowls and litter box there. This will allow each cat to grow accustomed to the other's scent.

- When you're ready to let them be in the same room, make it a fun experience by having enough treats and toys to go around. In case of a brawl, spray them (gently, and not in the eyes) with a water bottle.

- Never leave your cat and dog alone together until they're fully acclimated to each other's presence. Keep the dog in his crate when you're gone or unable to supervise—and keep the cat out of that room.

INTRODUCING DOGS: While not as territorial as cats (generally speaking), some dogs can feel anxious or upset having to share their space (and your attention) with another.

- You'll want to supervise the pets for at least the first week, until you are comfortable with their relationship. Keep them in separate rooms when you are not at home.

- When the new dog is in his crate, keep the old dog out of the room or area, and never let the old dog enter that crate when unoccupied.

- Establish mealtime as a positive activity that they share. Start by feeding each dog (or a cat and dog) on either side of a baby gate, within view of each other. Gradually move their food bowls closer until both pets seem relaxed. Then remove the gate.

- Rather than doling out punishment, heap praise on your pets (dogs and cats) for appropriately interacting with each other. Show equal amounts of affection to all.

RESCUE CARE

Designating a safe space in your home for any new dog or cat is important. But it's vital for a rescue animal, who might need extra time to adjust to the new surroundings. The animal may have had several different homes (including a noisy, stressful shelter), leaving her understandably anxious.

If you have kids, show them how to respect their new pet's boundaries; for example, they need to understand why it's important not to take toys away from an animal, hug her when she doesn't want to be hugged, or enter the pet's safe space without you.

HOW TO
MAKE YOUR HOME PET-PROOF

Your home is replete with items that are potentially toxic to your pets. It's your job to protect them from letting their curiosity get the better of them. The solution? Learn the common culprits along with the signs of possible poisoning.

SAFETY STRATEGY

Being prepared and informed is absolutely in order.

BE PROACTIVE: Keep contact information for your vet, the nearest animal emergency room, and the 24-hour ASPCA Poison Control Center (888-426-4435) in a prominent spot so all members of the household, as well as dog walkers, can act in case of an emergency.

KNOW THE DANGERS: Below are the most frequently reported causes of pet poisoning in the U.S., but this list is by no means exhaustive. Use common sense in keeping your pet safe.

LEARN THE SIGNS: The symptoms include mild stomach upset, nosebleeds, lethargy, loss of appetite, nausea, vomiting, blood in the stool, seizures, and kidney failure; seek help at the first sign of the above, or if you have reason to believe your pet has ingested something poisonous.

POTENTIAL HAZARDS

Make sure everyone in the family has this information.

MEDICATIONS: According to the ASPCA, over-the-counter and prescription medications for people rank at the top of the pet-poison list.

- Pets snatch pills from nightstands and snap up medications that fall on the floor (another reason to teach the "drop it" command).

- Some of the most dangerous drugs include aspirin and other everyday drugs (such as ibuprofen).

- Vitamin and mineral supplements also pose risks, particularly those containing iron and vitamin D.

FOOD: Most everyone knows chocolate is potentially toxic to dogs (dark chocolate especially so). The same is true for cats. Other foods are just as harmful to both animals:

- Avoid caffeinated beverages; alliums (onions, garlic, chives); yeast bread doughs; alcoholic beverages; or any foods containing xylitol, a sugar alcohol found in many sweets and also toothpaste.

- Macadamia nuts, grapes, and raisins can lead to acute kidney failure in dogs.

- Canned tuna can cause severe inflammation in cats.

- Raw and undercooked meats pose the same problem to pets as to humans.

- Mind the garbage; it can contain moldy foods as well as possible choking hazards.

HOUSEHOLD CLEANERS: Pets are yet another excellent reason to swap out all chemical products with those that are nontoxic.

- Exposure to bleach and ammonia-based cleaning solutions is particularly hazardous; never use where pets are likely to frequent.

- Some pets are fond of eating bar soaps, which can trigger stomach upset.

PLANTS: Know the types of plants that are inside and outside your home.

- A photo list of the 700-plus poisonous plants can be found at *aspca.org*. These are among the more common: Easter lilies (deadly to cats, even in small doses), English ivy, azaleas, begonias, clematises, daffodils, delphinium, hyacinths, lupine, oleanders, rhododendrons, sago palms, and tulips.

- If it turns out you have a poisonous plant, you have a couple of options: Give houseplants to pet-free friends; for outside plants, put up a barrier such as chicken wire fencing or prickly plants to keep your pets away, or have those in the front yard and pets in the back.

- Other common toxins that may be lurking in your yard include mushrooms (pick those up right away), snail and slug bait, cocoa-bean mulch, and compost; always keep those and all gardening supplies out of reach.

ANTIFREEZE: Some pets can't resist this sweet solution. Clean up spills in the garage or on the driveway right away. A mere teaspoon can kill a 10-pound cat; 1 to 2 tablespoons are lethal to a 10-pound dog. There is an antidote, but it must be given within 12 hours.

HOW TO
KEEP YOUR PET HEALTHY

Having pets boosts owners' immunity, lowers blood pressure, encourages exercise, and reduces stress and depression. In turn, stroking dogs and cats can lower their blood pressure, lessen their anxiety, and help with their pain relief. Read on for more ways to keep your pets happy and healthy for life.

SCHEDULE CHECKUPS

Reevaluate your pet's care once a year to be sure it is addressing her needs.

ROUTINE VISITS: For the utmost in prevention and early detection of possible problems, dogs and cats should see the vet at least twice a year, more often for puppies and kittens.

- Discuss any concerns you have regarding your pet's weight and ways you can help maintain, or regain, the ideal.

- Depending on the pet's age and overall health, your doctor may advise certain blood work or other diagnostic procedures.

WHEN NEEDED: Don't wait for wellness appointments to address any health concerns with the vet, as early detection is often the key to successful treatment. See opposite for the more common warning signs.

> **TIP**
>
> Have your pet microchipped, then have your vet scan the chip once a year to ensure it is working properly.

STAY CURRENT ON SHOTS

Talk to your vet about putting your pet on the right vaccine schedule based on her age, overall health, location, and lifestyle.

RABIES VACCINE: Every state requires dogs to have rabies vaccines in order to get licensed; some states also require this of cats, even those who never venture outside.

DISTEMPER COMBINATION: While the distemper vaccines are different for dogs and cats, they are required in some states—and highly recommended by many vets. Once a kitten or puppy has completed the first year's vaccinations, the animal will typically need a booster shot only every three years.

SECONDARY VACCINES: Depending on your pet's location and situation, your vet may also suggest so-called secondary immunization.

- If your dog spends time at dog runs or a day-care center, ask about the bordetella (or "kennel cough") vaccine, which also cross-protects against other respiratory diseases (in fact, many doggie day cares require this).

- You might also consider the vaccine for leptospirosis, a rare but serious bacterial infection that dogs can pick up by drinking or splashing around in stagnant water (such as a pond).

- Secondary vaccines for cats include those targeting chlamydophila (or pneumonia) and leukemia, the latter being particularly important for cats who go outside or are exposed to other cats that do.

PRACTICE PREVENTION

Keep up a medication regimen throughout the year, not just during warmer months. Always buy the medicine directly from your vet, who can prescribe the right protocol.

TICK WATCH

Tick-borne diseases in canines are typically treatable if caught early enough but potentially deadly if not. After any possible exposure, feel for bumps everywhere on your dog's face and body, including around the ears and the folds of the neck. If you find a tick, remove it right away—it can take as little as four hours for an infection to set in.

TO REMOVE A TICK

Using pointy tweezers, grasp the tick gently but firmly near its head. Pull upward in a slow but steady motion to remove the whole tick and discard. Swab the bite area with rubbing alcohol.

WHAT TO LOOK FOR

It can take three weeks or longer for dogs to show any symptoms, which can vary in type and severity. Common ones include stiff and swollen joints, limping or lameness, loss of appetite, fever (103°F), lethargy, or seizures. At the very first sign, call your vet to discuss testing and treatment options, so you can get your dog back to being healthy.

HEARTWORM: This disease has been reported in all 50 states for both cats and dogs. Though easy to prevent, it is difficult to cure—and can spread to people through contact.

FLEA- AND TICK-BORNE ILLNESS: Ticks tend to get all the attention, but fleas can also pose a health risk beyond the usual scratching.

- Because fleas are found everywhere, and have implications for both dogs and cats, it's important to give your pet protection—even if ticks are not a concern. Tapeworm and flea allergy dermatitis, or hot spots, are the risks for dogs, secondary anemia for cats.

- Ticks are problematic in certain parts of the country, and only for dogs (there are no known health risks for cats). If you live in a tick-prone area, or will be traveling to one, discuss the best protocol (oral, topical, or even a combination) with your vet.

ARTHRITIS: Older pets may require medications for arthritis and other age-related aches and pains, and your vet can suggest a treatment plan to help alleviate any suffering.

ADMINISTER MEDICATION

Not all dogs and cats have a problem taking medicine. If that doesn't describe your pet, however, try these vet-approved methods. Follow up with praise and other rewards.

PILLS AND TABLETS

1. First, offer a bite or two of a food your pet enjoys (cheese, peanut butter, chicken) without the medicine, then sneak it into the food. (This will keep him from avoiding treats entirely.)

2. If that doesn't work, or if your pet is on a restricted diet, try this: Gently push the pill into your pet's mouth, at the very back of the tongue, then hold her head high (stroking her to keep her calm) until she swallows.

LIQUIDS

1. Try mixing it into her regular meal. Many liquids now come in a surprising range of flavors (bacon, beef, and salmon among them), so your pet may have no objection at all.

2. If that doesn't work, or if the drug cannot be taken with food, do this: Pull out the side of your pet's cheek and, with a syringe or teaspoon, squeeze or pour the medicine into her mouth. Avoid tilting her head back or forceful squirting, which can cause choking.

WATCH FOR WARNING SIGNS

Dogs and cats can mask medical problems with admirable stoicism, so it's up to you to be on the lookout for subtle signals. Call your vet right away if any of the following applies.

- Give your pet a thorough once-over each month, feeling for any unusual lumps on the face or body, and looking for skin sores, a dull or scaly coat, or more than the usual discharge from the nose, ears, or eyes.

- Pay close attention to changes in your pet's activity level, appetite, and attitude. Same goes for unexplained weight gain or loss.

- If you notice excessive drooling and/or very bad breath, or if your pet seems to be dropping food or chewing on one side only, periodontal disease may be the problem—which, as with humans, can affect overall health.

- Excessive wax or odor in a dog's or cat's ears can signal an ear infection, as can a pet who seems to be tilting or shaking his head, or frequently scratching his ears.

- A pet who is hiding, crouching, or seems more needy (and/or vocal) than normal is possibly trying to send a message.

- Cats who stop their usual grooming may also be waving a red flag.

MARTHA MUST

I highly recommend looking for a veterinarian who practices what is known as integrative medicine, which combines the best of both conventional and alternative therapies. This approach should also focus on wellness and disease prevention, and on teaching and informing pet owners so they can better ensure their pet's health. As such, be sure to ask questions and demand helpful answers.

HOW TO
NURTURE PETS

Your pet is most content when right by your side. Make the most of that together time by providing a combination of mental, physical, and social stimulation. Thinking beyond your pet's normal routine is the best way to keep you both from falling into a rut.

MENTAL STIMULATION

You can stimulate all five senses by feeding your pet via interactive toys and activities.

- Try giving your dog a meal in a hollow rubber chew toy (such as Kong brand) or a puzzle toy that requires moving the pieces with his nose or paws.

- Put your cat's dinner in a puppy-size Kong toy, or sprinkle kibble in cardboard boxes or bags. This encourages the cat to fish the food out, which triggers natural hunting instincts.

- Adding ice cubes to their water bowls will also give dogs and cats some new playthings.

- There are myriad interactive toys for dogs and cats that are worth experimenting with to see which ones appeal to your pets.

PHYSICAL ACTIVITY

Aim for activities that trigger instinctual behavior such as hunting and exploring.

FELINES: Cats are fairly self-sufficient, but you'll still want to make sure they get enough exercise (at least 15 minutes a day) to satisfy their inner predators.

- Cats love climbing, so have a vertical structure (such as a cat tree) or two around the house for them to enjoy.

- They also love hiding; try offering several boxes and rearranging them regularly.

- Be sure to build in playtime with your cat, when they can chase a string toy or catnip ball.

- Laser pointers and battery-operated mice prompt predatory behavior.

CANINES: Dogs need more exercise, preferably outdoors.

- Add intrigue to your daily walks by hiding treats along the route, encouraging your pet to sniff and search.

- Make an obstacle course by having your pet sit at each parked car or lamppost, or walk figure eights around trees.

- Try a play-training class, which uses games to teach and reinforce obedience, or join a dog-sport club, which allows your dog to engage in the type of behavior it has been bred for (get information at American Kennel Club, *akc.org*).

SOCIAL INTERACTION

Canines need more interaction than cats, which are, for the most part, just fine at home with you.

- Take your pet to the local dog park or drop-in day-care center, and make regular playdates with other dogs.

- Visit your local pet store or other places where dogs are likely to be; even a brief sniff will brighten your pup's day.

- People count, too; have your pet tag along with you when picking up the kids from school and while running errands. She'll love being out and about.

ALONE TIME

When dogs are left to fend for themselves for long periods of time, they may try to create their own entertainment in the form of destructive chewing or barking. There are ways to help avoid that:

- Exercise your dog before leaving; a tired dog is less likely to get bored.

- Hide treat-dispensing and/or rugged chew toys around the house.

- Play classical music (or set the TV on a pet channel) while you are away.

- Use a webcam with an app that lets you see and talk to your pets from afar; some are equipped with laser pointers to get them moving.

- Hire a dog walker (or ask a friend or neighbor) to take your dog on a midday stroll.

HOW TO
TACKLE PROBLEM BEHAVIORS

Today's pets are an extension of the family and are often expected to behave as such—you don't want your pup jumping on friends whenever they stop by. But rather than trying to fight their centuries-old inclinations with punishment, the prevailing wisdom is to use those instinctive behaviors in putting an end to disorderly conduct.

BASIC TIPS AND TRICKS

Training a pet requires persistence, consistency, and a fair amount of tough love. That can be hard on an otherwise doting pet parent—at least initially, when you're just getting a handle on the necessary skills and steps. This is never more true than when teaching a new puppy basic commands. Instead of going alone, consider seeking out obedience classes—also great for providing socialization—or hiring a private trainer. To find a qualified behaviorist, ask your vet for a recommendation; fellow pet parents are other good resources. That said, the following are common dog and cat problems that can crop up over time, along with expert-backed solutions that you can try yourself before calling in reinforcements.

COMMON CAT BEHAVIORS AND SOLUTIONS	
SCRATCHING ON FURNITURE	Cats scratch to groom their claws, mark their territory, or handle stress, so give them a more appropriate outlet like a scratching post. Whenever your cat starts to scratch the furniture, gently redirect her to the post and reward her with treats and affection. Until she learns to use the post, you may want to trim her nails regularly (see page 372-373) and protect your furniture with double-sided tape (or a product such as Sticky Paws).
WAKING YOU IN THE NIGHT	Don't respond to all the meowing, pacing, and/or rubbing up against you at night— they're just craving your attention. Caving will only make matters worse. Also, avoid feeding or playing with a cat first thing in the morning (use an automatic feeder instead); keeping your bedroom as dark and quiet as possible will also help the cat stay calm.
JUMPING ON COUNTERS AND TABLES	Cats love exploring high places. Satisfy their instincts by getting them a cat tree or other perch (rubbing it with catnip to make it more enticing). This way, they can climb safely, without accidentally breaking something or stepping on a hot stove. Each time she goes to the tree, reward her with a treat or by playing with her favorite feather or string toy.

COMMON DOG BEHAVIORS AND SOLUTIONS

JUMPING ON PEOPLE	Turn away when your dog jumps up on you, as he is begging for attention. When his front paws are back on the ground, use the "sit" or "down" command and reward with a treat. Start by using a leash to practice approaching different members of the household each day, then introduce visitors in this way, too. Eventually your dog will automatically obey, without the need for a treat.
IGNORING THE "COME" COMMAND	It's very important to teach every dog this command, as it could save her life (when running into a busy street, for example). To teach it, keep your dog on a short leash while saying "come," praising and rewarding when she listens. Advance to a longer leash and intermittent treats, and then move off-leash (and treat as needed).
BEGGING FOR FOOD	Ignore all the whining and pleading—and never feed the dog from your plate. There'll be no turning back. Rather, teach him the "go to your place" command: Each time your dog approaches, say the command while moving him to an assigned spot—such as his dog bed—and then rewarding with a treat. He'll eventually go there on his own.
CHEWING ON THINGS	Dogs are always going to chew, but you can make sure they gnaw on the right things. Anytime she starts chewing on something "bad," redirect her to something "good," such as a toy or bone, and provide positive reinforcement to teach what's permitted and what's off-limits. Make sure to have toys available while you are gone, too.
DIGGING IN THE GARDEN	This is most likely a sign of boredom. Whenever your dog starts digging, introduce another activity, like a game of fetch, or hang a rope toy from a tree that he can tug on. Never let him see you digging in the garden, and consider also spraying the area with a mix of water and lemon juice (most dogs dislike citrus scents).

HOW TO PROVIDE SEASONAL CARE

Certain times of year bring new challenges when it comes to caring for your pet. Follow these suggestions to keep them safe and thriving in all kinds of weather.

SUMMER STRATEGIES

Taking a few sensible precautions will ensure your pets can have fun in the sun.

- Make sure dogs and cats have access to fresh drinking water throughout the day.

- Adjust your schedule during the summer months, limiting outdoor activities and walks to early morning and late evening. Whenever pets are outside, they should have a place to stay out of direct sunlight.

- Watch out for blazing-hot sidewalks and roadways. While dogs' paws are tough, they can still get burned. Try to walk on grass whenever possible, or at least stick to the shady side of the street.

- Never leave pets in a parked car; even with all the windows rolled down, the temperature can rise quickly to dangerous levels. (Some states have even passed laws against this.)

- While trimming long fur is fine, don't take off too much. Their insulating fur actually keeps them cool in the summer (and warm in the winter).

- Long coats also help prevent against sunburn and skin cancer. Apply a pet-specific sunscreen to any nonpigmented areas such as bellies or ears (but keep in mind that products containing salicylate are toxic to cats).

WINTER STRATEGIES

Even when the temperature plummets, you can encourage your pets to be active.

- Notice if your dog is shivering after a brief stint outdoors. Many dogs do just fine without having to bundle up, while thin-skinned and short-haired breeds (greyhounds, Weimaraners, French bulldogs) may benefit from a warm coat or sweater—so long as the outerwear doesn't restrict movement.

- Ice and snow can be hard on pets' paws, but so can the deicing salts used to melt them. Stick with pet-friendly products or regular sand from a home-improvement center on your own steps and walkways. Keeping the nails and the hair on pads well trimmed and groomed will also help.

- Booties can protect delicate paw pads, though some dogs refuse to budge with them on (borrow a friend's set for a similarly sized dog to see how your dog reacts). Otherwise, topical ointments like Musher's Secret and Aquaphor can offer protection against the elements.

- Don't let the shorter daylight hours deter you from getting out with your pet. You can keep track of him when it's dark by using flashing-light collars and reflector harnesses. Also consider putting bells on the collar or harness so he always stays within earshot.

- Cold temperatures can exacerbate arthritis, yet it's important to continue to provide some regular exercise to keep those joints moving. Try three shorter walks instead of one longer one.

- There are ways to give young and old dogs alike an indoor workout—playing fetch, for instance. Puzzle toys and other mental stimulation counts, too.

HEATSTROKE

Dehydration and heatstroke can strike fast, even when it's not excessively hot.

LEARN THE SIGNS

The following symptoms can be mild or severe.

- Excessive panting or drooling
- Difficulty breathing
- Rapid heart rate
- Wobbliness or stupor
- Difficulty standing
- Vomiting or nausea
- Seizure or collapse

WHAT TO DO

The key is to cool down the pet's temperature as soon as possible.

1. Get the pet into a shady area and provide water right away (though don't force him to drink).

2. Spray lightly all over with cool (not cold) water, concentrating on ear flaps, armpits, and groin.

3. If possible, put pet in front of a fan.

4. Take him to the vet to get checked out (even if he seems better).

MARTHA MUST

During the winter, I leave a bowl of tepid water and a cloth by the entrance for wiping off my dogs' paws after each outdoor time, to keep their paws from stinging. For the same reason, I take fragrance-free wipes on snowy walks and keep packages in the car.

HOW TO
GROOM YOUR PET

If you establish a grooming habit early on, when your pet is still young, you'll have a much easier time sticking to it as he grows (older cats and dogs can even learn to love it). Approach grooming in the spirit of spending quality time bonding with your pet— and improving his quality of life.

BRUSH COAT REGULARLY

Brushing is essential for all breeds (even those with short hair), as it keeps their coat shiny and healthy.

- Make brushing your cat or dog a weekly event, using treats to make the process more enjoyable (if necessary).

- Long-haired and double-coated breeds like shepherds and huskies may need brushing daily to keep their fur from matting; if mats do occur, cut them out with blunt scissors.

- Always brush in the same direction as the hair growth, using a slicker brush or a pin brush, which is more gentle on longer hair.

- It's a good idea to brush them outside, to avoid spreading dander in your home, as a courtesy to people with pet allergies.

BE DILIGENT ABOUT DENTAL HEALTH

While dogs and cats aren't prone to getting cavities, they can develop painful gum disease that may lead to loss of teeth.

- At first, just let your pet lick toothpaste off your finger once a day. Use a pet product, never human toothpaste. After about a week, start rubbing the paste on the gums.

- Next, introduce a toothbrush that's designed for animals (or use a soft-bristle infant toothbrush). Some fit over the finger and may be easier to maneuver than traditional types.

- Brush daily if you can, or at least once a week. The animal's tongue does a good job of scrubbing the inside of teeth. Just carefully lift your pet's lips and brush the outer surfaces, particularly the teeth along the cheeks.

CLIP NAILS WITH CARE

This can be a tricky task to do at home, since your pet will most likely be none too eager. That said, it's entirely doable—and can be another bonding opportunity. See opposite for more tips on clipping a cat's nails. For dogs:

- Choose clippers that are easy for you to handle. Guillotine versions often have a built-in guard against removing too much. The cross-cutter variety looks more like scissors.

TIP

White furry faces (dogs and cats) and certain smush-nose dog breeds (bulldogs and Pekingese) are often prone to harmless rust-colored tear stains. Temper the discoloration by applying cornstarch with a moist towel, avoiding the eye itself, then brushing it out.

- If your pet is really resistant, have a partner hold his muzzle while you work, or have your vet or a groomer do the clipping for you.

- Clip less than you think you should; a good rule of thumb is to cut only the curved portion of the nail. Always leave at least 2 millimeters between the end of the nail and the quick (the flesh-colored segment).

- If you do cut to the quick, apply cornstarch or flour with a moistened cotton swab to stop the bleeding. Call your vet for other guidance.

BATHE AS NEEDED

Most dogs need a good sudsing at least monthly, more often if he is prone to getting sweaty or muddy. Cats are self-grooming, so it is up to you to determine when a bath is called for (some long-haired breeds can get sticky or smelly). Introduce the ritual gradually: Place pet in a dry sink or tub (lined with a nonslip pad) and reward with praise and treats; add a little warm (not hot) water the next time, and the next, until your pet is comfortable enough for a full cleaning.

BRUSH OUT THE COAT: Besides removing excess hair, brushing dry fur will remove any snarls much more easily and gently than when it is wet. See opposite page for more brushing tips.

CLEAN THE EARS: Dampen a cotton ball or gauze pad with pet-specific ear cleanser and gently wipe just the visible parts; never go inside ear canal with a cotton swab. Place clean cotton balls in each ear to keep out bathwater, since moisture can lead to infection.

LATHER AND RINSE: Use warm water (hot water can encourage shedding) and pet-specific products only; a conditioner can help soothe dry, itchy skin. The head should be the last part you wash and the first you rinse (as this is what dogs like the least); cover their eyes with your hand or a cloth to prevent soap from getting in. Rinse well.

DRY THOROUGHLY: Wrap short-haired pets with a towel and rub vigorously—they'll love this part. To avoid tangles, pat or press longer-haired pets in sections with the towel. Let your pet dry naturally, or use a blow-dryer on the cool or warm setting (and never point it at the face). When your pet is dry, brush her coat once more, and offer praise, cuddles, and treats as just rewards.

TIP

If you don't have a hand-held showerhead, you can find one made for pet baths to attach to your indoor or outdoor faucet; this helps you reach every part of the animal's body.

CLIPPING TIPS FOR CATS

The key is to take your time. In feline handling, haste definitely makes waste—and you may end up never being successful.

1. Massage each of your cat's paws gently, moving slowly so you don't startle your pet. After touching all four paws, give her a treat so she thinks of this as a pleasant activity.

2. Once your cat is accustomed to your touch, introduce the clippers. You may want to start by touching the clipper against her paw pads (without clipping) for a few times, giving her treats after each time.

3. Begin by clipping only one or two nails: Gently press on the pad to extend one nail, then trim just the white tip above the quick (see opposite for how to treat the quick if cut). Reward her with a treat.

4. Continue to acclimate your cat to the practice gradually. Cut more nails each time, until you can do all four paws in one sitting. If your cat panics, stop immediately and consult your vet or groomer.

HOW TO
KEEP A CLEAN HOUSE WITH PETS

A clean home naturally starts with a clean pet. Follow the grooming regimen on pages 372–373, putting an emphasis on brushing (outdoors, if possible), to reduce shedding and dander. Then take a targeted approach to keeping your dwelling looking and smelling its best, no matter how many muddy paws are running underfoot.

FEEDING AREA

For practical reasons, feed your pet in a tucked-away space, such as the laundry room or a kitchen's corner.

- Keep dry kibble in a tightly sealed bin.

- A dog who gobbles down his meals, making a mess as he goes, might be doing so to keep other pets from getting his share; better to feed multiples in separate areas.

- Another way to reduce kibble spillage is to place a tennis ball in the center of the dry-food dish—he'll be forced to slow down and eat around it. If you are shopping for a new bowl, purchase one with a raised center, for the same results.

- Or ditch bowls altogether and use a puzzle feeder, which distributes dry food one piece of kibble at a time.

- Wash food bowls after each use, and water bowls at the end of each day, in hot soapy water.

- To minimize odors, spray the area with a solution of 2 cups water, 1 tablespoon white vinegar, and 1 teaspoon baking soda.

PET BEDDING

Regular laundering will prevent odor buildup. The same applies to your own bedding if your pets like to snuggle on or under the covers.

- Wash fabrics and cushions every week in hot water and a non-chlorine-bleach detergent.

- Once a day, pick up fur with a lint brush, and spray area (not bedding) with the baking-soda-vinegar mix, as described above.

- Don't forget to launder the liner for travel carriers if used on a regular basis; otherwise, clean at the end of each trip.

LITTER BOX

This is often the source of unpleasant smells, but that doesn't have to be the case.

- Place the box in a confined space, such as a bathroom or closet, and prevent odors from spreading with an activated carbon air freshener.

- Choose a litter product that doesn't simply mask odors but eliminates them on a molecular level.

- Scoop out and throw away the waste every day, and top off with new litter as needed.

- Once a week, scrub the box with a rag or dedicated sponge, using fragrance-free dishwashing detergent and warm water; dry thoroughly.

- Line the box with deodorizing liners, if your cat is okay with it, before pouring on the litter. If he dislikes liners, sprinkle baking soda on the box before adding litter.

- Place a litter mat in front of the opening of the box (or cut one out of a regular doormat), so the cat can leave without a trace.

MARTHA MUST

Create fur-free zones with expandable willow fencing (sold at garden centers). Attach two or three large eye screws to both sides of the doorjamb; sand unfinished ends of fencing and link into eye screws.

TIP

If your pets are allowed on upholstered furniture, train them (with treats and cuddles) to stay on just one spot, preferably lined with a cozy throw that can be washed in the machine. Removable slipcovers are another pet-friendly, easy-care option.

HOW TO
TRAVEL WITH PETS

If taking your pet on vacation is non-negotiable, you'll need to add an extra layer to your preparations. Before you commit, take a step back: Is your cat or dog up to the journey? Will she feel safe and sound in an unfamiliar hotel? Some cats and dogs might be happier (honestly!) staying behind.

BEFORE YOU GO

Get your pet used to her carrier, since most types of commercial transportation require one, and you may feel safer driving with her in a protected place. Leave the carrier out and open for a few weeks before you depart, placing treats in it now and then. When she goes inside, give her lots of praise and more treats.

TRAVELING BY CAR

Pets are just as prone to serious risk as children when roaming freely in a car. Plus, some dogs and many cats deal with anxiety when traveling. Heed these tips.

BUCKLE UP: Cats and dogs should always be restrained in the car—this is true whether you are driving two miles or 2,000.

- For larger dogs, buy backseat harnesses; smaller dogs can be strapped into a raised doggie car seat that allows them a safe view.

- Cats, who are natural climbers and explorers, should always travel in crates.

GO FOR A TEST RIDE: Get your pet accustomed to the restraint and the ride before driving to your destination. If you'll be using a crate, start feeding and treating while the crate is still in your home. After a few days, move the crate into the car; feed meals here and/or offer treats without driving anywhere. Then use it on short trips with big rewards.

AVOID CAR SICKNESS: If your pet is prone to getting carsick, ask your vet about medication. Otherwise, the following steps will help to stave off nausea and other side effects.

- Hold off feeding your pet a meal for three to four hours before long-distance travel.

- Ride with the windows open, even if only every now and then, to keep the air fresh.

- Take plenty of rest stops to let them stretch their legs and do their business.

TRAVELING BY PLANE

Always check with the airline for specific policies and requirements.

- Small pets (typically 19 pounds and under) are allowed to travel in the cabin, under the seat in front of you. Make sure to abide by the airline's rules regarding the type and size of the travel carrier, as well as medical records.

- If cargo is your only option, always check the pet-safety records of the major airlines at *transportation.gov/airconsumer*. Book a direct flight. Note: Many airlines now prohibit snub-nosed breeds from traveling at all—inside the cabin or not.

- For in-cabin travel, exercise your pet for at least 15 minutes before boarding to ease anxiety, longer for larger dogs flying cargo.

- Never give your pet sedatives before flying, as these can slow breathing.

- Don't feed her for four to six hours before departure.

- Place frozen water in the tray inside the crate and/or attach a water bottle with a nozzle, so she can stay hydrated.

PACKING FOR PETS

No well-traveled pet should leave home without these:

- Sturdy, well-ventilated carrier or crate (labeled with owner's ID)

- Leash, collar, and permanent and travel ID tags

- Health certificate from a vet (often required when crossing state lines)

- Medications, medical records, and a vet contact

- Paperwork for international travel (check *www.aphis.usda.gov* for guidelines)

- Pet food and bowls, plus a water bottle or bowl with nozzle for travel crate (if using)

- Favorite bedding and toys

- Grooming supplies, including a dental kit, pet wipes for spot cleaning, and non-toxic pet sunscreen

- Pet flotation device, if you'll be near water

BOARDING YOUR PET

Putting your pet in another's care takes some deliberation. Here's a handy checklist to help make the boarding experience a secure and stress-free time for the both of you.

ASK QUESTIONS

Before deciding on a kennel, interview the owners on issues that are important to you. Find out what happens if a pet becomes ill, if they work with a veterinarian or emergency clinic, and if the animals are ever left alone.

GET THE REQUIRED PAPERWORK

As a general rule, you'll need to make sure all vaccinations are current and bring proof when you drop off your dog.

■ Most kennels also require a clean fecal report to show your dog doesn't have worms.

■ If you're concerned about over-vaccinating your pet, some places will accept titers (or blood tests that stand in for the shots) from vets, and/or offer owners the choice of signing a waiver assuming the risk should their pets become ill while there.

KEEP UP WITH PARASITE PREVENTION

Almost every facility will require you to treat your dog with a monthly flea and tick preventive. Schedule a treatment just before your dog checks in.

VISIT YOUR VET

Even if a facility doesn't require a veterinarian's clearance, you may want to schedule a checkup for your dog within 30 days of boarding. This is especially helpful if your dog is elderly or has chronic health issues.

BRING ESSENTIALS

Bring your dog's regular food, to reduce the risk of dietary upset.

■ Also, make sure to provide enough medications to last the entire stay, bringing the prescription in its original container so the staff can follow the vet's directions and avoid getting mixed up with another dog's prescriptions.

INFORM ON INTAKE

Advise the boarding facility of any known allergies and other medical or behavioral conditions.

DEVISE A PLAN

You'll need to provide contact information for your general vet and any specialists, as well as any insurance policy information.

■ For older dogs (or younger ones with known medical issues), you may want to draw up a formal statement (like a DNR for pets) that indicates your preferences in case of emergencies.

PREP YOUR PET

Dogs can sense when you are worried, which in turn makes it hard for them to bond with their temporary caregivers. Make drop-off a positive experience.

■ Bringing the dog's bedding and favorite toys will help alleviate any anxiety.

■ There are also homeopathic products that can be sprayed on their bedding or added to their water during their stay to help them stay calm and happy.

TIP

When picking up your dog from the facility, hold off on feeding or giving him water for at least four hours (ice cubes are fine for a pet who seems thirsty). All the excitement of seeing you and being home again can lead to gulping down food and water—and then nausea and vomiting.

TEMPLATES

CRAFT AND CREATE: SEW AN APRON WITH HIDDEN SEAMS

See How to Sew an Apron with Hidden Seams, page 163.

1. Assemble pattern from *marthastewart .com/1078591/apron*, using the image at right as a guide.

2. With a ruler and a craft knife, trim left side of each sheet at vertical crop marks. Repeat process to trim bottom of each sheet. Using remaining crop marks as guide, align design, then tape sheets together.

3. For the neck strap, use one 20-inch piece of 1-inch twill tape or ribbon. For the waist straps, use two 44-inch pieces of 1-inch twill tape or ribbon.

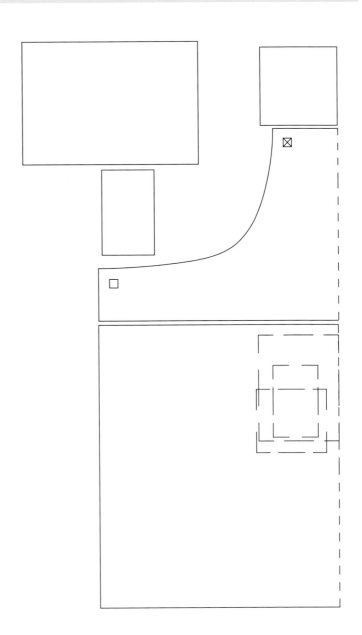

CRAFT AND CREATE: SEW FABRIC FLOWERS

See How to Sew Fabric Flowers, page 170.

1. Photocopy template and increase size by 25%.

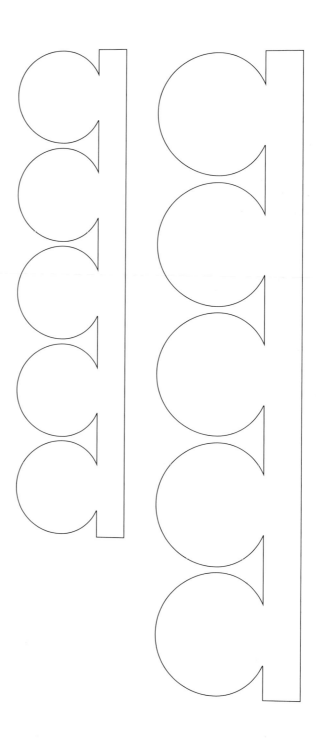

CRAFT AND CREATE: KNIT A BLANKET

See How to Knit a Blanket, page 187.

1. Knit the pieces, and then sew them together as explained on page 187.

2. (Optional) For a crocheted edge, insert a crochet hook into the hole on the selvage at the beginning of your work. Wrap yarn over the hook, pull it through the hole, then repeat into the next hole, first wrapping yarn over hook and then pulling hook through second hole. You now have two loops on your hook; pull more yarn over the hook, then pull hook back through the two loops. This is the first crochet stitch. Repeat with the next two holes in the same manner, until the entire piece is finished; cast off as for knitting on page 181.

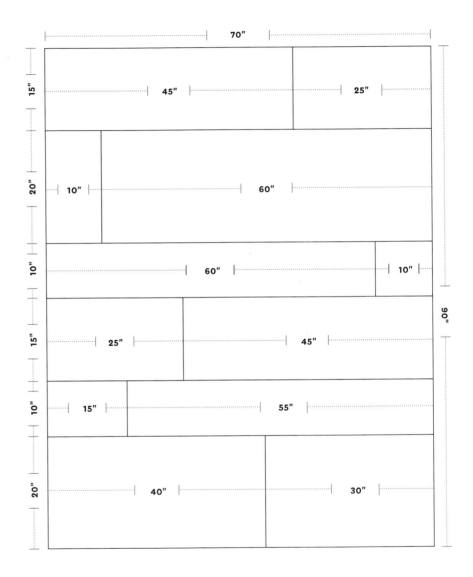

hi

CRAFT AND CREATE: EMBROIDER A BLOUSE
See How to Embroider a Blouse, page 191.

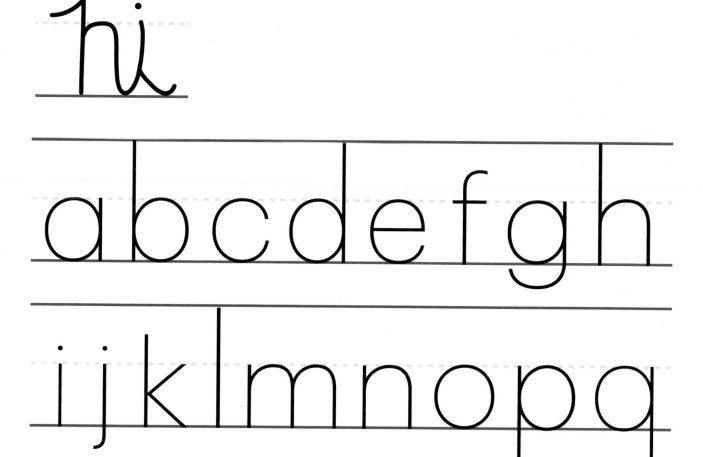

abcdefgh

ijklmnopq

rstuvwxyz

CRAFT AND CREATE: EMBROIDER SAMPLERS
See How to Embroider Samplers, page 192.

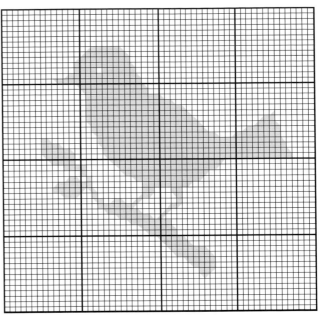

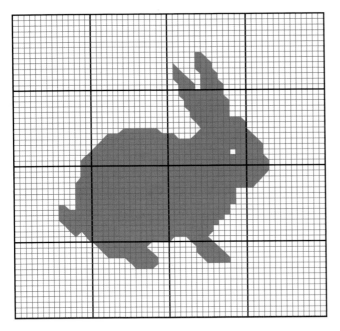

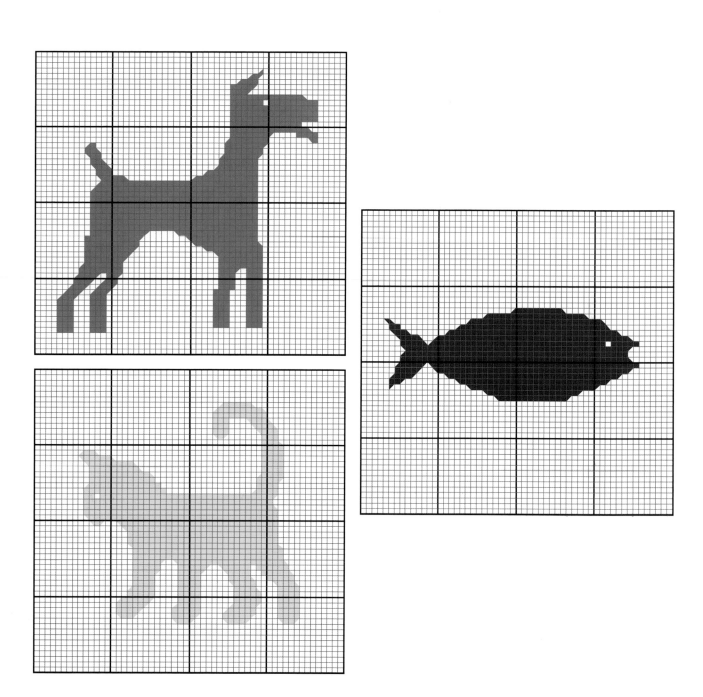

CELEBRATE: POP-UP CARDS

See How to Celebrate Valentine's Day, page 325.

1. Photocopy template at desired size.

2. Trace onto paper for the folded piece.

3. Using bone folder, score along dotted lines, then fold along lines.

4. Unfold, cut out, and refold (for Heart Card, cut out and refold large heart piece, then use small heart template to cut three single hearts from a contrasting paper. Score and fold, and attach to folded large heart piece with double-sided tape).

5. Position the folded piece inside base card so it pops. Secure with double-sided tape.

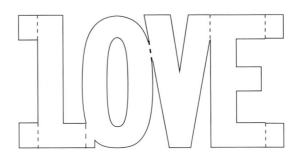

CELEBRATE: AIRPLANE AND LOCKET GARLAND CARDS

See How to Celebrate Valentine's Day, page 325.

1. Photocopy template at desired size, and cut out.

2. Trace two copies onto heavyweight colored paper (but only one copy is necessary for the image with keyhole). If paper's color or embellishment is single-sided, be sure to flip template before tracing the second copy so the paper's design or color will appear on front and back.

3A. AIRPLANE: Sandwich ribbon between plane and 3 heart pieces (spacing as desired), and secure all with double-sided tape. Leave about 4 inches of loose ribbon trailing, and secure end of ribbon with tape inside envelope.

3B. LOCKET: Secure the key pieces together with double-sided tape. Use screw punch on hole of key. Stick the pieces of lock base together with double-sided tape, sandwiching one end of cord between layers. Thread loose end of cord through hole in key, and secure with a knot. Attach keyhole heart with double-sided tape, and cut keyhole through top heart and lock base.

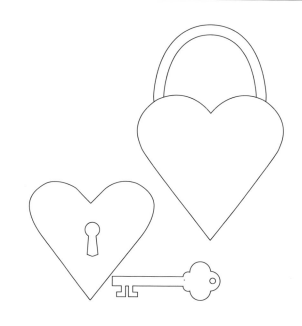

CELEBRATE: LOVEBIRD GARLAND CARD

See How to Celebrate Valentine's Day,
page 325.

1. Photocopy template at desired size, and
cut out.

2. Fold heavyweight colored paper in half,
and align bird template with beak at folded
edge. Trace bird and wing, and cut out (leaving
connection at beak).

3. Using ⅛-inch screw punch, make bird eyes
where indicated on template. Cut small slit
between tail and body to allow bird to rest
on cord.

4. Attach a wing to each bird with double-
sided tape. Cut two card bases to desired
size, score in middle, and fold in half. One will
be used for cord; the other, as backing: On
one card, cut ¼-inch slits (for cord) approximately 1½ inches from both outer edges for
cord to thread through. Feed cord through
slits, and cut so it bows slightly at center.
Secure on back with tape. Using the slits at
their tails, place the birds on the cord. Affix
birds' beaks to that card with a small amount
of glue. Attach the second card base with
double-sided tape.

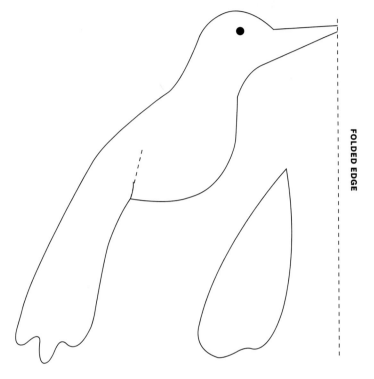

FOLDED EDGE

CELEBRATE: PAPER-BAT MOBILE

See How to Celebrate Halloween, page 339.

1. Photocopy template at desired size on 8½-by-11-inch paper, and cut out.

2. To make one whole bat, fold sheet of heavyweight black paper or card stock in half widthwise. Then place template's straight edge along fold, and trace outline.

3. Cut out along traced line, and unfold. Then fold bat's wings where template's dotted lines indicate. Repeat for each bat.

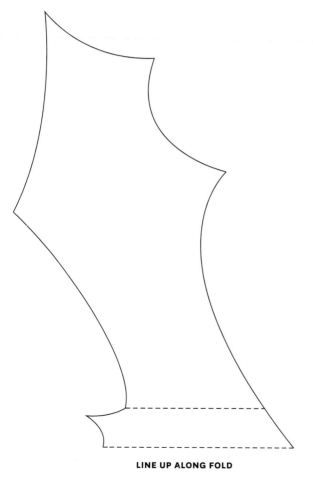

LINE UP ALONG FOLD

CELEBRATE: HANDMADE HANUKKAH DREIDEL PLACE CARD

See How to Celebrate Hanukkah, page 352.

1. Photocopy template at desired size.

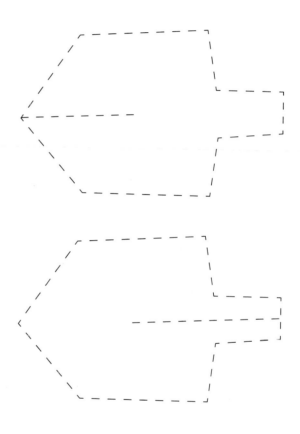

INDEX

W

wallpaper
  cleaning, 126
  for refreshing/embellishing, 97–101

walls
  cleaning, 126
  maintenance, 58, 89
  painting, 88–93
  wallpaper, 97–101

wall studs, 80

wardrobe. *See* clothes

washing. *See* cleaning

watering wands, 205

water marks, 63

water valves and pipes, 46

wax stains, 61, 63, 126, 128

weatherizing, 56

weather-resistant fabrics, 106

weeding, 213

weekly tasks
  cleaning, 119, 124, 128
  organizing, 11
  pet grooming, 372

whetstones, 293

windows
  cleaning, 127
  curtains, 110
  drafts, 56
  glass panes, 66
  ledges, 82

  screens, 57
  shades and blinds, 111

wine, 240, 242–43, 291, 328
  as gift, 328
  stains, 128, 132–33

winterizing, plants, 216–17

wood floors
  cleaning, 124
  maintenance, 60–61

wool
  clothes, 140
  upholstery, 106
  yarn, 174

wrapping gifts, 317, 318–19

wreaths, 350–51

wrenches, 46

Y

yarn, 174–75, 180

yearly tasks
  chimney cleaning, 64
  cleaning, 124
  organizing, 11
  pet care, 364

yoga, 269–71

Z

zone storage. *See* grouping principle

CREDITS AND ACKNOWLEDGMENTS

IMAGE CREDITS

COVER: Ryan Liebe

BACK COVER: Marcus Nilsson

COVER OBJECTS: Scissors (Martha Stewart), Trowel (Sneeboer), Whisk (Martha Stewart), Paintbrush (Purdy), Hammer (Anvil)

ABRANOWICZ, WILLIAM: 79 (right), 91, 96, 360

ABRANOWICZ, WILLIAM/ ART + COMMERCE: 367

ALLEN, LUCAS: 41, 101 (left)

AMOS, ANTHONY: 67

AN, SANG: 339 (right), 346, 347, 351 (right), 354, 355

AVSAR, BURCU: 20 (right), 146, 328 (left)

BAGI1998/ISTOCK: 47 (Level)

BAIGRIE, JAMES: 74, 75

BAKER, CHRISTOPHER: 186, 187

BARBERA, PAUL: 151 (top right)

BATES, HARRY: 144, 145, 147, 159 (Running Stitch, Backstitch, Slip Stitch), 177, 180, 181, 182, 183 (How to Increase, How to Divide), 189

BATES, HARRY, AND NOLA ROMANO: 159 (Catch Stitch)

BELLO, ROLAND: 344

BERISHA, FADIL: 242

BERNHAUT, JUSTIN: 101 (right), 326

BIALES, SCOTT: 276

BOOTZ, ANTOINE: 106, 336

BORDWIN, ANDREW: 128

BRACKETT, AYA: 312

BRENNER, MARION: 275

CAUSEY, JENNIFER: 195 (left)

CAVANAUGH, CHELSEA: 21 (left), 83, 109

COPRID/ISTOCK: 47 (Tape)

COSTELLO, PAUL: 223

DE LEO, JOSEPH: 22, 24 (left), 164

DEWAR, NICK/KANG, DAVID: 105

DIMEDROL68/ISTOCK: 46 (Wrench), 47 (Scissors)

DISCAN/ISTOCK: 136

DISCHINGER, FRANCOIS: 38

DOLAN, JOHN: 208

DONNE, TARA: 222, 281

DRUMMOND, PIPPA: 173

DYER, AARON: 32, 36 (right), 81, 82 (right), 191, 193 (top), 289, 290, 335 (left)

ESTERSOHN, PIETER: 232

FIELDS, DIANE: 24 (right), 25 (right)

FORMULA Z/S: 327

FRANCIS, KATE: 49, 52, 57, 59, 64, 66, 71, 107, 108, 110, 111, 139, 150, 163 (bottom), 165 (Pom-Pom Illustrations), 166 (Duplicate Stitches Illustrations), 183 (How to Finger Knit), 193 (Diagonal Pattern, Chevron Pattern, Chinese Staircase), 277, 280, 349 (left)

FRIEDMAN, AMANDA: 270–271

GALLAGHER, DANA: 349 (right)

GARDNER, BRYAN: 51, 126, 129, 184, 185, 244, 230, 258, 267, 319

GENTL AND HYERS: 333 (left)

HOM, RAYMOND: 140, 209, 310

HOME DEPOT: 12, 42

HRANEK, MATTHEW: 93, 103, 308

HUBA, JOHN: 272

HUBBARD, LISA: 102

INGALLS PHOTOGRAPHY: 220, 237, 269, 324

ISAGER, DITTE: 27, 199, 279

ISTOCK: 47 (Hex Keys)

JEANSON, THIBAULT: 62, 95

JOHNSON, STEPHEN KENT: 78

JUENGEL, KARL: 46 (Power Drill, Hammer, Screwdriver, Staple Gun), 47 (Tape Measure, Utility Knife, Putty Knife), 204 (Bedding Rake, Loppers), 205 (Shovel, Spade, Spring Rake, Trowel, Watering Wand)

KRAUTTER, MIKE: 20 (left)

LAGRANGE, FREDERIC: 216, 217, 235, 372

LEE, JASON: 151 (bottom left)

LENZ, VANESSA: 127

LEWIS, STEPHEN: 338 (right)

LIEBE, RYAN: 2, 8–10, 44–45, 68–69, 99, 112–113, 120, 121, 130–131, 134, 141, 152–153, 157, 163 (top), 175, 195 (right), 202-203, 204 (Hedge Shears, Secateur), 205 (Hori Hori), 236, 238–239, 241, 262–263, 282–283, 316–317, 333 (right), 358–359, 375

LOOF, PERNILLE: 15, 30 (right), 31, 335 (right)

MALOSH, DAVID: 250, 296

MATHIS, KATE: 14 (right), 34, 82 (left), 160, 161, 329, 339 (left), 357

MCNAMARA, CHELSEA: 330

MILLER, JOHNNY: 36 (left), 40 (right), 86 (right), 104, 148, 162, 219, 252, 255, 286, 315, 328 (right), 352

MOSS, LAURA: 371

NGO, NGOC MINH: 37, 138, 188, 190, 194, 218, 325

NILSSON, MARCUS: 16, 18, 19, 207, 224, 249, 291, 295, 340, 343

NORMAN, HELEN: 86 (left)

NOVAK, SHANA: 65

OKADA, KANA: 306

PEARSON, VICTORIA: 215, 362

PEDEN + MUNK: 213

PIASECKI, ERIC: 79 (left), 88, 92 (left)

PIASECKI, ERIC/OTTO: 76

PICAYO, JOSE: 259

POULOS, CON: 231, 292

PRINCE, DAVID: 260

PRINCE, MICHAEL/GALLERY STOCK: 377

PUGLIESE, LINDA: 246, 320, 353

QVC: 204 (Japanese Weeder, Hand Cultivator), 205 (Garden Fork, Hand Saw)

RAESIDE, PAUL: 265

RANSOM, JAMES: 170, 171

REIKA/SHUTTERSTOCK: 47 (Assorted Hardware)

ROEMER, EMILY KATE: 197, 198, 332, 348

ROMEREIN, LISA: 54, 92 (right)

SCHLECTER, ANNIE: 26, 28 (left), 29, 40 (left), 56, 118, 122, 166 (Hats), 167, 234

SEARS, KATE: 28 (right)

SEPTIMUS, MATTHEW: 60, 210

SERHII, KUCHER/SHUTTERSTOCK: 47 (Pliers, top)

SMOOT, SETH: 21 (right), 25 (left), 87, 192, 256, 266

SOHN, JULIANA: 225

SOWDER, JEFF: 228

THOMPSON, MARTYN: 84

ULIN, PIA: 100, 125

UPTON, SIMON: 154

VALIANT, JONNY: 14 (left), 137, 143

VANG, MIKKEL: 100 (left)

WARD, SARAH ANNE: 168, 169

WEIBULL, LENNART: 30 (left), 200

WILLIAMS, ANNA: 351 (left)

WILLIAMS, MATTHEW: 72, 116, 165 (top), 350

YANES, ROMULO: 305

YASU + JUNKO: 338 (left)

YELLOW CAT/SHUTTERSTOCK: 47 (Pliers, bottom)

ADDITIONAL CREDITS

TEXT CONTRIBUTIONS BY: Evelyn Battaglia

ART DIRECTION BY: William van Roden

This book was produced by

 MELCHER MEDIA

124 West 13th Street · New York, NY 10011 · melcher.com

FOUNDER, CEO: Charles Melcher

PRESIDENT, CRO: Julia Hawkins

VP, COO: Bonnie Eldon

EXECUTIVE EDITOR/PRODUCER: Lauren Nathan

PRODUCTION DIRECTOR: Susan Lynch

SENIOR DIGITAL PRODUCER: Shannon Fanuko

ASSOCIATE EDITOR/PRODUCER: Victoria Spencer

ASSISTANT DESIGNER/EDITOR: Renée Bollier

ACKNOWLEDGMENTS

MARTHA STEWART AND *MARTHA STEWART LIVING*:

A book of this magnitude required the expertise of many of our talented colleagues. Thank you to the *Martha Stewart Living* team of past and present for inspiring us with every issue. Editors Susanne Ruppert, Nanette Maxim, and Bridget Fitzgerald worked to create a how-to manual that readers could turn to again and again. Proving that they actually could do everything were Evelyn Battaglia, Lauren Nathan, Victoria Spencer, and Renée Bollier. William van Roden designed the pages, with Kevin Sharkey offering his creative guidance, and Ayesha Patel and Megan Hedgpeth contributing their impeccable style. Special thanks to Melissa Ozawa and Ryan McCallister, whose knowledge and generosity were invaluable. We would also like to thank Chad Wagenheim, Carolyn D'Angelo, Charlie Melcher, Kim Dumer, Stacey Tyrell, Mike Varassi, Alison Vanek, Laura Wallis, and Robin Gericke for all of their support. This book starts a new partnership with Houghton Mifflin Harcourt, and we look forward to publishing many more beautiful books with Deb Brody, Stephanie Fletcher, and the whole team.

MELCHER MEDIA:

Melcher Media gratefully acknowledges the following for their contributions: Jess Bass, Amélie Cherlin, Cheryl Della Pietra, Sharon Ettinger, Shannon Fanuko, Dave Kang, Karolina Manko, Anya Markowitz, Emma McIntosh, Jy Murphy, Michael Quinones, Josh Raab, Nola Romano, Gabrielle Sirkin, Do Mi Stauber, Christopher Steighner, Nadia Tahoun, Katy Yudin, and Gabe Zetter.